*The Ralph Nader Study
Group Report on the
Interstate Commerce
Commission and
Transportation*

THE INTERSTATE COMMERCE OMISSION

The Public Interest and the ICC

Robert C. Fellmeth PROJECT DIRECTOR

GROSSMAN PUBLISHERS NEW YORK 1970

Copyright © 1970 by The Center for Study of Responsive Law
All rights reserved, including the right of reproduction in whole or
in part in any form.
Published by Grossman Publishers, Inc.
125A East 19th Street, New York, New York 10003
Published simultaneously in Canada by
Fitzhenry and Whiteside, Ltd.
Library of Congress Catalogue Card Number: 70–112514
Printed in the United States of America
First printing

Director & Co-author:
ROBERT C. FELLMETH

Special Consultant:
RALPH NADER

Investigators & Co-authors:

Ronald E. Berenbeim, A.B. Cornell University, M.A. Oxford University, Second-year law student at Harvard University

Gerald J. Billow, A.B. Dartmouth University, third-year law student at Harvard University

Richard E. Brodsky, A.B. Brown University, second-year law student at Harvard University

Alan E. Kear, A.B. University of Pennsylvania, third-year law student at the University of Pennsylvania

Edward C. Pachniak, A.B. University of Wisconsin, second-year law student at Harvard University

Jonathan A. Rowe, A.B. Harvard University, second-year law student at the University of Pennsylvania

Economic Consultant:

Professor John A. Marlin, Baruch College, City University of New York

Statistical Consultant:

Professor Damodar Gujarati, Baruch College, City University of New York

Secretary:
Mrs. Jill D. Fellmeth

Photographer:
Mrs. Constance Heiman

Other Staff:
Mohan Mehta
Andrew Condey
Lewis Dars
Robert Najman
Steven Ezon
Professor Josephine Olson

Foreword

As the oldest independent federal regulatory agency, the Interstate Commerce Commission has set longevity records in its systematic failure to protect or further the public interest in surface transportation. Long ago, the ICC found itself surrounded by a special interest constituency that viewed the agency as an opportunity for protection from competition and for insulation from consumer demands. Regulatory power became a commodity for transport interest groups to manipulate in their internecine struggles for ICC grants of authority or approvals of rates. The resolutions of these conflicts were very often at the expense of the public interest in an efficient, low cost, and safe transportation system.

Both shippers and passengers have endured the relentless erosion of highway and rail transport services with few remedies at their disposal. The massive irrationality and cost of these services, where they have not been discontinued altogether, reverberate throughout our economy with concrete effect on the cost of consumer goods, the mobility and safety of the populace, the location of economic enterprises, and the use of human and natural resources.

For generations the ICC has operated as a shield, protecting and preserving economic groups from the discipline of the marketplace, yet has declined to institute the pro-public interest pattern of regulation that was its original *raison d'être*. Long before it became a pattern of our political economy, the ICC and the transport industries forged a corporate state that utilized public power for private pursuits. (These private pursuits were often so parochially defined that they undermined the overall health of the industry of which they were a part.) All of the now-familiar trappings of such a condition appeared early in the ICC—routine movement of personnel into the industry, absence of rigorous Congressional scrutiny, heavy political overtones to agency decisions, rigid barriers to a citizen-consumer access to and participation in ICC proceedings, wholly unjustified secrecy, poor analytic and fact gathering performances, failure to base decisions on reasoned explanations, and a gross dereliction in helping to shape a far-sighted transportation policy.

By way of covering over this regulatory degradation, the ICC has extruded a stream of complexity which only the special claimants on the agency have mastered. The public has lacked representatives to wade through this material and find the basic issues.

Herewith the following report. As is so frequently becoming the case, investigating students are assuming the role that their elder professional peers have so long abandoned. Whether or not the ICC can stand sustained, skilled, citizen inquiry will be tested in part by this report and its aftermath of action. For now, it is sufficient that these seven law students relate the details of their dismaying findings and concrete recommendations to those persons who long for the emergence of that sustained, skilled citizenship.

Seven law students from Harvard and the University of Pennsylvania were chosen for this project, partially because of their backgrounds in statistics, computer science, economics, anti-trust law, rate regulation, accounting, and other disciplines relevant to the operations of the ICC.

They began the study in late 1968 by compiling and reading all available reference material. They studied the Interstate Commerce Act and the ICC and court decisions interpreting the Act. They reviewed and outlined the agency regulations. Two students compiled an annotated bibliography of law-review articles from the past decade on the ICC and surface transportation generally. Economic texts, conference transcripts, and major articles in economic journals were examined. They then gathered and read Congressional hearings, the agency's annual reports for the past ten years, agency press releases and newsletters, speeches by Commissioners over the past several years, news articles and magazine articles, including a continuous survey of the major trade press. They read and discussed government and professional studies of the agency, examined agency publications, including cost studies and formulas, job descriptions, personnel resumes, *et al.* They went to the Departments of Justice, Transportation, Agriculture and Defense, and reviewed all available pertinent reports concerning the ICC.

The students began interviewing in June of 1969, completing over 500 different interviews by September, 1969. Over 100 of those interviewed were ICC officials and employees. Other people interviewed included truck drivers, carriers, shippers, railroad workers, union members, consultants, government officials in other federal departments, and attorneys, Interviews averaged about two hours in length and some were followed up by subsequent visits.

Ron Berenbeim, Bob Fellmeth, and Ed Pachniak undertook various field trips throughout 1969 to study ICC enforcement procedures and to conduct research into specific problem areas. Chicago, Indianapolis, Philadelphia, New York, and Denver were all visited at least once.

The students also conducted several formal surveys. Richard Brodsky sent two sets of questionnaires to the schools where the ICC recruits young attorneys. Gerald Billow sent detailed questionnaires concerning ICC administrative procedure to every attorney ICC Practitioner in Washington, D.C., and others surveyed some sixty middle-level staff through standardized questions during initial interviews. They sent detailed three-page questionnaires to a sampling of some 200 shippers in order to test the nature and impact of competitive conditions, service, rate discrimination patterns, access to the regulatory forum, etcetera. Finally, Jonathan Rowe and Bob Fellmeth surveyed over 1300 trucker drivers on the issue of driver and vehicle safety. Some of the questionnaires used are presented in Appendices.

With the aid of numerous consultants, officials of the Department of Transportation, faculty of Baruch College of the City University of New York, and faculty of the Harvard Law School, they conducted four separate statistical analyses by computer. Three of these studies attempt to refine past evaluations of the cost and competitive structures of the rail, water carrier, and motor carrier industries. The fourth study analyzes the nature and impact of crucial aspects of ICC rate regulation policy. The data selection procedures, ratio selections, and formulas were decided upon in consultation with numerous experts.

In addition to the half million pieces of data handled by

various computers, numerous surveys were conducted by hand. Special studies and investigations were conducted on a number of subjects, including a survey of pipeline, rate bureau, rail, motor carrier, and water carrier annual reports, railroad advertising, private car company rates of return, enforcement data, Commission travel vouchers, etcetera.

In addition to much of the data and material produced by the inquiry itself, the investigators are publicly releasing for the first time to our knowledge portions of the following documents: the undisclosed Civil Service Commission Report on the ICC, the suppressed Inventory of Motor Carrier Authority study on motor carrier regulation, the 1966 way bill results, much intra-agency communication, details of secret agency personnel evaluation procedures, compilations from secret reports and surveys, and internal carrier memoranda.

RALPH NADER

Contents

Introduction

The impact of the surface transportation system of the United States on the consumer, the environment, and the national economy is not always apparent. Except for certain clearly affected areas discussed at length in this work, such as boxcar shortages, safety, home moving, and passenger train decline, much of the effect of transportation is hidden. A product picked from the shelf will not display information about transportation cost. Yet transportation is a significant part of the expense of almost everything we buy. A television set requires not only transportation of the set to your home and from the manufacturer to distributor to retailer, but its parts, the tubes and cabinet and wiring, must be carried to the assembly plant. Further, the glass and metal and wood must be carried to subassembly plants for the manufacture of the parts. Often, as is the case with timber, the logs must be transported to a factory for cutting before they can be transported to a subassembly plant to be crafted into a cabinet to be shipped to the assembly plant. And then the machines, and their replacement parts, which gather and mine and cut various natural resources, must be transported to their points of operation. Transportation accounts for from 15 to 20 per cent of our Gross National Product.

A monopolistic and inefficient transportation system has a direct and substantial impact on product costs and inflation. Transportation favoritism for large shippers can pervasively affect the plight of small business. The system has a substantial impact on indirect costs and inefficiencies, decisions on where to locate manufacturing plants or what kinds of natural resources to utilize, and on other economic decisions involving the consideration of transportation costs. Plant location decisions, particularly, can and do have an indirect but pervasive impact on urbanization, pollution, and inflation.

There are very few subjects about which so much is written and so little known. Yet there are very few areas more important to the economic health of a nation. Interstate commerce is esoteric and complex, but it is too important to leave entirely to the transportation industry, large shippers, or an unexamined Interstate Commerce Commission.

The importance of the transportation system is difficult for the consumer to perceive in all its manifestations, and the public is unlikely to take an active interest in an area it does not understand. The interest of the transportation industry in public transportation policy, however, has remained steady and intense through the years. There have been few public upheavals of interest and concern comparable to the Granger movement of the late nineteenth century over railroad rebates and concessions, but industry interest in profit maximization and in expansion has remained unchanged.

The primary *theoretical* function of the Interstate Commerce Commission is to represent the diffuse public interest vigorously as a counterforce to highly organized transportation interests. It was Congress' intent that the ICC do more than serve as judge or arbitrator between those transportation forces which might find themselves in conflict. Supreme Court interpretation of the Interstate Commerce Act further indicates that the agency's purpose is to serve as the aggressive and independent representative of the general public interest.

The industry view of the function of the ICC was expressed shortly after the establishment of the agency in 1887. In 1892 Charles E. Perkins, President of the Chicago, Burlington and Quincy Railroad, wrote a letter to his friend Richard Olney, Attorney General of the United States, recommending that the embryonic five-year-old Commission be abolished. Olney's reply was a masterpiece of impropriety and prophecy which deserves attention in any study of the Commission:

. . . My impression would be that looking at the matter from a railroad point of view exclusively it would not be a wise thing to undertake. . . . The attempt would not be likely to succeed; if it did not succeed, and were made on the grounds of the inefficiency and uselessness of the Commission, the result would very probably be giving it the power it now lacks. The Commission, as its functions have now been limited by the courts, is, or can be made of great use to the railroads. It satisfies the popular clamor for a government supervision of railroads, at the same time that the supervision is almost entirely nominal. Further, the older such a commission gets to be, the more inclined it will be found to take the business and railroad view of things. It thus becomes a sort of barrier between the railroad corporations and the people and a sort of protection against hasty and crude legislation hostile to railroad interests. . . . The part of wisdom is not to destroy the Commission but to utilize it.

The Interstate Commerce Omission

1 / The Commission

Who Rules the ICC?

The ICC was set up by Congress as an agency of experts to protect and represent the public interest in matters of transportation in interstate commerce. In fact, the agency is predominantly a forum at which transportation interests divide up the national transportation market. The Commission handles thousands of operating rights and finance cases every year, and is to a large extent defined by this huge caseload as a passive arbitrator for vying commercial interests. Even the possibility of imaginative resourceful *regulation* of surface transportation within the context of these cases is precluded by the attitudes and points of view of the men in position to regulate aggressively: the Interstate Commerce Commissioners.

Crucial to an understanding of the Commissioners' attitudes is an understanding both of the pre-appointment backgrounds of the Commissioners and the appointment process.

Although the appointment process ostensibly works to provide a Commission that will serve as the expert arm of Congress in the area of surface transportation, a greater interest for both the President and Congress is served by the chance to pay off political debts and provide jobs for political supporters. Therefore, two important qualifications for a Commissioner are his political connections and his political party. The ICC has eleven members, and statute requires that there be a 6–5 split in the Commission between Democrats and Republicans, depending on whichever is the majority party in Congress.

The nature of the process insures that every Commissioner has his benefactor, be it the President or a Senator or a Representative. A brief political road map of the ICC illustrates the political affiliations and transportation experience (or its lack) of the present Commissioners.

Virginia Mae Brown, wife of James V. Brown—an attorney with practices both in West Virginia and Washington—was a close associate of former West Virginia Governor Barron for many years in the Attorney General's office in Charleston and in the Governor's office. Her regulatory experience was limited to the West Virginia Public Service Commission. In 1964, Lyndon Johnson, trying to broaden his appeal among the nation's female voters, was looking for women to appoint to high federal office. Mrs. Brown, a loyal and active Democrat, was his choice.

The new "temporary permanent" Chairman, George Stafford, was the choice of Senator Frank Carlson of Kansas. At the time he was chosen, Stafford had been an Administrative Assistant to Senator Carlson for seventeen years. Before that, he was a Kansas Republican worker for five years. When asked at his confirmation hearing by Senator Magnuson whether he was a Republican or a Democrat, he replied honestly that he was a "Frank Carlson Republican."

Dale Hardin of Peoria, Illinois, is a Republican. He is a former FBI agent. After a term as Congressional Liaison Officer in the ICC, he served as a counsel for the U.S. Chamber of Commerce, the Transportation Association of America, and the American Trucking Association. At his confirmation hearings, it was announced that the late Senator Everett McKinley Dirksen's illness prevented him from presenting Hardin to the Committee. Dirksen was known as Hardin's patron Senator.

Laurence Walrath of Florida was appointed in the 1950's as Senator George Smathers' appointee. Walrath, as a Jacksonville attorney and an ICC Practitioner, had previously been Senator Smathers' campaign manager.

John Kennedy was doing a favor for Governor "Mike" DiSalle of Ohio when he appointed John W. Bush to the Commission. Mr. Bush had served as an official in DiSalle's administration for several years, Mr. Bush created quite a stir when, as an ICC Commissioner, he was elected as a delegate to the 1964 Democratic National Convention in Atlantic City. His wife, the former Mrs. Dorothy Vredenburgh, was the Secretary of the Democratic National Committee and the official reader of the Convention roll.

Willard ("Joe") Deason was Lyndon Johnson's roommate at Southwest Texas State Teachers College. He worked in the National Youth Administration in the 1930's, under

Lyndon Johnson. He worked as an executive for KTBC and KTEV in Austin, Texas. And, finally, he raised "Him" and "Her," LBJ's famous beagles. He was named an ICC Commissioner in 1967. (One lobbyist familiar with the ICC said that Deason was named so that President Johnson could maintain a close watch on what was going on in the ICC.)

Georgia's Rupert Murphy came to the ICC under the wing of Senator Walter George. Murphy, who had made a livelihood representing large shipping interests, is a Democrat. Another Senatorial patron was Richard Russell, although, when appointed, Murphy was *not* Russell's first choice from Georgia for the job.

Kenneth Tuggle, Republican Commissioner from Kentucky, was brought to the ICC through the efforts of Senator John Sherman Cooper, but it is reported that Tuggle was in reality another "Dirksen man."

Richard Nixon's first appointment to the ICC was Donald Jackson. This was a "Presidential," as opposed to a "Senatorial," appointment. Jackson was a former Congressman, a colleague of Nixon's in the clubby *Chowder and Marching Society*, and, like Nixon, a member of the House Unamerican Activities Committee. After leaving Congress, Jackson was a TV newscaster in California.

President Nixon's latest appointment to the Commission is Robert A. Gresham. He is another former FBI agent and lobbyist. He was the minority staff director for the House Appropriations Committee, and was apparently sponsored by Representative Bow of Ohio, ranking minority member on the Appropriations Committee, and other senior members of the Committee. Interviewed soon after his appointment, he said: "I consider myself an expert in budgets, but not in the regulation of surface transportation—if I said I was, I'd be telling a tale." [1]

The appointment process and the Commissioners' backgrounds indicate what the President and Congress feel are important qualifications for the leadership of the ICC. Certainly knowledge of the problems and experience in the field of transportation are thought unimportant. Only three of the present Commissioners, Hardin, Walrath, and Murphy, had any experience at all related to transportation. Experience in the area of public regulation of private industry seems even less important. With the exception of

Mrs. Brown, none of the Commissioners had experience in this area. What does seem important is political contact and alliance. That is the only area in which all Commissioners are similarly well qualified.

There is one final criterion for appointment. Most appointees are quietly "cleared" by industry groups before selection. In effect, the clearing process means prior approval by the American Trucking Association and the Association of American Railroads, sometimes by other carrier associations, and, on occasion, relevant labor interests.

Knowledge of the Commissioners' backgrounds does enable one to predict what these people's attitudes toward regulation will be. Does experience as counsel for the U.S. Chamber of Commerce, the Transportation Association of America, or the American Trucking Association engender a healthy skepticism of industry demands? Does experience representing carrier interests or large shippers before the ICC foster a balanced perspective toward industry interests? The point to be made both about the three Commissioners with some transportation experience and those without it, is that little in their collective backgrounds suggests that they entertain even the slightest suspicion that the interests of the transportation industry (or industry in general) and the public are not identical. Nowhere is there a hint of a healthy skepticism toward industry claims.

Commissioners who come to their jobs without the wariness of industry that is essential for aggressive regulation will not have to question their assumptions in their new positions. The rhetoric and behavior of the Commissioners demonstrate that they believe the public interest is served by serving transportation interests. They further assume that the various transportation interests are adequately and appropriately represented so that the Commission, acting as a passive body, can shape from the arguments and interests before it a national transportation policy in the public interest. Both of these assumptions are open and clear. In a speech before the Annual Meeting of the Railroad Public Relations Association in the Fairmont Hotel in San Francisco on June 10, 1968, Commissioner Kenneth H. Tuggle delivered a speech entitled *The Public Interest—Where Does It Lie and Who Is Its Spokesman?*

Assuming a qualified Commission and an adequate record, it might be said that, in a given case, the public interest lies wherever the Commission finds it. It is not arrogance to say the Commission necessarily speaks for the public. *But so do the advocates of the special interests* and of the other governmental agencies who appear before us. All are part of the scene, all are necessary to the scene, and, in a sense, *all really speak for the public.* . . . With all the diverse voices raised in loud cacophony before it, the Commission, by according more or less weight here and there and by adding a few notes of its own, seeks to convert the din into a symphony recognizable as harmonious in terms of the public interest. (Emphasis added.)

If one believes that neither the Commission nor the special industry interests necessarily "speaks for the public," and that the theoretical purpose of the ICC is to represent the public interest aggressively, it is necessary that the Commission be structured so as to be able to accomplish this task. The structure should be such that people making decisions concerning the allocation of ICC resources are independent of political forces and independent of excessive industry group influence. It also might be appropriate to consider the wisdom of separating the judicial and prosecutorial functions of the agency. This hypothetical restructuring is unrealistic, however, because political and industry influences are so pervasive that unless there is basic reform outside the purview of the agency itself (campaign contributions, "political" appointments, lobbying, *et al.*), label switching will have little impact.

At present each of the ICC's operating bureaus has a specific framework of responsibilities. These basic responsibilities, or similar ones, will continue in some form regardless of the fate of the present ICC.

As of June, 1969, the eleven Commissioners were named by the President and confirmed by the Senate for staggered seven-year terms. The rest of the Commission consisted of 1906 staff members—1438 in Washington and 468 in the field offices around the country.*

The work of the Commissioners themselves is divided in several ways. First, various boards of employees are authorized to decide certain cases not involving issues of "general

---

* See Appendix 8 for a discussion of the position of black employees within the ICC.

transportation importance." There are currently sixteen such boards, organized according to the particular section of the Interstate Commerce Act they are authorized to adjudicate. These boards were created in the 1960's in order to free the Commission members for issues of transcending, or "general transportation" scope. Second, there are three divisions of the Commission, each of which administers a separate section of the Interstate Commerce Act, and is authorized to decide cases on behalf of the entire Commission, in issues not of general transportation importance. The three divisions are as follows: *Division 1*, Operating Rights Division, headed in 1969 by Commissioner Rupert Murphy of Georgia; *Division 2*, Rates, Tariffs, and Valuation Division, headed in 1969 by Commissioner Laurence Walrath of Florida; and *Division 3*, Finance and Service Division, headed in 1969 by Commissioner Kenneth Tuggle of Kentucky.

The Chairman, according to the old system which expired January 1, 1970, had only general responsibility for the overall management and functioning of the Commission, but did not serve for more than a one-year term. Primary responsibility for the budget and internal management of the ICC was vested in the Office of the Managing Director. The Chairman was and is responsible for the legislative liaison and public information functions of the Commission. Under the new system, the Chairman will be named by the President to serve as permanent Chairman of the Commission.

The staff of the ICC is divided into five bureaus and four offices, including the Office of Managing Director. Each bureau is headed by a director and divided into sections headed by section chiefs. Certain boards of employees are off-shoots of bureaus and offices, but have independence from the bureaus and offices to which they are assigned due to their quasi-legislative or quasi-judicial functions. The field organization of the ICC is divided into six geographical regions, each region headed by a Regional Manager, who reports not to the Chairman, but to the Managing Director.

Under the system prior to January 1, 1970, the *Office of the Managing Director,* with 165 positions in Washington and seventeen in the field, was responsible for the day-to-day and week-to-week operation of the Commission. The functions of the Managing Director were budgetary, personnel, administrative services, systems development, and

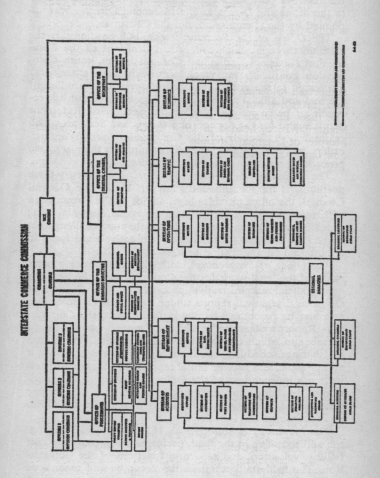

field control. The six Regional Managers reported directly to the Managing Director. The Managing Director was appointed by the Commission, not the Chairman.

The *Office of the Secretary*, with 145 positions, is the medium through which orders and decisions of the Commission (divisions, individual Commissioners, entire Commission, boards of employees, joint boards, and examiners) are issued to the public. The Secretary is the custodian of the seal and official records of the Commission and its proceedings; he is responsible for the Section of Reference Services and for the Section of Records and Services which maintains all dockets of the Commission, serves reports, orders, and notices, and generally administers the *pro forma* procedural requirements of the Commission.

The *Office of the General Counsel*, with twenty-three positions, is the Commission's lawyer. Under the General Counsel, the office provides legal advice to the Commission with reference to its jurisdiction, functions, and activities; it defends the Commission's orders if they are challenged in court. The General Counsel is not an active participant in the internal administration process of the ICC.

The *Office of Proceedings*, with 422 positions, performs much of the legal work for the Commission in the agency's quasi-judicial administrative proceedings. The Section of Opinions drafts final reports under a streamlined procedure and files its recommendations in petitions to the Commission. Report writers confer with the Commissioner or Board Member to which the case has been assigned. The Section of Hearings schedules, conducts, and processes hearings; it also prepares and releases initial reports. The Hearing Examiners are independent of the Office according to the provision of the Administrative Procedure Act: they have higher status and salaries than the attorney advisors in the Office of Proceedings.

The *Bureau of Accounts*, with 183 positions in Washington and sixty-five in the field, performs the accounting, cost finding, valuation, and reporting functions of the Commission. The field staff examines the accounts and records of regulated carriers in order to ascertain whether a given carrier is in compliance with regulations and statutes administered by the ICC. Eighty-nine of the 183 positions are filled by accountants.

The *Bureau of Economics*, with thirty-two positions, performs mathematical, statistical, economic, and related analytical work. The Bureau advises the Commission as to the effect of its proposed decisions on the economic condition of carriers, shippers, and consumers, as well as the general economy. The Bureau contains fifteen economists, one cost analyst, one mathematical statistician, and four statisticians. The remaining eleven are clerical employees.

The *Bureau of Enforcement*, with forty-one positions in Washington and thirty in the field, including thirty-six attorneys, negotiates agreements with carriers violating the law, guides investigations of violations, and prosecutes violations of the ICA in court. Occasionally, the Bureau is requested to appear in an ICC proceeding to develop facts in the "public interest."

The *Bureau of Operations*, with seventy-four Washington positions and 356 field positions, keeps abreast of the operations of the industries under ICC regulation. Its work involves investigating for economic violations, administering the rules and regulations relative to insurance protection, and administering the rules and regulations relative to the car service provisions of the Act. In investigations, the agents report to Section chiefs in Washington, who then turn investigative reports over to the Bureau of Enforcement for evaluation for possible prosecution.

The *Bureau of Traffic*, with 246 positions in Washington, performs duties relative to the filing of tariffs and rates by regulated carriers before the Commission, suspends rates pending determination of their lawfulness and confers with shippers and carriers in reference to rate policies.

Legal Machinery

The administrative-legal procedures of the ICC are generally used to settle three kinds of disputes, corresponding to the Divisions of the Commission. First, operating rights cases, the vast majority of which are disputes over what firms will carry what commodities in what areas. Second, rate decrease cases, which are disputes between modes, or among carriers within a mode, as to who will carry particular commodities. Third, finance cases (mergers, consolidations), which are disputes over who should own pieces of the transportation industry and how large those pieces should be. These disputes, which make up the majority of the Commission's caseload, are primarily between private transportation interests. Even in those few kinds of cases that are not, private interests are well represented and defended since decisions will invariably affect them.

ICC settlements of disputes presented and framed by special beneficiaries necessarily affect the public interest. Virtually every ICC decision rearranges—if perhaps insignificantly—the transportation picture. Virtually every decision determines how goods and passengers will be transported. As individual ICC decisions combine to describe the national transportation system, the ICC defines national transportation policy. If the public interest can be identified with the satisfaction of the transportation needs of the public, then it is fair to conclude that the ICC speaks to the public interest only secondarily, to the extent that the public interest is served by the satisfaction of the demands of the transportation industry. The ICC places the cart before the horse. The Commission should clearly identify the nation's surface transportation needs and compel the several industries to serve those needs. Instead, the ICC responds to the demands of the industry—through the issues framed in the caseload—and only if satisfaction of those demands complements the needs of the transportation public, is the public interest served.

When a dispute arises and is found to come under ICC jurisdiction, it is assigned by the Chief Hearing Examiner to be processed either formally (in the "Formal Docket" with a hearing and oral argument) or informally (through the "modified procedure"). Hearing Examiners handle formal dockets, and the Section of Opinions is responsible for the modified procedure.

Upon completion of the formal hearing and arguments, the Hearing Examiner may issue an initial report. If he does, the disputing parties have an opportunity to present exceptions and objections, and if they fail to do so, the examiner's report becomes the decision of the Commission. If the opposing interests do raise objections, a division of the Commission issues a decision. If the Examiner issues no initial report, the division makes the initial decision. It is possible to appeal a given decision, either to the specific division involved, or to the entire eleven-member Commission in matters of General Transportation Importance as set out in the ICC's General Rules of Practice.[2]

The Deputy Director of the Section of Opinions oversees

the Commission's modified legal procedure, in which approximately 100 attorney advisors make the initial determinations concerning controversies. As a rule of thumb, unopposed cases, and most cases in which the opposition is limited to a few parties, go through the modified procedure.

After an attorney advisor makes his recommendations and refines them, if requested, to satisfy the Review Board or Division assigned the case, the Board or Division issues an initial decision. Parties may appeal by right to the appropriate Division. They may ask for review of the record, petition for further submission of evidence, or request an oral hearing. As with the formal procedure, after final decision by a Division, parties may seek further review before the entire Commission if the case involves issues of General Transportation Importance.

The ICC is not a forum for the poor man. It is extraordinarily expensive to make and present a case before the ICC. Costs to a litigant include attorney's fees, witnesses' expenses, consultant fees, and printing. The least expensive case opposed will generally cost about $3000 for these fees alone, while more complicated cases often run into the hundred of thousands of dollars.

The Bee Line Express Company of Birmingham, Alabama, a small carrier specializing in service to small towns, spent approximately $1500 for an application in which the Commission granted limited authority to serve Albertville, Alabama (population 5037) but declined to approve service to Boaz, Alabama (population 3078). The Shipley Transfer Company, of Baltimore, spent $9000 in attorney fees to process its applications for operating authority in liquid latex. The company did not obtain satisfactory grants despite strong shipper support. The Yeary Transfer Company's estimated litigation expense to safeguard its rights under an agricultural exemption amounted to between $15,000 and $20,000. A study of merger applications approved in Volumes 57 and 59 of *Motor Carrier Cases* found that the average price paid for operating rights by the largest group of motor carriers was $45,852—that paid by other carriers was $12,157. Such costs rest heaviest on the small carriers.[3]

The Commission provides a legal arena for disputes among business interests. Neither small carriers nor individual consumers can afford even to enter the arena. Two clear examples indicating whom the ICC almost exclusively serves are its failure to provide for a consumer or public interest representative in adjudications and its inadequate use of the ICC rule-making function.

In controversies before the Commission, issues and arguments are presented by means of an adversary system. Interests are clearly identified: attorneys specializing in ICC practice argue the cases for their respective clients whether the case concerns rates, finance (mergers), or extensions of authority. When the profits of private interests or industries are involved, those interests will have adequate representation. But there is no specific representation of the public interest, in spite of the fact that the expense and complexity of Commission proceedings prohibit the participation of the general public. In major rate cases, where a consumer representative is necessary to press for rates that reflect efficient operations, there is no one who performs this role. The Department of Transportation has intervened on several occasions to "represent the public interest," but has made it clear that regular D.O.T. intervention will not be forthcoming.[4] Only recently, in major merger cases, has the Commission realized the necessity for participation of an adversary to represent interests not provided for by private parties. The Bureau of Enforcement has been asked to enter to "develop the facts." Even so, their participation has been limited in comparison to that of the private interests * and erratic at best. The Bureau of Enforcement simply is not structured to represent the public and consumer interest on an *ad hoc* basis.

The Commissioners are well aware of the pressing need for some means of consumer representation. The authority to create formal procedural mechanisms to represent the public can be found in 49 U.S.C. 16 (12), † but the Commission has chosen to ignore it.

* In the recent C & NW-Milwaukee Road merger (F 24182) argument before the full Commission, the ICC's Bureau of Enforcement was allotted five minutes, the City of Milwaukee five minutes, and the applicants *two hours*.

† "The Commission may employ such attorneys as it finds necessary for proper legal aid and service of the Commission or its members in the conduct of their work, or for proper *representation of the public interest in investigations made by it or cases or proceedings pending before it,* whether at the Commission's own instance or upon complaint . . . and the expenses of such employment shall be paid out of the appropriation for the Commission." (Emphasis added.)

Another factor indicating that the ICC is essentially a forum within which competing transportation interests work out their competitive squabbles is that only about twelve out of thousands of proceedings in the ICC each year are rule-making (ex parte) hearings. Ex parte hearings are investigation and rule-making proceedings, initiated by the ICC, that could perform many important functions in the public interest. By creating rules, the Commission can approach problems aggressively; it can encourage exhaustive presentation of all the considerations pertinent to an issue by all interests (including the consumer), rather than respond to the narrow scope of a formal complaint. These proceedings allow the Commission to deal with a possible problem area before it becomes a national transportation crisis. In short, rule-makings are a means by which the ICC can affirmatively make transportation policy.

Part of the reason why there are so few rule-making hearings when this tool provides a unique opportunity for the Commission to place its resources at the disposal of the public interest is, according to Commissioner Tierney, that rule-makings are very expensive, since they require independent studies from the ICC staff. Money and staff are generally not available to perform this function,[5] due to the ICC's own choice of priorities. The ICC is under-budgeted, yet it is the Commission's responsibility to petition for greater funding to perform the necessary rule-making functions or to shift its priorities. It has done neither.

The Organization Men

The "personality" of the bureaucracy is an invisible force that plays an extremely important role in defining and controlling the administrative process of the ICC. Perhaps fifteen men—heads of the Sections in the Office of Proceedings, and several others, including members of review boards—seem to be the real transportation experts and policy makers in the ICC. In innumerable ways their influence seeps into the various levels of ICC procedure to affect actual policy formulation. Few ICC staffers whom we confronted with this conclusion denied its importance.

The attitudes toward transportation of the men in this upper staff are similar. They have generally been in the Commission in one capacity or another for at least thirty

years.* They share a protective attitude toward the transportation industry. They are afraid of change. The image
they have of transportation is set not in the booming 1960's
but in the days of the Great Depression. These men are in
positions of great responsibility and their presence is felt in
many ways.

First, they are policy advisors within the Commission.
Some make policy through formal decision mechanisms—
those on the review boards and members of the Policy Review Committee. † Others submit memoranda to Commissioners and staff when asked to do so.[6]

Second, they train young men on the way up in the Commission. The formal training sessions for young attorney
advisors are prepared by the heads of the Section of
Opinions. Young attorneys thus learn the law from men who
bear much of the responsibility for past ICC transportation
policy (be that good or bad) and it is inevitable that the
philosophy of the supervisors will rub off on the initiates.
Another factor in this perpetuation of the ICC's transportation philosophy is that the "teachers" are responsible for
promotions. Commissioners rely upon the recommendations
of the select few "teachers" in appointing their staff.

Third, the young attorneys are "socialized" by considerable contact with hearing examiners and attorney advisors
within the Commission. Bertram Stillwell, Director of the
Office of Proceedings, indicated there is "quite a bit" of
contact; they eat together and take coffee breaks together.
They become friends. They are all part of the same Commission; mixing is unavoidable.[7]

To a much lesser extent the same kind of influences are
at work on hearing examiners. Often they have come to their
positions through the attorney advisor route. But hearing

---

* The top staff members of the ICC—Directors and Deputy of
Assistant Directors of the Bureaus and Offices—have been at the ICC
for an average of twenty-nine years. Directors have been at the ICC
for an average of thirty-one years. The average tenure of the five
top officials in the Office of Proceedings is thirty-four years. Thus it
is inconceivable that the top bureaucrats at the ICC should *not* have
developed an attachment to thirty-year-old methods and concepts. See
Appendix 5 for a detailed run-down of these statistics.

† The Policy Review Committee of the Office of Proceedings provides top-staff-level advice and analysis for the ICC. Significantly, it
is made up of career bureaucrats with a stake in the regulatory
status quo. Thus, chances of significant regulatory policy changes are
minimized by the very structure of this Committee.

examiners have more independence in the decision-making process because they are generally more experienced than attorney advisors. As a group, hearing examiners perpetuate the 30's "personality of the bureaucracy." *Half* are now eligible for retirement.[8] The stasis of attitudes implied by this fact is unfortunate: these men developed their conception of the needs of national transportation years ago; they tend to stay on until they retire or die. There is little the ICC can do about inadequate performances by hearing examiners, since their independence is safeguarded by the Administrative Procedure Act.

That the staff heads have considerable informal influence over policy is undeniable. Their influence on the younger staff, and therefore on future policy, is also considerable. They readily admit that it is difficult to find and keep new men with initiative, since an attorney advisor's work is none too glamorous [9] and private practice beckons. Former ICC attorneys told us that work was generally uninteresting, that individual attorneys received no personal recognition, and that imaginative thinking went unrewarded.

Some ICC officials deny that there is a prevailing view on "transportation policy" in the Commission; rather, they assert, everything depends on the issue.[10] If that assertion is true, it was certainly not proved during our experience with the Commission. As an example of the archetypal and omnipresent "personality" of the bureaucracy, responses to a standard series of questions were virtually identical throughout the Commission. Q: What would be the result of deregulation of motor carriers? A: Chaos. Destructive competition. Q: Are you aware of any facts and figures, studies, or reports that support your conclusions? A: No. Q: Well, how do you know? A: We remember the 1930's.

The Regulatory-Industrial Complex: ICC and Industry

The existence of "personal" lobbying in Washington is a well recognized fact. The ICC is particularly susceptible to it for several reasons. First, the industries with a stake in ICC policy are identifiable and definite. Second, they stand to gain or lose a great deal, since even with a passive ICC they compete for favors with other carriers or transportation modes. These industries use the ICC to implement new policy whenever they find it impossible to deal under the table with potential adversary transportation interests.

Finally, the combined transportation industries account for over 15 per cent of the nation's GNP. Their lobbying interests, therefore, are enormous and highly active.* There is little doubt that some contact between the ICC and the transportation industries is necessary and desirable, particularly that confined to formal informational exchange. But the massive industry press † and ICC publications can easily assure the necessary exchange of information, and those needs that cannot be met by publications could be met by ICC sponsored seminars in Washington and regional transportation centers. The Commissioner's argument that they need extensive personal contact with industry for the purposes of information collecting is a bit disingenuous since they are rarely seen soliciting consumer views, labor or truck drivers' views, or the views of small shippers, etc.

The ICC Canons of Conduct, say that "members and employees of the Commission shall not solicit or accept, directly or indirectly, any gift, gratuity, entertainment, favor, loan, or any other thing of monetary value, which might reasonably be interpreted as being of such a nature that it could affect their impartiality," [11] and that "members and employees shall avoid any action, whether or not specifically prohibited therein, which might result in, or create the appearance of, . . . affecting adversely the confidence of the public in the integrity of the Commission." [12]

The reasoning behind this provision is clear. The ICC is, by Congressional command and Supreme Court interpretation, the guardian of the public interest. As an independent regulatory agency with a substantial adjudicatory function, it is under special obligations to avoid excessive friendship or favors from litigants before it. Even contact can give the

---

* The incredibly powerful American Association of Railroads, divided into numerous divisions, the mammoth American Trucking Associations with many subgroups (e.g., regular route, irregular route), the Water Carriers, and several rate bureaus, all have their own lobbyists. In addition, ICC Practitioners and the Motor Carrier Lawyers Association, as well as numerous transportation "consultants," maintain close personal relations with ICC officials on behalf of a variety of specific carriers and clients. The former group is even allowed to maintain offices right in the ICC's headquarters in Washington, D.C.

† There are seven major, regular publications of the transportation industry. The three most popular are *Railway Age, Transport Topics,* and *Traffic World.* In addition, there are over ten minor magazines and periodicals, as well as numerous special publications.

appearance of impropriety if it is too extensive, informal, personal, and private. These limitations apply to any government officials with adjudicatory authority, and should apply to all relations with trade associations, since these interests are in almost perpetual litigation before the agency.

During the summer of 1969 it was revealed that members of the ICC, traveling to industry functions at public expense, were receiving free hotel rooms, meals, and other expenses from the industries that the ICC regulates. After the initial publication of some of the facts concerning this practice in *The New York Times,* the Commission Chairman, Virginia Mae Brown, announced a prohibition against accepting money or in-kind benefits from regulated industries. Since this behavior is explicity prohibited by the ICC Canons of Ethics, the purpose of this pronouncement must have been to assuage declining public confidence in the integrity of the Commission resulting from the disclosures. But the acceptance of in-kind benefits—certainly an impropriety—is not the only behavior which causes loss of public confidence in the Commission. Recurrent industry-ICC contact at conferences and conventions creates an impression of partiality, regardless of improprieties, and adversely affects the confidence of the public in the Commission's integrity.

Commissioners have often failed fully to consider the implications of particular excursions. On June 24, 1967, one year after the filing of the petition in an important case against the Southern Pacific, Commissioners Kenneth Tuggle, Williard Deason, and Paul J. Tierney boarded a *private* car on the Southern Pacific for a trip between San Francisco and Portland, Oregon. The purpose of the trip, which included a picturesque ride through the Cascade Mountains, was to inspect the railroad's facilities between those cities. While Commissioner Tierney denies that the trip had anything to do with railroad passenger service (the "adequacies" issue) it is obvious that that was no time to be taking a privileged trip on the Southern Pacific.

Another trip that might better have been avoided was Mrs. Brown's recent excursion (June 17, 1969) to Minneapolis, Minnesota, for a luncheon address before the Accounting Division of the Association of American Railroads. At that time the ICC was completing for publication its important *Investigation of Costs of Intercity Rail Passenger Service.* A key issue of that study was proper railroad accounting procedure. In fact, the study criticized the accounting methods then in use, but its criticism does not negate the obvious impropriety of mixing with businessmen whose deepest financial interest was at stake, while the study was as yet unpublished.

The Commissioners' contact with industry cannot cause them to lose an objectivity or sharpness that they never possessed, but clearly little insight is gained at these meetings. And any "sharpness" that *might* develop in the absence of constant industry contact is thwarted. The trips are an aspect of the small favor process which, on a cumulative basis, adds to industry's informal connections to the agency.* The chance to return to (and speak in) the home state at government expense is an obvious small gratuity to a Commissioner, and industry gladly obliges. Mrs. Brown, for instance, has visited her home state on nineteen separate occasions at government expense (on "official business") since fiscal year 1966.

The payment of Commissioners' miscellaneous expenses by industry has built up over the years to a level that seems to violate General Accounting Office standards against the augmentation of agency appropriations from "outside sources," as well as the agency's own canons. Commissioner Murphy has estimated that "no more than 25 per cent" of his past travel expenses had been paid by industry groups.† A conservative estimate of direct industry supplement to the Commission since 1966 based on Commissioner Murphy's admitted percentage and our own accounting would be well over $10,000.

* Law firms keep file cards on Commissioners' birthdays, anniversaries, hobbies, *et al.* Contact is constantly maintained through luncheons and golf dates. The power of access to a legal representative or Commission staff member who has a personal, informal relationship with a Commissioner should not be underestimated. The upper staff is often wined and dined as vigorously as are the Commissioners.

Small favors, so small that they do not seem clearly to involve impropriety, accentuate this process. A bottle of whiskey at Christmas time, scores of ashtrays and calendars—it is unlikely that these gestures drastically affect a Commissioner in a given decision, but we cannot help feel that the cumulative effect of this process annihilates whatever little hope there might be of an appointee developing an independent, challenging role *vis-à-vis* industry.

† See *The New York Times*, August 24, 1969, p. 1. Mr. Murphy told the *Times* reporter that he "never did feel too sure about it, but . . . knew it was the practice."

Industry regularly pays for luncheons, hotel rooms, even for a hairdresser for Madame Chairman. Commissioners and upper staff are commonly transported around at their convenience by corporate jets, private rail cars, and pleasure yachts.

The loss of any critical distance that might still exist between regulator and regulated, and improprieties or the appearance thereof, are not the only issues at stake with regard to Commission travels. Taking these trips is simply not a useful or efficient way for a regulator to learn about transportation.

On the spot examination of surface transportation meccas in the popular convention spots of Hawaii, Puerto Rico, or the Bahamas does not seem worth the expense or the time of the Commissioners. Nor does the effort to maintain personal contacts with industry leaders, all of whom often visit the capital and have powerful spokesmen permanently in Washington, D.C. Nor does the opportunity to present agency views and ideas seem to justify, even if all other things were equal, this expenditure of effort and time of a group responsible for the regulation of almost one-fifth of the nations's GNP.

It is difficult to assess the impact of the perpetual absence of one to three of the Commissioners from Washington. There is, perhaps, very little impact: they might do little if back in Washington. But the side effects of these trips are clearly wasteful. For example, there is the writing of the speeches delivered at these events. The public is paying quite a lot of money for these speeches: since 1966, Commissioners and staff have turned out over 4000 pages (over one million words) to be delivered by traveling Commissioners. Although none of the speeches serves to develop policy or treats its subject with any depth, they are all different. Another side effect is the expense of the trips themselves. (See Appendix 3 for a compilation of two Commissioners' travels as illustration.)

Whatever a reader's judgment about the inappropriateness of some of these trips, or about wasted resources, one can't help wondering why the Chairman of the ICC found it necessary to visit Hinton, West Virginia in September of 1967, at taxpayer expense, to attend the State Water Festival and crown "Queen Mermaid II."

Another indication of Commission regulatory attitudes

is the constant flow of employees and Commissioners between agency and industry. The manner in which agency officials lay down the regulatory cudgel and pick up the industrial cudgel by changing jobs indicates that they feel an identity between the two roles. In addition, a surprising number of ICC officials have admitted receiving job offers from various industries or their counsels while in government employ. Perhaps it is understandable that young attorneys leave the ICC for jobs as practitioners or industry representatives, for many of them frankly view their ICC employment as training for industry or industry-connected employment. And it is perhaps justifiable that certain employees—like tariff examiners—leave their jobs for industry where comparable work receives greater pay.* It must influence a high Commission official's judgment to know that he may get a lucrative industry position when he retires from the Commission. And Commissioners are certainly aware of that possibility. In addition to their own job offers, they know what happened to their predecessors. The following is a description of the "fate" of the last eleven Commissioners to leave the ICC.

Owen Clarke, left 1958
    V-Pres., C&O-B&O Railroad
Robert W. Minor, left 1958
    Senior V-Pres., Penn Central Co.
Anthony Arpaia, left 1960
    V-Pres., REA Express, now retired
John H. Winchell, left 1960
    now retired, Washington, D.C.
Donald McPherson, left 1962
    ICC Practitioner, Washington, D.C.
Clyde E. Herring, left 1964
    ICC Practitioner, Washington, D.C.

* Because of the difficulties in proposing a solution to this problem, its impact on middle-level decision-making has not been emphasized. In addition to the influence that alluring job offers might have over middle-staff personnel, most of the personnel in the Bureaus of Traffic and Operations, as well as many in Accounts, have been hired *from* industry. As with the case of young attorneys, this process is understandable. There are simply few alternative sources of qualified manpower.

Abe M. Goff, left 1967
  now retired, Moscow, Idaho
Everett Hutchinson, left 1965
  ICC Practitioner, Washington, D.C.
Howard Freas, left 1966
  Ass't to Pres., Southern Railway System
Charles Webb, left 1967
  Pres., Nat'l Ass'n of Motor Bus Operators (NAMBO),
  Washington, D.C.
William H. Tucker, left 1967
  V-Pres., Penn Central Co.

The dangers of such interchange are apparent. First, there is the public loss of confidence in the ICC's independence and integrity. It is not unreasonable for the public to wonder whose interest a Commissioner is serving when one week he is the regulator and the next the regulated, particularly when Commissioner and staff admittedly receive private offers while still in government employ.

Second, there is the effect that the knowledge of available industry jobs has on the Commissioner's regulatory attitude and independence. Since the Commissioner can in fact wear either hat—regulator or regulated—he must blind himself to inherent conflicts of interest. Aware that the door to industry employment is open, a Commissioner may keep it ajar by passive regulation that does not step on industry's toes.* Or, preferring another term as regulator, a Commis-

---

* The reality of this possibility is well recognized by the regulators themselves. It is illustrated rather bluntly by the following letter from a member of the Federal Power Commission to President Kennedy in 1963, announcing his unwillingness to accept another term on the Federal Power Commission:

> Ordinary men cannot administer [the regulatory] law today in the face of pressures generated by huge industries. . . . The big problem in the regulatory field is not influence peddling and corruption as that word is commonly understood. . . . But abandonment of the public interest can be caused by many things, of which timidity and a desire for personal security are the most insidious. This commission, for example, must make hundreds or even thousands of decisions each year, a good many of which involve literally scores and hundreds of millions of dollars in a single case. *A commissioner can find it very easy to consider whether his vote might arouse an industry campaign against his reconfirmation by the Senate.* (Letter from Howard Morgan to President John F. Kennedy, January 23, 1963, quoted in Louis M. Kohlmeier, *The Regulators,* Harper and Row, New York, 1968, p. 82.) (Emphasis added.)

sioner will be hesitant to arouse industry antagonism that might make reconfirmation difficult. How proper would it be for a corporate defendant in a civil or criminal action privately to offer a lucrative job to a district court judge? ICC decisions often involve matters of greater economic consequence than most court proceedings, are subject to general adjudicatory standards, and are given generally greater credibility by courts of appeal than are district court decisions.

In addition to informal contacts, small favors, and job interchange, industry groups have an institutionalized influence on agency policy-making and information-gathering mechanisms. There are seventeen groups, committees, or liaison activities in which the ICC participates with industry. There are a number of others with various governmental agencies. There are none consisting of consumers, and there are no consumer representatives on any of these groups. (Appendix 4 lists all seventeen.)

Industry's chance to help formulate regulations, standards, and detailed policies at the initial stage, where policy is still in a relatively malleable state, is far more useful than the opportunity given any consumer representatives who might be aware of the issues involved. Public access might be possible at a public hearing stage, when amendments could be proposed or expressed in letters to the agency. As things stand, however, programs and policies harden progressively as they surface from within the agency.

Sleepy Watchdogs: Congress and the ICC

The ICC's relations with Congress are extremely important, if for no other reason than that the ICC was created by Congress as the expert agency in the area of surface transportation. If the ICC operates at optimum functional efficiency, it 1. does the will of Congress as clearly set forth in the ICA; 2. sets explicit standards of regulation which are clear enough for the Congress to understand and approve through acquiescence; and 3. brings to Congress' attention the need for changes in the ICA where policies set by Congress are considered by the ICC to be deficient for current or future regulatory problems. The theoretical role of Congress is fulfilled through overseeing * ICC en-

---

* This "overseeing" or supervising function is called "Congres-

forcement of the Act, through the receipt and consideration of legislation recommended by the ICC as its expert, and through legislation generated at its own initiative.

Proper Congressional supervision of the ICC requires that two conditions be met. First, the men responsible for examining the agency and its appropriation requests must be generalists. That is, they must not further reflect the special interests already represented throughout the agency's ranks. Second, they must have the time and resources to examine and evaluate the agency in some detail. Unless questions are framed with a specificity that forces direct answers and detailed confrontation, the agency can avoid scrutiny and will feel no need to set policy on a basis that could be publicly justified under a cross examination.

Of all the Committees that, for various reasons, deal with the ICC, the Surface Transportation Subcommittee of the Senate Commerce Committee is in the best position to accomplish the task of supervision. It has the regular assignment of ICC oversight, and its members represent large, general constituencies. But even though good intentions are apparent, manpower is woefully inadequate. The Subcommittee staff is quite small, largely made up of one counsel with several assistants, and the turnover on those positions is fairly rapid.

The Subcomittee itself has ten members, but only a few have any time to attend to ICC matters. At the Oversight Hearings in June, 1969, Senator Vance Hartke of Indiana, Chairman of the Subcommittee, did by far most of the questioning, and only three other Senators—Prouty, Pearson, and Hansen—were present.

Even those Senators and Congressmen who are interested in what is going on in the ICC are too busy to maintain the kind of close touch with technical matters that the ICC's limited attitude toward its own discretionary powers would require. For example, Senator Hartke had three committee hearings on the day of the ICC "oversight" hearings, and had to go to them, despite the priority he gives the ICC.

Still, the Surface Transportation Subcommittee—due to the competence of its overworked staff and the persistence of its Chairman, Senator Hartke—is able to conduct occa-

---

sional oversight"—not to be confused with the more common use of the word "oversight" to mean error or omission.

sional, brief oversight hearings of some intensity. The better questions by the Chairman are greeted by long silences or nervous glances from the Commissioners. But the Commission still views these occasions as rather unpleasant periods it must endure and then ignore. It understands that the Senator must appear antagonistic so the folks back home will know he is doing the job. Hostile questions are accepted as part of the game.

The kind of scrutiny that can compel policy change is, perhaps, impossible without a major change in personnel at the upper staff level. But supervision that effectively brings to light the full impact of ICC policies as they betray the public interest could have at least a partial impact. The hearing necessary for this task would require several weeks of vigorous questioning—six to eight hours each day. The kinds of questions which must be asked would require a full-time staff of fifteen to twenty full-time attorneys *and economists*. Although this procedure would mean substantially increasing the present staff, we are talking about the oversight of an agency responsible for regulating a substantial portion of America's GNP, probably the single most important part.

The ICC is "quasi-legislative" as well as "quasi-judicial" in nature. It has the power and the authority to set standards and establish new policy. However, the Commission does not see itself in this light. Generally, when a matter in transportation becomes critical, where it is necessary for some branch of government to step in and protect the public interest, the ICC is either silent or looks desperately to Congress to be told what to do. Thus, in the area of small shipments, rail passenger service, household movers, conglomerates—areas which demand technical skill, for which purpose the ICC and other "expert" agencies were set up —the ICC is usually unwilling or unable to lift a regulatory finger.

For example, Commissioner Tuggle said at the "oversight hearings" before Senator Hartke in June, 1969, that: "[I]n the academic sense, we do not create or recommend policy. . . . The only policy Congress has enacted—and we are a child of Congress, they created us to do certain things. They only delegated to us certain powers and prerogatives." An analysis of the record reveals that the ICC rarely proposes detailed legislation to Congress that might give it needed authority. Most of its recommendations are for technical changes in the ICA, and most are initiated through industry pressure. Those that are proposed for the benefit of an unorganized group are usually modified by industry at the formative stage within the agency.

The bills the ICC does recommend to Congress have two places of origin—the staff of the Commission and industry.* The staff bills reach the ICC through the Legislative Counsel and a committee of ICC Commissioners, and are generally sent up to the Hill—without revision year after year. Industry bills are suggested to the Commissioners on an individual contact basis, and are approved by the Commission before they are sent up to the Hill.

The ICC's passive interpretation of its legislative role is particularly unfortunate since its expertise and supposed independence make it uniquely able to propose revisions in the ICA for the public interest. Matters which affect the interest of regulated industry are brought to Congress' attention anyway, by registered lobbyists. But where "only" *citizens'* complaints are at stake, the Congress must depend on the ICC to bring problems to its attention. If the ICC is silent, the problems fester in inattention. Only when severe do they reach Congress' attention, and not usually through ICC initiative. Even those bills the ICC does send to Congress languish there for years before Congress either passes them or the ICC removes them from the Hill's consideration. One Commissioner admitted to us that Commissioners do not spend enough time simply educating Congressmen about the gaps in the ICA which hinder effective regulation.

Political pressure by special interest groups on individual Congressmen is another important factor curtailing effective Congressional protection of the public interest in transportation matters. This pressure is particularly strong in the House, where an interest group concentrated in a particular district can have a great impact. Further, general industry trade association campaign contributions of $500 to $5000 are more important in a House election than in a million-dollar Senate campaign.

Trucking and railroad executives traditionally are big givers to election campaigns, and these executives have a

* Until 1957, the ICC never recommended legislation to Congress on a regular basis.

great deal of business before the ICC. It does not require a great leap of imagination to see why the trucker or the railroad man or the freight forwarder or the barge man or the big shipper would attempt to have "his" Senator or Congressman intercede before the ICC on behalf of his interest.

These pressures are generally accepted around Washington: in the words of one federal judge: "The practice of seeking personal and poltical favors from kings and public officials is a sport as old as government itself." [13] What may not be necessarily known to all is, who has given what to which elected official's campaign. In fact, these facts may never be known to anyone but the giver and the receiver, because of the lax provisions of the federal law requiring Senators and Congressmen to file with the Senate and the House lists of their campaign contributors. For example, some Senators and Congressmen escape the law by listing all contributions as coming from "Friends of Senator X": since all that is required is a listing of contributions to Senator X personally, Senator X can claim simply that all his contributions came in one bundle from a legal intermediary. Also, since no corporations are allowed to give in the corporate name to a political campaign, and individual contributions are limited to $5000 for a single campaign fund, many industry associations create financial arms which secretly channel contributions to candidates. Labor unions operate in much the same way.

The members of the Senate Commerce Committee and the House Interstate and Foreign Commerce Committees have received large amounts of legal campaign contributions from ICC-regulated industries and labor unions in these industries. In 1968, the Bus Industry Public Affairs Committee of Washington, D.C., James T. Corcoran, Secretary-Treasurer, gave the following members of the Senate Commerce Committee the following contributions: Howard Cannon of Nevada, $200; Warren Magnuson of Washington, $200. Members of the House who received bus money were then Representative Melvin Laird, $200; the ranking Republican on the important (roadbuilding) Public Works Committee, William C. Cramer, $200; three Republican members of the House District of Columbia Committee, William Harsha of Ohio, Gilbert Gude of Maryland, and Joel Broyhill of Virginia, the total of $375. Finally, California Democrat B. F. Sisk of the Rules Committee received $200, and Colorado Republican Donald Brotzman of the Commerce Committee received $200.

The rail labor campaign fund, the Transportation Political Education League of Cleveland, Ohio, was also quite active in 1968. Among Representatives receiving contributions from this source were Nebraska Republican Glen Cunningham (Commerce Committee), $1000; Maryland Democrat Samuel Friedel, second-ranking Democrat of the Commerce Committee, $500; California Democrat John E. Moss (Commerce Committee), $1000.

Granddaddy of all ICC-regulated-industry campaign funds in 1968 was that of the American Trucking Associations, the Truck Operators Non-Partisan League, of Washington, D.C.—$73,456.50 was the sum "distributed" in 1968 by T.O.N.L. The discovery of this wholesale giving campaign, when a major bill in Congress desired by the truckers was pending, produced a sharp reaction against the trucking industry, and actually led to the defeat, through Congressional inaction, of the truck-sponsored bill to increase the size and weight limits of trucks on federal highways. The boldness of the entirely money "distribution" was illustrated by the remark made by the Treasurer of T.O.N.L., Frank Grim: "We do what we can for those on the committees who might help us." [14] *Des Moines Register* Washington correspondent Nick Kotz read through files in the House of Representatives Clerk's Office and came up with the following list of recipients of trucking money:

House Public Works Committee Chairman George Fallon (D-Md.), $1000; Subcommittee Chairman John C. Kluczynski (D-Ill.), $3000; members John Blatnik (D-Minn.) and William H. Harsha (R-Ohio), $1000 each; Senate Public Works Committee member and Senate Minority Leader Everett Dirksen (R-Ill.), $2000; Sen. Mike Monroney (D-Okla.), a member of the Senate Appropriations Subcommittee on Public Works, $2375; Sen. Baker and Sen. Caleb Boggs (R-Del.), each $1000; House Public Works Committee Democrats Robert E. Jones (Ala.); Frank Clark (Pa.); Harold Johnson (Calif.); W. J. Bryan Dron (S.C.); Arnold Olsen (Mont.); Roy Robert (Tex.); and James Kee (W.Va.), each $500. House Public Works Committee Republicans James Gover (N.Y.); Roger Zion (Ind.); Charlotte Reid (Ill.) and Charles Halleck (Ind.), each $500.

Sen. Alan Bible (D-Nev.) and Sen. Peter H. Dominick (R-Colo.), $1000 each; Reps. John D. Dingell (D-Mich.) of the

Commerce Committee and B. F. Sisk (D-Calif.) of the Rules
Committee, $1500 each; Tom Steed (D-Okla.) of the Appropri-
ations Committee and Samuel N. Friedel (D-Md.) of the Com-
merce Committee, $1000 each. Morris K. Udall (D-Ariz.),
Interior Committee; John Brademas (D-Ind.), Education and
Labor; Brock Adams (D-Wash.), Commerce; and Julia B.
Hansen (D-Wash.), Appropriations, $500 each.

Transportation Subcommittee Chairman Friedel received
$1000 in October, 1966; $250 in May, 1968; and $750 in April,
1968.

Other Subcommittee members and the amounts they were
given: Dingell (D-Mich.), $1500 in May, 1968; Samuel Devine
(R-Ohio), $1000 in 1966; Albert Watson (R-S.C.), $1000 in
January, 1968 and $500 in 1966; Adams, $500 in March, 1968
and $500 in 1966; Daniel Ronan (D-Ill.), $500 in 1966; and
Glen Cunningham (R-Neb.), $500 in 1967.

These members of the full Committee had also received cam-
paign contributions from the truckers, each getting $500: Reps.
Lionel Van Deerlin (D-Calif.), 1966; Fred Rooney (D-Pa.),
1966; John Murphy (D-N.Y.) May, 1968; John Jarman
(D-Okla.), April, 1968; Ancher Nelson (R-Minn.), 1966; and
James Harvey (R-Mich.), 1966.

The late Senator Everett Dirksen was the recipient of
many contributions from ICC-regulated industries, as well
as two personal contributions in 1968 from key industry
lobbyists—$500 from Charles Webb, President of the Na-
tional Association of Motor Bus Operators, and an ex-ICC
Commissioner, and $1000 from Thomas M. Goodfellow,
President of the Association of American Railroads. This is
especially significant because of the great influence Dirksen
is said to have had with two of the eleven Commissioners,
Kentucky's Kenneth Tuggle and Illinois' Dale Hardin.[15]

Some recent attempts to raise money for party coffers
have been rather ingenious and have created great political
debts in favor of regulated industries. The Democratic
Party's paean of praise to the Great Society, *Toward an
Age of Greatness,* was produced in 1965 by a Washington,
D.C. public relations firm, Maurer, Fleisher, and Zon Associates. This 176-page book, which looked like a rather
permanent version of *Life* Magazine, had full-page advertisements at $15,000 per page, sold to the nation's biggest
corporations. Sixty-nine out of the 176 pages were sold to
corporations yielding over a million dollars for the Party's
coffers. Several of these corporations were domestic airlines

regulated by the Civil Aeronautics Board. Three were railroad companies regulated by the Interstate Commerce Commission: the Southern Railway System, the Union Pacific, and the Milwaukee Road. One was a trucking firm regulated by the ICC.

The Southern's two-page advertisment is of special interest. It contains the text of a message from the President of the Southern System, D. W. Brosnan, and is a blatant attempt to lobby Congress through Democratic purse-strings. The message concerns the exemption from minimum rate regulation given motor carriers for the shipment of agricultural goods. It urges Congress to broaden the exemption to cover the railroads, to allow the Southern Railway to use its new aluminum boxcars in the transportation of grain products, and, incidentally, to gain a firm foothold on the market for the Southern. The message concludes: "The lawmakers of our country should have the foresight and courage to correct this sorry situation." [16] In the 1964 Democratic Convention program, which brought in $1,335,-000 in advertising revenue, there were five pages of railroad advertising and sixteen of truckers.*

Another profitable method of raising corporate money for the two major parties has been the Convention program. Regulated industries represent the fifth, sixth, and eighth biggest contributors to Party coffers since the 1960 Conventions. The railroads come in fifth, but lead the regulated industries, with thirty-one separate advertisements since 1960. Next come the airlines, with twenty-seven; and in ninth place overall come the truckers, with nineteen. Had it not been for the passage of the "Williams Amendment" barring tax deductions for these contributions, the level of contributions would have been higher.

Transportation industries have tried to use even more direct means than contributions to influence politicians in their own behalf. An Atlanta attorney named Robert B. Troutman, Jr., recently sued the Southern Railway System for

* The expenditure of substantial sums for this purpose, as well as for "public" lobbying (such as astronaut Wally Schirra's ads on the "greatness" of our railroads and the need for "equitable" regulation thereof, and ATA ads—notoriously deceptive—concerning truck safety) raises questions about ICC maximum rate policy, since these items are not clearly excluded from general expenses, which justify rate increases. Because this is a monopolistic industry, the public is paying for these lobbying efforts.

$150,000 for services in twice going to President John F.
Kennedy to attempt to overturn an ICC ruling barring the
railroad's low rate for shipment of grain. After Troutman's
meetings with Kennedy, the Justice Department filed pleas
in court which led to the overturning of the ICC order. The
jury awarded Troutman $150,000 for services rendered,
after having heard what the *Washington Post* called "rare
admissions about a big corporation's use of political influence." [17]

The informal political game at the ICC works like this:
motor carrier X applies for additional authority, say, to
carry widgets from A to B; motor carrier Y protests; there
is a hearing, and a recomended report from the examiner;
and the case goes to the Division for decision. But motor
carrier X is worried that he might not win the certificate, so
he calls up his Senator, to whom he may have given $250
for last year's election campaign. The Senator is anxious
to impress MC-X, because he'd like to live up to last year's
$250 friendship, and although he dutifully tells MC-X that
he has no control over the decision by the independent ICC,
he tells MC-X that he'll do what he can do, anyway. He
may write a formal letter to the Commission, which is answered by the Congressional Liaison Officer. This is a formal "status check," or he may simply call his favorite Commissioner. (It is interesting to note that there is no one
central record-keeping area in the ICC where these requests
for status checks are totaled.) If a formal status check is
made, the C.L.O. writes the Senator that a hearing has been
held and that a decision is forthcoming, etc.

The purpose of these contacts may be simply to speed up
a decision. The truth is, of course, that a $1-million-a-year
business means almost a hundred thousand a month, and
a quick decision means, potentially, more money. This kind
of status check ends up in the Commissioner's "tickler file,"
wherein the Commissioner, at the very least, promises the
Senator that he will find out the result of the case about an
hour before it is announced to the press, so that the Senator
can call and tell the constituent with the million-dollar application either that he has won (thus creating the impression that without the Senator's help he would have lost)
or that he has lost (thus reassuring the constituent that even
though the Senator did all that he could do, it wasn't in the
cards) before the official announcement is made. This is

the core of ICC politics on a day-to-day basis, and it is important for all concerned: the Commissioner, through a little extra diligence, has done a favor for a Senator whose support he might need for reappointment; the Senator, with the Commissioner's help, has apparently done a big favor for a helpful constituent; and the carrier, if successful, makes more money as a result of the speed-up of his application.

PR: The ICC and the Public

Since public relations is the reality of Washington, the ICC seeks to project an image of concern for the general public interest. The esoteric nature of the transportation industry and its indirect impact on the public effectively insulate the agency in most cases from direct public pressure. In the specific areas where policy impact is more direct, the consumer's major contact is through letters—particularly in the case of home moving complaints. But even there most of the public knows little about the ICC. The agency does not actively publicize its existence, its annual report is clearly not written for general public consumption, and neither are its news releases or reports.

Nevertheless, the ICC has developed certain fundamental protective mechanisms in order to shield itself from general scrutiny by other than special interest groups with which it regularly deals. The two mechanisms consist, first, of the projection of a consistent agency position or "line" and second, of the careful control of information release concerning agency documents, reports, and decisions.

One of the indications of an entrenched bureaucracy is the development of a self-interest perceived by the bureaucracy itself. One of the clearest signs of such a perceived self-interest is the development of a standard bureaucracy "line" consisting of stock answers to questions that frequently come up before the bureaucracy. These answers frequently miss the point of the question posed, but stated often enough and with sufficient invariability they can achieve the status of hard "facts," rather than opinions or theories. The consistency of adherence to the agency line throughout the ICC adds to the credibility constant repetition gives it.

A study of the information published by the Commission in various media, including its Annual Reports, Congressional hearings, and official reports on substantive matters, reveals a remarkable constancy in the ICC's responses to various official and unofficial inquiries.

Although the ICC does not have any formal relations with consumers' groups, the Commission always publicly states that its regulation adequately protects the public interest. When pressed to state exactly how the public interest is represented in the administrative process, the spokesmen for the Commission say that the adversary process brings out the necessary facts by which the ICC can make a decision and protect the public interest. In addition, the ICC usually states that intervention by the Bureau of Enforcement in various cases further protects the consumers' interests. The Bureau of Enforcement is referred to constantly, in interviews, public statements, responses to Congressional inquiries, and Congressional hearings.

In the area of competition, the Commission usually states, when asked, that there is adequate competition within and among the various modes of transportation, but that excessive competition would be "destructive," driving out the smaller carriers. Whenever asked to substantiate either the claim that there is substantial competition or that destructive competition is a likelihood at the present time, the Commission usually sidesteps the first question by stating that the National Transportation Policy compels the ICC to protect the stability of the regulated industries, and refers to conditions of "1935" to answer the second question. The ICC officially considers the competition among the various modes to be "keen," pointing to "the acquisition of new, larger, and specialized equipment; the search for new methods of pricing; and various means for providing more efficient service." [18]

The usual Commission response to consumers' complaints about home moving is: "Sorry, no jurisdiction." When it is acknowledged that there is a problem—underestimation, late deliveries, damaged deliveries, etc.—the problem is seen in terms of "eliminating the continued friction between the household goods movers and the shipping public," not in attempting to insure maximum service to the shipping public.[19]

In response to complaints about rail passenger service, the ICC points to declining passenger figures and increased deficits, and although sometimes admitting downgrading by the industry, states that the railroads have been unable to compete with the airlines over the past decade. The ICC very rarely if ever sets up the problem of competition with the motor bus, but prefers to see it in terms of the inability of the passenger train to compete in speed of service with the airlines. Asked about steps the ICC could take to improve the situation, the stock response is that ICC jurisdiction is limited, and that the ICA gives them no alternative but to allow train discontinuances when an undue burden on interstate commerce is shown.

There is no official channel through which consumer complaints reach the Commission. We were greeted by many in the agency's bureaucracy as though we were the first citizens they had ever encountered in their offices (citizens meaning anyone who has no special interest at stake at the ICC). In fact, there is reason to believe that we were the first group to spend a great deal of time asking specific questions of people down to the middle and lower levels of the bureaucracy. Our inquiries probably constituted the first real test of the agency's information control mechanisms when confronted by representatives of the general public, or at least by investigators with no special axe to grind.*

It was clear from the beginning that the agency approach to our study was one of at least official welcome. Chairman Brown, with some sincerity, promised full cooperation. Managing Director Schmid was assigned the task of gathering our initial information requests. Mr. Schmid assured us that his door was always open to us. We were not hindered in any way as we conducted our interviews of agency personnel. This cooperation was extended throughout the summer.

As the study proceeded, however, it became clear that the agency was becoming increasingly uncomfortable.†

* Of course, there are also journalists and an occasional professor. But the journalists have deadlines to meet, operate alone, and rarely reach beneath the surface level of argument and rhetoric. Indeed, most journalists, with some exceptions, are easily induced into becoming the servants of the bureaucracy.

† For example, the *Journal of Commerce* printed an editorial entitled "Whose Guardian Angels" about us early in the summer. Although almost completely inaccurate, the article was based on a private meeting among some ICC upper staff, Ralph Nader, and Robert Fellmeth. It was apparently written by the agency itself,

Agency staff were remarking to journalists that the study could "crucify" them. Many of the agency staff we interviewed appeared exceedingly nervous. One official simply walked out in the middle of an interview. As this fear, which we could not understand at first, increased, the agency began to erect various defense mechanisms.

First, it denied the vast majority of specific requests for information made via the formal mechanism (in writing with appeal to the ICC Secretary and the Chairman). As the study progressed, more and more information requests were denied. The nature of the denial process underscored to most of us the importance of the long-standing informal contacts the industry had been able to engender within the ICC, for our own limited informal contacts enabled us to obtain privately a great deal of information the ICC would then officially deny to us. It was amusing to request a document that we held in our hands and have an official tell us that the document, or the information it contained, did not exist or that it was confidential. Most items were easy to obtain if we simply walked into the office of some official with whom we had talked previously, and asked for the document; the same document requested formally would often be denied. Since this formal request process is the route most of the public must take, their requests are generally subject to the more stringent controls of formal release.

The formal denial of information was generally framed within the context of the more general exemptions to the Freedom of Information Act. Under the Act, all information must be disclosed unless specifically exempted. Unfortunately, several of these exemptions are framed in language which the ICC (and other agencies) use to avoid the purpose of the Act entirely. Particularly subject to abuse are the so-called "investigatory file" exemption, the "internal rule and procedure" exemption, and the "inter-office memorandum" exemption. Despite a legislative history limiting the applicability of these exemptions, the ICC was able to invoke the terminology of these general provisions to avoid compliance with the Act. Some of our requests

---

without so much as a phone call by the *Journal* to determine its accuracy. The *Journal of Commerce* and many other publications have become little more than extensions of agency public relations.

were borderline with regard to several of these exemptions, but most were not.

The fear of the agency was underlined most clearly late in the summer when a delegation of four Commissioners quietly petitioned Senator Magnuson and staff to deny us the correspondence we had requested between Congress and the agency, although these documents are explicitly subject to disclosure under current court interpretation of the Freedom of Information Act.

In addition to denying us information that is known to exist, the agency makes a habit of collecting information designed more clearly to serve industry requests for information than public requests. As the substantive discussion of this report illustrates time and again, by *not* collecting relevant information in the boxcar shortage area, by not compiling way bill data for two modes and not releasing it in meaningful form for the rail mode, by not checking industry cost figures, not compiling motor carrier concentration data in meaningful form, *et al.*, the agency fails to serve the information needs of decision-making in the public interest. Further, the agency fails to keep data concerning enforcement activity and detected violations of law by type. It refuses even to count its complaints from consumers by category.

As the study progressed, we began to encounter increasing resistance in ways other than the failure to collect, or direct denials of, information. We first observed that many of our interviewees felt it necessary to have a stenographer present to record verbatim what was said. (It is doubtful that industry guests received the same careful monitoring.) We also noticed that many of our interviewees, if not most, wrote memos for their files (with several copies) explaining what was said at each interview. Undoubtedly, most of this paperwork occupied far more agency time than we did ourselves. Visits by industry rarely produce detailed memos to the file. Further, a directive * was issued, indicating the scrutiny to which personnel talking to us were subjected. Those employees who were cooperative expressed the belief that there was a likelihood of retribution for

---

* At the beginning of the summer, agency personnel were told by the Commission to clean up their offices, remove documents from general view, and be careful what they said to us—precautions "necessary" for us but not for industry visitors.

knowing failure to adhere to the agency "line." Retaliation would take the form of denial of within-grade step increases (normal pay raises), unpleasant work assignments, harassment, even dismissal.

A comic example of the importance the agency attached to our study was provided when we requested simple permission to photograph ICC travel vouchers. The vouchers had been finally released to the public. In somewhat predictable fashion, however, the agency accompanied its much heralded and publicized release of the vouchers with the instruction that they were not to be removed from the room in which they were kept—not even to take an arduous journey across the hall to the Xerox machine. Since we preferred not to spend many hours copying the voluminous records verbatim, we requested permission to snap pictures of the pages with a Minox camera. We were told to make the request in writing. Although puzzled why anyone would want to require us to copy it all down by hand rather than simply photograph it, we complied, presenting a handwritten request to Chairman Brown.

Mrs. Brown then proceeded to have a discussion among all ten Commissioners as to whether the vouchers could be copied by hand or photographed. On two occasions Mrs. Brown's office was asked whether permission was granted or denied to take photographs of the vouchers. On both occasions, the office staff responded that the entire Commission had not yet decided the issue. Disbelieving, the Task Force members pressed Mrs. Brown's staff: was it true that all ten Commissioners had to be polled on a matter of such triviality, when certain train discontinuances could be decided by a Division of three Commissioners? The answer, apparently, was yes. Finally, twenty-nine hours after the initial request, Mrs. Brown informed the Task Force by letter that the Commission had decided to grant permission to photograph the vouchers (by which time almost all had been hand copied).

Up Against the Wall

Many ICC officials privately feared that this report would concentrate more than anything else on personal or private indiscretions of agency Commissioners and staff. Agency personnel responded to us with tales of employee behavior ranging from drunkenness to extra-marital affairs. Such information, unless directly relevant to official duties, was of no interest to us. In addition, we were given innumerable tips concerning petty conflicts of interest and ex parte contacts. At least one of the latter was an eyewitness account of a railroad lobbyist talking a member of a quasi-adjudicatory ICC body into changing his decision. But the structure of the agency, its relations with Congress and the industry, and the background of its personnel make such contacts inevitable. The formal illegality of such behavior, as with private, pre-rule-making conferences with industry, and failure to rotate examiners under the Administrative Procedure Act and other statutes, is not the crux of the problem. Nor did we feel the many tales of bias, cronyism, and party politics of critical importance.

The crucial element impeding ICC performance of its statutory duty by even the most minimal standards is the cumulative effect of many years of acculturation with industry. The impact of years of influence peddling, incestuous job interchange with industry, lack of appointment integrity, *et al.*, can be dramatized by considering their effect on one particular case. During our study of the ICC we discovered a set of relationships we feel are worth describing for this purpose.

We discovered that the Managing Director of the ICC, Bernard F. Schmid, had a rather close relationship with the U.S. Freight Company, a holding company under ICC regulation, with several huge freight forwarders as subsidiaries. We discovered that about three years ago, Mr. Schmid was offered an executive position with the Freight Forwarders Institute, Washington, D.C.-based lobby for the freight forwarding industry, and located at the same address as the Washington office of the U.S. Freight Company. We discovered that Schmid, among other ICC officials, had been a fairly frequent guest on the U.S. Freight Company yacht, "Natamor," docked at the Capital Yacht Club, off Maine Avenue in Washington, D.C.* We were told that Mr. Schmid also attended U.S. Freight Company cocktail parties and was friendly with members of the U.S. Freight "family." And we discovered that Mr. Schmid frequently called up U.S. Freight officials in New York City

---

* This appears to be in violation of the ICC Canons of Conduct, 49 C.F.R. 1000. 735–41, "Gifts, Entertainment, and Favors."

to inform them of the activities of rival freight forwarders
in the ICC.[20]

The next set of facts that we discovered puts this relationship, similar to many between industry and the ICC, in
a slightly different perspective. It has to do with a discovery
by an ICC investigator in Chicago, Frank E. Lawrence, of
an elaborate system of bribery by subsidiaries of the U.S.
Freight Company. These companies were allegedly violating the ICA by giving gifts to shippers to induce them to
place their freight with the forwarder. The significance of
such a plan was indicated by the Interstate Commerce
Commission in a press release of July 18, 1969, entitled
"ICC Cautions Carriers on Gifts to Shippers."

When Agent Lawrence discovered this apparent violation
of the Elkins Act in 1967, he compiled the evidence in the
form of the usual "compliance survey" demanded of special
investigators. Reputedly, Lawrence's survey contained an
unusual amount of detailed evidence documenting the existence of warehouses filled with goods for bribery purposes.
Despite the documents that he sent to Washington, D.C.,
Lawrence did not hear from his ICC superiors for almost
a full year on this matter.

In 1968, after the retirement of Agent Lawrence's former
superior in Washington, Edward Murphy, Mr. Lawrence
asked the new Chief, Joel Burns, about the case. Mr. Burns
told Agent Lawrence to investigate the matter further.
After Mr. Lawrence had done this, Mr. Burns told him not
to follow up the investigation, not to file an "investigative
report," but to file only a memorandum on the investigation, an unusual and puzzling request. Mr. Burns explicitly
told Mr. Lawrence, after receiving the memo, not to do
anything more, to drop it completely. In addition, we were
told that this matter never reached the Bureau of Enforcement, to which investigative reports are supposed to be
sent so that an attorney can decide whether or not to prosecute, given the evidence gathered.

From that point forward, Lawrence was subjected to
completely different treatment than he had grown accus-
tomed to in his nine years of satisfactory performance at
the ICC. His next compliance survey and most of his subsequent submissions to Washington were returned to him
with hypercritical comments. Then Mr. Lawrence received
word that he had been denied his in-grade pay increase.

Shortly thereafter (in August, 1969), he received word that he was being dismissed from the ICC because of "substandard work."

After we began investigating the basis for Mr. Lawrence's dismissal, we discovered that the Lawrence file had been moved into the Chairman's office. During this period Managing Director Schmid retired from the ICC on four days' notice. Shortly thereafter, the dismissal action against Mr. Lawrence was rescinded.

According to the *ICC Manual of Administration*, "Overall management of field operations, at the Washington level, shall be the responsibility of the Managing Director." [21] The Managing Director has the responsibility of "[s]ecuring and allocating the necessary resources (funds, *personnel*, and materials) to accomplish approved programs." [22] (Emphasis supplied.) Further, while the Regional Manager, who is responsible to the Managing Director organizationally, has initial responsibility for "approval of all requests for personnel actions initiated by program directors within the region," the following proviso is added: "all actions pertaining to professional and technical positions [are] subject to further review and approval by the technical bureaus and the Managing Director." [23] Joel Burns, Chief of Rail Investigations, and Mr. Lawrence's immediate superior in Washington, told us that decisions as to whether an investigator would be transferred from one region to another were made by the Managing Director and the Director of the Bureau of Operations.

Soon after Mr. Lawrence turned in the report on the U.S. Freight Company subsidiary in Chicago, he began receiving "adverse personnel actions" from the ICC management in Washington. These actions had to be approved by the Managing Director, according to the *ICC Manual of Administration*.

As soon as Mr. Schmid left the ICC, charges against Mr. Lawrence were dropped. The ICC has done nothing about the U.S. Freight bribery, which continues into 1970. It has failed, even though confronted with substantial evidence, to prosecute for the $1 million (at least) in fines the government stood to collect; and has failed as well to press criminal charges which would have been quite appropriate.

2 / The Industry

Glossary for Chapter 2 [1]

1. Cost. In economic terms, a foregoing required to secure an objective usually measured in money. The expense, both cash and non-cash, required to sustain the operation of a transportation enterprise.

2. Common Cost, also alternative cost, joint cost. Cost incurred by or associated with transport operations involving several services or types of traffic. Examples are railroad maintenance-of-way expense for both freight and passenger service; highway land acquisition for automobiles, buses and trucks; investment in airline ramp equipment used to load both passenger baggage and air cargo.

3. Cost Ascertainment, also cost-finding procedure. The processes involved in first, gathering basic cost information, and second, in analyzing it.

4. Cost Structure. The composition, and sometimes behavior of expenses associated with and inherent in the technology and institutions of each mode of transportation; useful in determining the relative capabilities and economic characteristics of the several transport types.

5. Fixed Cost, also constant, threshold, indirect, overhead, shut-down, or residual cost. Also "burden."

Fixed costs have no relationship to volume; they are unaffected by increases or decreases in production. They are incurred by an operation as a whole, can be avoided only by total abandonment, and cannot be traced to particular units of traffic. Fixed costs are the minimum costs incurred when an organization commits itself to existence: interest on investment, supervisory staff, insurance, and land are examples. Since there is no relationship between these minimum establishment costs and the amount of work accomplished, it follows that these costs cannot be meaningfully associated with any specific unit of output.

Fixed costs can be arithmetically unitized, *i.e.*, expressed in amounts per ton mile, per passenger mile, per hundredweight, etc. Such a division is only a numerical exercise; it in no way describes either costs that would be added by new business or saved by reduced business.

6. *Fully-Distributed Cost,* also fully-burdened, fully-apportioned cost. These terms can be used only in connection with unit costs, and represent the sum of variable cost per unit plus an arithmetic division of fixed costs per unit. If the magnitude of fixed cost is substantial, the "fully-distributed" cost has little relation to what will be saved or incurred as volume fluctuates. In the special sense used by the Interstate Commerce Commission, "fully-distributed" cost includes railroad out-of-pocket costs plus all remaining revenue needs necessary to cover fixed costs, passenger-train and less-carload operating deficits and return on investment after federal income taxes.

7. *Joint Cost,* also by-product cost. This cost is experienced where the production of one article results *ex necessitate* in the production of another. In transportation the classic example is backhaul or so-called "empty return": in all modes except pipelines the production of transportation service in one direction creates capacity in the reverse direction, since equipment and personnel become available and incur cost in returning to point of origin.

8. *Out-of-Pocket Cost.* See variable cost. Sometimes used to define that part of variable cost whose behavior is readily measured.

9. *Per cent Variable.* Refers to the relationship between variable and total cost at a given traffic volume. If costs are 90 per cent variable, by definition 10 per cent of cost is fixed.

10. *Semi-Variable Cost.* This term is sometimes used to describe expenses which respond with less sensitivity to traffic volume fluctuations, *i.e.*, in less than direct proportion, or in stages or steps. Cost of this type has a fixed portion at zero production or traffic volume.

11. Total Cost, also full cost. The grand total of expenses requisite to produce transportation, *i.e.,* the sum of fixed and variable expenses. Usually expressed in aggregate terms, but can be used to derive unit cost at the total expense level.

12. Unit Cost. Expense expressed in terms of output units: car mile, vehicle mile, available ton mile, cars or tons handled. With respect to specific commodities, the expense associated with the several outputs required to handle the traffic, expressed in cost per hundredweight (cwt.).

13. Variable Cost, also direct, out-of-pocket, avoidable, escapable, product, assignable, directly assignable, added traffic, marginal, traced, prime, or separable cost. Variable costs include all costs not fixed. They are usually assumed to fluctuate in some relationship to traffic volume, but may be influenced also by other factors. Variable costs include some expense which is difficult to measure, such as wear and tear on highway road surfaces or railroad track structure, but difficulty in measurement is irrelevant to the rest of variability which hinges solely upon whether or not the expense level changes.

Cost Structure

RAIL

Rail systems require an enormous initial capital investment.* Their high fixed threshold cost is not easily divisible

* Traffic structures, rights of way, roadbeds and other large initial costs last many years. The decline in the value of these investments over time is compensated for by the introduction of new fixed costs in recent years. Specifically, the need for substantial investment in computerized hardware, new super-capacity car types, more powerful engines, *et al.,* has created new depreciation bases and new fixed charges on indebtedness. Despite this trend, some 60 per cent of rail investment is still in structures and road and only about 40 per cent is in movable equipment.

The impact of the rail cost structure is evident when one examines the traditional index of annual capital turnover. During the Depression, the ratio of revenues to capital investment reached 1 to 6 as turnover was nil. In the 1950's it climbed to 1 to 3 and even 1 to 2 as volume and utilization improved. As of 1968, it has slid back a bit to approximately 1 to 2.5. The industry is still relatively bound by its heavy fixed cost requirements. Note that automobile manufacturers often achieve 8 to 1 ratio, food chain stores sometimes reach 12 to 1 and more. Only electric power plants are comparable into small operational units and hence is not adaptable to varying levels of traffic. After the initial investment, however, the most significant rail expense characteristic is at the other extreme: the short term cost varying directly with the quantity and type of traffic carried.

The expense structure of a rail system, with its threshold cost characteristics, presents some special problems. First, it creates a significant barrier to entry into the industry, to be discussed below. Second, it means a potential excess capacity condition. Some of the railroad physical plant, particularly roadbeds and track, will not be utilized most efficiently until there are very high levels of traffic volume. Given the long life of much of the physical plant and its lack of flexibility, any reduction in pre-existing traffic will accentuate the excess capacity problem. The plant cannot be readily reduced in size to meet lesser traffic demands in a short period of time.*

Our own study of rail cost structures (discussed in Appendix 9) reflects these problems. The ICC recognizes, at least in part, the high fixed cost characteristic of the rail mode. It estimates "out-of-pocket" expenses on a very structured formula. Out-of-pocket cost is 80 per cent of fully-distributed cost. The basis for this figure, which one D.O.T. economist described as "mystical and absurd," was a post-World War II study. Much has happened to the rail mode since that time. Our own results indicate that the ICC variablility formula underestimates fixed costs. And we have conducted a second study in order to determine if the inclusion of other variables through multiple regression † might facilitate the creation of a standard formula which could be easily applied to individual carriers with greater precision. When we take the assets, miles of route, and density of a carrier, we can predict with fairly remarkable

---

to rail turnover, and even they often exceed rail levels. Of the other transport modes, only pipelines approximate this characteristic. Water carriers are the next closest, often achieving a 1 to 1 ratio, with airlines and motor carriers following.

* This phenomenon creates some thorny problems in rate regulation as railroads attempt to cut rates below costs in order to attract more traffic to an existing structure. ICC policy in his area is discussed in Chapter V.

† Multiple regression enables us to predict how one set of numbers will vary according to a formula based on *combination* of other variables.

accuracy the terminal cost/GTM (Gross Ton Miles) of individual carriers. The same principle can be applied to the aggregation of all fixed costs/GTM. The automatic adjustment of ICC knowledge about the cost variability characteristics of carriers as they vary individually and as each varies over time according to operational characteristics (*e.g.*, density, miles of route) which statistically affect variability, could be a substantial improvement on the ICC's present approach.*

MOTOR CARRIER

Motor carriers, in contrast to rail, require a trivial initial capital investment. The cost elements are highly divisible and hence highly adaptable to quick changes in traffic flow. This means that there is no necessity for a continued serious excess capacity situation.† There are, of course, very high fixed costs in the construction of highways, but these are irrelevant to the cost characteristics of the industry since the society at large has provided this element of long-run capital expense. The carriers pay a portion of the maintenance costs in the form of various user charges.

Unit costs in the motor carried industry decline significantly with increases in the length of haul and in the size of the shipment. This, of course, is because of the *relatively* constant terminal costs (billing and collecting, pickup and delivery, *et al.*) for a shipment, regardless of distance traveled or size of load. Since these costs amount, on the average, to some 40 per cent of the total cost of operation (including terminal platform charges which will not increase with distance), their distribution over more units

* Knowing precise variability for a firm would enable the ICC indirectly to judge the degree of excess capacity. More important, it would enable the ICC to determine with greater precision whether an individual carrier is in fact pricing commodities below marginal cost (theoretically illegal). That the ICC does not concern itself with cost considerations in its rate policies will be made apparent below, but if the agency is to begin to consider specific cost characteristics on a defensible basis, it must do more than change its policy. It must utilize modern techniques of statistical analysis and seek precision. Even with a policy change toward the serious consideration of cost, new formula approaches are impossible unless the present accountant dominated Bureau of Accounts and Cost Finding Section adds economists, statisticians, etc.

† The major exception to this rule is the possibility of empty backhauls with uneven traffic flow.

of operation amounts to a substantial cost reduction on a ton mile basis.

The line-haul costs make up the remaining 60 per cent of motor carrier expenses. Slightly over one-half of that is devoted to fixed expenditures per year, such as depreciation, insurance and license fees. The rest is made up of direct operating costs, such as fuel, tires, drivers' wages, and maintenance expenses. The line-haul cost is highly variable according to traffic levels. Much of the terminal expense is variable as well, since it is based on the number and value of trucks owned or leased, a factor easily adjustable to variations in traffic flow.

The regression study of the leading text [2] suggests that, despite the flexibility of capital costs, expenses are not exactly linear with regard to traffic levels. For although there is not a threshold cost related to firm size, there is a "fixed cost per unit of geographical size." That is, as the number of route miles increases, terminal, supervision, and maintenance costs increase for the same level of traffic. Asset size, operating revenues, and GTM are all irrelevant to this factor.

Thus, the only fixed cost—terminal expenses related to the geographical extent of the route—can be reduced on a unit basis through greater density of traffic. This is the only optimum structural characteristic relevant to a competitive cost advantage *within* the motor carrier mode. The asset size of a firm is believed to be relevant only insofar as larger carriers tend to have longer average runs.* The few small firms with long average lengths of haul are able to achieve costs equally as low as the larger firms with the same haul length.

Our own study attempted to ascertain the formula for cost change with increase in volume. The ICC assumes a static 90 per cent variable formula. There is little doubt that the ICC formula, based on a small sample a number of years ago, is correct in its assumption that motor carrier costs are more highly variable with changes in volume than

---

* Robert A. Nelson, *Motor Freight Transport in New England, A Report to the New England Governors Council*, Boston, 1956. The Nelson study revealed a less significant +0.33 correlation between cost/GTM and operating revenues (as a measure of size), and this was explained by a +0.45 correlation between operating revenues and the average length of haul.

are rail (or water carrier) costs. But the static 90 per cent
figure is crude, of disputable validity, and generally irrelevant to specific carriers. A comparison of the different samples reveals marked differences, for example, in the slope
and in the constants between some of the sample groups.
Generally, there is evidence that the 90 per cent is too low
for motor carriers just as the 80 per cent is probably too
high for the rail industry. In the rail formula, we demonstrated the possibility of introducing other variables, such
as density, in order to ascertain yearly formulas for variability on a firm by firm basis according to operating characteristics which statistically affect variability. The motor
carrier data indicate that the subdivision of carriers into
elementary groupings depending on the type of operation
involved would further refine the system, since there are
some marked differences in slopes between the groupings.
It might also be useful to square one of the terms to test for
curvilinearity for yet greater precision, and, further, to cube
one in order to test for an "S" pattern.

WATER CARRIER

Water transportation, like rail, requires a fairly large
capital investment. However, turnover is higher than for the
rail mode due to public financing of rights of way.* Despite
higher equipment costs than with motor carriage, the water
carrier industry does not have the excess capacity problem
of the railroads because it has the motor carrier industry
characteristic of divisible units of operation and cost. Costs
are closely associated with the numbers and value of barges
and tugs which can be adjusted to varying traffic levels.

Because of the industry's cost characteristics, utilization
of carriage facilities is an important measure of efficiency.
Since each unit of operation (barge, ship) is capable of
carrying a great deal of produce, water carriage requires a
significant volume of traffic. Unit costs are reduced if the
high terminal costs are spread over a great distance relative

---

* Like motor carriage, much of the fixed, threshold costs are
borne by nature (the ocean, lakes, and rivers) or by society at large
(subsidized harbor facilities). Nevertheless, each operating unit requires a significant percentage investment relative to output or turnover. In addition, terminal costs are extremely high, particularly for
seaport harbors. Loading is another substantial expense, especially
when mechanization is impossible (not bulk or containerized). However, line-haul costs are extremely low.

to the lower line-haul expense—thus extremely long hauls are the most efficient. Finally, rising labor costs for water carriers place a premium on mechanization of loading facilities.

Perhaps because the degree of variability for water carriers is different for different kinds of operations, the ICC has generally avoided making any static percentage formula. Our study found that the water carrier degree of variability seems to be somewhere between rail and motor carrier. We believe that separate regression studies, including density as another independent variable, for each of the various types of operation (lake, river barge, coastal, *et al.*) will enable the ICC to determine just where between motor carrier and rail a particular water carrier's per cent of variability lies. In addition, it would be wise to consider time series studies of individual carriers in order to further refine the measure by time span.

PIPELINE

The construction of the initial pipeline plant requires the outlay of a high, fixed threshold cost. The unit of operation is not as divisible and movable as it is for motor and water carriers. Most of the cost cannot be adjusted to a decline in traffic volume. The threat of excess capacity, therefore, demands the construction of a plant which will have full and assured utilization for optimum efficiency.

Like the cost structure of the rail industry, the long-run plant expenses and the short-run line-haul costs (*e.g.*, pumping) are significant. The cost of transport varies most significantly with the length and diameter of the pipe.* The larger the inside diameter of the pipe, the lower the unit cost. These savings apply not only to the distribution of similar fixed costs over a greater traffic volume, but to reduced line-haul unit costs as well. The costs which vary with the length of the line are linear past a distance of 175 miles.†

* Meyer, *et al.*, *The Economics of Competition in the Transportation Industries*, p. 128. The authors define the principal cost components in terms of relationship to 1. line diameter (depreciation on pipeline, cost of laying line, steel, pipe coating, block valves, corrosion protection, property taxes, maintenance); 2. horsepower (electric power, pumping station costs); 3. length of time (tankage, surveying).

† Costs per barrel mile vary from .04 cents for a 10″ diameter line. *Op. cit.*, p. 127, amounts are in 1954 dollars.

According to calculations from the 1967 annual reports of the respective carriers, the average pipeline firm has the following features:

Trunkline mileage	1310 miles
Gathering line mileage	530 miles
Barrels delivered from the system	75,560,000 barrels
Operating revenues	$11,050,000
Operating expenses	$6,261,000
Net income	$2,898,000
Assets	$5,771,000

COMBINATIONS

Intermodal combinations can achieve significant cost savings by using the inherent cost advantages of various modes. Combination motor carrier-rail movements, popularly termed "piggyback" operations, are increasing most rapidly. The primary advantages of the piggyback method is its economy and simplicity: it eliminates some terminal costs, yard expenses, and delays. Also, switching costs en route can be minimized through over-the-road truck movement where low volume traffic makes switching operations more expensive. The decreased loading and unloading times, in addition to yard and switching bypass, enables the piggyback shipment to move with a speed comparable to highway transport.

The second most prevalent combination, transportation via rail and water, is a necessity where bulk commodities must be transported significant distances beyond the geographic reach of rivers, lakes, or coast line. The least used combination is motor carrier-water carrier, despite some theoretical cost advantages.*

Subsidization

The subsidization and taxation system affects the competitive structure of the transportation industry. Subsidization, to the extent that it is unrecovered by taxation, results in a cost advantage that a mode or carrier would not otherwise have. Thus it necessarily affects the inherent natural advantage of each mode. It also can favor a given locale

* Seatrain Lines, for example, a pioneer in this area, suspended its Atlantic service in October, 1966.

if the subsidization is in right of way construction. Both of these impacts are extremely important and may be adjusted fairly easily. It is useful to understand the subsidization basis for the present intermodal competitive structure in order to be able to measure the degree of resource misallocation it causes and to estimate the possible impact of a different system.

The subsidization pattern can also affect more subtly the cost structure of a mode: it can erect or remove barriers to entry, create or diminish a possible problem of excess capacity, produce or reduce economies of scale. For example, if a right of way—the construction of which involves a substantial commitment of financial resources—were built by government, with user taxes collecting the expense involved over time, the cost structure of the mode could be drastically changed *vis-à-vis* what it would be without the public capital investment. The result could mean low barriers to entry, a diminishment of excess capacity problems, and somewhat of a reduction in economies of scale.

RAIL

Although the railroads received substantial governmental aid through initial land grants, they have received little subsidization assistance since. The Transportation Act of 1958 did authorize low interest loans to the railroads but the amount involved was not substantial.

WATER CARRIERS

River and harbor development by the Army Corps of Engineers is the primary source of subsidy to the water carrier mode. Up to 1960, the Corps of Engineers had spent some $5.7 *billion* on such projects. In addition, another $3 billion has been authorized for expenditure to extend inland waterways.* The Coast Guard has spent $1.7 billion on similar projects and the Tennessee Valley Authority has spent another one-quarter to one-half million dollars. The total aid comes to about $7.1 billion.

Water carriers rarely if ever pay user charges for these

---

* Two-thirds of this amount has been allocated to two specific projects. One will make 450 miles of Southwestern rivers navigable into Oklahoma heartland (the Arkansas River-Verdigris River Project.) The second will widen and deepen the Trinity River connecting Dallas-Fort Worth to the Gulf of Mexico.

expenses.* Further, since these projects are often viewed as multi-purpose in nature, commercial water carriers are viewed as marginal beneficiaries. Finally, water carriers, unlike railroads, are not subject to the full burden of maintenance of way costs or property taxes on their publicly owned rights of way. Estimates of appropriate user charges for public investment vary, usually between one-half to one mill per ton-mile.†

If water carriers were required to pay for a portion of these public subsidies, even on a marginal benefit basis, the railroads and pipeline modes would acquire additional bulk traffic, particularly petroleum and coal. Since utilization is more crucial to rail than to water carriage efficiency, where units of operation are more highly divisible and where costs are easier to adjust to changing traffic flow, it might be wise to extract user taxes—at least on a limited marginal use or benefit basis. The water carrier argument that water-borne coal movements would be lost to railroad carriage, resulting in power plant relocation and development closer to mines and further from waterways where most are located, is two-edged. The social cost of maintaining the present system manifests itself in greater overall inefficiency, as well as in increased power plant concentration near urban centers. In other words, why should the public subsidize a less efficient system than would exist without subsidy? Why should it subsidize its own pollution?

A second aspect to the subsidy patterns is not of direct concern here but must be mentioned. That is, even if one grants the wisdom of public subsidy discrimination between modes, the basis for specific subsidy programs is another question. These subsidies are geographic and highly susceptible to political pork-barreling. As one author mildly put it: ". . . water resources and navigational developments have traditionally been based as much (if not more) on political grounds as on economic grounds. Consequently, examples of uneconomic investments are legion." [3]

* There are occasional but quite minor pilot and lock fees.
† A memorandum of the Transportation Association of America estimated that the cost of unrecovered operations and maintenance expense amount to $64 million and that new construction costs amounted to $138 million. This was for 1964. If these figures are correct, the estimate above is a bit low, and actual cost is closer to 1.4 mills per ton-mile (increasing previous average costs of three mills by 47 per cent).

Some of the projects will cost the general public more than they will save the shippers in the region. Further, they displace other pre-existing transportation structure and misallocate resources at large.*

MOTOR CARRIERS

In 1965, 14.3 billion dollars were spent on the United States Highway System. Expenditures on new construction totalled some $8.4 billion. Some 70 per cent of the highway expenditures and 50 per cent of the construction expenditures were borne by state and local governments.[4] It is generally believed that state governments recover a high percentage of their investment from users, with commercial motor carriers paying much of their share. The three kinds of taxes generally involved—registration fees, motor fuel taxes, and structure taxes—are all framed to tax heavier vehicles more severely. Thus, many believe that the heavier vehicles pay at least a substantial amount of the marginal construction and maintenance costs associated with their use. However, most evidence indicates that this is not the case. The rate of increased taxation as motor carrier vehicle weight increases does not even approach the rate of damage necessitating maintenance as weight increases.

The 30 per cent and 50 per cent proportions subsidized through federal aid programs amounted to a cumulative subsidy of $20.7 billion by 1960. Projected totals through 1975 reach upwards of $62 billion. Fifty-eight per cent of this federal input is directed at the interstate system alone. There is little doubt that motor carriers have used the public rights of way to improve speed and service.

Whatever the view as to motor carrier contribution toward state and local highway expense, their contribution toward this federal highway expenditure is only partial. Even with a generous marginal benefit analysis, the pavement damage † caused by heavy trucks is not paid for.

* For a discussion of the uneconomic aspects of the current construction orgy along the Arkansas-Verdigris Rivers for the benefit of petroleum interests at a public cost of over one billion dollars, see *National Transportation Policy*, A Report Prepared for the Committee on Interstate and Foreign Commerce, U.S. Senate, by the Special Study Group on Transportation Policies in the United States, January 3, 1961, otherwise known as the "Doyle Report," pp. 95–96.

† The pavement damage caused by a sixteen-ton tandem-axle load is 7450 times as great as the damage caused by a typical auto (one-

". . . there is considerable evidence that the heavy diesel trucks do not pay the full costs attributable to their differential wear and relative use of the highways." [5]

The increasing use of heavier loads and regular violation of federal weight limits * has probably increased the gap between taxes collected from motor carriers and incrementally based costs from federal highway outlays. The total federal subsidy is approximately in the $200 to $300 million range.† The subsidization by state and local taxes is probably less and very difficult to determine with certitude.

Even if the total subsidy to motor carriers amounted to $400 million or more, its elimination (through higher user taxes) would have little impact on the competitive position of the trucking industry. A $400 million figure or more would just exceed one mill per ton-mile when extended over total motor carrier ton-miles. In an industry with an average revenue rate of seventy to eighty mills per ton-mile, such an addition would have an insignificant effect on competitive position.

It is important to remember that the subsidization and user tax patterns are critical to the cost structures described above. The fact that rail rights of way are not publicly owned and financed is responsible for much of the high entry barrier, high average cost relative to marginal cost characteristics of the industry. The same holds true with pipelines. On the other hand, the capitalization and to some extent the subsidization of motor carrier and water carrier rights of way create relatively low barriers to entry and lowers operating costs.

The recent pattern of federal highway, airport, and

---

ton axle load), see Highway Research Board, *The AASHO Road Test: Proceedings of a Conference,* May, 1962, Special Report 73, p. 422. Note also that damage increases at an accelerating rate as weight increases beyond the 32,000 pound legal limit. Our research, some of which is presented in Chapter VIII, revealed evidence of excessive and illegal loads beyond this limit as a common practice.

* See Chapter 6.

† The Bureau of Public Roads has allocated 21.3 per cent of the federal outlay to heavy trucks on an incremental cost basis (p. 23). Multiplying this times the total federal outlay for a year and subtracting the $650 to $750 million in taxes (post-1965) to federal coffers from motor carriers, gives us a figure somewhere in this range.

waterway appropriations, as well as projected trends, is depicted in the chart below.[6]

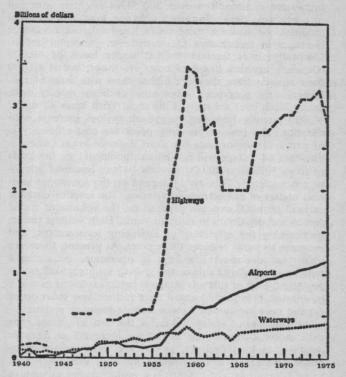

Billions of dollars

Inherent Advantages

After subsidization, a second aspect of concern with regard to intermodal competition is the inherent advantage of each mode (by distance, load, and commodity type) in comparison to competing modes. The cost inherent advantage is important because, without *intramodal* competition, a mode's inherent advantage defines the degree to which it can exercise monopoly power. There has been a great deal of research done on this subject, and there is substantial agreement as to basic inherent advantages.

HIGH-VALUE COMMODITIES

The inherent cost advantage in the transportation of high-value commodities over 200 miles is either with rail or piggyback, depending upon distance, load, and terminal facilities. As distance increases, a line-haul cost advantage increases in significance to override any terminal deficit. Generally, it is thought that at under loads of 40,000 pounds, piggyback line-haul costs are lower, but at 40,000 pounds and above they are higher than with straight rail. Hence, any piggyback advantage declines rapidly with heavy loads over substantial distance. With loads of under 40,000 pounds, however, piggyback savings increase with distance. The precise breaking point for cost efficiency is of particular importance for short distance loads (where a line-haul advantage will not be as significant) or for loads of from 30,000 to 40,000 pounds (where line-haul advantage is unclear). This would depend on the somewhat variable matter of rail terminal expenses. The level of cost for carload terminal expense depends on the volume of traffic served and proximity to railroad yards. High volume traffic, maximizing the efficiency of switching locomotives, and nearness to yards reduces these costs. At present, there are many uneconomic rail sidings in operation, indicating a remaining margin of substantial growth for piggyback transportation. Part of this advantage is being exploited as many businesses, previously located near rail sidings, move to or expand near locations on the interstate highway system.

At distances of under 200 miles, the cost advantage rests with motor carriers. The advantage increases as distance declines, as load declines, and as the value of the commodity increases. If the commodity is of *extremely* high value (diamonds, etc.), there is a motor carrier advantage for hauls of longer than 200 miles (because of the time factor discussed below).

Water carriage is at a cost disadvantage relative to rail or piggyback transportation for high-valued goods. The package freighter is at best able to approximate the highest piggyback costs. Motor carriage is the most expensive means of transport for high-value commodities. Pipeline transportation is not yet technologically feasible for these goods. Air freight is not yet able to compete on a large-scale basis.

Apart from cost, inherent advantage considerations must

include an evaluation of speed, damage, and service. In terms of high-value commodities, motor carrier transportation is superior in these respects. Piggyback would constitute the next speediest mode with rail and water carriage following.

According to a study of Intermodal Competition by R. L. Banks and Associates,[5] "railroads do not enjoy the speed advantage frequently imputed to them over trucks." Numerous studies seem to place the average intercity rail line-haul speed at between thirty-five to forty-five MPH. Intercity motor carrier speeds are now averaging forty to fifty MPH over the less congested, flatter runs. Switching, classification, and extra loading requirements also substantially delay rail shipments. Finally, loss and damage and the inability to provide point to point service on all occasions gives the rail mode a significant speed and service disadvantage.

Many of the rail service deficiencies are not inherent in the mode and can be minimized through intelligent management and imaginative innovation. Further, piggyback transportation enables the bypassing of much of the rail terminal delay and damage and provides flexible point to point service. Only the relatively small line-haul speed differential over rail is sacrificed.[7]

Water carriage suffers from markedly lower speeds in transit of from ten to fourteen knots.

Generally, high-value traffic should be carried by piggyback or rail depending on load and distance. If inventory cost demands speed, or if switching cars in straight rail transportation might result in nonrecoverable damage,

† Efficient Allocation of Truck, Piggyback, and Rail Traffic, by Size and Value of Equipment (according to Friedlaender).

Size of shipment (tons)	High-value commodities			Low-value commodities		
	Truck	Piggyback	Rail	Truck	Piggyback	Rail
1	226[a]	226–369	369[b]	220[a]	220–340	340[b]
5	132[a]	132–497	497[b]	123[a]	123–363	363[b]
10	121[a]	121–709	709[b]	105[a]	105–380	380[b]
15	107[a]	107–1148	1148[b]	89[a]	89–412	412[b]
20	91[a]	91–1882	1882[b]	73[a]	73–407	407[b]
30	43[a]	43[b]	—	30[a]	30–420	420[b]
40	43[a]	43[b]	—	29[a]	29–537	537[b]

a. Maximum efficient distance in miles.
b. Minimum efficient distance in miles.

piggyback should be favored. If speed is unimportant or disadvantageous * or if there is substantial bulk, water carriage can possibly be used if available on an extremely efficient basis. If the distance is under 200 miles (depending upon load) † motor carriage is appropriate, particularly if high speed is important.

BULK COMMODITIES

The inherent cost advantage for the transportation of bulk commodities rests with water carriage. The closest cost competitor is pipeline transportation. Rail transportation is substantially more expensive (10 to 500 per cent more expensive per ton-mile on a line-haul basis). Motor carriage is a distant fourth except for very short distance of small load hauls.

As distance increases, pipeline costs approach water carriage costs.‡ Further, pipelines are beginning to experiment in the transportation of bulk commodities aside from oil. Coal and several other ores can be transported through a liquid medium. Where high volume operations can justify pipeline construction, competition with water carriage over long distances is possible.

Rail transportation is necessary where lack of water or seasonal conditions (icing) inhibit water carriage and where a pipeline alternative is precluded by insufficient volume or commodity type.

In terms of service, water and rail are somewhat comparable. Water, however, is slower, particularly in terms of line-haul speed. Pipeline transportation of solid bulk commodities requires special equipment for conversion to and reconversion from a liquid medium. Other service considerations parallel those for high-value goods.

The cost advantages of two of the modes and the main combination method of transport have been nicely capsulized by Ann F. Friedlaender. Both low-value and high-value commodities have been computed. It is necessary to note, however, that the figures are highly deceptive with regard to low-value goods. This is simply because of the

---

* For example, a shipper might wish to use carriage facilities as storage while he arranges for sale.

† See footnote on page 55.

‡ This is primarily due to the cumulative effect of increased circuity via water.

exclusion of pipeline and water transportation, the two most efficient modes for this traffic.

PASSENGERS

According to one leading source, the cost for the leading modes of passenger transportation rank as follows in cents/passenger mile:

private passenger car	0.42 to 0.50
rail coach	1.3 to 1.4
intercity bus	1.25
plane	1.8 to 3.2 *

It should be noted, however, that these costs are in terms of passenger seat miles, with auto costs assuming six seats. More than two passengers are necessary for advantageous auto costs even on a marginal cost basis. Otherwise, near capacity on the other modes, particularly rail and bus, would render them less costly. The plan expenses rise significantly on a passenger mile basis as distance decreases from 1000 miles. Finally, indirect and social costs are not relevent to this ranking.

Both speed and safety considerations favor the most expensive mode, air travel. These advantages increase with distance of trip.† The other three modes are roughly comparable in speed, with passenger trains roughly equivalent to bus and auto. In terms of safety, however, trains rank higher than auto or bus. The great dangers of automobile travel are a counterbalance to its speed advantage, but a general lack of concern for safety together with the automobile's convenience and flexibility upon arrival at destination make it immensely popular.

Optimum Features ‡

To what extent concentration is necessary in order to create carriers of adequate size for optimum efficiency can

---

* Costs are in 1955 cents. Private passenger costs are marginal costs. Plane costs are for jet transportation at distances in excess of 1000 miles. Since publication of this table, plane costs have declined, but still do not approach bus or rail costs for distances under 800 miles. Source: Meyer, *et al., op. cit.,* Table 33, page 158.

† See Meyer, *et al., op. cit.,* Table 22, p. 134. Note that plane safety records have improved measurably since the publication of this study.

‡ The computer studies referred to in this section are still in progress and will be released in a refined form in an academic journal later this year.

be determined by looking at the optimum features of the various transportation industries. To the extent that present carriers deviate from the optimum size, or to the extent that there is no optimum economic size, ICC entry barrier and merger policy are either detrimental or unnecessary to an efficient mode.

OPTIMUM FEATURES WITHIN RAILROAD INDUSTRY

The optimum size of a rail carrier in terms of miles of track, assets, or traffic flow is still unsettled. It has been suggested that a high GTM/miles of track, or density in traffic, is desirable. (This is a way of expressing track utilization.) Some studies and recent experience with mergers indicate that there is an optimum maximum size for a railroad and that a number of carriers may have exceeded it by substantial margins. One theorist has placed the limit in terms of employees at the 20,000 mark, with significant financial losses occurring past that point.

Our own computer study of the optimum features of carriers in the railroad industry found that—briefly—there are no consistent economies of scale by the four measures of company size used: assets, operating revenue, gross ton-miles, or length of main run (track). This finding is moderated in two respects. First, it applies only to the size range in our sample, all Class I carriers.* The range involved here, however, is substantial. Second, there is no clear evidence of economic loss due to large firm size according to our measures. Nevertheless, the statistical lack of correlation of efficiency with firm size does not justify increased concentration and carrier size (mergers) on the basis of increased efficiency from alleged "economies of scale."

OPTIMUM FEATURES WITHIN MOTOR CARRIER INDUSTRY

There seems to be substantial agreement among experts that there are no appreciable economies of scale in the motor carrier mode, *i.e.*, the size of a firm is not of itself an advantage.

Professors Myer, Peck, Stenason, and Zwick conclude that differences in unit costs between firms should depend on the length of the average haul. This conclusion rests on the assumption that the average *size* of haul does not vary significantly between firms; therefore, the only other ele-

* Railroads with more than $5,000,000 in annual operating revenues.

ment affecting unit costs which does vary between firms must be responsible. Previous studies by Robert A. Nelson and Merill J. Roberts are cited to support this conclusion. The Nelson study of 102 New England carriers produced a very high coefficient of correlation of +0.82 between length of haul and cost per ton mile. Other experts have expressed the view that high density of traffic over authorized route gives an individual firm a cost advantage.

Cost characteristics such as fixed *v.* variable costs, excess capacity, *et al.*, within the mode will inevitably vary within the confines of the preceding discussion depending upon the commodities transported and the legal classification of the firm. Firms are categorized as "common carriers," "contract carriers," or "private carriers." Common carriers are licensed to serve the general public, contract carriers to serve specific shippers on a regular basis, and private carriers are shippers carrying their own products.

A primary cost characteristic differentiating the private and contract carriers from the common carriers is a higher terminal expense for the latter group. Private and contract carriers have more specialized loading facilities and do not have to provide diffuse terminal facilities for service to the general public.* On the other hand, some experts have stated that private and contract carriers average 11 per cent higher ton-mile line-haul costs than common carriers. The reason for this is lower average loads on private and contract carriers, since they are legally precluded from soliciting traffic for return trips.

According to experts, the lower terminal costs of the large-scale private and contract operations offset the higher line-haul costs at distances up to 300 miles. Below this point the private and contract carrier can effect lower unit costs than the common carrier. And yet there are some puzzling aspects to these observations. First, there is a great deal of private and contract carriage at over 300 miles. It is estimated that over one-half of all ton-miles carried 200 miles or more are by private or contract carriage. This

---

* Most of the terminal expense advantages of contract and private carriers are advantages that are due to the consistency and kind of traffic carried. If the common carriers had this traffic they could easily develop identical facilities. For example, they could simplify billing and collecting procedures to the now contract-served shippers. Common carriers have the immense advantage of return traffic.

traffic should not exist in a competitive system if private and contract carriage were in fact less efficient and costly than common carriage.

Why do the supposedly efficient private and contract carriers haul over one-half of all traffic at above 300 miles? Professors Meyer, *et al.*, vaguely attribute it to "the interaction of managerial practice and regulatory policy." [9] The fact is that while common carriers are theoretically more efficient at these distances, rates do not reflect this advantage. ICC regulatory policy requires that shippers be treated equally regardless of potential lower cost, large volume-long distance, traffic. "Value-of-service" rate-making results in high rates on high-value commodities regardless of the cost of transport involved. Rather than pay these high rates, shippers resort to contract or private carriage. Both of these latter practices are discussed in Chapter 5.*

A large-scale regression analysis of motor carrier optimum features was organized and conducted by the authors with the same goals in mind as the rail study above. In addition, we hoped to be able to do a more detailed breakdown of the cost components of different types of motor carriage and an examination of the effects of deregulation on efficiency through the isolation of separate samples.

Our motor carrier study found, in brief, that gross ton-mile, operating revenue, and asset measures of carrier size have no consistent correlation with carrier efficiency. Only household carriers come close to showing economies of scale. Size as measured by miles of route did correlate with efficiency increase to some extent, indicating a direct cost

* Note that the existence of the contract and private alternative does not mean that there is a competitive system despite the general shift to these latter carriers. There is still a substantial margin of monopoly power for the common carrier to exploit (generally due to regulatory restraints on contract and private carriers) before it becomes advantageous to choose another kind of carrier. Further, these other forms of motor carriage are completely impractical for a great many shippers. Contract carriers are limited by the ICC to the number of shippers each may serve. This puts small shippers at an immediate disadvantage. Further, unless a shipper's business is steady enough (not seasonal) to create a steady traffic flow for maximum utilization, and more importantly, large enough so that backhaul capacity can be utilized, the shipper is going to have to use common carriage. The major reason there has been a shift to contract and private carriage is because common carriers, setting rates in collusion, have set prices so far above cost for many items that despite these disadvantages it will pay for many to seek alternatives.

of ICC restrictions on routes, and of the values of route extension favors to be fought over before the ICC.

Operational features tested included traffic density, average haul multiplied by average load, and owned (versus leased) vehicle use. Density increase does not improve efficiency, although average haul multiplied by average load does. This indicates that although there are unit cost and efficiency advantages in high load, long distance transport, it is relatively easy to adjust units of operation to volume regardless of density. This, plus the lack of economy of scale evidence, precludes any rational basis for increasing carrier size because of improved efficiency per se. Thus, the motor carrier merger movement is motivated either by a desire to expand simply for the sake of increased size, or for increased assets, or because merger allows the amalgamation of operating authority grants for more monopoly power which would be reflected in the rate structure.

The final operational variable, owned vehicle use, indicates increasing efficiency with the utilization of leased vehicles and drivers (owner operators). This further emphasizes the conclusions of various experts as to the low natural barriers to entry into the industry for new firms. The major entry factor is ICC authorization to operate. Since possession of this authorization is all that is needed to set up a lease-haul arrangement with pre-existing owner operators, it takes on great value where protection from competition by the ICC allows monopoly profits.

OPTIMUM FEATURES WITHIN WATER CARRIER INDUSTRY

The cost characteristics of the water mode require the maximum utilization of the barge or ship for greatest efficiency. The chief impediments are insufficient, untimely, or inconsistent traffic volume, slow speed or excessive time in transit, less than capacity loads, and excessive time loading or unloading. This last factor can be additionally crucial since terminal costs while in harbor are often substantial, thus demanding quick turn around times.

There have been few if any studies of the potentially optimum features of a water carrier. Aside from what can be imputed from the cost reduction advantages of full utilization, little is known.

Our own study of the optimum features of the water

carrier industry found briefly, that carriers do not show increasing efficiency as size increases—with size as measured by gross ton-miles, operating revenue, or assets. As with motor carriers, publicly owned and maintained rights of way inhibit efficiency improvement through merger of carriers using the same route. There is an increase in efficiency with longer routes of operation. Once again, route restrictions impede optimum efficiency and constitute a valuable commodity to be bid for before the ICC.

Concentration Levels

One of the most important considerations involved in judging the impact of ICC policy toward competition is the level of concentration for the respective modes within "relevant markets." The standard index of concentration is the concentration ratio, which sets out what percentage of a given market a number of percentage of carriers have acquired. In traditional antitrust terms, the capture of 50 per cent or more of the business within a "relevant market" by one firm would be, at a minimum, cause for an investigation into potential monopoly power. An oligopolistic (small numbers or shared monopoly) condition can exist with 50 per cent or significant business domination by ten or more firms.

The concentration ratios for the United States, or for various regions, can indicate high concentration and possible monopoly power, but a great number of firms and low concentration levels for various regions does not necessarily indicate *lack* of monopoly power. This is because vigorous competition in the transportation of artichokes from Salinas to Los Angeles will not help a shipper who wants to send gravel from San Diego to Santa Barbara, if there is no competition for the latter commodity between the latter points. The concentration ratio figures alone for the Far West will not reflect this factor. Therefore, it is necessary to consider concentration on the narrow basis of route or point to point and specific commodity markets, as well as on regional bases.

We have no computer study to help us in the evaluation of concentration levels. In the rail, water, and oil pipeline modes, detailed statistical study is unnecessary since cursory examination of statistics indicates very high concentration, with substantial monopoly power by individual carriers.

With motor carriers, the concentration levels by relevant market are closely tied to the system of restrictions described below (since they define the limits of a carrier's competitive opportunity through the very detailed and complex allocation of authority grants). Since a "relevant market" over which a motor carrier can exercise monopoly power can be defined in the narrow terms of a single, highly specialized commodity over a given route, it is possible to create an infinite number of them. Since we have no definitive, comprehensive data on the number of relevant markets in this regard (although we know there are potentially millions of them), we can extrapolate by hand on an indirect basis from related data.

CONCENTRATION WITHIN THE RAILROAD INDUSTRY

Although we found no comprehensive, detailed study of competition within the rail industry, we did find numerous tangential surveys and commentaries. Taking the 1967 statistics,[10] we were able to make some fundamental calculations of concentration levels ourselves.

| | NATION | | EAST | |
	Number	Traffic %*	Number	Traffic %
Freight	13	61%	5	72%
Passenger	13	65%	5	93%

| | WEST | | SOUTH | |
	Number	Traffic %	Number	Traffic %
Freight	5	49%	3	75%
Passenger	5	55%	3	35%

* Traffic per cent is in terms of GTM of freight for the freight statistics and passenger miles for the passenger statistics. The use of operating revenue instead of GTM yields similar results.

The rather marked concentration levels indicated by the above statistics suggest an oligopolistic industry. The fact of extremely high economic barriers to entry guarantees the maintenance of a given level of concentration for a substantial time. The current financial pressures in the economy (*e.g.*, tight money) make the barriers even more significant. Further, the above statistics are drawn from the rail industry *before* the latest round of mergers (due to the lag in data collection by the ICC). The thirteen carriers hauling 61 per cent of the nation's rail freight are now ten in number, the five top carriers in the East hauling 72 per cent are now three in number, and so on. And there have been no signals from either the ICC or the industry that the trend will soon abate. Quoting from the Association of American Railroads' own publication concerning developments in 1968 and prospective plans: [11]

> The merger pace quickened in 1968. On February 1, the Pennsylvania and New York Central formed the 19,200-mile Penn Central and the New York, New Haven and Hartford was included on January 1, 1969. The C&O/B&O gained control of the Western Maryland, the Norfolk & Western acquired the Erie Lackawanna and the Delaware and Hudson, the Chicago Great Western was merged into the Chicago & North Western, and the C&NW and Missouri Pacific were granted joint control of the Alton & Southern. On January 3, 1969, the New Orleans & Northeastern was merged into the Alabama Great Southern. Some twenty-three Class I railroads are involved in other acquisition plans.

This tightening structure of oligopoly, protected by natural barriers to entry, is even less competitive than it seems, for, as mentioned above, having four or five firms to choose from in a region does not mean that choice exists on a commodity type basis or on a point to point basis. One of the leading texts on the economics of transportation analyzes the more detailed patterns of competition as they existed in 1956. The authors took the thirty most traveled passenger routes. They found four competitive carriers on two of the routes, three competitive carriers on eleven, two competitive carriers on fourteen, and a single carrier on three of the routes. The selection of the major passenger routes for the analysis is more than generous, however, since over 75 per cent of *freight* ton-miles originate from points of insignificant population. These points of origin are mostly near sources of raw materials and are admittedly "usually . . . served by one road." [12] The authors acknowledge this fact but suggest that the thirty passenger routes in their analysis are still relevant since the average shipment of "428 miles" will travel at least a portion of its journey between the major passenger cities. They argue that the opportunity to switch at these points creates a competitive situation of sorts. This judgment ignores the fact that firms can set rates for that portion of the journey where they do have complete monopoly power and then can, at a point of possible competition, lower rates to or below the level set by competitive roads thus making it uneconomical to switch at that point. In any event, the monopoly condition is significant to the extent it does exist on the main freight routes which do not parallel the passenger routes. Finally, even at those points of greatest competition referred to by the authors, much has happened since 1956. Many of the thirty routes surveyed in 1956 are now dominated in close to monopolistic fashion by a single carrier.*

All of the above is in addition to the question of interlocking ownership and the existence of railroad rate bureaus which are allowed to set rates in collusion. The judgment of Professors Meyer, Peck, Stenason, and Zwick that the rail industry had moved into a state of oligopoly in 1956 would be overly generous today. There is little doubt that even without rate bureaus (*i.e.*, merely considering the matter of service competition), the rail industry has moved from oligopoly to a substantially monopolistic structure over much of the crucial point to point traffic markets.†

CONCENTRATION WITHIN THE MOTOR CARRIER INDUSTRY

There have traditionally been a large number of small firms engaged in motor carriage. This is undoubtedly due to the cost characteristics of the motor carrier industry, particularly the small initial capital requirement and the lack of economies of scale. Over the past several decades, however, there has been a steady change in the concentration levels of the industry.‡ The Lorenz Curve analysis presented in the chart on p. 86 [13] illustrates the concentration level and trend.

Also illustrative of this concentration are the declining numbers of carriers. For although motor carrier traffic and

* See, for example, the main intercity Eastern routes, now dominated by the Penn Central.

† Department of Transportation economists and Department of Justice officials have admitted that probably one-half or more of all point to point routes are close to complete monopolies, and that most traffic travels under this condition for a substantial part of the haul. The dangers of oligopoly or monopoly structure are not confined to the increased likelihood of collusive pricing (a present fact because of rate bureaus and agreements). Of course the enforcement of collusively determined rates against independents becomes easier when there are a few large firms involved, but moreover, the oligopolistic or monopolistic structure can independently affect whatever competition might exist outside the area of rates (*e.g.*, for service), and facilitates concerted action generally (lobbying, etc.).

‡ This comment, of course, is applied only to the motor carriage operations under regulation by the ICC.

revenue volumes have grown significantly since the advent of comprehensive regulation in this area, the number of regulated carriers has declined greatly—from an estimated 26,167 in 1939 [14] to 15,125 in 1968.[15] An examination of rarely released statistics reveals that while the numbers of general commodity carriers decreased, the size of those remaining have increased. Those general commodity carriers with assets of over ten million increased from sixty-four to 137 between 1957 and 1965.[16]

This trend toward concentration and larger firm size is not the result of optimum growth under competitive conditions. Ease of entry into the industry is rendered impossible by ICC operating authority requirements and specific restrictions attached thereto. By not granting new authority commensurate with transportation growth and volume, the ICC increases the size of the average carrier.*

There have been no comprehensive studies of point to point competition within the motor carrier industry. Concentration based on carrier market share by ICC region would be particularly irrelevant, if for no other reason than because their regional divisions are based on the location of carrier main offices—not on groupings of carriers as they compete. The twenty groupings used by TRINC (a division of Dun and Bradstreet) come much closer to matching the carriers as they actually operate by region. An analysis of 1968 data shows that for one-half of TRINC's regions, market share is dominated by from three to six firms. This indicates substantial concentration when one considers the fact that actual markets are divided within TRINC's regions according to specific route restrictions and by infinite commodity limitations.

As with the rail concentrations above, this shift into an oligopolistic and now substantially monopolistic structure does not directly affect rates already set in collusion. It makes the mechanism for rate collusion more effective but

* ICC merger permissiveness, in combination with the need to combine in order to expand operating authority (the result of restrictive ICC regulation), greatly contributed to motor carrier concentration. In 1963, thirty-four firms were purchased by or merged with other firms; in 1964, thirty-one; in 1965, forty-two. More striking, Pacific Intermountain Express once consisted of thirty small firms, United-Buckingham Freight lines once consisted of seventy small firms, Consolidated Freightways Corporation of Delaware once consisted of ninety small firms.

its chief impact is on a loss in service competition and in more collusive behavior generally.

CONCENTRATION WITHIN THE WATER CARRIER INDUSTRY

Concentration is extremely high within the non-maritime water carrier industry. The ICC divides the mode into five regions: Atlantic and Gulf Coast, Great Lakes, Mississippi River and Tributaries, Pacific Coast, and Intercoastal.

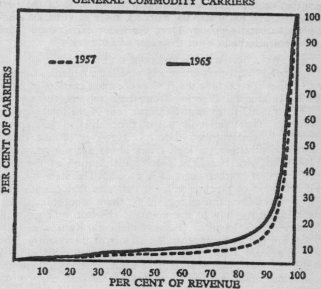

INDUSTRY CONCENTRATION OF GENERAL COMMODITY CARRIERS

There is little competition between carriers of different regions. Within the Atlantc and Gulf Coast region, two carriers collect about 50 per cent of the operating revenue. Within the Great Lakes region, one carrier collects 66 per cent of the revenue. Within the Mississippi River and Tributaries area, almost one-half of the region's operating revenue goes to four firms and two-thirds (67 per cent) goes to seven firms. Within the Pacific Coast region, two firms collect almost one-half of the operating revenue, and four collect 65 per cent of it. Within the Intercoastal region, one firm collects 100 per cent of the operating revenue.*

The above computations are from 1967 data. Concentration has not decreased since that time. The carriers involved are merely the Class A carriers, but this group hauls over 90 per cent of the freight hauled by non-maritime water carriers. Further, it does not include concentration increase from the recent creation of holding companies. Finally, as high as these concentration levels seem, they are in reality much higher. Further restrictions segment the markets within each region, and on much if not most of the port to port, specific comodity markets, there is virtually complete monopoly power. Thus, the water carriers are more concentrated than even the railroad industry.

CONCENTRATION WITHIN PIPELINE INDUSTRY

As of 1967 there were ninety pipeline companies submitting annual reports to the ICC as common carriers in interstate commerce. Figuring from these reports, the top six (77 per cent) firms control 36 per cent of the total pipeline mileage. These ratios do not of themselves suggest an exceedingly concentrated industry. However, unlike motor carriers, pipelines (at least trunk lines) are not geographically flexible. Thus, the specific distribution of the lines in terms of market demand is crucial. The state by state distribution of pipeline mileage indicates that despite only moderate concentration nationally, there is substantial concentration, usually to the point of absolute monopoly, in many specific localities. Texas, Oklahoma, Kansas, and Illinois are the least concentrated sectors of the country. This is significant since these areas contain the most pipeline mileage and pump the most barrels. But even here the situation on a point to point basis is at best oligopolistic with from one to four firms operating between most points.

There were four mergers in 1967 and the total number of reporting carriers has declined in number from ninety-four in 1963 to ninety in 1967. During this same period, mileage, diameter size, output, and revenue have all been increasing. Most of the increase has been accruing to the larger firms, increasing the trend toward concentration in the industry.

* These findings are computed from 1967 statistics based on annual reports filed with the ICC. See *Transport Statistics in the United States*, ICC Bureau of Accounts, Part 5, Washington, D.C. (1968).

Competition Between Industries

The industry claims—as it points to relatively substantial market shares of the rail, motor carrier, water carrier, and pipeline industries in freight carriage—that brisk competition between these industries makes up for the lack of competition within each of them. Such a claim is not warranted. First, although there is no formal inter-industry rate fixing, there is a certain amount of oligopolistic "price leadership" (see Chapter 5). Second, a particular mode may have an inherent advantage for a given commodity, and thus be able to raise its rates and profits. And finally, a particular mode may be the only one available in a given location.

Thus, intermodal competition is severely limited and virtually useless as a check on monopoly power pricing in the freight area—even though it is clearly more substantial (see Appendix 10) than the non-competition that exists within the various modes.

With regard to passenger transportation, however, intermodal competition is more rigorous. The private auto enters the picture, and so does vigorous competition from a mode regulated by a different regulatory body, the Civil Aeronautics Board.

Appendix 11 contains tables drawn from the very thorough 1967 travel census. The data there set forth not only relevant market shares by various measures, but break down a mode's clientele by distance, family income, occupation, education, *et al.* Briefly, the auto dominates on trips up to 500 miles. With the demise of the auto, for one reason or another, however, we might see a boom in bus and train travel, both of which exceed air in person-night market share for up to 200 miles, with rail continuing to hold on to a respectable market share *vis-à-vis* air on up to 1000 miles.

The rather strange increase in rail market share, progressing steadily upward from .7 to 5.9 per cent as distance increases to 1000 miles does not make complete sense. Nor does the fact that buses have their largest market share at 200 to 500 miles. Part of the answer can probably be found in the rate regulation philosophies of competitive regulatory bodies, each allowing discriminatory pricing to drive the other out. Since airlines maintain the most useful and extensive monopoly power, they have the advantage. Thus, the CAB will subsidize short haul air carriers or allow larger air carriers to price longer hauls well above cost for higher profits where there is monopoly power, in order to subsidize shorter distance hauls, thus driving buses and trains out of their most lucrative market, short to medium hauls.

Variation Levels

In a competitive transportation system, efficient carriers will drive out the inefficient. Innovation, better service, and lower rates will be encouraged and rewarded. Those carriers failing to utilize their facilities (or lower costs) at a rate comparable to their competitor's will be driven out. Wide variation in efficiency levels between competitors will not endure.

In order to measure the level of competition indicated by this measure, we have conducted a variation study of all the modes. High levels of variation should suggest lack of competition *and* the protected maintenance in operation of relatively inefficient carriers. Low variation levels should suggest either a competitive system, or uniform levels of inefficiency.

RAIL

For the ratios we are using, a value of one indicates a significant spread of values. As this coefficient increases past one, the amount of variation becomes increasingly severe. The variation involved with various coefficient values can be imputed from the values as they pertain to the spread in, say, absolute size or value or cost. As immense and varied as this spread is, most values fall in the one to one-and-one-half range.

The coefficients of variation for many of our indices, however, substantially exceed even this very high level.

No.	Index	Coefficient of Variation
22	Gross Tons/Total Vehicle Capacity	3.18
23	Freight Vehicle Miles/No. of Freight Vehicles	3.20
21	Gross Ton-Miles/Main Run Length	.735
27	Gross Ton-Miles/Main Run Length and Network Mileage	.619
28	Revenue Need	.833
31	Cost Rate	1.21

MOTOR CARRIER VARIATION

As mentioned earlier, in a competitive industry, those firms failing to utilize facilities, or failing to achieve low cost transportation, will be driven out by the more efficient. Coefficients of variation should be quite low.

Our separate samples gave us some interesting comparisons. The degree of variation seems consistently related to the degree of regulatory limitations imposed by the ICC. Just as concentration seems to increase the coefficient of variation, regulation does too. Thus, general freight irregular route carriers have the lowest variation in revenue/GTM, followed by the regular route (more restricted) general freight carriers, followed by high interline carriers (not only route specified runs, but generally shorter as well), followed by contract and finally by household movers.

The same holds true with the mean values, particularly the revenue/GTM or (cost/GTM) figures. The very lowest is the unregulated agricultural sample, next is general freight irregular route, then general freight regular route (route specified), and then high interline, contract, and finally special and household carriers. Unit rates and unit cost increases with the degree of regulation.*

WATER CARRIER VARIATION

Our water carrier variation study demonstrated exceedingly high variations within the industry. The significance of this lies in the fact, as outlined above, that a competitive industry would not permit great variations in efficiency or cost for like services. The impact of these results is somewhat clouded by the fact that the industry has few companies in even theoretical competition, and they vary in terms of vehicle types, operating conditions, etc. However, we have taken several steps to minimize this bias.

Coefficients of variations are extremely high for everything except for operating ratios, indicating that there is a wide diversity in efficiency levels and that the less efficient are not driven out but are able to adjust revenue to meet costs regardless of efficiency. Not only is there a lack incentive for efficiency, but the costs, due to monopoly power

* Lack of regulation seems to drive down cost and rates, but the industry favors regulation and abhors competition. The reason is suggested by the profit (cost/revenue) data which show the agricultural group (less regulated) the least profitable (an expected result of competition), with contract carriers the most profitable.

pricing, are easily passed on. Undoubtedly, some of the variation is accountable to differing kinds of traffic (*e.g.*, tons/aggregate capacity will differ for the same utilization with different weighted traffic). But generally homogenous commodity types minimize this. In any event, variations are so pervasive and so great, exceeding 100 per cent by utilization ratios and close to 300 per cent by cost of revenue need measures, that they cannot be explained away by differences in type of equipment or region.

PIPELINE VARIATION

Standard deviation levels are extremely high for all indices relevant to rates or revenue. Cost data are less varied and utilization indices are substantially uniform (both in ratio form). These patterns suggest the existence of monopoly power within the mode limited by competition from the other modes. Some locales and some commodities enable the extraction of substantial revenues over cost due to the margin provided by the mode's inherent cost advantage. Thus, operating ratios are widely distributed from 40 to 190 per cent.*

* It has also been suggested that cost hiding by parent corporations or a desire to drive out another mode is responsible for these revenue deviations.

3 / The Corporate Conglomerate: Consolidated Menace

The 1960's witnessed some of the most important developments in the history of transportation: changes in the patterns of ownership throughout the transportation industry included mergers, purchase by holding companies, and investments by carriers in areas entirely unrelated to transportation. All these developments pose profound challenges to the ability and willingness of the transportation industry to maintain a competitive system.

These challenges are perhaps clearest in the railroad industry. Railroads were characterized by overbuilding from the start, and the earliest merger movement began in the form of links to local traffic centers. For example, the former Pennsylvania Railroad was comprised of what were once 600 individual railroads. During a peak sixteen-month period in 1899–1900, one-sixth of the nation's rail mileage was absorbed by other lines. Finally, the Supreme Court held in *Northern Securities v. United States*, 193 US 197 (1904), that the Sherman Antitrust Act applied to railroad consolidations using the holding company device. The anti-consolidation thesis was continued in *U.S. v. Union Pacific Railroad*, 226 US 61 (1912), and by the passage of the Clayton Act in 1914.*

* Section 7 of the Clayton Act, as originally passed, "prohibited the acquisition by one corporation of the *stock* of another corporation when such acquisition would result in a substantial lessening of competition *between the acquiring and the acquired companies,* or to tend to create a monopoly in any line of commerce," *Brown Shoe Co. v. U.S.*, 370 US 294, 312–13 (1962). (Emphasis in the original.)

The industry at that time was in need of consolidation. Overcapacity caused many railroads to indulge in sometimes ruinous competition as they offered rebates, cut prices below costs, and engaged in other activities designed to attract business which would recoup at least some of their unusually high fixed costs. Of course, in areas where no competition existed, the railroads charged near-monopoly rates to shippers who had no alternative means of transportation.

World War I highlighted the weakness of the rail system as well as its importance, and continuing problems of inadequate car supply and distribution of service brought on government take over of the railroads in 1917.

Largely as a result of this experience, the Transportation Act of 1920 set up the goal of an adequate and financially healthy transportation system. Included was a provision in Section 408 for preparation and adoption of a plan for consolidation of the railroad properties of the United States into a limited number of systems. Such consolidations were rendered immune from the antitrust laws if approved by the ICC as "promoting the public interest." The ICC was not to force these mergers, but to allow only those mergers which it had approved as part of its master plan.

Harvard Professor William Z. Ripley was commissioned by the ICC in 1920 to draft such a plan. He presented his plan to the ICC in 1921. The ICC issued its tentative plan, 63 ICC 455 (1921), but there followed several years of disagreement over the details of the plan. In 1925 the Commission asked Congress to repeal the master plan provision of the 1920 Act, and repeated the request unsuccessfully for the next three years. Finally, in 1929, the ICC reluctantly issued the complete plan.[1]

Between 1920 and 1929 there were few mergers, as the railroads waited for the supposedly forthcoming master plan before thinking seriously of beginning merger application. 1929, of course, was the year of the stock market crash and the beginning of the Great Depression, during which few railroads were financially strong enough or optimistic enough to undertake large acquisition plans.

In 1940, the idea of a national plan was dead, and the 1940 Transportation Act did away with the requirement that the ICC produce a plan for rail mergers and approve no mergers not corresponding to the plan. In its place, Congress allowed the ICC to exempt rail mergers from the antitrust laws if "consistent with the public interest," and included as criteria in the ICC's determination the following factors:

1. The effect of the proposed transaction upon adequate transportation service to the public; 2. the effect upon the public interest of the inclusion, or failure to include, other railroads in the territory involved in the proposed transaction; 3. the total fixed charges resulting from the proposed transaction; and 4. the interest of the carrier employees affected." [2]

Statistics show that few mergers were consummated between 1929 and 1945; among other reasons, of course, was the Great Depression. The ICC to this day points to this period of merger inactivity as proof that any general Transportation Act or plan is inimical to the industry and that the Commission can therefore only accept merger applicants, one at a time, without attempting to assert an overall direction. In fact, no real plan was ever given a sufficient test.

The most recent merger movement began in 1959 with the approval of the Norfolk & Western-Virginian merger, 307 ICC 401 (1959). The movement now includes virtually every major Class I railroad, and the pace of merger proposals increased significantly in the 1960's. The approval of the Penn Central merger in the mid-60's was a watershed, for it meant that a carrier with significant market power could be created despite the resultant loss of interrail competition. The approval of the "Northern Lines" merger will have similar effects in the Northwest. [3]

Whereas the Transportation Act of 1940 made it clear that the principal economic justification for a rail merger should be better service to shippers, it is apparent that rail mergers, which originate in the corporate board rooms of railroad companies and holding companies, are proposed for reasons other than improved service capabilities. [4]

First, psychological factors should not be underestimated. The results of large mergers are large companies, with tremendous assets and market power. It simply feels better for a railroad executive to be a big executive in a giant carrier than in a smaller carrier forced to compete with other small carriers. Mergers make news, and executives on merged carriers become celebrities in financial circles. They can hobnob with the great and the near great.

Second, it is no secret that businessmen want a great deal of market power in a given economic area in order to control price and service without competition. The Sherman Act, and other antitrust legislation were aimed at curbing this natural anti-competitive proclivity in other areas of the economy, but the Transportation Acts of 1920 and 1940 effectively exempted rail mergers from strict antitrust prosecution.

Third, mergers mean larger combined assets. Larger combined assets mean greater opportunities to invest railroad money in diversified interests outside the railroad field. For example, the Penn-Central Company owns significant non-rail real property across the country, and has been estimated to be the largest single owner of real property in the United States.* The spreading out of operations may bring greater return on capital for the merged carrier, thus bringing greater dividends to the stockholders—many of whom are the directors and officers proposing the merger.

Fourth, the railroads claim that mergers will allow for significant cost savings which can be passed on to the shippers, and thus the consumers. One of the greatest causes of financial loss to the railroads is overcapacity: railroads cannot reduce the costs of track and road and loading facilities even when the level of traffic (and therefore of traffic income) is reduced. Where that happens, a merger might in fact save the railroads money by allowing them to reduce capacity. For example, where there are two parallel tracks each used to one-quarter of capacity (but incurring heavy depreciation and maintenance costs), abandoning one and shifting all traffic to the other will decrease excess capacity on one track, and the abandoned track will no longer need to be maintained. However, the possibility that a merger which decreases capacity will result in lower rates for shippers or consumers is highly speculative for several reasons. First, reduced capacity is a possibility only where the merger is between two companies that cover the same route, not between two that combine end-to-end to make a third route, longer than either of them. For example, the Northern Lines merger will result in the abandonment of only 500

* See Appendix 22 for a discussion of the non-rail estate holdings of the Penn-Central and other major carriers.

miles of road in a 26,500-mile system, according to officials of the new merged carrier.[5] Second, reduced expenses can be achieved only where greater size will *in fact* mean greater economy. Simply producing a *large* carrier is no guarantee of such saving; on the contrary, study after study, apparently ignored by the ICC, has shown that after a certain point the increasing size of a carrier detracts from its ability to operate efficiently.

D.O.T.'s Robert Gallamore did a study of whether proposed cost savings had in fact been achieved in major mergers. He concluded that, in fact, greater costs have been the result:

. . . in most circumstances, there have been difficulties in achieving merger savings. Merger is not a panacea. The summary picture is that the larger, more recent, and more complex mergers have produced the least favorable results. The particular configuration of routes involved does not seem to make as much difference as the overall size of the consolidation. . . . But the overwhelming evidence is that size and complexity of a merger plan are the qualities that can lead to extra costs, rather than savings, in the wake of consolidation.[6]

The major danger from mergers is the growth of excessive market power. Giant merged carriers like the Penn-Central have virtually eliminated interrail competition in many areas. The preservation of interrail competition between major population centers was recommended by the Doyle Report, but scant attention has been paid this need by the ICC.[7] For example, the Penn-Central merger resulted in the loss of interrail competition in thirty-two urban areas.[8]

Where the railroads have a monopoly, either point-to-point or by commodity, the dangers of the lack of competition are obvious. Either the merged lines will attempt to charge monopoly prices, thus increasing the need for maximum rate regulation; or they will attempt to achieve monopoly profits by reducing service—without lowering their rates—to shippers who are totally dependent on their service. In view of the 1940 Transportation Act, and the requirement that the ICC consider the effect that mergers will have on levels of service offered the shipping public, this last result would appear to be highly undesirable. However, where competition between railroads has been destroyed by piecemeal mergers, it is virtually inevitable.

The argument that there is enough intermodal competition (from trucking, ships, air freight, etc.) to offset the destruction of competition within the railroad industry (intramodal) is sometimes accepted by the ICC. Yet its staff study entitled *Railroad Consolidations and the Public Interest* states:

It is clear that, despite its importance, intermodal competition may possibly be inadequate to provide, in the public interest, the full benefits which should flow from competition. The main competition for certain types of traffic moving over certain routes must be intramodal, since effective intermodal competition in these cases is not present.* [9]

The problem with many of the mergers which have already been consummated is that where the resulting economies have not developed, it is too late for the government to disentangle the merged lines. The idea that the ICC can review mergers over a five-year period after their consummation to make sure that the desired economic effects have taken place is encouraging only in theory, since the damage will already have been done. It is also questionable whether the ICC will have the capacity or will to force changes in the merger arrangements years after they have been consummated. The immutability of these transactions only points up the fact that the ICC must take an extremely careful look at railroad proposals before ruling on them. It is not promising, therefore, to hear from an ICC accountant that the Commission "usually just listens to the proposal, shrugs its shoulders, and approves the merger." [10]

The Supreme Court has taken note of the difficulties inherent in the Commission's reconsidering the merits of a merger years after approving it. The Court stated that the belief that a merger could be "unscrambled" if hoped-for results do not occur is "blinking at reality." The fact is that traffic trackage, terminals, etc., as well as financial and corporate structures can and will, beyond doubt, be quickly combined, changed, abandoned, or consolidated. The Court concluded: "Our experience with . . . mergers, and common sense as well, indicate that the 'scrambling' goes fast but the unscrambling is interminable and seldom effectively accomplished." [11]

---

* The questions of intermodal competition, and the monopoly pricing which results from the lack thereof, is discussed more fully in Chapters 4 and 5.

There is an additional question as to how close to strict antitrust policy the ICC must adhere in deciding whether or not to approve a particular merger. The Commission's decisions under Section 5(2) are, of course, exempt formally from antitrust law. However, the question of competition was not entirely mooted by the Transportation Acts of 1920 and 1940. As the Supreme Court said in *McLean Trucking Co. v. U.S.*, 321 US 67 (1944), the ICC "must estimate the scope and appraise the effects of the curtailment of competition which will result from the proposed consolidation." In a later case, the Supreme Court clarified the ICC's duty under Section 5(2). Quoting from a 1959 case, the Court said in *Seaboard Air Line R. Co. v. U.S.*, 382 US 154, 156 (1965):

Although Section 5(11) does not authorize the Commission to "ignore" the antitrust laws, *McLean Trucking Co. v. U.S.*, 321 US 67, 80, there can be "little doubt that the Commission is not to measure proposals for [acquisitions] by the standards of the antitrust laws." 321 US, at 85–86. The Commission remains obligated to "estimate the scope and appraise the effects of the curtailment of competition which will result from the proposed [acquisition] and consider them along with the advantages of improved service [and other matters in the public interest] to determine whether the [acquisition] will assist in effectuating the overall transportation policy." 321 US, at 87.

In a later decision on the procedural aspects of the Penn-Central merger, *Penn-Central Merger Cases*, 389 US 486 (1968), the Court alluded to the fact that the merger would eliminate interrail competition in thirty-two urban areas.[12]

With respect to the lessening of competition where it now exists between the roads to be merged, the Commission pointed out that it will retain continuing power over reductions in service and facilities which are not specifically approved in the merger plans.[13]

Thus, the importance of the ICC's five-year control over merger approvals cannot be overestimated, since the Supreme Court makes it quite clear that the ICC has met its ultimate obligations to antitrust policy solely by retention of control. The ICC must remember that Supreme Court approval of the Commission's exercise of administrative discretion does not mean either that the Court approves specifically of the ICC's merger decisions, or that the ICC, once having decided these cases, is bereft of specific future responsibility for making sure that the operations of the railroads meet the demands of the National Transportation Policy.

In virtually every merger application, the railroads claim that costs can be decreased so as to enable the merged lines to reduce rates or increase service. In analyzing the various cost savings claims, two factors must be kept in mind.

First, the carriers usually claim that the proposed savings will be unattainable except through a merger—despite the admission during testimony by a leading economic consultant that the costs savings, for example, from the "Northern Lines" merger "might be physically possible without merger."[14] Considering the economic result when competition between railroads is destroyed, the possibility of seeking less burdensome alternatives to mergers should be fully investigated.*

Second, in spite of elaborate claims made by the carriers at merger hearings before the ICC,[15] there is no guarantee that the desired economic results will occur. As stated above, the ICC retains a surveillance of the merged carriers for five years, but this regulatory function is highly academic.

The result may be, as D.O.T.'s Robert Gallamore calls it, "unguarded optimisim" at the merger hearings.[16]

The proposals made by the railroads to lessen their costs through merger are generally similar from case to case—outlined as follows:

Elaborate maps are usually submitted purporting to show how a particular yard in the map can be moved to another area miles away, or can be enlarged to two or three times its original size. Accompanying the diagram is a set of figures, prepared by the railroad economists, showing estimated cost savings from the physical changes portrayed. There is little or no follow-up by the ICC as to the accuracy

* At the 1969 Oversight Hearings before Senator Hartke's Subcommittee, Commissioner Tuggle recognized this possibility but stated: "It is exceedingly difficult to get two carriers who are arm's length competitors all the time" to so agree. However, were the ICC to accept the basic policy of antitrust law and insist on a less burdensome alternative to the public interest—realization of the same benefits without the dangers of reduced competition—then it probably would not be so "difficult" for the ICC to get such "competitors" to come to such an agreement.

of these claims, and, of course, no way to assure that the facilities will actually be moved.

In this connection, the railroads proposing certain benefits should be held to a reasonable standard of certainty: if most of the proposed economies are not attempted by the merged carrier, the ICC should compel specific performance of these changes. At the very least, the ICC should assign high uncertainty value to claimed benefits which are, in effect, highly speculative.

Actually, many of the savings from yard costs should be able to be produced without a merger. Yards can be enlarged or shared, as can tracks, without the loss of competition between railroad companies. The objection that such arrangements might benefit one line over another could be answered by requiring the carrier receiving the greater benefit to bear a greater burden of the expenses involved.

Applicants often say that by merging they will be able to route traffic over the combined best track of the individual carriers. The resulting routes may be shorter, or the grade may be less severe. The claimed result is better service. There are no hard statistics on how a merger will actually affect use of the best track. There are so many factors going into the rating of a track that it may be impossible for a railroad to choose the "best" route with any great precision. Even if it were possible, it is still questionable how much could actually be saved that could not be saved by separate carriers sharing track.

The applicants sometimes present to the ICC a proposed timetable showing the speedier operations that will result from the merger. The Justice Department, a frequent critic of major mergers on grounds of preserving competition, cast some doubt on the credibility of such schedules when it recently undertook its own study of one such schedule and found that the time savings had been effected or even surpassed *before the merger had been approved*. In the "Northern Lines" case, the applicants stated at the initial hearing that the fastest Chicago to Seattle time by either the Great Northern or the Northern Pacific was seventy-six and one-half hours, and that the merger would reduce the time to seventy and one-half hours. By the time of the filing of the exceptions, the Northern Pacific had already pared its time to fifty-eight and one-half hours, and the Great Northern to fifty-nine and one-half hours. Obviously, this is another area where the ICC should look at railroad prognostications with great care, because predicted results are not proven results, and may be accomplished in any case without a merger.

The railroads also usually claim that the merged carrier will help ease the car supply shortage. This argument is always mentioned, because as seen in Chapter 9, the railroad industry has had car supply shortages for decades, and the ICC tends to look favorably on claimed solutions. Commissioner Kenneth Tuggle, at the Oversight Hearings in June, 1969, admitted to Senator Vance Hartke that despite mergers, the car supply shortage still brings many complaints to the Commission.[17] Still, the readiness with which the ICC accepts this argument was exemplified at the oral hearings before the full Commission into the C&NW-Milwaukee Road merger in August, 1969. On ICC document had recommended to the Commissioners that they not forget the Penn Central merger, which had only exacerbated the car supply problem. During the argument by Edward K. Wheeler, attorney for one of the applicants, Vice Chairman George Stafford leaned forward and in a sincere tone asked the lawyer whether the proposed merger would solve the car supply problems of the two roads. Wheeler hastily assured Vice Chairman Stafford that such would be the case. The Vice Chairman leaned back, obviously pleased. The hearing continued.

Mergers could help alleviate faulty distribution of freight cars, if one central controller equipped with extensive computers could shuttle cars back and forth as they are needed. However, the failure of the Penn-Central Company seems to prove that the *decentralization* of car allocations was more efficient.

Another argument made in favor of mergers is that the railroad industry is generally characterized by stodgy management, and that through mergers it may be able to shake up the *status quo* in the carriers' offices. It is hypothesized that by combining the managements of the two carriers, there will result a larger enterprise being managed by the best men from each of the old carriers. This may or may not be true, but a *Railway Age* article suggests that is not.[18] An article in that trade magazine in 1969 suggests that the top men in the to-be merged roads may feel that their jobs are in jeopardy, and because they are so competent, they often find other jobs before their status becomes subject to the whims of new management. Thus, the managerial group which finally goes to the newly merged carrier is comprised of those men who could not make the grade elsewhere; this possibility, which is not at all unrealistic, should be cause enough to cloud the importance of such claims made at merger hearings before the ICC.

As a matter of fact, Professor Kent Healey of Yale has suggested that managerial effectiveness is limited after a railroad reaches 20,000 employees, and that above that level, railroads are subject to extra-managerial cost due to greater size.[19] The operations of the carrier simply become too far-flung for managerial efficiency. Thus, when a merged carrier like the "Burlington Northern" (product of the Northern Lines merger) with 50,000 employees whom it guarantees lifetime employment, announces that it intends to cut no more than 500 miles of road, the claims that it will save $40 million through "economies . . . [in] a lot of areas" have to be greeted with a great deal of skepticism. Yet the ICC approved the merger on those terms.[20]

The railroads also claim that by increasing their size through mergers they will be better able to afford expenditures for research and development. The transport industry as a whole has generally been less than aggressive in R & D expenditures. For 1960, for example, transport industries spent 0.7 per cent of their total revenues on R & D, while the average for all industries in the U.S. was 4.2 per cent. The railroads had an even worse record than the transport industry as a whole: they spent 0.07 per cent, 0.06 per cent, and 0.07 per cent of their total revenue on R & D in 1960, 1961, and 1962.[21] Professor Ann Friedlaender argues that the cause of this low expenditure is not only lack of entrepreneurial initiative, but is also due to the regulatory constraints and market constraints existing in the railroad industry.[22]

Given the lack of price competition from other railroads or other modes of transportation, there will be little or no spur for the merged companies to develop new methods of providing better service to shippers. Improved research methods may result from mergers, but merged railroads will not necessarily provide better R & D than unmerged lines.

In conclusion, the ICC must, in evaluating the case made by the applicants, approach their claims and arguments with a healthy skepticism. As stated by Mr. Justice Brennan:

Ultimately, however, the reason reliance upon the estimates of railroads of their own best interests is objectionable is simply that the best interests of the railroads are not necessarily consistent with the public interest, and it is the latter which the Commission is directed to advance. . . . The commendable industrial statesmanship demonstrated by the railroads on many occasions in these recent proceedings only serves . . . to aggravate the danger that 'grows out of the tendency of these giant corporations to compromise their own differences at the expense of the unorganized public.'. . . The regulatory agency must be the bulwark against such compromise.[23]

There is a special "politics" of ICC merger decisions, arising from the interplay of parties and persons in the process. The setting or "scenario" of a merger generally goes by the following basic pattern: the railroads propose the merger; the Justice Department opposes the merger on the grounds that it unduly restricts competition; the ICC approves the merger (thirty or thirty-four mergers have been approved by the ICC); and the Courts rule on the ICC decision. Often the merger proposal is sent back to the ICC for further reconsideration, often to include the fate of other carriers that would be crippled by the economic power of the merged line. Thus, the ICC's role in the proceedings is basically a passive one.

The Merger Process

INITIAL MERGER HEARINGS

The parties argue the merits of their proposed merger before an ICC hearing examiner. The examiner travels to the various places affected by the merger and takes the testimony of interested persons or groups. Hearing examiners generally are not accompanied by accountants or economists to help them understand the complex data (maps, graphs, exhibits, and economic details) being presented by the proponents of the merger. Recently, in the Rock Island and Milwaukee mergers, the hearing examiner had one economist present; however, in the "Northern Lines" hearings, the examiner heard the case himself without technical support.

The size of the record from a merger hearing can be overwhelming, and clearly beyond the capacity of a single examiner, or perhaps even an examiner and an economist to handle. For example, in the consolidated proceedings involving acquisition of the Rock Island Line, the hearings lasted from May, 1966, to August, 1968; cross-examination covered 47,893 pages of testimony; the entire record covered 100,000 pages. No recommended report has yet issued from the hearing examiner. It is estimated by one close observer of the merger situation that the case will take another eight to ten years, through the ICC and up to the Supreme Court.[24]

One examiner reported that in cities like Chicago, opponents of the mergers are usually overpowered by the railroads because the railroads have highly paid consultants at their disposal, while municipalities opposed to the merger do not have such technical help in the preparation of their case. In small towns, the situation is worse, as local interests are even less able to bring to their side economic consultants, lawyers, and accountants. Thus, it is important that hearing examiners be provided with adequate technical support at the actual hearings, since the ICC is virtually the sole representative of the public interest in such proceedings.

With or without technical help, the hearing examiner's own competence or energy may play as important a role as anything else in his ability to reach an informed decision in a complex merger case. The examiner's role is to search out the "facts" and the issues presented in a particular case. Because of the magnitude of the task, some examiners may be tempted simply to accept the elaborate testimony of the applicants as the basis of his report.

Sometimes opponents of a particular merger react with outrage at what appears to be a clear bias on the part of the examiner. In the "Northern Lines" merger (recently approved by the Supreme Court over the Justice Department's opposition), the Justice Department criticized the handling of the arguments in opposition to the merger. In its exceptions to the examiner's report, the Justice Department stated that "The affidavits disclose a shocking, extreme, and undisciplined personal bias in favor of the merger. It is a bias which resulted in an unfair hearing and an unreliable report to the Commission." The Justice Department continued that the remarks of the examiner during the hearing "betray[ed] a dismaying gullibility" to the applicants' presentation. The examiner's attitude toward the public was "clearly hostile and impatient." Further, "this basic attitude—that industry-sponsored witnesses are all-knowing and wise and that others are naive or ill-informed—must certainly account for the examiner's unfair conduct of the hearing." Finally, the Justice Department admonished the ICC, saying: "The public trust was not given to the Commission to be handed over bodily to the carriers."[25]

In the "Northern Lines" merger hearings, the State of Minnesota also criticized the conduct of the examiner:

Applicants have to be admired for the way they have parlayed their faults into assets for merger: Lack of cars, when others have surplus; refusal to transit inter-line; refusal to short-haul traffic to retain traffic from competing modes; refusal to coordinate; neglect to speed up service (until recently); neglect in car repair. All this, and applicants' plea that other modes are taking away their business, is heeded by the examiner!

On the examiner's report, Minnesota commented: "From the melange of this report it is apparent that the examiner accepted *in toto* the theory and arguments of applicants on all those matters which are pivotal; and peremptorily, briefly, or with mistaken grasp, overruled the points raised by Minnesota." The State concluded: "[T]he examiner merely parroted what applicants said in their pleadings, evidence, and brief, and the intervenors in support.[26]

THE ROLE OF THE JUSTICE DEPARTMENT

The Justice Department often appeals ICC approval of mergers to the Court of Appeals and to the Supreme Court. Justice usually argues that the anti-competitive effects of the particular merger overshadow the cost benefits envisioned by the applicants.* The Department is hindered, however, by the lack of adequate manpower and funding to fully contest mergers. It cannot pay adequate witness fees to transportation experts, and it also cannot assign men to exclusive handling of a particular merger. In addition, of

---

* For example, in oral argument before the Supreme Court in the "Northern Lines" merger, Assistant Attorney General Richard McLaren said that the ICC had given mere "lip service" to their statutory responsibility to disapprove unnecessarily anti-competitive consolidations.

course, the Department is prevented from basing its argument on the value of competition alone by railroad merger exemption from the antitrust acts.

Although the Justice Department represents the people of the United States in merger proceedings, the ICC often treats the Department as if it were the Commission's prime adversary. For example, the Commission refused to approve the "Northern Lines" merger the first time it heard the case. Subsequently, the carriers requested a rehearing for the introduction of new "facts," relating to cost savings predicted for the merger. The Justice Department repeatedly requested that the ICC invest the Department with the Commission's own powers to investigate the carriers' new data, so that the Department could test the new claims against its own calculations—which showed that cost savings claimed through merger could be achieved by the carriers without merger. The ICC denied all these requests for independent investigation power, despite the importance of determining these cost savings as accurately as possible. The ICC justified this refusal by saying that "there comes a time at which we must honor our concomitant obligation to complete our proceedings upon a rail merger application within a reasonable time." Needless to say, the ICC subsequently approved the merger, and it was recently approved by the Supreme Court, over the protest of the Justice Department.

The crunch comes when the Supreme Court defers to the expertise of the ICC. If the Commission has ignored the anti-competitive nature of the merger, the Justice Department's protests are of little avail.* And, of course, Supreme Court approval of such mergers as the Penn-Central and the Northern Lines only encourages the ICC to continue such policies.

SHIPPER SUPPORT

The carriers must produce shippers to support the merger in testimony before the ICC. The Commission then asserts that the shippers are an effective advocate of the consumer in these proceedings. In the "Northern Lines" merger, the State of Minnesota argued that the testimony of shipper

* For example, see the comments by Mr. Justice Douglas in his partial dissent in *B & O R. Co. v. U.S.*, 386 US 372 (1967), discussed later in this chapter.

witnesses "was without qualification, foundation, and merely mimicked applicants." [27]

The applicants usually submit to shippers in their area a summary of the arguments in favor of the proposed merger. Included is a notice of the time and place of the hearings. Since an individual shipper does not have the resources to investigate the proposal to see if the postulated effects will in all probability take place, he tends either to support the merger or remain silent. There are a number of reasons why a shipper will testify in favor of a merger that will produce a monopoly power situation in the rail mode. First, the shipper might assume that there is sufficient competition from other modes of transportation in the area to protect him from the results of the destruction of interrail competition. Second, he might be a large shipper with many plants, and think he has enough leverage to exact services from a larger, merged carrier; in fact, he may have been offered concessions in return for his support. Third, the shipper might have no other means of shipping, and he might fear that a "sick" carrier will abandon his needs. Fourth, he might believe that the merged lines will indeed be able to save money and despite diminished competition, pass their savings on to the shippers. Fifth, the shipper could hope that a railroad with increased monopoly power might grant him a privileged rate for its services.

The fact is that the legal departments of the railroads often write the testimony which the shipper later dutifully delivers at the ICC hearings. The Justice Department chronicles this habit in its exceptions to the examiner's recommended report in the "Northern Lines" merger. One shipper admitted that he read the testimony almost verbatim from remarks prepared by the applicant carriers. Another said that although the railroads urged him to say what he thought, in the next breath they "strongly urged" him to follow their "model" testimony.[28]

During the hearings in the Seaboard Cost Line merger, the president of a shipper called the Justice Department and asked them to do something about the merger, as he feared the combination would result in much poorer service. Yet on that very day, an agent of this shipper had testified before the ICC wholeheartedly in favor of the merger. When the shipper president was informed of this, he fell silent, and then mumbled something about "too much friendliness" between his agents and the carrier.

The argument might be made that shippers are adequately organized for protesting rate increases, so they should be equally well-organized to fight mergers, if it were in their interest to do so. The fact is that they are not. As was mentioned, in small towns local shippers simply lack the economic resources to organize an effective case against the mergers. Left to the ICC, *their* interest is left virtually unprotected.

LABOR SUPPORT

Organized labor used to intervene in merger hearings and often provided some opportunity for a record to be made. The ICC is required by the Act to give weight to "the interests of the carrier employees affected." The carriers often admitted that some of the savings to be had from the merger were from the layoff of excess employees in the new carrier. Since the Penn-Central merger, however, labor has been less of an obstacle. The Penn-Central was a very *touchy* merger, and Stuart Saunders of the Pennsylvania Railroad knew that he would need all the help he could get. He therefore negotiated a contract with labor in which they could keep a "fireman" on each train. (A fireman used to stoke coal on the old locomotives, and "featherbedding" is the most accurate term to describe his present work on today's diesels.) Labor was delighted and decided not to vigorously oppose the Penn-Central merger. As contracts with other carriers have come up, similar deals have been worked out. Result: greater costs to the railroads, undoubtedly passed on to the consumers.

THE FORMAL HEARING

Once the merger has been processed through the initial hearing stage, it passes on to the Commission. Most mergers are certified as of "general transportation importance," and are thus argued before the eleven-member Commission. But Division 3 Chairman Kenneth Tuggle, and his attorney advisor Robert Brooks, play a dominant role in the Commission's decisions. Where cases are argued before the entire Commission, it is Tuggle's Division 3 that is assigned the basic analysis of the proposal. Commissioner Tuggle is a commanding figure, the most experienced man on the Commission, having served continuously since 1953. He takes a very limited view of the ICC's role, claiming that the Commission cannot take an active part in working out a truly national approach to rail consolidations. This attitude is indicated by his testimony before the Senate Transportation Subcommittee in June, 1969:

Senator Hartke: I think there is a growing concern on the part of a lot of people that a very broad view of the national economy should be given very careful regard before granting these mergers. Do you view that as your role or do you believe that you are so limited by legislative restrictions that it is not possible for you to give that type of consideration?

Commissioner Tuggle: We can't give a single case national consideration. As the law is now, a merger proposal has to be started by the carriers. We have no authority to start that. Until something comes before us, there is nothing we can do.

Senator Hartke: Do you feel the law should be changed?

Commissioner Tuggle: No, sir. I see no reason to change it. I think it is adequate now. Let me add just this observation: I don't think that you can get together any eleven men in the United States who can sit up here in Washington and draw lines on a map and make a viable, practical, efficient, economical national rail network. It just couldn't be done.[29]

Given Commissioner Tuggle's view that "[the ICC] can't give a single case national consideration," it is no surprise that mergers like the Penn-Central and the "Northern Lines" have been approved by the ICC, despite the view of many observers that the ICC should consider other options besides the creation of giant merged lines in the rationalization of the "crisis" of overcapacity.

Partisan politics and the political process outside the ICC also play a role in merger applications and proceedings. Actively involved in many merger controversies are the Justice Department (and thus the Executive Branch), the D.O.T., and occasionally the public—as in the Penn-Central debate, when a highly vocal segment of voters (New England and New York commuters) saw a pending merger as an apparent solution to their local transportation problems.

From the very beginning, the Penn-Central merger was seen as a dangerous proposal by experts outside the industry. Not only would the East be sealed off from competition between railroads for future years by the massive Penn-Central's market power, but, equally important, the merger would have extraordinary precedent value. Other large-scale mergers would be encouraged across the country, since other lines would—and subsequently did—argue either that their merger would be necessary to compete with the Penn-Central, or that their merger would be no worse than the Penn-Central in terms of market power created.

The interagency merger study committee appointed by President Kennedy never officially decried the Penn-Central merger, but it is known to have discussed it and advised the Administration not to support it.

The Justice Department opposed the merger in the initial hearings before the examiner. The case went up to the Supreme Court on a procedural issue in which certain parties unsuccessfully sought to force the ICC to join consideration of this merger with consideration of the C&O-B&O merger in the same general region.

When the case came back to the Commission, the Justice Department had apparently already prepared a brief seriously attacking the decision of the hearing examiner in favor of the merger. As the date for filing of briefs came closer, the New York Central and the Pennsylvania grew a little worried. They had already succeeded in quashing labor's opposition by agreeing to the extra firemen described above. At some point in this period, the railroads discovered that they would receive the support of many New England and New York political leaders, and therefore greatly improve their case before the ICC, if they would agree to take over the ailing New Haven Railroad. The New Haven was in its dying days. Service was at an all-time low. The states had been subsidizing the road, and the issue of the New Haven Railroad was a hot one in New England.

It was a bitter pill for Messrs. Saunders (Chairman of the Board of Penn-Central) and A. E. Perlman (then President) to swallow, for neither wanted a losing enterprise to tack onto their new giant, which had financial problems of its own. Eventually, though, they gave their tacit approval to this idea, and the ICC used the condition of take over of the New Haven as a major justification for approving the merger. That the Penn Central has not lived up to its promise of improved service on the New Haven is ironic, since aside from this promise, the merger had, in fact, little economic justification.

Despite having apparently placated both labor and the

New Haven passengers and their Congressmen, Messrs. Saunders and Perlman decided to take their case to the top in an attempt to prevent the Justice Department from opposing the merger in its brief to the ICC. A meeting was scheduled at the White House with Saunders, Perlman, and then Attorney General, Robert F. Kennedy. It was at this meeting that Kennedy decided that the Department would not oppose the merger. One of the possible reasons for his decision was the fact that he was considering announcing his candidacy for the United States Senate. The merger was politically popular in the Northeast because of the New Haven issue. He may have wanted to be sure to be on the right side of the tracks on this issue.

With the time for the filing of briefs close at hand, the Justice Department wondered whether it would have time to revise its brief. Then, Donald Turner was named the new Chief of the Antitrust Division. The Justice Department requested more time from the ICC for writing the brief, and permission was granted.

The final brief of the Justice Department was more or less neutral to the merger. At oral argument, the Justice Department attorney was asked by the ICC whether the Department opposed the merger. He answered that with certain conditions—*i.e.,* the inclusion of the New Haven Railroad—the Justice Department was not opposed. The ICC then asked if that were the *Administration's* position, and the answer was in the affirmative. The merger was approved by the ICC.*

It has become apparent in the few years since the Penn-Central merger was approved, that the merger was unsound in a number of ways. The Penn-Central is seeking a rate increase of 6 per cent in the freight area, and service has deteriorated so badly that officers are kept busy traveling around the country pleading with shippers to stay with the railroad through the "transition" period.[30] And the excuse for the approval of the Penn-Central merger, the continuance of the New Haven through attachment to the

---

* The ICC's asking if this approval by the Justice Department represented the approval of the Executive Branch is interesting. Nowhere in the Interstate Commerce Act is it stated that mergers must be favored by the President. If the ICC were using the Administration's approval as a "crutch," it makes the decision much less sound, and shows the extent to which the ICC is sensitive to political pressures.

merged carrier, merely compounded the mistake. A much sounder economic arrangement would have been the disapproval of the Penn-Central merger, and the financing of the New Haven Railroad through government subsidies; this latter condition has already developed in the New York-Connecticut area. The public is stuck, however, with the Penn-Central merger, and they will continue to pay long after the New Haven is taken over entirely by government operations.

Another criticism of the ICC's decision in the Penn-Central merger is that having taken care of the New Haven issue (Commissioner William Tucker personally went to New Haven for the hearing on the inclusion of the New Haven as a condition of approving the Penn-Central merger; Commissioner Tucker is now Vice President of the New Haven region of the Penn-Central Company), and winning the approval of New England politicians, New York State politicians and public opinion in general, the ICC proceeded to ride roughshod over the effect that the merger would have on *other* parts of the country, including central Pennsylvania, which, after inclusion of the three minor railroads (Erie-Lackawanna, Delaware & Hudson, Boston & Maine) in the N & W, is virtually bereft of rail competition.[31] This point is noted by Mr. Justice Douglas in his discussion of the merits of the Penn-Central merger:

What satisfied Section 5(2) (c) of the Act apparently is the opportunity to salvage the New Haven situation. This, I admit, is a relevant consideration if there is to be a merger. But if salvaging the New Haven so as to maintain the economy of New England is relevant, then what about the economy of the cities and counties stretched along the lines of these two roads which will be merged? What degree of obsolescence will they suffer? [32]

The Interstate Commerce Commission is fond of asking its critics, "How do *you* know what the 'public interest' is? We call it the way we see it." However, the term the "public interest" is not as nebulous as the ICC suggests.

It is in the public interest, for example, that shippers and passengers be provided with adequate service from the various carriers, and that the basic stability of the transportation industry as a whole be protected. Only a self-regulating, competitive system or extremely close regulation could promote the public interest in these areas. But the ICC has

placed far greater emphasis on preserving the economic
health of individual carriers than on preserving a competitive system, and it has failed to provide an alternative of
meaningful regulation.

Standards of acceptability for particular mergers are
vague or nonexistent. The ICC takes each case as it comes
along, ignores the objections of transportation economists,
adopts the rather loose standards of the 1940 Transportation Act, and accepts without scrutiny the cases made by
the applicants. It has approved thirty out of thirty-four proposed mergers so far, creating enormous areas of monopoly
power and virtually ignoring the public interest. The Commission has consistently failed to combine the considerations
of adjacent mergers which, taken together, have a comprehensive economic effect on whole sections of the country.
For example, the ICC refused to combine consideration of
the Penn-Central, the N&W-Nickel Plate, and the C&O-
B&O mergers, despite the fact that looking at the three mergers together would have enabled the ICC to take a more
comprehensive view of the Eastern railroad picture.

This refusal to consider the three Eastern merger proposals together came under heavy criticism from the Supreme Court in *Baltimore & Ohio R. Co. v. U.S.*, 386 US
372 (1967).

Mr. Justice Brennan, concurring with the opinion of the
Court *per* Mr. Justice Clark, states that "It is difficult to
understand exactly what the ICC is arguing" when the Commission claims that the consideration of the Penn-Central
merger "would amount to a consolidation of the proceedings
in Penn-Central with the N&W inclusion proceeding, and
that this would constitute a return to the 'master plan' approach for railroad unification unsuccessfully tried under
the Transportation Act of 1920. . . ." [33] Mr. Justice Brennan concedes that there is no longer a *requirement* that the
ICC develop a master plan for mergers, but he adds: "That
the ICC is no longer told to plan does not mean it is unable
to do so when planning is necessary to fulfill its duties." [34]

. . . [T]he agency has wide latitude in fashioning procedures,
and a broad power to condition its approval of proposals. *In
other words, the ICC is not the prisoner of the parties' submissions.* Rather, the agency's duty is to weight alternatives and
make its choice according to the judgment how best to achieve

and advance the goals of the National Transportation Policy. [Emphasis added.] [35]

Mr. Justice Douglas, one of the leaders on the Supreme Court in the area of economic regulation, has equally sharp words for the ICC's failure to take a coordinated approach to the merger situation. He states: "The Commission has ample authority to insure a coordinated approach to railroad consolidations; it is not strait-jacketed by a disjointed case-by-case approach. Yet the contrary attitude of the Commission is evident in this case." He adds that the ICC's refusal of the Justice Department's request to consolidate the three merger proceedings suggests "a subservience of the Commission to the railroads' estimates, the railroads' proposals, the railroads' evaluation, the prophecies of the future." [36] Douglas goes on to say that he considers the ICC decision "irresponsible," [37] and then discusses the "many crucial issues, necessary for evaluation by the Commission, [which] are not even exposed in this record, let alone appraised." [38] These "crucial issues" include:

1. Who the beneficial owners of the merged line are. (This question is considered later in this chapter.)
2. What effect the merger will have on communities within the merger area, and on rail competition outside of the merger area, and on rail competition within the merger area.
3. What effect the merger will have on national transportation policy, both inside and outside the government.
4. What effect the merger will have on employment, plant location, and other economic matters within small communities along the merged line.
5. What interests will control the new carrier, how powerful their control will be, and whether their interests are antagonistic to the area being served.

The point is clear: the ICC, in approving the merger of two carriers which together account for "51 per cent of the assets, 50 per cent of the trackage, 52 per cent of the operating revenues, 75 per cent of the revenue passenger miles, and almost 53 per cent of the railroad employees in the Eastern area," paid scant or no attention to factors relevant to the public interest, and merely acceded to the wishes of the railroad companies.[39]

Besides drawing the fire of Supreme Court justices, economists, and shippers, the ICC has not fared well in the eyes of other government units and agencies. The Senate Subcommittee on Antitrust and Monopoly stated in its 1963 report, *The Railroad Merger Problem:*

Despite the fact that as early as 1958, it became obvious that the railroad industry was headed for an attempted realignment and reorganization among trunkline carriers, the Interstate Commerce Commission has made no effort to investigate the scope and impact of this vast developing rail reorganization. Instead, it has chosen to hide behind a restrictive interpretation of the 1940 Transportation Act, and assert that it has no planning or policy functions with respect to the guidance and initiation of railroad consolidations, and that its only power is to approve or disapprove these transactions, as they come before it, on a case-by-case basis, based strictly upon the evidence in the record before it.

And, D.O.T.'s *Western Railroad Mergers* study drew these conclusions about the effect of the ICC's piecemeal approval of merger applications:

The results of the rather random manner in which recent mergers have been proposed and approved are twofold. First, there has been no real overview of the public interest in rail mergers. Stated somewhat differently, the mergers proposed and approved were simply not the best of possible and more efficient alternatives. Second, the adversary process, far from resolving the merger issue in each case, has, if anything, created additional intra-industry conflict.[40]

It is not as if there have been no plans by which the ICC could develop a long-range view of the merger situation. There have been plans put forward. The ICC has ignored them.

In 1962, President Kennedy set up an interagency group which was to study the merger problem in the railroads and the airlines. Sitting on the panel were the Chairman of the Council of Economic Advisers, an Undersecretary of Commerce, the Assistant Attorney General in charge of the Antitrust Division, and an Undersecretary of Labor. This group disbanded after the assassination of John F.

Kennedy, when plans were being developed for the Department of Transportation. But while it existed, the group came up with a set of criteria which they recommended to the ICC for use in merger applications.

These criteria, released to the ICC on March 6, 1963, were:

1. Will the proposed merger restrict effective competition in the provision of transportation services in the areas affected?

2. Will the proposed merger permit an economically more efficient use of resources, through fuller utilization, over a period of time, of plant and equipment and/or reduction of indirect costs per unit of output, which will reduce costs while maintaining or improving the general quality of service offered to users?

3. Can the economies sought by the proposed merger be achieved by alternatives more easily revocable which promise to be of comparable effect in accomplishing the improvement in overall efficiency?

4. Will the cost and quality benefits resulting from the merger be reflected in benefits to the public?

5. Will the proposed merger, with the increased market power of the merged carrier, have substantial undesirable repercussions on other carriers in the industry?

6. Will the proposed merger serve the long-run interests of both the public and the carriers concerned, or is it merely an attempt to meet a short-run crisis arising either because of unfavorable economic conditions in general or a particular transitory problem?

7. Is the merger proposed, in part, because of the imminent failure of one or more of the merging carriers, and is it the most appropriate solution to this difficulty?

8. Are the legitimate interests of existing creditors and equity holders of the merging carriers adequately protected?

9. Does the merger provide adequate protection and assistance to affected employees and take into account community employment effects?

10. Will the proposed merger serve other objectives of public policy, including a reduction in public subsidies? [41]

Yet in *no* case did the ICC ever *mention* these criteria.

A second set of standards was suggested to the ICC by the Department of Transportation. In January, 1969, the D.O.T. published its booklet entitled *Western Railroad Mergers*, pointing out the problems of past mergers, and suggesting that before any merger is allowed among the remaining lines west of the Mississippi, an overall view should be taken of the region and the available and potential transportation facilities. The D.O.T. suggested six different plans which the Department felt would cause minimum harm to small carriers and still retain maximum competition in competitive markets. None of the mergers then being proposed by the carriers before the ICC were included by D.O.T. in the six possible groupings.

The ICC simply ignored the study, claiming it was not "official" D.O.T. policy. ICC officials downgrade the status of the report, and it has never been given serious attention by the Commission.

Commissioner Kenneth Tuggle's response to a question from Senator Hartke at the June, 1969, Oversight Hearings shows in clearest form the attitude the ICC takes toward the idea of adopting a comprehensive national, or multiregional approach to the problems posed by merger proposals. Commissioner Tuggle said: "Some of these regional matters [like the Western Rails study by D.O.T.] being mentioned were tried back in 1920, and they failed." [42]

The fact is that the ICC did not promulgate standards for rail mergers until 1929, and then the Depression interrupted everything. The ICC never gave fair trial to a truly coordinated approach to mergers, and Congress soon repealed the "plan" provision of the ICA. If the public is to avoid paying for the lack of coordination in rail mergers for years to come, the ICC must take a "hard line" toward mergers, placing the burden of proof that the merger is necessary on the carriers; the Commission should listen more closely to the Justice Department, and require competing carriers to seek available alternatives to mergers. Shared trackage and shared car supply are among the many ways in which carriers legitimately suffering from overcapacity could save excess capacity without destroying the competitive structure of the rail market.

What is needed is the ICC's understanding of the role it must play for there to be an efficient transportation system in this country. Its timidity with regard to Eastern rail merger proceedings has proven costly to the American public, but there is still time for the ICC to rescue to some extent a sorry record in the merger area. It can adopt a stiffer approach to future Western merger proposals, insisting on more than "paper proof." It can begin to heed the call of experts in transportation economics, and adopt meaningful, articulable standards for approving or disapproving mergers.

D.O.T.'s *Western Railroad Mergers* makes it clear what the ICC role has to be:

What then of the future potential of railroading? How will the industry be organized and what role can it be expected to play in the transportation system? How exactly will different kinds of mergers, or no mergers, affect the industry's performance? What other factors co-determine the future? Not a great deal is known about these subjects, but what is clear is that *the future can and will be determined by conscious decisions—many of them to be made by public regulators. Thus, there is an obligation on the regulators to analyze the impact of their decisions.* [Emphasis added.] [43]

In many cases, the damage has been done. The ICC has authorized the creation of financial and operational giants, with little understanding of what has been approved. The Commission is unaware of who controls the railroads it has allowed to merge, and apparently does not care. Vast market power has been created, endangering shippers, and, inexorably, every citizen—because poor service to shippers will inevitably be reflected in higher prices to consumers.

Who Owns the Railroads?

Although the ICC is entrusted with approving stock transactions in which one carrier seeks financial control of another or the owners of one seek to own another, and though it has the authority to investigate ownership (§12(1), §20(50)), the ICC has not exercised this authority, and has no real idea who owns the railroads. Obviously a person or a company owning a substantial interest in two carriers can control their respective policies, and obviate the pure competitiveness of the carriers. The ICC is supposed to guard against these developments.

The 1963 report, *The Railroad Merger Problem,* bemoaned the lack of ICC action in this important area.

It should appear that at a time when there is a dedicated attempt to concentrate vast holdings of railroad wealth, the Commission has no records and no detailed facts as to what financial controls are being exerted and developed, and has no specific knowledge of the actual influence over the policy of the railroads by insurance companies, commercial banks, investment banks, and other financial institutions, except as may be brought out in the individual cases.

Further, in the Penn-Central merger, the ICC was specifically requested to look into the complex patterns of ownership of the two carriers to determine who owned the two lines, and what effect these patterns of ownership would have on the public interest. *The ICC refused to investigate this matter.*[44]

There is a great deal of known interlocking ownership in the railroad industry. Most spur lines * are now owned by the larger rails which regularly use the track. Terminals, rail yards, and switching facilities are also owned by these large lines. When the owner-carriers get together to discuss the managerial problems of such properties, they have a natural forum for planning concerted actions to protect their own and thwart competition. The government has dealt with this danger in other sectors of the economy through rigid enforcement of antitrust laws.

There is also a great deal about the ownership of the railroads that is *not* known. According to the ownership statements of the railroads, the vast majority of the outstanding stock of publicly-held lines is in the hands of various so-called "Street Names," *i.e.*, investment houses like Cudd & Company; Perc & Company; Merrill Lynch, Pierce, Fenner & Smith; Sigler & Company, etc. There is some stock held by Swiss banks, which means that the true owners will probably never be known. Thus, it is more than possible that an investor or a group of investors can buy stock in more than one competing railroad through one of these

---

* Short lines connecting to the main road, usually serving individual shippers or small towns.

investment houses and later exercise some control over the policies of competing lines. The ICC would never even know of the arrangement. In other words, the investor group could enjoy many of the benefits of a merger without ever having to go through the cursory examination which the ICC requires in a merger hearing. Such influence is perfectly feasible, because with a large, publicly held corporation, a small percentage of active stock can often control the corporation. ICC personnel admit that in some cases even as little as 5 or 6 per cent of the stock would yield its owner a great deal of influence in the carrier's decisions.

The Supreme Court in *North American v. SEC*, 327 US 686, 693 recognized the power of these less than obvious binds. "Historical ties and associations, combined with strategic holdings of stock, can on occasion serve as a potent substitute for the more obvious modes of control. . . . Domination may spring as readily from subtle or unexercised power as from arbitrary imposition of command. To conclude otherwise is to ignore the realities of intercorporate relationships."

Our own survey of the ownership patterns of railroad stock underline the need for explicit information as to who owns what. Based on information made available, we have learned that of the seventy-six main (Class I) rail carriers in 1967, the stock in each of fifteen carriers was fully owned by less than ten individuals. More important, twenty-five of the carriers, or about one-third, were each owned in full by less than fifty persons. Influence through the ownership of a large piece of the corporation is more than a possibility with these carriers. Going further, we find that thirty-seven of the major carriers are owned in full by less than 1000 stockholders (that is, about one-half of the Class I carriers in the country) and that forty-eight (or almost two-thirds of the nation's carriers) are each fully owned by less than 5000 persons. Even among these latter carriers, influence by two to three key men with a large proportion of the stock is quite likely. The ICC has made no effort to determine the proportion of ownership in the hands of a limited group of persons.

In the Rock Island merger proceedings, Examiner Nathan Klitenic tried to discover the true owners of the carriers that were attempting to merge. Klitenic asked the "Street Names" in which the real owners held railroad stock. Although at first the investment companies argued that they were not allowed to disclose the names of their investors, under threat of application for subpoena they agreed to give the information. This information is still being compiled, but so far we have learned that Klitenic has simply found another layer of anonymity under the cover of which the true investor or group of investors can still hide. It was found that the "Street Names" were often holding the stock for large investment banks. For example, Sigler & Company holds much railroad stock for the Manufacturers Hanover Trust Company. Many of the shares of Carother & Clark are held in trust for a group known as Investors Mutual, Inc. Cudd & Company holds stock for the Chase Manhattan Bank. Ing & Company holds shares for the First National City Bank of New York. Ferro & Company holds shares for the Fidelity Fund.

The ICC should assert its jurisdiction to force these second-level owners, in turn, to indicate the individuals for whom they have purchased, but Examiner Klitenic is being met with opposition within the Commission. Divison 3 Chairman Kenneth Tuggle, when asked by us about this situation, simply asked us whether we would like to have our investments made public. He further said that since the first examination has turned up no evidence of any particular individual or individuals holding large portions of the railroads, the ICC should do no further "snooping."

Commissioner Tuggle entirely misses the point. An individual or a corporation purchasing a share or a block of shares of stock in a manufacturing company is entitled to the security of privacy, limited, of course, by the requirements of the Securities and Exchange Act. The same person or corporation buying railroad stock, however, should be subject to closer scrutiny, because the country has an interest in preventing competing utilities from being controlled by identical interests, and in finding out exactly who is the actual owner that benefits from the stock. The public has entrusted that interest, that responsibility, to the ICC.

It is relevant to consider the words of Mr. Justice Douglas, concurring in *Baltimore & Ohio R. Co. v. U.S.*, 386 US 372, 444, where he discussed one of the "many crucial issues" ignored by the ICC in its approval of the Penn-Central merger:

What is the nature of this cartel? What financial interests control it? Only one of the largest stockholders is known. The remaining largest stockholders are brokerage houses and Swiss banks holding nominal title for their customers. The beneficial owners are unknown, and apparently of no concern to the Commission. *The Commission was specifically requested to determine who are the beneficial owners of the stock and who would control the merged company. The Commission refused to accede to the request.* Nor did the Commission consider it relevant that, through interlocking directorates, the proposed directors of the merged company are directors of and interested in corporations which deal with the railroads or that the control of railroads is steadily being concentrated in the hands of banks, insurance companies, and other large financial interests. [Emphasis added.]

A related method of effecting control over more than one carrier at a time is the practice of some directors of sitting on more than one carrier's board of directors. The ICC is specifically entrusted with the responsibility of deciding whether a person can become a director of more than one line. It has generally ignored this responsibility.

Some indication of the lack of ICC concern was evident in our attempt to find the records of such approvals. Several ICC staffers, including staffs of commissioners, expressed surprise that approval was even necessary. Apparently, such approval is routine, as statistics of an earlier year indicate. In fiscal year 1961 for example, five applications to hold the position of officer or director in one or more railroads were pending at the beginning of the year and 243 new applications were received during the year. Of these, a grand total of four were denied, one was dismissed, and 231 were granted, while twelve were pending. Similarly, of 4883 such applications between 1936 and 1961, 4808 were granted in whole or in part, two were dismissed, and only fourteen were denied. George E. Leighty, then Chairman of the Railway Labor Executives' Association, commented on this situation in testimony before the Senate Judiciary Committee hearings on rail mergers in 1962:

[T]here can be no doubt but that such one-sided approval exceptions to the Interstate Commerce Act prohibition against the holding of the position of officer or director of more than one railroad or sleeping car company, unless approved by the Commission, has tended to centralize control in the railroad industry to a degree that permits valid questions to be raised concerning the adequacy of present protection of the public interest against monopoly.[45]

Also evident are interlocking directorships with other industries than railroads. On the subject of the proposed Penn-Central merger, George Leighty warned of this phenomenon:

Concentration of control over the railroad industry becomes much more dangerous when it is recognized that the control over these railroad corporations themselves is also being concentrated into a steadily shrinking number of banks, insurance companies, and other large financial interests which control the railroads through ownership of their stocks and bonds. This pattern of control becomes ever more ominous when one notes that through interlocking directorates, control over the railroads ties in directly with control of the major corporations in other industries, so that the Nation's largest shippers now, in effect, appear to share with the dominant financial interest the power to make the ultimate decisions concerning the future amount of railroad service that is to be available in this Nation.

Interlocking directorates are being used to attain monopoly power by people whose interests are clearly not those of the public. Leighty urged a study of the extent to which this concentration of control is impeding the service and efficiency of the railroads. The ICC has never answered the challenge.

In the recent *Illinois Central-Gulf Mobile and Ohio Railroad* merger, F.D. No. 25103, *et al.*, many of these same questions came up. In that case, the Columbus and Greenville Railway Company filed a motion to dismiss the merger application on the basis that all of the parties to the merger had not been ordered to testify. Its brief contended that the Brown Brothers Harriman interest should be compelled to testify because of their historic control of Union Pacific Railroad, and through the UP, the Illinois Central.

A complex web of the control relationship is spun. Union Pacific is alleged to own 27 per cent of Illinois Central stock outright. Other Illinois Central stock is widely held. Although the UP offered to put its IC stock in a "trust" for the purpose of expediting the merger, Columbus and Greenville felt that the historic control would still be felt by IC officers, in that these officers would be most susceptible to the suggestions of those who would someday resume voting interest.

Brown Brothers Harriman has allegedly controlled Union Pacific (only 3 per cent of UP stock is actually owned by them, but that was apparently enough to put a member of the BBH law firm on the board of directors of the Illinois Central) since 1890. In that year, it is alleged that Harriman's purchase of stock in UP allowed him to block its reorganization. E. H. Harriman became the chairman of the executive committee a year later. Control was maintained over the years through the principal offers of UP. Among them were his sons W. A. Harriman, E. Roland Harriman, his close associate Robert S. Lovett, and his son Robert A. Lovett. Harriman's law firm was Clark, Carr, and Ellis, a firm which was also closely tied to the UP. Members of the firm continually served as general counsel to the UP. In 1938, W. A. Harriman was able to completely alter the composition of the UP's board of directors.

Clark, Carr, and Ellis were also employed by the IC. The opponents in the IC-Gulf Mobile and Ohio merger alleged that the Harriman interests have been able to control IC decisions since the 1880's. More recently, Wayne A. Johnston, who was president of the IC from 1945–1966, is reputed to have admitted that before major decisions of the IC were made he would "put on his hat and go down to see 'Big Brothers' "—meaning the senior partners of Brown Brothers Harriman and Company. The present president is reported to have said that the Union Pacific and the partners of Brown Brothers Harriman selected him as president of the Illinois Central.

A direct example of policy influence is alleged in the Illinois Central's inaction in relation to the Union Pacific's attempt to merge with the Rock Island. IC had intervened in other merger proposals in its area, claiming that a substantial loss of its traffic would result. In the opinion of the Columbus and Greenville Railway, the UP-Rock Island merger threatened much more serious loss to the Illinois Central than other mergers it *had* opposed.

In summary, the Columbus and Greenville alleged that the Brown Brothers Harriman interest have controlled the UP with only 3 per cent of its stock for over sixty years, and through UP's 24 per cent of IC, they also control IC. The C&G charged that these interests would now be gaining control over the Gulf Mobile, and Ohio. Therefore, the C&G charged, the ICC could not even consider the application because the real parties in interest were not before it as applicants, and under Section 5(2) (a) of the Interstate Commerce Act the merger could not be approved.

The allegations above have not been proved, but some novel legal issues were asserted, and without a comprehensive study the ICC really has no idea how stockholdings and joint directors may be concentrating control of the railroads into a few hands.

The reply of the Justice Department to the brief by the Columbus and Greenville Railway Company agrees that the ICC must look much closer at the ownership of the railroads in order to fulfill its statutory duty to oversee "control" transactions.

The *ability* of one carrier to influence the affairs of another is the core element of the control issue, and the element at which the statute is directed. . . . The question is whether one company may influence the other if it chooses, for, *e.g.*, by obtaining a voice in the management of the company (*e.g.*, through the election of directors, or by careful and deliberate use of stock voting power) day to day direction need not be at stake. Influence on major decisions such as whether to oppose a merger proposed involving other carriers, where to locate a major terminal, the location of which might help one carrier or hurt another, with whom to join in promotional rate and service arrangement, etc., are enough to affect transportation service, and enough to justify the exercise of commission jurisdiction over the control relationship.

The Interstate Commerce Commission has been remarkably oblivious to the issue. As a start, the ICC should undertake a large-scale study of who really owns the railroads, and then begin to sift out how they are controlled and to what ends. The ICC should enforce its power to reject applications for joint directorships between railroads and between railroads and other industries. The ICC must regulate a discernible industry if it is to provide for an effective national transportation system. At the very least, the ICC should investigate who has control of applicants in merger proceedings. If not, one seemingly innocent merger may be a mask for a far more complex extension of power.

The Trucking Giants

Railroad mergers, because of the expense involved and the extent of the current merger wave, are the most critical at the present time. However, the ICC must also approve truck mergers, bus mergers, water carrier mergers, and pipeline company mergers, although the latter two occur very infrequently.

It is possible that the ICC has even less idea of the scope and effect of trucking mergers than it does of railroad combinations. There are no statistics which accurately portray the concentration or competitiveness of the trucking industry. It is, however, apparent that the trend of mergers and acquisitions over the past twenty years has significantly fostered concentration in the industry. There are increasingly fewer trucking companies, the average company is growing larger, and the largest companies are capturing greater proporitons of the total business volume of the industry. In conjunction with entry barriers and tight restrictions, described below, many carriers appear to have substantial monopoly power.

If there is any ICC policy toward motor carrier mergers, it seems to be to allow large carriers to take over small ones. If nothing else, it is thought that fewer carriers will present less adjudication before a Commission that styles itself overworked. Included in this hypothesis is the ICC's "failing carrier" doctrine—that it is in the public interest for a large magnanimous carrier to take over the poor failing one and strengthen it, thus providing better service to the shipper.

In fact, there is absolutely no evidence that greater size means greater economy in the motor carrier industry. All previous studies have shown no natural advantage with larger size (see Chapter II for [new] discussion of this point). The elimination of interchange * and the accession

* Trucking companies are allowed by the ICC to operate only on very specific restricted routes. A trucker authorized to carry from Chicago to Denver must therefore transfer his Oakland-bound load to another carrier at Denver. This practice is called "interchanging," or "interlining," and is costly in both time and efficiency: the second trucker must arrive in Denver at exactly the same time as the first trucker for maximum efficiency on both lines, and the time taken to transfer the shipment from one truck to the other adds to the total time of the run.

of more territory to be serviced appear to be the main reasons for the carriers to merge. Due to the Commission's practice of granting restrictive operating rights, a carrier whose business is good and who wishes to expand to a wider service area must go through a long and costly proceeding before the ICC in order to extend his certificate. Motor carriers find it easier to buy out or "merge" with a small or failing company that already has a certificate authorizing service on the hoped-for route. For example, some years ago seven large trucking companies applied for merger approval into a single firm, Associated Transport. The rationalization for the merger was that single-line through-service from Florida to the Northeast was needed. The merger was allowed. It did not seem to occur to the ICC that the economic disadvantages of "interlining" are the result of ICC geographic restrictions and that the need for East Coast through-service could be filled without further concentration. Removing geographic restrictions would accomplish the same end.

Because of the ICC, the simple freedom to do business in a particular area has been warped into a saleable commodity. There is little doubt that many "firms" given operating authority for a specific commodity over a specific route simply make a quick "sale" of the ICC-granted favor for a profit. Needless to say, the consumer eventually pays for this process, for the trucker considers the cost of his certificate—whether acquired through ICC hearings or through purchase of operating rights from another carrier by means of merger—as an expense which he must make up in the prices he charges. Higher rates are easy to impose because he has monopoly power provided by ICC protection from competition (see Chapter V for full discussion).

Motor carrier mergers are questionable not only because of the system of restrictions, the lack of economic advantage in size, and increase in monopoly power, but also because consumers often lose the benefits of competition following a merger approval. As with the railroads, consumers complain that the newly enlarged trucker is harder to communicate with, less responsible to small shippers, and less eager to carry small shipments. Small towns may experience drastic deterioration of service.

For example, suppose firm A carries goods from Elgin, Illinois to Chicago. Firm B carries the same goods from

Rockford to Elgin. If the ICC approved their merger, we now have a carrier that can deliver along the entire Rockford to Chicago route. As a "common carrier," * the carrier is theoretically required to transport anything which he is offered, if he has the capacity. As might well happen, the new carrier will attract so much Rockford to Chicago traffic that Elgin to Rockford traffic will be of less and less importance to him. Without the spur of competition, he is less likely to offer special services, more likely to cut back on the number of trips in the less profitable run, and in general more likely to provide poorer and more expensive service to the area.

At present the ICC relies heavily on the testimony of the applicants for motor carrier merger. Employees of the ICC are bored by motor carrier merger hearings, and most are treated by the ICC's modified, non-oral procedure. That is, the case for the merger is submitted on the briefs, without oral argument. There is no careful examination of the interrelationships of various mergers, no plan, no clear standards, no consideration of the merger's impact on the public or on competition.

The Bus Industry: Merger to Monopoly

Two bus lines, Greyhound and Continental Trailways, dominate the intercity bus industry. These carriers grew to their present sizes through a series of mergers with smaller lines. Little research has been done on the effects of these past mergers, and present merger activity is relatively calm.

A recent ICC decision concerning Greyhound showed a refreshing amount of post-merger control, using reasoning which perhaps could be applied elsewhere. In the *Mt. Hood Stages* case, Docket No. Mc-F-9136, it was proven that Greyhound had engaged in certain predatory practices for the purpose of forcing a small bus line to allow itself to be taken over by a Greyhound. Mt. Hood was a bridge carrier in the route from San Francisco to Spokane, going from Klamath Falls to Biggs. For many years, Greyhound had an informal agreement with Mt. Hood in which the two carriers provided interline passenger service with a minimum of inconvenience for the passenger.

* A transportation firm that holds its services out to the public on a first-come-first-served basis.

Schedules were coordinated, advertising for the other's line was evident in stations, and sometimes the transfer of lines merely meant that a new driver would come aboard at each end of the Mt. Hood stretch.

After some years, Greyhound decided that it wanted to take over the Mt. Hood leg of the trip. It made overtures to Mt. Hood concerning a merger, but Mt. Hood refused. Greyhound then began taking steps at ruining Mt. Hood. First, Greyhound quit selling Mt. Hood tickets at its terminals and also discontinued advertising of the interline service. Next, Greyhound unilaterally changed its schedules, so that a person interested in going from San Francisco to Spokane had to wait up to three hours at the end of the Mt. Hood route. Finally, Greyhound instituted its own San Francisco to Spokane route through its own operating territory. The route was 110 miles longer, but it was faster than having to wait for the Mt. Hood layover.

Mt. Hood protested, and the ICC claimed jurisdiction. It said that Greyhound had gotten its routes on the coast only through other mergers which had received ICC approval. The Commission stated that Greyhound repeatedly offered assurances during merger proceeding that it would not engage in predatory practices. The Commission said that it had conditioned its previous approvals at least partly on these assurances, and that it still had the power to revoke its approvals and undo the mergers. Greyhound quickly entered into a new agreement with Mt. Hood.

Similar reasoning can be applied to any ICC merger approval, and the ICC should exercise revocation powers whenever it appears that the promises of the merging carriers have been in bad faith.

The fundamental question remains, however: whether the ICC can justify a system of restrictions which protects monopoly power where there is no economic advantage inherent in greater size. Here, as with rail and motor carrier mergers, the ICC has failed to set a rational policy. Enforcing the prohibition against predatory pricing, as virtuous as that action might be, does not affect the fact that the merger policy of the past decade has resulted in a passenger industry dominated almost entirely by two firms—only partially in competition themselves.

Transportation Companies

The ICC is entrusted by law with the approval of mergers between the various modes of transportation. These have been feared by the trucking industry for many years, because the truckers are afraid that the railroads will eventually absorb them. It is certainly possible that a railroad that finds itself losing traffic over a certain route to a small trucking outfit or a small barge line would be tempted to buy it out. But the ICC has interpreted the National Transportation Policy to require that some competition exist between the various modes, since there is increasingly less competition within them. The Commission further interpreted the National Transportation Policy to mean that the ICC should encourage this intermodal competition, so that each separate mode can survive within the transportation system. Thus, the ICC has been somewhat reluctant to grant mergers between the various modes. If a railroad owns a trucking concern, that fact must be included in its annual report. Such ownership is generally limited to trucks operating in spokelike patterns from rail stops—so-called supplemental and auxiliary service or "drayage." Rarely is a railroad allowed to purchase a long-haul trucking concern.

It is interesting to speculate about the possibilities of intermodal ownership, however. Professor Donald Turner has suggested that a transportation conglomerate might be able to provide the best all-around door-to-door transportation service to shippers. Having five or six of these intermodal carriers competing in each region might, it seems, prove to be the most efficient competitive system possible.

The ICC's reluctance to allow intermodal mergers is only clearly manifested in the policy of prohibiting rail-truck mergers. There is a great deal of common ownership between all of the other modes—a phenomenon the ICC has generally ignored. This situation is particularly puzzling given ICC reliance on competition between the various kinds of transportation as the last bulwark against total monopoly power. Penn-Central owns an executive airline company, a water carrier and, most recently, Buckeye Pipeline Company, the fifth largest pipeline in the nation. Bus lines have numerous financial interests in commercial airlines, and so on.

Big Brother and the Holding Company

Beyond the intermodal merger, there is yet another level of corporate consolidation: the conglomeration movement. Conglomerates, which include diverse transportation and non-transportation industries in one huge super-corporation, play a critical role in the nation's economy. Rail conglomerates include Northwest Industries, Inc. (Chicago and North Western Railroad); Boston & Maine Corporation (Boston & Maine Railroad); Illinois Central Industries (Illinois Central Railroad); Kansas City Southern Industries (Kansas City Southern Railway); Katy Industries (Missouri-Kansas-Texas Railroad); Mississippi River Fuel Corporation (Missouri Pacific Railroad); Seaboard Coast Line Company (Seaboard Coast Line Railroad); and Santa Fe Industries (Atchison, Topeka & Santa Fe Railway Company).* Rio Grande Industries, Inc., and Seaboard Coast Line Industries, Inc. exchanged their shares with the Denver Rio Grade Western Railroad and the Seaboard Coast Line Railroad respectively, creating those companies in order to include non-railroad concerns in their conglomerates. Further, the boards of directors of the Boston and Maine Railroad, Penn-Central, the Union Pacific Railway, and the Southern Pacific Company recently approved plans for submission to their shareholders of parent holding companies for the purpose of non-transportation diversification.

There are now fourteen holding companies which own railroads as well as other concerns.[46] In many cases, the holding company is first set up, then it buys out the railroad by a transfer of stock, then it proceeds to purchase interests in other concerns. In other words, the holding company is set up for the sole purpose of allowing the railroads to invest capital in other ventures. Northwest Industries and Illinois Central Industries are two examples which fairly closely followed this model.

Water carriers have for some time been part of larger corporations, and oil pipeline companies are usually sub-

* Conglomerate mergers comprised over 71 per cent of all mergers from 1960 to 1966 (Reilly, Conglomerate Mergers, 61 Nw. U.L. Rev. 522, 529 (1966). Recently released data by the Federal Trade Commission indicates that this trend is accelerating. Eighty-three per cent of the mergers during 1967 were conglomerate in nature (FTC News Release, March 18, 1968).

sidiaries of integrated oil corporations. Motor carriers, too, have recently been diversifying into other areas and are themselves being purchased. Just under 50 per cent of Class I railroad assets were or will soon be owned by conglomerate firms.

But the ICC has yet to formulate a policy concerning this kind of conglomeration. Section 5(2) of the Interstate Commerce Act requires approval by the ICC of the acquisition of a carrier by a holding company only when the company already owns a carrier or is seeking to purchase more than one at a time. The ICC has recommended to the present Congress that the Act be changed to include the acquisition of a single carrier by a non-carrier holding company within its jurisidiction.

The argument for diversification of the railroads is that the railroad industry has such a low rate of return on investment that the railroads must invest in higher profit industries in order to help subsidize the rail operation and to attract more capital. Supposedly, this new capital will be used in the transportation sector.

One danger is that the management of the holding company will be much more interested in increasing profits than in maintaining its rail plant. There are many indications that the railroads are anxious to get out of the railroad business, and if allowed to invest elsewhere they may "bleed" the carrier into poverty.

The conglomerate, in its eagerness to invest profitably, is tempted to fail to replace worn out obsolete plant and other rail assets. Needed track repairs are "deferred" while rail revenue is used to invest in computers. Such activity presents basic policy questions to the Commission.

A strong counterargument to the "need to attract capital" argument is the ease with which the railroad industry has attracted capital in the past. Their low rate of return has persisted for many years but rail stocks have maintained a stable price range. The investor in rails is interested less in glamour than in stability. Presumably there will continue to be a sizable demand for stable investments and it can even be argued that the railroads do a disservice to their owners by attempting to become excessively growth conscious. Diversification offers excellent opportunities for the railroads to create self-fulfilling prophesies. Goods produced from another investment presumably must at some time be transported. There would be a great temptation to favor such products by charging unduly low rates. Because of this, the railroads will show even lower profits, and will thus gain added credence in their requests for overall rate increases. On the other hand, the lower transportation costs of the goods will produce higher profits for them on their outside operations. These higher profits will be used to justify further investment into other industry.

The extent of conglomerate interplay with most holding companies can be seen in a typical example, the Philadelphia and Reading Corporation (C&NW Railroad). The company produces industrial products through Lone Star Steel Company (steel tubular goods, cast iron pressure pipe, concrete reinforcing bars, ingots, slabs, skelps, coke by-products, and chemical derivatives) and Universal Manufacturing Corporation (ballasts, or small transformers used in fluorescent lighting fixtures, and insulated wire). Consumer products are chiefly produced by Union Underwear Company, Inc. (yarn, cloth, shirts, underwear, and elastic web), and Acme Boot, Inc. (the nation's largest producer of leather boots and shoes). Fruit of the Loom, Inc., franchises certain items of apparel under its trade name. It is impossible for the C&NW, controlled by this holding company, to refrain from the carriage of all these products.

There is now a proposal by the C&O and Norfolk & Western railroads before the ICC for a giant merger to "balance" against the Penn-Central to the North. Together, the two carriers own an estimated 80 per cent of the land that produces bituminous coal in this country. Currently, they lease this land to mining companies, the mining companies mine the coal, and the railroads carry it to industrial centers where it furnishes coke for steel. If this merger takes place, the emerging carrier will have the power to *set the price for bituminous coal* simply by adjusting the rentals for the various mining companies. The Justice Department has not intervened.

The opportunities for discriminatory favoritism of a conglomerate's own manufactured goods in transportation, as well as the danger of cost hiding mentioned above, led Congress long ago to write into law the so-called "commodities clause" (see Appendix 1). This provision explicitly prohibits a railroad from carrying any commodity (except for timber) in which it has a financial interest. In addition, Congress recognized the cost-hiding danger as far back as 1933, when it enacted Section 5(5) of the ICA. In 1940, Section 5(5) was amended slightly and made applicable to motor and water carriers.

Despite these dangers, the Commission has yet to make clear that it will apply the same powers of inspection and examination of holding company records as it presently exercises over straight carriers. It professes bewilderment at the problems of conglomeration and the movement toward investment in non-transportation industries. Others have been studying the area for some time—there have been Congressional suggestions to set up an interagency committee to study the effects of diversification in the regulated industries—but as yet there has been no formal action.*

The Commission *has* prepared a staff report on the problem. It is not known what conclusions were reached, because the Commission alternates between denying that it exists and claiming that as a staff report it is exempt from public inspection under the Freedom of Information Act. From interviews with various Commissioners and with the Bureaus of Economics and Enforcement, the authors assume only that the report was inconclusive. One is reminded of a similar staff report, *Railroad Consolidation and the Public Interest,* which, when released to the public, caused the ICC great embarrassment. That report admitted that the ICC was doing an uninformed job in acting on railroad mergers. It is understandable that the ICC would be reluctant to issue a similar appraisal of its diversification understanding. Nevertheless, both the ICC and the public would benefit from publication of the document together with discussion and debate of the opinions expressed.

A corollary aspect to general diversification into non-transportation investments is the growing trend toward sub-

* Chairman Staggers of the Committee on Interstate and Foreign Commerce introduced two legislative proposals to amend Section 5(2) of the Act. Mr. Stagger's amendments would require prior Commission approval of an acquisition by a non-carrier of control of a single carrier.[47] In addition, Representative Keith of Massachussetts, a member of the House Commerce Committee, introduced a bill which would place a freeze on further take overs of transport carriers by non-carriers until a government study can determine whether such mergers are in the public interest.[48]

Even the Common Carrier Conference—Irregular Route of ATA has inaugurated a study of the competitive impact of rail conglomerates on the regulated motor carrier industry.

sidiary ownership. Congress responded to the cost hiding
and related dangers here through the passage of Section 10
of the Clayton Act. Section 10 prohibits carriers from doing
more than $50,000 worth of business per year with a sub-
sidiary unless it engages in open bidding for this business.

However, the ICC still fails to look very closely at the
railroads' consolidated balance sheets and income statements for evidence of profit hiding activity, and is overly
impressed with what the railroads call their net railway
operating income, as computed by the railroads. People in
the industry intimate that a great deal of profit hiding goes
on, and the relevant statistics look very suspicious. For instance, an analysis of the financial data of private car companies shows great and unexplainable disparities in the
rates of return on investment for similar types of railway
cars. Mileage, average capacity, type of goods carried, all
could not explain it. Whether there is cost and profit hiding
of various sorts at least should arouse the suspicion of the
ICC.

Net rents (a factor added or subtracted before net railway operating income is computed) also show interesting
variations. Many railroads make money renting properties
to others while paying small rents for operating facilities
themselves. Other railroads charge themselves far more than
they charge others. It is quite possible that the losing railroads have sold their land to dummy corporations and then
pay excessive lease amounts, virtually to themselves.

The Justice Department is conducting an investigation of
its own into Section 10 violations by the carriers, apparently
unsatisfied with ICC enforcement efforts. This is not surprising. Although the ICC theoretically requires the carriers
to list all companies in which they have an interest and to
list all dealing with such companies, there is little follow-up.
In the last two or three years, the ICC's Bureau of Accounts
could only remember detecting four to six instances in which
it thought that there were violations, and the Bureau of Enforcement could only remember two or three times in which
it sent these along to the Justice Department for prosecution.

To begin with, since the ICC doesn't even know who
owns the carriers, it is possible that the owners of a supply
or equipment or steel company that does a great deal of
business with a railroad or motor carrier could also be the

owner of the railroad or motor carrier. The ICC would not detect the connection.

Second, the ICC's detection process begins with the review of data submitted by the carriers. The staff of the Commission could think of no case in which it found that a carrier had not reported its ownership of a subsidiary, although a field investigator told us that he knew of many such cases. He said he has since quit trying to report them to the Washington headquarters, because nothing is ever done.

The assistant chief of the Bureau of Accounts admitted that he does not even look for violations by what he called "closely held" motor carriers, because he thought that the ICC had a tacit agreement with the Justice Department not to tackle such cases. When the Justice Department expressed surprise upon hearing about an agreement to which it was supposed to be a party, the ICC expressed its gratitude to us for clearing up a long existing "misunderstanding."

It is interesting to try to find where the records of the competitive biddings are kept. It took us three days to find someone in the Commission who had even heard of them. One doubts whether they are rigorously scrutinized, even if they are sent in by the carriers. (We were finally assured that most of the carriers who do more than $50,000 worth of business with a subsidiary in any given year do submit reports of competitive bidding arrangements.) Although eventually we did get to see some reports sent in by railroads, an ICC staffer in the Bureau of Accounts somewhat red-facedly could only produce three such reports sent in by motor carriers in the last five years.

Our own examination of the limited carrier records available indicate that the seventy-six main railroads in 1967 invested approximately 10 per cent of their total assets (an extremely large total including road and equipment) in affiliated companies, quite apart from the entire holding company issue discussed above. The entire amount involved in these unregulated and virtually unknown investments reached $3,186,381,746 in 1967.[49]

By allowing the railroads to bypass the commodities clause restrictions, by ignoring the enforcement of Section 10 of the Clayton Act, by accepting at face value and without verification the cost data of the carriers in almost every agency proceeding to which they are a party, and by refusing to set a clear policy regarding subsidiary control, affiliate investment, or holding company ownership and diversification, the ICC has abdicated its basic regulatory responsibilities. The agency has set policy through inaction, letting the natural interplay of interest group preferences determine the competitive non-structure of the transportation industry.

Since the Commission has very little knowledge about the ownership of any of the modes, especially the railroads, it cannot adequately judge the effects of its merger policies on the modes themselves. Further, since it knows virtually nothing about the relationship of the carriers to industry at large, it is even less capable of making complex and subtle judgments about the impact of various decisions on all of the interrelationships now extant.

The ICC should realize that transportation cannot be viewed in the same light as other industries. The ostensible purpose of the ICC is to preserve and regulate a transportation system that will service the common carriage needs of the citizenry. To allow the transportation industry to be swallowed up by monopolies and conglomerates, and be made subject to the marketplace and its profitmaking assumptions, is antithetical to both the public interest and the avowed purposes of the ICC.

4 / The Protection Racket

Congress passed the Interstate Commerce Act in 1887, setting up the Interstate Commerce Commission as a check on the then powerful railroads. The task of the ICC was to prevent the railroads from abusing their monopoly power, especially their practice of granting concessions to large shippers while gouging small shippers. The emphasis was on *maximum* rate regulation. It was not until the Transportation Act of 1920 that the ICC was charged with exercising some control over entry into the transportation industry. The ICC was given the power to limit the establishment of new railroads and to control the extension or abandonment of railway lines by granting or denying certificates of public convenience and necessity. The Act also introduced the concept of inherent advantage, the foundation of minimum rate regulation. During the economically perilous thirties, Congress gave the ICC power to control entry into the motor carrier industry, which was still in its infancy. The Commission grasped this power and used it strictly to limit entry into the motor carrier industry by defining "public convenience and necessity" so as to impose an almost impossible burden of proof on applicants for motor carrier operating authority.

In order for an applicant to obtain a certificate of public convenience and necessity, it must show specific shipper need for its services, *i.e.*, that existing carriers cannot provide "adequate service." "Adequate service" is defined *by the ICC* to mean capacity and equipment to handle the freight traffic on a particular route or in a particular region.* Whether or not an existing carrier is inefficient and

* In this respect it should be noted that the ICC is prohibited from restricting the right of a carrier to add to its equipment and facilities by the proviso of Section 208 (a) of the ICA. Thus, existing carriers can block an application by adding on more equipment, and, there-

has high costs and rates is rarely considered. Indeed, in *Wellspeak Common Carrier Application*, 1 M.C.C. 712, 715-16 (1937), the ICC held that evidence that a prospective carrier could and would charge lower rates was *inadmissible as irrelevant*. Similarly, the Commission considers it insignificant that a prospective carrier could provide better service: *The only criterion is whether existing carriers have enough equipment to handle the freight load.**

Regardless of what may have been the merits of control of entry into the motor carrier industry in 1935, it is noteworthy that the high barriers to entry were imposed by the ICC and not Congress; the words of the Act do not call for such tight restrictions.† Whatever the justification for the ICC interpretation in 1935, the shocking fact is that this approach represents an administrative response to conditions that no longer exist.‡

Restrictions

Once motor carrier authority is granted, restrictions are placed on each firm so that it is not even in direct competition with other authorized firms. The Interstate Commerce Act gives the Commission discretion in fashioning restrictions on grants of authority."Section 208 (a) of the Act" as interpreted by the Commission, "requires that certificates issued under 206 and 207 specify the service to be rendered thereunder." The ICC regards as broad "the power to attach terms, conditions, and limitations" to certificates conferred by Section 208 (a). As the ICC puts it: *"From the beginning of federal motor carrier regulation, restrictions gen-*

---

fore, have all the traffic they want regardless of their efficiency or the quality of their service.

* See Appendix 12, "Control of Entry: *De facto* Discrimination," for a discussion of the effects of the ICC's restrictive entry policies on black truckers.

† Admittedly, Congress has not amended the Act to define "Public convenience and necessity." But it is not unreasonable to assume that "public convenience and necessity" changes as economic conditions change.

‡ The trucking industry is no longer in its infancy, it has had over thirty years to develop and mature. The Depression of the thirties, which so hampered its initial growth, ended thirty years ago and was replaced by a continually expanding economy which in large part depends on a viable trucking industry to transport its raw materials and finished products. In today's economy, the supply of carriers certainly does not outstrip the demand for carrier service.

erally have been imposed to protect already authorized carriers from unintended or unwarranted competition . . ." [*Emphasis supplied.*] [1] Restrictions according to type of vehicle, point of origin, point of destination (even to specific road), area, and particular commodity, combine effectively to carve out grants of jurisdiction in which carriers operate with a minimum of competition.*

In the early 1960's the Interstate Commerce Commission, acting through its Bureau of Economics, determined to find out how extensive restrictions and other limitations of authority actually were. By October 2, 1964, the Bureau had "developed a preliminary profile of the motor carriers of property industry based on information contained in the inventory of motor carrier authorities (IMCA)." [2] (On January 21, 1965, the Commission voted to phase out the IMCA profile, apparently for "budgetary reasons." Effective use of the inventory of operating authority would have provided essential information as to the number of firms in each transportation market. As a result of its discontinuance, such knowledge is unavailable or fragmentary. However, the data developed by 1965 give *some* indication of the scope of restrictions.)

The IMCA profile concludes that the 91,335 grants of authority, 31,645 or 34.6 per cent were restricted. But the study employs the term "restriction" in a technical and misleading way. Specifically, IMCA "restrictions" refer to basic limitations on equipment, service, tacking and interchange, operation, auto-carriers, and certain miscellany. *Supposedly* unrestricted carriers—unrestricted as to the six generic limitations above—are in fact further restricted by routing.† Routing limitations include carriage between terminals serving specified points only; between two specific areas or points; between specific terminals serving no intermediate points; etc. An ICC granted authority will be thus limited, for example, to operations between San Jose, California and Tempe, Arizona—perhaps limited to a *specific* highway, perhaps prevented from serving any towns or shippers between those two points. Of the 88,483 grants to regular and irregular common carriers, 14,150 or 16 per

* The constant battle between carriers within the halls of the ICC to guarantee that potential competitors do not intrude within these grants comprises 70–80 per cent of the Commission's caseload.

† See Appendix 13.

cent are fundamentally unrestricted as to both routing limitations *and* generic "restrictions."

But even certificates without "restrictions" and "routing limitations," the so-called 16 per cent fundamentally unrestricted, are severely limited by commodity descriptions. Obviously carriers with the same restrictions, operating on similar routes or in the same areas, are not competitive unless authorized to carry the same commodities. The IMCA profile indicates that there is an extremely small number of grants that provide comparable service, and even those do not reflect the full extent of what is called "commodity fragmentation." Commodity descriptions in carrier certificates were considerably more limited than the broad Bureau of Budgets groupings used for the IMCA profile. In fact, less than 1 per cent of actual commodity descriptions were completely compatible with the broad categories. Thus even *within* a generic commodity classification, there may be little competition. For instance, two carriers of "farm products" are not competitive if one is limited to fruits and the other to vegetables, or if one carries peaches and the other pears. Grants of authority are ludicrously narrow: a survey of specific commodity restrictions reveals that one carrier is limited to "*exposed* film," another to "*unexposed* photographic paper." Carriers have certificates restricted to flexible pipe or plastic pipe or lead pipe, ad infinitum.

It is true that carriers often hold several grants of authority along the same routes and that grants provide for commodity clusters. Clustering of commodities within grants, and multiple grants, tend to enlarge the scope of carrier authority. The broader the authority held, both in terms of commodities, and routes and restrictions, the more poten-

NUMBER OF CARRIERS, GRANTS, AND GRANTS PER CARRIER OF
MOTOR CARRIERS OF PROPERTY HOLDING PERMANENT AUTHORITY
FROM THE INTERSTATE COMMERCE COMMISSION, BY CLASS OF
CARRIER, DECEMBER 31, 1964.[3]

Class of carrier	No. of carriers	No. of grants	Average no. of grants per carrier
Class I	1208	40,858	33.8
Class II	2502	19,195	7.7
Class III	10,191	31,282	3.1
TOTAL	13,901	91,335	6.6

tially competitive is the carrier. Limited multiple grant authority is common.

Commodity clustering within grants is less common. 295 of 1305 grants in a sample studied in the IMCA file "provided for the transportation of more than one commodity, and therefore contained clusters." Within the 22.6 per cent of grants that contained clusters, "clusters ranged in size from two commodities to fifty-five, the average being 3.45 commodities per cluster." [4]

While the IMCA study throws some light on commodity fragmentation, clustering, and multiple grants of authority, it does not indicate the total number or percentage of *carriers* severely limited to commodity restrictions because these charts characterize only grants of authorities and carriers often hold several. J. C. Nelson reports on an earlier study, before the recent trend toward concentration, which concluded that:

A 10 per cent, stratified, random sample of intercity truckers subject to ICC jurisdiction was taken by the Board of Investigation and Research in 1941. . . . The BIR sample of certificates as of 1942 disclosed that 62 per cent of the regulated truckers had been limited to special commodities; that approximately 40 per cent of such carriers (other than those operating specialized equipment) had been limited to one commodity or commodity class, with 88 per cent limited to six or less; and that, in 1941, the carriers limited to special commodities conducted about two-fifths of the total regulated operations. [5]

Nelson further comments:

. . . In its replies to a Senate Small Business Committee questionnaire in 1955, the Commission acknowledged that the same types of restrictions as disclosed by the BIR study were still to be found in operating authorities. [6]

Considering the IMCA enumeration of commodity classifications, there is no reason to think a comparable pattern is not in existence today.

The total number of commodity descriptions, restrictions, and routings is astounding. Their possible combinations are even more so. *Theoretically, every ICC grant might easily be so limited by these factors as to be distinct from any other grant*. Of course, carriers do face limited competition in terms of service. Only a survey of available service in a specific area and an analysis of the cost and rate structure of the carriers operating there could determine the actual restraint of competition resulting from restrictive grants.* Much evidence (see Chapter 2 and Robert A. Nelson's 1956 study of New England) [7] suggests that restraint is severe, and that the trend is toward more restraint and less competition. Growing numbers of trucking firms are able to exercise absolute monopoly power for specific commodities over specific routes—regardless of rate levels or service quality—as a result of ICC protection from competition.

The ICC has justified its restriction of competition among motor carriers by arguing at various times that: 1. Common carrier services can be required from certified carriers in exchange for protection from competition; 2. The assured profits resulting from reduced competition will finance and encourage adequate investment and technological progress; 3. Fly-by-night operations will be screened out and chaotic conditions will be avoided; and 4. Duplications of investment and excess capacity will be avoided.†

In fact, empirical evidence demonstrates that these objectives have not been secured by regulation, and that other harmful effects result from the carving out of monopolistic areas of transportation.

Limiting competition does not assure the performance and availability of common carrier services. Even a cursory examination of the small shipments and household moving problems makes this apparent. Hundreds of complaints each year are received from shippers who are denied service for less than truckload shipments. Motor carriers seek to escape transporting low density, high risk freight such as furniture, and to avoid the out-of-the-way towns and cities. The ICC's response to this latter problem is, as Commissioner Stafford

* In a brief survey of the information available, J. C. Nelson indicates that only fragmentary data on the number of firms in each market exists. While "a considerable number of regulated truckers still operate on dense traffic routes between large, relatively close population centers," there are many dense traffic routes and markets where competition is very light. Equally important is the competitive trend. "In many markets, the number of effectively competing certified truckers has been drastically lowered by dropouts, mergers, and numerous denials of new entries and extended services," p. 401.

† Yet in spite of its highly restrictive control, the ICC has not exercised its Congressional mandate to make racial hiring policies a test of motor carrier fitness. See Appendix 14: "Blacks Within the Industry."

admits, tacit recognition of the carrier's failure to perform its common carrier duty. The Commission has prohibited free use of the Interstate Highway System by motor carriers because of its fear that, given the choice, carriers will refuse to service towns and cities on traditional routes, if these towns and cities are not also on or near the new super highway.

In the household moving area, there are numerous instances of favoritism for large institutional shippers at the expense of small shippers. The moving companies have national accounts to move all the employees of a large corporation like General Electric. Should one of these accounts request transportation for its employees' goods, the household mover will reroute a van originally scheduled to pick up the household goods of a small family shipper who had made arrangements to move weeks before the national account. The small family shipper's household goods will be unloaded and placed in a warehouse in order to service the national account, resulting in an inordinate delay in the delivery of his goods. This practice is an abuse of the common carrier duty, and is an example of the very discrimination the Interstate Commerce Act was designed to eliminate. Other abuses, such as failure even to answer damage claims, manifest attitudes and practices by these carriers that are inconsistent with common carrier duty.

Again contrary to ICC contentions, restricted entry does not encourage innovation and technological change, but in fact makes it unnecessary. Without competition or ICC pressure, there is no inducement to advance technologically in order to reduce costs. Carriage is guaranteed regardless of efficiency and quality of service. Illustrative of this contention is the fact that the advantages of piggybacking and containerization, which were first developed in the 1920's are only now being implemented and exploited—*nearly fifty years later*.

The ICC's principal fear is that removal of entry control into the motor carrier industry will lead to the chaotic conditions which were so prevalent in the industry in the 1930's that Congress felt it necessary to pass the Motor Carrier Act of 1935 (which gave the ICC control over entry). The Commission argues that free entry will spur an upsurge of financially irresponsible motor carrier firms and lead to an excess of carriers which will result in rate wars and cutthroat competition. These fears have little basis in reality.

First, despite ICC efforts, the fact is that *even with control of entry* not only do fly-by-night operations exist, but they flourish—*i.e.,* gypsy, gray area traffic. Artificially high rates caused by ICC regulatory policies make it possible for unauthorized and often irresponsible motor carriers to capture traffic from authorized carriers simply by offering lower rates. Lower rates resulting from competition would preclude entry by gypsy firms, since the only advantage they have to offer *is* lower rates. Second, ICC concern with the dangers of financial irresponsibility from fly-by-night operators seems inconsistent with its present enforcement efforts, *e.g.,* The Bureau of Enforcements prosecution program against insurance violators. Third, removal of entry control does not preclude the requirement and enforcement of adequate safety and insurance standards, which would control what the ICC views as a significant danger of free entry.

It is certainly true that ICC control of entry has precluded the chaos of rate wars and cutthroat competition. In fact, ICC regulation has fostered the other extreme: rate collusion, price fixing, and absence of competition. All evidence indicates that the deregulated model of transportation results in neither rate wars nor cutthroat competition, but rather in healthy stimulation and competition resulting in better service.

That free entry—and the competition it engenders—entails some duplication of investment is an economically recognized fact; but the duplication is counterbalanced by the benefits of competition—lower rates being the most obvious. What the ICC fails to recognize is that its regulatory policies result in substantial excess capacity without the benefits of competition. Often carriers with limited commodity authority, or restricted routings and delivery points, are unable to fill their trucks with authorized commodities. Partially loaded trucks are responsible for much of the under-utilization of capacity. Since most carriers are only permitted to carry certain commodities, they often end up carrying less than full carloads of one or a few commodities. Less than truck-load shipments are inefficient. Extended commodity authority would provide greater opportunity to complete the load. Empty backhauls are also responsible for substantial excess capacity. Obviously there is nothing more inefficient than driving an empty truck.

Some figures are available to suggest the extent of excess capacity among regulated carriage. In a study of the New England transportation system conducted by Robert A. Nelson, motor carriers reported that on the average 17.2 per cent of total miles operated were empty in 1954; and that when only intercity miles were considered the number rose to 60.5 per cent. The great majority of carriers indicated that their operations would be more efficient in terms of more full carloads if their certificates were broadened.[7]

Ten years later, the ICC's unpublished Inventory of Motor Carriers reported substantial under-utilization of capacity. It concluded "that backhaul movement has not been authorized for 19 per cent of grants." [8] The IMCA study supports the proposition suggested by the Nelson findings, that the greater the scope of authority, the less the likelihood of empty or partially empty hauls. "Only 10.3 per cent of grants analyzed for the fifty largest common carriers did not contain backhaul authorization." [9] "For all common carriers, it appear that less than 1.0 per cent of both general commodity grants and household goods authorities lack backhaul authority." [10] *

Not only do ICC regulatory policies fail to achieve their objectives, but they also have other, harmful economic consequences. The number of trucking firms has decreased as a result of ICC regulatory policies. On the one hand, an almost impossible burden of proof on applicant carriers has limited entry to a minimum; on the other hand, the ICC has been willing to approve both mergers between carriers and the purchase of one carrier's authority by another.

---

* Our own studies (see Chapter II), as well as Friedlaender's study, further substantiate the excess capacity and inefficiency problems caused by regulation. Friedlaender writes: "Most carriers operate through points that they could not legally serve, leap-frogging between non-contiguous points and areas. Regular route carriers were, and still are, required to follow specified highway routes, which often lead to circuitous and inefficient operations. A good example of this was the carrier operating between New York and Montreal via Reading, Pennsylvania, a detour of some 200 miles. Similarly, a carrier operating between the Pacific Northwest and Salt Lake City was permitted to haul commodities eastbound but not westbound." (P. 113.) See also Friedlaender, p. 88 for utilization table.

Decrease in the number of firms substantially limits point to point competition, especially in those markets where original competitors were few. Some decline in the total number of carrier firms in the nation since 1935 may be justifiable, but the ICC seems to be unaware of or at least unconcerned about, the possible dangers of this change in the market structure. It has made no studies to ascertain optimum market structure for particular regions, taking into account *inter alia,* the dangers of concentration. As the number of firms has decreased, the size (assets) and traffic volume of firms has increased, but there is no indication that larger firms are more efficient.

Chief among the dangers presented by large firms and increased market concentration is the possibility that the decline in the number of firms will result in oligopoly or near-monopoly in many transportation markets. James C. Nelson presents some of the available data and concludes that while

a considerable number of regulated truckers still operate on dense traffic routes between large, relatively close population centers . . . , even on many routes, generating fairly dense traffic flows, the number of general commodity motor carriers authorized to give single-line service varies from two or three up to six or ten common carriers.[11]

The second danger is price fixing. "The dominance of very large firms obviously has facilitated concerted action on rates." [12] Rate agreement is more easily reached among a few large firms than among small ones. Moreover, "with fewer and larger firms, the rate suspension and minimum rate procedures can be utilized more effectively to thwart independent action." [13] James Nelson reports that in a study done for the Senate Small Business Committee in *Trucking Mergers and Concentration,* Professors Walter Adams and James B. Hendry found that by 1956 the extent of concentration in the motor carrier industry was "disturbing." [14] Concentration has increased steadily since that study.* [15]

A third danger of market concentration is that only large firms can take advantage of value of service pricing to distort the rate structure. Small firms are merely able to maximize revenues from value of service pricing. However, the breadth of authority held by large firms allows high reve-

---

* See Chapters 2 and 3 for details of the concentration process.

nues from value of service carriage to subsidize low revenues from rates adjusted downward to meet competition. Therefore, uncompetitive shipments subsidize competitive shipments, distorting whatever "inherent advantage" a competitor might have.

Such pricing has both intramodal and intermodal effects. First, the lower, subsidized rates of large carriers can drive out small motor carriers even if the latter are more efficient. (There is no need for the subsidized rates to reflect large carrier costs or a profit margin comparable to what small carriers must have on this traffic in order to survive.) Second, and more important, low subsidized rates of large motor carriers have been able to attract traffic from railroads even though the railroads can move the traffic more efficiently. This diversion of traffic to motor carriers "has contributed importantly to the decline of the railroad common carriers in the spheres of traffic and haul in which they have substantial cost superiority." * [16]

Since rates are maintained by a combination of ICC protection and motor carrier concerted action, there is no significant rate competition in the motor carrier industry. What competition does exist takes the form of service competition. The range of the quality of service—*i.e.*, service competition—is difficult to evaluate. † If continual innovation—introduction of cost-saving and safety features to meet shippers' needs—is any indication of service competition, the inevitable conclusion is that service competition is not rigorous. Whether or not regulated carriers provide "better" service than exempt carriers has never been determined. But one question is settled. If regulated service is superior, it is not superior enough to justify the high costs of common carriage. Shippers simply do not want this "extra" service at the rates charged. Proof of this contention is "the large and continuing diversion of regulated commodities to private carriers [and] the widespread shipper use of gray area for-hire operations. . . ." [17] Shippers are willing to sacrifice "better" service for lower rates.

So-called service competition (more runs of less than full truckloads) is only one of many indications of ineffi-

* See Chapter 5.
† It has been suggested that service competition consists solely of carriers providing more runs for shippers. The result is, of course, more runs of less than full truckload.

ciency in the motor carrier industry. Unnecessary mileage, high costs, empty mileage, and partial loads strongly suggest an inefficient system of transportation. Figures are not available as to the percentage of total hauls that are partially full or the percentage of usable capacity in fact used during less than full load shipments. Taking into account both empty and partially full hauls, authorities have estimated that 50 per cent of capacity is unused.* [18] But regardless of the numbers, it is clear that there is substantial under-utilization of capacity.

Unnecessary added mileage on trucking routes leads to inefficiency. Gateway restrictions, restricted use of the Interstate Highways, and circuitous regular routes increase mileage unnecessarily. For instance, a carrier providing service between eastern Pennsylvania and eastern Virginia is forced to travel a circuitous route through western Virginia in observance of a gateway restriction. A trip down the Atlantic coast would save up to 60 per cent in mileage and a comparable amount in time.† [19] The inefficiency of this practice is patent; its justification is to prevent that carrier from winning traffic from carriers who already hold direct route authority.

Inefficiency combined with high costs result in high rates whether or not profits are exorbitant. Regulation adds significant expense to the ordinary costs of transportation.‡ The added costs of rate bureau membership must be reflected in rates. The administrative costs of securing, adding to, or protecting grants of authority before the ICC are very great. Aside from filing fees, the costs of attorneys, consultants, and witnesses, make hearings very expensive.§ Naturally, these costs are reflected in higher rates.

* Admittedly some excess capacity is not an expression of inefficiency resulting from ICC regulation but rather an expression of such industry conditions as seasonal demand and the special requirements of specialized shippers.

† In one case elimination of the gateway would reduce mileage from Lancaster, Pennsylvania to Falls Church, Virginia by 144 miles. Gateway total: 262. Direct: 118.

‡ There are indications that the "ordinary costs" of regulated traffic are higher than they need be. James C. Nelson reviews some of the evidence as to line-haul costs, labor costs, the costs of terminals and buildings, and sales costs in his "Entry Control of Surface Transport," p. 410.

§ See Chapter 2. Further, the fact that entry controls have pro-

Not only is the rate structure of regulated motor carriers of freight unnecessarily elevated, but it is also economically irrational. Value of service pricing—possible only because rates are fixed by concerted action—assures that rates do not reflect the costs of transportation.* Very high profits on some commodities subsidize the transportation of others. Very low subsidized rates divert traffic from other carriers or modes able to carry the commodities at lower cost.†

Deregulation

The four objectives of regulation ‡ could be achieved in a competitive non-restricted transportation situation, which would avoid the negative effects § of regulation. This conclusion is strongly suggested by an analysis of empirical studies of the motor carriage of agricultural commodities. Because these commodities are exempted from regulation by Section 203 (B)(6) of the ICA, their transportation

---

tected exorbitant carrier profit levels gives the ICC authorization certificate a value per se. Thus, they are sold and purchased. The ICC becomes a distributor of favors, which are sold at profit. The carrier acquiring the new authority merely passes the cost on to the consumer. A variation of this theme can be found with the auto driveaway business. Three companies dominate this business, having been given authority after the enterprise was declared illegal by the ICC unless with certification. The result, according to several sources, has meant that all previous operators, unable to get their own authority, were forced to accept franchise arrangements with one of the three companies given the proper authority. And although the large companies do very little except market the authority granted them by the ICC, they extract up to 40 per cent of the gross take of their previously unregulated "franchises." The franchises are forced to increase rates to pay this fee.

* Besides moral suasion, the ICC only has one incentive at its disposal to induce low costs and efficient operation by motor carriers: downward rate pressure. Until its recent recognition of the importance of and necessity for cost-based rates, the ICC rarely gave even implicit indication of its understanding of this incentive.

† For a complete discussion of the consequence of rate distortion, see Chapter 5.

‡ Assurance of common carrier service, assurance of adequate investment and technological progress, avoidance of chaotic conditions of destructive competition, avoidance of duplication of investment and excess capacity.

§ Unhealthy market concentration, service rather than rate competition, inefficiency (excess capacity and high costs), high rates, irrational rate structure.

provides a good model with which to examine the effects of deregulation.

Economist Walter Miklius conducted a thorough study of exempt agricultural transport in 1966.* He came to four primary conclusions: 1. In the competitive (exempt from regulation) sector the quality of service was superior to that in the regulated sector. Specifically, there was no need to interline, and therefore no delay or damage. Equipment was available to meet peak periods. Exempt carriers had better time schedules. Shippers said that, in general, they got better, more personalized service. Exempt truckers exercised more care in handling cargo and in checking temperature and humidity than their regulated counterparts. Finally, exempt carriers were willing to load and unload at multiple points; 2. Competitive rates were generally lower than regulated rates; † 3. Perhaps most importantly, the competitive rate structure seemed to be patterned closely on the costs of providing services; and 4. "The available evidence from the competitive sector [that he compiled], conclusions of studies, foreign evidence with non-regulated trucking ‡ are all *inconsistent with the hypothesis of 'excessive competition'.*" (Emphasis supplied.)

No study contradicts Miklius' findings and conclusions. § In fact, other economists have supplied data to substantiate his position. Using figures from a study [21] of exempt agri-

---

* Miklius' study, entitled "Agricultural Exemption," was made for the Department of Transportation and is unpublished. While taking into account many primary studies, Miklius relied heavily on his in-depth study of transportation in California published in 1965. In the California study, besides studying extensive cost data, Miklius conducted numerous interviews with shippers, carriers, and truck brokers. See Walter Miklius and D. B. DeLoach, *Interstate Trucking of Exempt Agricultural Commodities, California*, ERS 216, Washington, D.C., USDA, 1965.

† This conclusion is consistent with USDA studies of the deregulation and reregulation of frozen fruits and vegetables and fresh and frozen poultry, discussed below.

‡ Canada and Australia.

§ The ICC has not even conducted an inquiry into the agricultural exemption to explore the effects of free entry, unrestricted carriage, and rate competition. Relying on recall of the 1930's experience rather than investigating today's economic controls and restrictions for the motor-carrier industry, the Commission offers a one word argument—"chaos." Adding insult to injury, without any hard studies to support its position, the ICC has the audacity to petition Congress to repeal the agricultural exemption.

cultural traffic in the three-state area around Washington, D.C., R. N. Farmer concluded that the exempt industry was quite stable.

An extensive sample of exempt carriers studied suggests that the firms are in fact quite stable and long-lived. Three-quarters of the firms surveyed had been in business over five years, 60 per cent over ten years, 40 per cent for fifteen years and 8 per cent over thirty years. . . . These figures compare favorably with survival rates in many more concentrated economic areas, and they do not suggest that competition in this sector has the effect of forcing prices below costs for long periods.[22]

As might be expected, the evidence also indicates that investment in the exempt carrier industry is not only adequate to provide equipment to meet capacity, but also to provide modern equipment to increase efficiency.[23] In one of his studies, Miklius found that there was no difference in the age of equipment of regulated and exempt truckers sampled at a border inspection station.[*][24]

Several studies indicate the magnitude of the effects of regulation on the rate structure, by contrasting deregulated rates. The Department of Agriculture conducted a study to analyze the effect of deregulation of the transport of several commodities which had been placed within the agricultural exemption. Both regulated and non-regulated carriers vied for the newly deregulated commodities. Regulated carriers met the rate competition of exempt carriers. Rates were fixed by supply and demand forces, not concerted action. Specifically, the USDA studies revealed that truck rates charged by carriers during 1956–57, the first two years of free entry, were approximately 33 per cent below the 1952 rates on fresh poultry, and 36 per cent below the 1955 rates on frozen poultry.[25] Truck rates on frozen fruits and vegetables during 1957 ranged from 11–29 per cent below the regulated rates of 1955.[26] Follow-up studies revealed that the rates on the exempt agricultural commodities had remained relatively stable during the unregulated period while the rates on regulated commodities had gradually risen,[27] and that since 1958, when frozen fruits and vegetables were again placed under regulation,

* These findings are consistent with the notion that competition rather than protection spurs innovation. Carriers can attract shippers with either low rates or improved service, both of which are induced by innovation.

nearly all the rates on those commodities had risen markedly.[28]

The results of these studies have been inserted not as a definitive estimate of the rate cushion caused by regulation, but rather to show that that cushion is substantial. In any event, as James C. Nelson argues, "Although the USDA findings involved limited commodities and the deregulation effects pertained to relatively short periods, the restrictive design for entry control and minimum pricing, the lack of significant economies due to large scale operations in trucking, and the continuing traffic diversion from regulated common carriers to unregulated carriers all logically support the expectation that the tendencies observed in the USDA studies would be fairly general." [29]

In addition, our own study (see Chapter II) indicates lower cost and generally higher utilization for the agricultural sample, and affirms the specific cost-producing effects of route limitations.

Impact of ICC Regulatory Policies on the Consumer

Since transportation is a substantial part of the cost of retail goods, regulation's most direct and immediate impact on the consumer is high prices. The effect of high rates is multiplied because all raw materials, as well as the finished product, must be transported. In rate matters, the ICC acts only as an intermediary between carriers, or at best between carriers and shippers, and relegates the consumer to the background. Its main concern is to protect the economic position of the respective carriers—without regard to their efficiency.

In his study of New England transportation, Robert A. Nelson says that in M.C.C. 1864, New England motor rate increases (1955), the ICC ordered *all* carriers to raise their rates by 6 per cent. Admitting that some of the more efficient carriers did not need the increase, the ICC asserted that the increase had to be across the board in order to "preserve the highway common carrier industry in New England." [30]

The transportation of agricultural commodities provides a model for deregulation as an economically ordered and stable system, devoid of excessive competition. Irresponsible firms do not threaten the system; but even if they were a problem, direct regulations on safety and financial responsibility would be the proper remedy—not control of entry. The demand for transportation services is sufficient to attract adequate investment capital to maintain and advance the system, and to insure provision of services which is at least comparable to that engendered by the common carriers under regulation.

But most importantly, the agricultural model presents a competitive system with pressures to reduce costs and increase efficiency. Rates are set by competition, not collusion, and hence reflect the lowest costs incurred in providing transportation services. Not incurred are the administrative costs of rate bureau participation or of obtaining operating authority. Thus not only is the rate structure at the appropriate level, but it is rational: rates reflect costs. Competition allocates traffic to the carrier which can transport it most economically.

5 / The Rate Rape

In the United States, government regulation is not the assumed method of economic policy control. Competition within the market system is considered the most desirable mechanism for the allocation of resources. The market system is self-adjusting, efficient, and yet capable of immediate response to complex situations. But there are compelling reasons for the occasional departure from reliance on the market, particularly when certain assumptions underlying the market theory fail or become corrupted. Rate regulation of the transportation industry has been established when this failure is believed to have occurred. Rate regulation has had the following purposes: 1. to prevent the extraction of unreasonable profits when monopoly power exists; 2. to subsidize certain traffic or modes of transport found to be in the public interest; 3. to prevent favoritism of shippers based on bargaining power; and 4. to maintain stable and healthy expansion of transport facilities free from the ravages of rate wars.

Rate Bureaus: How Rates are Set

The rate bureau is an organization of either rail, water, or motor carriers operating in a given region devoted to the common formulation of a tariff.* The purpose and function of a rate bureau is to engage in organized price fixing. This activity, of course, explicitly violates a number of antitrust laws, but was conveniently overlooked until 1948. In 1948, the Reed-Bulwinkle Act was passed, amending the Interstate Commerce Act.[1] The new law legalized pre-existing practice and placed the bureaus under ICC

* The tariff, a collection of rates, is either published by the rate bureau or by a publishing agent. Note that a firm operating in more than one region will usually join all of the bureaus with jurisdiction over territory it serves.

regulatory control. Specifically, the Reed-Bulwinkle Act empowered the ICC to approve rate-setting agreements which furthered "the national transportation policy." It cautioned that every carrier should have "the free and unrestrained right to take independent action." Although these Congressional guidelines regarding rate bureau regulation were quite broad, they seem to imply a legislative intent to sanction the existence of collusion only when it *furthered* the public interest and guaranteed the opportunity for independent action.

Proponents of the rate bureaus argue that the possibility of publishing separate rates independent of the bureau, and of protest procedures with ICC review, preclude excessively high rates or monopoly pricing. In addition, they point out the tariff publishing cost and complexities * that would result from separate tariff issuance.[2]

The ICC supports these arguments. It generally phrases its affirmation of the bureaus with stock phrases about "stability of rates" and the necessity for protection against "cutthroat competition."

But the rhetoric about the rate bureaus is seriously belied by reality. First, the right to independent action as a safeguard against excessive charges and monopoly pricing is a myth. Walter Adams [3] comments that "in practice, this right is little more than a sterile gesture. To the rate bureaus, it represents a minor annoyance which cannot break down the self-imposed restraints 'born of history, habit, and strong mutual self-interest.' To the Commission, it represents no more than . . . a safety valve . . . which must not be allowed to undermine general adherence to the idol of rate stability. In other words, independent action is not to be encouraged, but tolerated—tolerated so long as it falls short of promoting genuine rate competition."

The ICC not only fails to encourage independent rate setting, but takes an active role in supporting rate bureau suppression of independent rate setting. Walter Adams, cited above, details the Southern Motor Carrier's case to substantiate this contention. In that case, the general manager of the rate bureau announced the open intention of

---

* The cost of publishing a tariff, according to rate bureau annual reports, runs from $30,000 to $300,000. The complexities would include difficulties for shippers in finding rates and ICC adjudication of rate protests.

enforcing absolutely uniform freight rates among the members. Suspension proceedings were filed against independently announced rates. Finally, "the conference used its power as a trade association to boycott recalcitrant outsiders who refused to go along with its rate policies." [4] The ICC nevertheless held that the protest proceedings in no way prevent or discourage independent action (but that boycott activities exceed the exception to the antitrust laws established by the Reed-Bulwinkle Act).

We have found that the expense of Commission litigation resulting from petitions for rate suspension and revocation, serve as a substantial deterrence to independent action.

A survey of the rate bureau annual reports (form RBO) reveals that the collective legal and political power available to the rate bureaus is immense. There are approximately eighty-seven rate bureaus or carrier agreements. Few of them require any major capital expenditures or extensive office facilities. Legal fees, clerk salaries, postage, and tariff publication are the major expenses. Yet the Rocky Mountain Motor Tariff Bureau collected $1,797,968 in fees and dues from its members in 1968; the Middlewest Motor Freight Bureau collected $1,416,332. Four other motor carrier rate bureaus collected over $½ million in dues and most of the others collected over $¼ million. In addition, most of these organizations have substantial incomes and assets apart from membership fees. The Southern Motor Carriers Rate Conference, a typical example, received $1,300,642 in "other receipts." Rail bureaus are no different, with the Transcontinental Freight Bureau and Joint Tariff Department collecting $1,033,287 in dues and another $488,760 in other receipts, or the Southwestern Freight Bureau (rail) with $1,285,663 in dues and $947,213 in other income, or the Southern Freight Association (rail) with $1,277,501 in dues and $1,777,524 in other receipts.

Where does all the money go? Much of it goes to "legal fees," or related expenditures. Some of it goes to conferences, conventions, speeches, carnivals, and ICC lobbying. A great deal of it is simply held in reserve. The collective power of one of these organizations naturally bent on its own survival is overwhelming in relation to the generally small independent carriers. A carrier independently setting a competitive rate must spend thousands of dollars defending it against the bureau's potent legal talent before the

ICC's Suspension Board. The fact that the burden of proof as to the rate's reasonableness is on the carrier proposing it (even if the proposal is for a rate reduction) makes challenge less costly and difficult than defense in any event.

The independent carrier's difficulty lies in the ease of challenge by a more powerful, legally oriented, collective bureau of each of his separate rate proposals. Since each tariff contains thousands of rates, the defense of a challenged tariff is a significant expense.

A study by James C. Nelson [5] discovered that the number of rate adjustments protested had risen from 567 in 1946 to 5170 in 1962 and the percentage representing protests against rate *reductions* increased in share from 40 per cent to 90 per cent. About 50 per cent of the protests were upheld through rate suspension and 70 per cent of those ordered suspended were ordered revoked.*

The great power of the bureaus is more fully apparent when one understands the now prevalent *automatic* practice of challenging a deviant or new rate as a matter of course. The recent comedy of the Yak Fat case illustrates this. A non-existent commodity (Yak Fat) is proposed for transport at a certain rate by a small, independent western trucker. Despite the fact that no one could possibly have any idea about a reasonable rate for the commodity's transport beyond certain limits, it is immediately challenged as an unreasonably low rate by numerous parties. Further, a rate bureau possesses numerous sanctions involving affirmative action. It can seek minimum rate orders to force rates up. In these latter cases the burden of proof shifts to the bureau. Nevertheless, alleged financial, legal, and political advantages seem to have given it a most successful record. For example, in Docket MC-C-1864, "New England Motor Rates Increases, 1955," the Commission granted a conference-sought 6 per cent rate increase minimum order as the hereafter lowest legal rate.[6] The order had no expiration date. Rate bureaus rarely seek minimum rate orders simply because their other powers make such orders generally unnecessary.[7] The same end is more easily achieved

---

* The increase in protest could indicate a greater number of independent challenges to bureau-set uniformity, as well as of increasing bureau enforcement. But the cause of increasing challenges would probably lie in an increasing and more tempting margin between rates and costs because of bureau collusion.

by intrarate bureau (rate increase) agreement accompanied by the suspension challenge threat to any who attempts to undercut.

In addition to the weapons possesed on a collective basis against independents, rate bureaus have the same natural advantages against rebels within the bureau itself. Our survey of 1968 Rate Bureau annual reports revealed that in seventeen of the motor carrier bureaus 15 per cent or fewer of the rate proposals are set independent of the bureau process itself, five of the bureaus set 25 ot 35 per cent of their rates on an independent basis, and only two bureaus, both rather small, set more than 35 per cent of the members' rates outside the bureau. Further, a number of even these rates are perfectly acceptable to bureau self-interest, since they tend to affect traffic for which a carrier has sole authority and hence do not undercut other members' or bureau monopoly rates.

Perhaps the most potent weapon of the rate bureau is the realization by carriers that cooperation with the bureau is collectively in their own interest. Even without financial and legal power, procedural advantages, and ICC friendship, this phenomenon alone would give the bureau much of the power it needs. Rate agreements are mutually profitable because a rate increase can only be profitable in most instances if all others in competition make the same increase. Likewise, a rate decrease is generally profitable only if all others in competition do *not* decrease as well. Thus, in an oligopolistic situation, advance knowledge about the action of competitors is crucial. The realization of this interdependence is accentuated and most apparent in the rate bureau setting. And the bureau members are soon aware that they do not operate within the framework of a zero-sum game. That is, they *all* can gain. Rate increases where there is little competition from another mode and favorable conditions of demand elasticity for a commodity's transportation can result in someone's gain, or everyone's gain, without anyone's loss.* These rates are increased. For commodities and markets where there is competition from another mode, lower than cost rates—financed by excessive

---

* That is, without loss by any of the members of the rate bureau. It is the consumer, ignorant of what is happening, who loses. The shipper, given optimum elasticity conditions, is able to pass the cost on to the public without difficulty.

profits where there is modal monopoly power—can drive out the other mode. The inherent advantage of the mode for the carriage of given commodities given distances provides the margin for financing the loss.

The net effect of the rate bureau * is to negate whatever elements of intramodal rate competition might remain from the increased concentration levels and regulatory impingement of recent decades. Further, the rate bureau causes the setting of rates at a level higher than they would otherwise be set. Finally, it results in the development of a sophisticated system of rate discrimination by commodity, mode, direction, distance, etc. in the interest of the mode, within the bounds of the mode's inherent advantages.

The ICC's Role

The ICC requires the filing of proposed tariffs thirty days before they take effect. It can declare a rate unreasonable or unlawful and prescribe a minimum, maximum, or specific rate on its own initiative or in response to protests. It can suspend some rates for up to seven months pending a detailed investigation and hearing.† The ICC has set forth regulations detailing with great precision the content and form requirements of various kinds of rate and rule tariffs.

That, however—contrary to common assumption—is the extent of the Commission's rate control mechanism. (See Appendix 5–2 of the original I.C.C. report for further details.) The agency refuses to examine rates for level or legality, other than as a matter of form. "Tariff examiners" spend years examining thousands of rates to see if the print size is correct, margins proper, and code references according to specification. Only if there is a protest are rates

---

* One shipper told us confidentially that the motor carrier rate bureaus, in combination with ICC-created restrictions and the inherent advantage of the motor carrier mode, created nothing more than a series of "mafias," able to extract outrageous and contradictory (*e.g.*, sometimes charging more for shorter runs) rates. Not only are many of the rates directly contradictory to the Interstate Commerce Act, but they provide extensive cover for massive corruption. Another shipper said that the situation was not much different than the so-called "protection rackets" that flourished in the 1930's.

† The first effect of these requirements is to impose substantial time and expense burdens on a carrier. These burdens, in addition to the rigidity of the rate structure, make it impossible for him to respond quickly to temporary changes in cost, technology, or demand.

examined—and protests are limited by the interstate carrier groups and their rate bureaus.

Thus, the effect of the ICC's rate-setting policy is highly academic, because it extends to such a small part of the rate structure. And the use of the Interstate Commerce Act in the limited areas in which protests do arise suggests the futility of giving the present agency the formula and computer capability to examine rates on its own initiative.

Section 2 of the Interstate Commerce Act prohibits personal discrimination: it declares illegal the charging of different rates for like services between different shippers.* Since it is possible to interpret "a like or contemporaneous service" or a "kind of traffic" quite narrowly, thus limiting the effect of this prohibition, the latitude taken by the ICC in its regulatory criteria greatly affects its enforcement.

Section 3 of the Act is even broader in scope, making it unlawful for any carrier subject to regulation "to make or give undue or unreasonable preference or advantage to any [shipper] in any respect whatsoever."

Section 4, the long- and short-haul clause, declares it unlawful to charge more for a short haul than for a long haul over the same route in the direction for the same commodity.† Although this provision seems as specific as Section 2 above, the interpretation of "like kind of property" and the special permission clause allows latitude for the flexible application of the provision.

In addition to these provisions, there are a series of miscellaneous specific criteria (such as a prohibition against

---

* It shall be unlawful for any common carrier . . . directly or indirectly, by any special rate, rebate, drawback, or other device [to] charge, demand, collect or receive from any person or persons a greater or less compensation for any service rendered, or to be rendered, in the transportation of passengers or property . . . than it charges, demands, collects, or receives from any other person or persons for doing for him or them a like or contemporaneous service in the transportation of a like kind of traffic under substantially similar circumstances and conditions. . . . (Emphasis added.)

† It shall be unlawful for any common carrier . . . to charge or receive any greater compensation in the aggregate for the transportation of passengers, or of like kind of property, for a shorter than for a longer distance over the same line or route in the same direction, the shorter being included within the longer distance, or to charge any greater compensation as a through route than the aggregate of the intermediate routes [except on special authorization by the Interstate Commerce Commission].

the raising of rail rates after lowering them to drive out water competition) and a number of general descriptive criteria. Rates are illegal if "prejudicial" or "unreasonable." The "inherent advantages" of the modes are to be considered within the framework of a Commission-determined "National Transportation Policy." Under the aegis of these provisions, the Commission has the authority to determine maximum or minimum rates, either by adjudicating protests by competing interests of rate increases or decreases, or on its own initiative.

The full policy of the ICC with regard to the "reasonableness" of rates is not entirely clear. The following observations, however, can be made: 1. The ICC, although it has the power to do so, rarely questions a rate or launches an inquiry on its own initiative—even when asked to do so. The agency prefers to assume a passive role, relying on the allegedly competing interests of carriers and shippers to evoke appropriate protests and arguments. It prefers to set policy on a case-by-case basis as cases arise within this formal framework. 2. The burden of proof of the reasonableness of a protested rate is with the party advocating a change in the existing structure. 3. The only consistent criterion accepted by the ICC as determining an unreasonable rate is that it must not be "destructively competitive" to traffic or to a mode the ICC seeks to protect.

At one time or another the ICC has used a variety of bases for rate policy. Relative cost or service capabilities of competing modes have occasionally been considered. National defense requirements have been a factor. Whether or not a rate is compensatory, as measured by the ICC's "out-of-pocket" cost formula, has been a rationale for rate rejection. But the most consistent basis for rate determinations has been a concern for the protection or perpetuation of a pre-existing market situation.

MINIMUM RATES

The context of ICC minimum rate policy is most apparent in the post-World War II efforts of the rail industry to lower rates to meet rising competition from water and motor carriers. In order to preserve a discriminatory rate system * the ICC has partially adopted the dual approach †

* Discrimination, as we are using the term, means merely a rate policy which departs from considerations of cost. Specifically, it in-

that rail rates can be reduced to out-of-pocket costs with bulk (low-value) commodities, but high-value commodities cannot be reduced below fully-distributed costs. "It is well established that what constitutes a 'proper return' on a high-grade commodity, such as cigarettes, is vastly different from a 'proper return' on a commodity of low value." [8]

The ICC allows reductions only to the fully-distributed level for high-value goods. This prevents much rail service in high-value traffic where railroads often have a marked inherent advantage.

The desire for the protection of the various regulated modes has degenerated into an open mother-hen philosophy. The economic inefficiency of preventing railroads from utilizing excess capacity not only mediates against rational inherent advantage considerations, but also costs money directly. The consumer, rather than the transportation system, pays for it in the end.

The desire to shield and "represent" their own "clientele" need not be inferred from the ICC's consistent representation of the "regulated industry view" against the Justice Department or the Department of Transportation, or from differing standards when competition with airplanes (regulated by the CAB) or unregulated traffic are concerned.*

This desire is openly expressed by the Commission in *Tobacco—North Carolina to Central Territory, Interstate Commerce Commission,* Division 2: [9]

---

volves the use of a state-granted or natural monopoly in a given area of traffic to extract relatively high profits while achieving lesser profits, or subsidizing other traffic.

† Revealingly, the ICC makes two specific exceptions to its insistence on fully-distributed cost pricing under the objection of another mode. First, where the regulated carrier or mode is competing with a non-regulated carrier, as long as these costs are compensatory, there is no official objection. (*Meats, Fruits, Vegetables—TOFC Transcontinental,* 316 ICC 585 [1962].) The ICC protective umbrella extends only to its perceived constituency, the regulated carriers. Second, there is at least one case which seems to recognize the economic wisdom of marginal (out-of-pocket to the ICC) rate making for motor carrier backhaul traffic. Additionally, of course, the failure of another mode to claim the impairment of its "inherent advantage" will usually cause the affirmation of a below fully-distributed level rate.

* The ICC has consistently applied a different standard when the protestant to a rate reduction was an unregulated mode: in four cases in 1959, two in 1962, the Big John case in 1963, two in 1965 and several more in the last two years.

Where, as here, carriers of competing modes of transportation propose reductions in their rates from levels not in excess of reasonable maximum rates for the sole purpose of attracting regulated traffic from one to the other, and the only result thereof to the respondents would be a net revenue loss for all the carriers concerned, the proposals constitute a destructive rate war which this Commission is empowered to avert. Any different conclusion would serve to impair, rather than foster, sound economic conditions in transportation and among the several carriers, and lead ultimately to large-scale dissipation of carrier revenues needed to preserve and maintain a national transportation system adequate to meet the needs of commerce and the national defense.

Specifically, the ICC feels that the maintenance of high rates on high-value commodities is essential because

The parties [do not] contend that they would be better off from a net revenue standpoint if the rates of both modes were reduced as proposed. The evidence is convincing that the opposite result would be inevitable. The rate relations between them would remain approximately as they are today so that no material changes in the traffic flow or volume could be expected, *and the net result would be a needless dissipation of revenue by both modes.*[10] [Emphasis added.]

Thus, the ICC acts aggressively to enforce monopoly power pricing, allocating the rewards between modes and among commodities. The entire framework of this rhetoric is most amazing, for it does not even pretend to consider the benefits of "less net revenue" for all concerned. The benefit, of course, is lower rates, increased incentive for greater efficiency in transportation and as a result lower commodity prices.

Since the ICC feels that lowering the rate will not take traffic away from the "clientele" of another agency, since it would rather not reallocate the market shares between these modes, and since it feels that lower rates for the transportation of these commodities will not attract sufficient increases in volume to justify a rate reduction for profit maximization, it will not allow rate reductions. The ICC is apparently not going to try to determine which carrier or mode does have the inherent advantage (the easiest way to do this is to allow rates to approach costs under competitive conditions and see which mode gets the traffic). Nor is the ICC, apparently, going to make even a substitute estimate. The Commissioners are concerned with profit maximization for all "their" carriers first of all, and next with the maintenance of the market share pattern that the present discriminatory and inefficient system has built up over the years. Thus, monopoly gouging of shippers is not only promoted, but required by the ICC—particularly where the shippers are most able to pass the cost on to the consumer.

The specific historical basis for minimum rate regulation is no longer with us. That is, it is no longer necessary to protect railroads from competition from other railroads since there is no longer a rail structure amenable to cut-throat competition. Not only do rate bureaus set rates in collusion, but ICC merger non-policy has given general monopoly power to most companies within the railroad in-dustry. Nor do the motor or water carrier industries require minimum rate regulation for "stability," since they lack either the potential for competition or the cost structure of rails which enable short-term reductions in rates without immediate loss. The ICC has now moved away from the protection of individual carriers within a mode, and is concerned almost entirely with the protection of one mode from incursions into its traditional traffic, or from alleged internal collapse.*

DISCRIMINATION

In addition to the protection of carriers from competition through minimum rate regulation (preventing rate under-cutting), and protection from inflation (or increasing in-efficiency) through liberal maximum rate regulation, the ICC has a subsidiary interest in the maintenance of the present discriminatory rate system. The present system re-sults in greater revenues to all the modes under ICC juris-diction than would otherwise be the case, and preserves the favoritism for agricultural traffic. This last consideration can explain most of the agency's decisions, particularly when the ICC acts to change a previous practice or permits challenge to an established share of the market.

Fundamentally, the protection of the discriminatory rate

* Thus, when the ICC refers to "cost-based rates," it does not mean the end of a discriminatory rate system, but merely that in a minimum rate case, the legality will turn on cost evidence. And usu-ally the cost evidence is directed at the probable effects of the reduc-tion on competing carriers, shippers, or other modes.

system is an act of faith by the ICC. There have been no comprehensive studies to determine if a discriminatory system is in fact desirable. There has been no discussion of alternatives. There has been no investigation into the total cost of the structure. There has not even been a thorough examination to see if the rate structure does in fact aid those commodities in whose name it exists, or to what extent it does so.

"Value-of-Service" Pricing

The Interstate Commerce Act, partially due to ICC support, has been interpreted to allow price discrimination in the form usually termed "value-of-service" pricing. Theoretically, the ICC maintains the position that it discourages and limits geographical price discrimination, and claims that, following the explicit tenets of the Act, it absolutely prohibits personal price discrimination (based on the identity of an individual shipper). In fact, there is massive discrimination in all of these areas and in other areas as well. The ICC attempts to conceal the nature and extent of discriminatory practices through the active suppression of relevant statistics.

In the one area of discrimination the ICC openly defends, value-of-service rate making, the actual statistics destroy any possible basis for the present system, even in the ICC's own terms of justification. Value-of-service pricing is a term applied to the present pattern of commodity-based discrimination. It began by the charging of low rates for agricultural commodities and raw materials and high rates for manufactured goods. The low rates served a highly beneficial function at the turn of the century—encouraging the development of the West, for the low rate on low-value bulk commodities enabled the subsidization of their transportation, minimizing the transportation advantage of eastern sources of agricultural products and raw materials in developed eastern markets. Since the sparsely populated West initially had little demand for these products, advantageous access to the eastern markets spurred the development and settling of the West. Meanwhile, the high rates on manufactured goods maximized the effect of transportation on their marketing and thus assisted the development of the infant manufacturing plants of the West. Since the federal government was generally committed over this period to a policy of encouraging the development of the West, this rate structure was understandable.*

The railroads supported the structure because it maximized profits. Specifically, it led to increased utilization of facilities in an industry where excess capacity is a common and damaging problem. The increased utilization occurred because the elasticity of demand for the transportation of low-value goods was high. That is, since the commodities were so inexpensive relative to bulk and density, the static cost of transporting them resulted in a greater proportional charge than was the case with high-value goods. For example, a $3 a-ton charge for the 500-mile transportation of a bulk low-value commodity like wheat bought at $6 a ton will affect the location of fields relative to various markets and thus the total amount of wheat transported over significant distances. Consignees (receivers) in market towns will be anxious to purchase more agricultural goods from farmers closer to town. But a $3-a-ton charge for the 500-mile transportation of radios worth $2000 or more by the ton will simply not matter as much. The shipper or distributor (receiver) will not care as much as the agricultural receiver if the price of transport is $10 a ton or even $20 a ton. Even if it cost *less* to transport radios, there would be little increased demand for radios. Therefore, by lowering the transportation expense on commodities where transportation cost affects volume of traffic, and raising it where it does not, railroads increase utilization and profits.†

There are several points which must be made about this system of rates. First, it can exist only where there is monopoly power, for the system involves the perpetuation of fundamental misallocations of resources which a competitive industry would not allow. Simply stated, if there were competing railroads, the railroad which set a highly profit-

---

* Many economists would argue that even within this context, general fund subsidies would have been more wise. The government, however, did not have the financial resources to accomplish the task by this means during this period.

† Note that there has been a diminishment over the last thirty years in the gap between high-value commodity and low-value commodity rail transportation profits. Nevertheless, there is still a substantial difference between profits for manufactured items versus bulk commodities, and the gap may have widened again in the last several years.

able rate on any high-value product would be undercut by a competitor in order to capture the traffic. Such lowering would occur on the traffic until a competitor determined that an underbid would not result in sufficient profits on the traffic to make its capture worthwhile. In other words, competition drives prices down toward cost.

Second, the misallocation of resources which theoretically occurs with this kind of monopoly-supported, discriminatory system, does not always manifest itself in a manner apparent to all. There are a number of decisions which are in fact based on transportation and which greatly affect the efficiency of the entire economy. A small but typical example shows the impact of the policy—a coal-source power utility has to make a decision about where to locate a power plant. If the transportation cost of the coal is subsidized by high-value traffic, the plant will be located further from the coal mines than if the cost were not subsidized. It will pay for the power company to haul tons of coal over long distances in order to heat water to turn turbines to produce electricity, which will then travel a relatively short distance, due to the subsidy, to users of electricity. The net effect of this is more transportation, or more transportation cost, than is necessary. Further, there is not only a dislocative effect to subsidized raw materials, but also to the excessively *high* priced transportation for the finished product. This further warps the location of the plant—pulling it yet closer to points of distribution than efficiency dictates. Since there is monopoly rate making, the railroads do not pay for the transportation inefficiency. They pass it on to the shippers. Since most manufacturers or distributors in competition are subject to the same disproportions for similar commodities in an area, or are little affected due to the overall small percentage of transportation cost on high-cost commodities, they can all pass the extra cost on to the consumer.

One result of this kind of inefficiency is the failure of raw material development in areas closer to the manufacturing plants and to points of distribution. That is, not only is the plant further from the location of raw materials and closer to points of distribution than cost, efficiency, or the natural dictates of the market would allow, but the manufacturer is less likely to provide adequate demand for raw materials closer to his plant, wherever it is located. Thus, more efficient locational development of raw materials is impeded.

Related to this are the indirect implications of the present policy as it affects plant location. For in reality, the movement of plants closer to distribution means the concentration of plants in *urban centers,* rather than decentralization closer to the location of the natural resources. This has significantly contributed to urban concentrations of industry, adding to population density and contributing to air pollution, congestion, and other urban ills.

Yet another kind of misallocation is caused by these rate differentials—the over-utilization of certain kinds of commodities due to the subsidization of their transportation. Thus, mining and lumber products have been over-utilized, to our ecological detriment, while manufactured goods have been under-produced. This kind of misallocation is general in effect, but also manifests itself in varying degrees on a commodity-by-commodity basis. That is, not only is more wood cut than should be cut because of its subsidized transportation, but fewer radios are sold than would be the case if rates were closer to cost.

Apart from the general effects of value-of-service discrimination, there are more precise, measurable aspects to the specific rate system now extant. One stated impact of the present value-of-service system has been rising overcapacity, particularly for the railroads. Since overcapacity means inefficiency and higher cost, the effects of this factor are reflected in across the board price increases and inefficiencies. Present under-utilization contradicts the original purpose of the discriminatory system from the railroad perspective. In addition, the cost structures of the motor carrier and water carrier modes have permitted increasing attack on railroad traffic from two directions. Motor carriers, although high-cost carriers, are able to compete for the railroad high-value traffic market because of the excessively high railroad rates for the transportation of these items. Thus the railroads lose both money and business.

Part of the excess capacity problem can be traced to the ICC policy of prohibiting higher rates in response to the higher costs of providing peak demand or irregular route service (off the main track or road). Thus, seasonal rate changes in response to varying volumes of agricultural traffic is prohibited.* This removes any incentive for the efficient development of natural resources in relation to optimum transportation utilization—something that pricing according to cost would automatically accomplish. But, the real cost, accelerated by the value-of-service system and traffic loss to motor carriers, is in railroad expansion of capacity.†

Our own studies tend to substantiate the notion that the value-of-service system has affected the under-utilization problem. For instance, the introduction of dummy regional variables in the examination of rail utilization measures reveals less utilization in the East. This is where the concentration of rail manufactured, or high-value traffic, is the greatest.

Decline in utilization must not be confused with productivity advances. In terms of output per man or per vehicle, the railroads have made remarkable advances, primarily due to technology in related fields. But increases in efficiency in this sense over time does not imply that efficiency is in fact increasing relative to the *use* of the better facilities. Railroads will point with pride to the increase in average carload tonnage over the years (except when seeking rate increases). And indeed these figures are impressive. For example, average carload tonnage has progressed from 1960:

* This policy is quite ironic since the ICC does allow innumerable rate distinctions based on mere competitive or locational advantages (see below) while it prevents rate response to the higher costs of certain traffic. This policy is self-defeating because the small farmer meant to benefit by the policy finds himself not with a slightly higher rate, but with no service at all as railroads suddenly "discover" (despite their common carrier obligations and the ready availability of cars for large shippers) that there are no cars available to service the small farmer.

† At least one expert also attributes overcapacity to a "fair return on fair value" rate policy. Ann Friedlaender writes that railroads do not like to lower rates on high-profit items without competitive inducement because of the chance of less volume increase than necessary to make up for lost revenue; thus they prefer "to hide excessive profitability by increasing investment in equipment and the modernization of facilities. These actions will reduce the observed rate of return and permit the railroads a constant rate of profit by curtailing replacement investment in periods of recession. . . ." (Friedlaender, pp. 79–80.)

1960—44.4
1962—45.4
1964—47.8
1966—50.1
1968—52.2

However, average car *capacity* has been increasing at a comparable pace:

1960—55.4
1962—56.3
1964—58.3
1966—61.4
1968—64.9

So while productivity per se has increased over time, utilization (productivity/capacity) has not so increased.

Ann Friedlaender's discussion of rail capacity utilization, although somewhat outdated by trends in the last four years, contains several viable conclusions. First, capacity utilization of rolling stock has not appreciably increased since World War II. Second, average traffic density "at no point approaches the estimated optimum level of density of 3 million ton-miles per mile of track required for efficient operations." [11] Third, Conant's studies have shown that density on "only 10.1 per cent of the lines could be classified as heavy." [12] Estimating from 1962 data another expert calculated that potential track capacity was approximately 3.5 times the actual use. [13]

The same problem of excess capacity affects the motor carrier and water carrier modes. In these areas, however, under-utilization is more directly traceable to the nature of ICC regulation itself, rather than to the rate structure of the industries.

Related to the question of excess capacity and inefficiency is the misallocation per se of traffic between modes because of the discriminatory system. Much of this results from the value-of-service system since motor carriers are allowed to be in a position to carry a great deal of traffic that they are not optimally suited to carry. For example, the fact that railroads are making extreme profits on high-value commodities enables trucks to undercut rail rates and carry much traffic even though it costs the railroads less to carry it. Likewise, the railroads carry bulk traffic that is more economically carried by water. The crucial condition enabling this kind of misallocation to occur is a total lack of intramodal competition. The existence of only intermodal competition means that the rate structures of the respective modes will be geared to compete with one another in such a way as to substantially negate whatever inherent advantage a mode might have.

Another specific kind of cost, alluded to above, that the present system entails as it operates, is the weakening of the motor common carrier *vis-à-vis* unregulated motor private carriage and contract carriage. The rate bureau and ICC enforcement of excessive profits for certain commodities even at relatively high motor carrier costs drives many shippers and manufacturers to maintain their own carriage or to engage a special contract carrier in order to undercut excessively profitable common carrier rates. This means that common carriers are deprived of the high-profit traffic on high-value goods.

One source describes the relationship of the value-of-service system, and the selective undercutting it engenders, with the decline of the common carrier as follows:

This progressive method of selective price undercutting is a process similar to that of the sun melting off the upper layers of an iceberg; to remain afloat, the bulk of the volume under the ocean has to rise to expose still more ice to still more melting. As the profits or "contributions to overhead" melted away from the traffic originally priced high on the value-of-service principle, railroads and motor common carriers were forced into general price increases. This in turn raised more traffic above the level where private trucks would become cheaper for shippers, and so the process continued.[14]

Since at least some volume is required to maintain private or contract carriage, as well as steady traffic and preferably some backhaul movement, only shippers with some size are able to provide for it. The small or inconsistent shipper and businessman must rely more on common carriage. If the small businessman transports high-value goods, this means that common carriers are going to have to charge him even more because of the loss of the revenue producing traffic from large shippers to private and contract carriage. Since there is no railroad siding or water facility in many areas, the small businessman is stuck with a high-cost mode which he must further subsidize to enable it to carry traffic in areas where other modes are better able to carry it. He cannot afford to provide private service (his own trucks) unless he is large enough to keep trucks in regular and preferably two-way operation. Even where there is, say, a rail alternative, ICC policy precluding rail rate reductions and competition will force him to pay the extra high cost of common carriage by motor carrier.

If there is a theoretical need for price discrimination by commodity, as there arguably was in the West of the late nineteenth and early twentieth centuries, there is none now.* Even if a need were to exist, there are compelling reasons why now the subsidization of certain kinds of traffic should not be financed through a discriminatory rate system. First, twentieth-century government has the general resources and administrative capabilities to subsidize directly virtually anything that needs to be subsidized. Second, a general fund subsidy does not result in the same degree of resource misallocation described above. Third, and most important, a direct subsidy is visible and measurable. It is less likely to establish its own vested interest and easier to remove when there is no longer a need for it.

Way Bill Evidence

In addition to general economic, plant location, and resource development costs, and to increasing inefficiency in the transportation system itself—all caused by the value-of-service rate structure, there are other losses caused by other forms of discrimination. The ICC is perfectly willing to admit the possibility of many of the above disadvantages— although there has been no effort to investigate or ascertain their extent—because the costs do not contradict their explanation of the system itself, that discrimination is based on commodity value. When the Way Bill Studies † of the Bureau of Accounts began to reveal incredible disparities in railroad profit levels (revenue/cost) for commodities of the *same* value, they were discontinued or reformulated.

* At least the same reasons do not compel it. The West is significantly developed, populated, and thriving. The Far West now has adequate markets, for western resource development and western manufacturing plants are as sizable, mature, and efficient as their counterparts in the East.

† The way bill contains basic information about a particular shipment: tonnage, revenue, data, commodity description, *et al.* For a number of years the ICC has collected a statistical 1 per cent sample of these bills.

The Way Bill Studies indicated that, quite apart from the extraction of monopoly profits on high-value commodities, there was additional and quite unrelated discrimination. There was discrimination between two carriers of the same commodity depending on distance, load, direction, and area served; that is, geographic and personal discrimination, both of which are officially condemned. Further, although the average statistics reflected a general value-of-service pattern, the disparities on a point-to-point and commodity-by-commodity basis were so great that many high-value commodities were transported at profit levels far *below* the profit levels for many low-value commodities, and vice versa. The data reveal that even the commodity-based discrimination itself cannot be explained away in terms of commodity value.*

The Way Bill Studies revealing some of these phenomena were last explicitly set out in 1961 in a document entitled "Distribution of the Rail Revenue Contribution by Commodity Groups—1961." [15] This document sets out on a commodity-by-commodity and region-to-region basis, the revenue/cost, average load, average haul, etc. for rail traffic from a 1 per cent way bill sample. The way bill data, easily collected, is fed into a computer which prints out the information for this report—popularly termed "the burden chart or report." 1961 was the last year this revealing and essential information about the nature and extent of rate discrimination was presented in this form. We were told by numerous ICC staff that "political pressure from the top," originating from the railroads, resulted in instructions to stop issuing the report. Up to 1965, the way bill data was still kept and published in raw form by the Bureau of Accounts.[16] Despite the ease of using a program to print out the desired information, the ICC required citizens seeking information about a specific profit level to rework the raw data through a twenty-step mathematical formula for each revenue/cost statistic for a given commodity from x region to y region in a given direction. Therefore, comparison of many profit levels from the post-1961 statistics are difficult. Comprehensive evaluations about the rate system are thus

* While ICC cost data are not perfectly precise in the measurement of a specific cost for a specific movement, the aggregate data presented by the Way Bill Studies indicate disparities which imprecision cannot explain away.

seriously hampered, despite the existence of a computer program readily able to provide the information.

A number of ICC staff members expressed private bitterness at the tactics used to suppress this vital information. One suggested that the railroads had probably argued that such information was not compiled for the other modes, and that collecting for just the railroads was unfair. But he added that similar information could be easily collected for the other modes as well to meet this objection. Another implied that the ICC does not like this information readily available to shippers who will begin to use the data as a basis for rate protests, constantly invoking issues of "burden," "discrimination," and "compensatoriness" that the ICC would rather not confront, particularly from their own data.

The data have recently been placed quietly under the aegis of the Bureau of Economics. The Department of Transportation has confidentially volunteered to take the data-gathering task from the shoulders of the ICC.

Figuring from the available 1961 statistics, we are able to analyze some of the details of the rate scheme. In 1961 17 per cent of rail rates, representing approximately 20 per cent of all traffic by tonnage, traveled at less than 100 per cent out-of-pocket costs. That is, it was subsidized traffic by ICC criteria. Further, most of these rates (over 10 per cent of all rates) were at levels below 90 per cent out-of-pocket costs. The data reveals increasing rates and tonnage traveling at under 100 per cent out-of-pocket cost levels. The ICC determined that in 1961, the estimated "annual loss" amounted to $226 million. Presumably, the ICC means that $226 million [17] was required to support the cost of this traffic.

A close examination of the kinds of commodities traveling at various levels belies the purported rationale and basis for the value-of-service system. For if high elasticity were the only factor, one would not see wheat, a bulk, low-priced commodity, and a necessity, as a contributor. Yet this commodity contributed more revenue above ICC out-of-pocket cost levels than any other commodity in 1961. Wheat is not an entirely isolated example. Wine, hardly a necessity, nor a bulk, nor a low-priced commodity, is "subsidized." West to East wine traffic went at 79 per cent of out-of-pocket costs.

Our point is not that there is no value-of-service system,

for there surely is, as the aggregate data still show. It is that commodity discrimination based upon the elasticity of demand for a commodity's transportation is not *all* that is involved. For while a value-of-service overall structure exists under this rule, there are many supplementary factors and forms of discrimination superimposed on this general form, and these other forms are explainable by theories other than straight commodity transportation elasticity.

Discrimination by Mode and Inherent Advantage

We have conducted a major computer survey of rate patterns in order to test several of our hypotheses. In so doing, we are releasing for the first time the revenue/cost, or profit, data (previously called the "burden chart") for the thirty commodity categories in our sample. The ICC has suppressed this information, as mentioned above, since 1961. In addition, we are attempting to compute for the first time revenue/cost statistics for motor carriers and water carriers on a commodity-by-commodity basis.

Appendix 15 contains a detailed explanation of the procedures used in the study. The explanation is coded into the summary forms through twelve footnote references. Some of the results are reprinted below.

The thesis of the study is that, quite apart from the value-of-service discriminatory scheme, there is massive discrimination based purely upon the monopoly power of a mode as it relates to other modes: the inherent and unique cost structure advantage of a given mode for a particular kind of traffic at particular distances, and/or locational advantages (*e.g.*, no water or road or track from a convenient point of origin or to destination) for one mode over another, can mean a substantial margin of monopoly power.

Market share, as the traditional measure of monopoly power, has been matched with the specific profit levels (revenue/cost) for each commodity. Profit levels increase as monopoly power from locational advantages increases from one region to another. (The regions are carefully matched between modes to enable comparison.) In addition, the levels of revenue/cost show the effects of inherent cost advantage of a mode on its profit levels for the transportation of various commodities: inherent cost advantage might not always vary directly with market share by region as locational advantages might, but is reflected in higher profit levels where market share is generally higher, and lower profit levels where market share is generally lower.

Thesis 1: Locational Monopoly Power Pricing. As market shares rise between regions for a given commodity, rates are fixed for higher profits by all three modes. This variation between regions is mostly attributable to differing locational advantages within the regions. Thus, there is discernible monopoly power pricing on this basis by modes. For example, flat glass, included below, has rail market shares in three different regions in 1961 of 34 per cent, 54 per cent, and 91 per cent; the corresponding profit levels are 211, 211, and 244, respectively. In 1966, market shares ran from 64 per cent to 68 per cent, 88 per cent, 93 per cent and 96 per cent; profit levels followed along from 138 to 155, 175, 197 and 206, respectively (see Sample 28 below). The patterns are scatter-charted in a rough style for ease of comprehension, with some freehand connections where useful.

Although the results seem mixed for most commodities, the trend is apparent upon close analysis. For example, computation of rail, water, and motor trends reveals that fifty-five generally follow the predicted course, revenue/cost rising with market share increase, thirty-nine are ambiguous, and twenty-six show a general downward pattern. The rest are either without data ("NST") or have no market share spread between regions for analysis.

There is substantial and surprisingly pervasive monopoly pricing based upon locational advantages of a mode. As market share increases for a mode from region to region, profit levels rise. Although there are exceptions to this rule, the trend is apparent.

One group of figures which does not reflect this monopoly power pattern is the motor carrier data on agricultural commodities, carriage of which is exempt from regulation. These commodities showed the least correlation to the market share increase, profit level increase pattern. Moreover, the occasional high-profit levels, usually in regions with little traffic volume, do not have the staying power of the other profit levels. They generally deplete between the 1962 and 1966 samples. Finally, overall profit levels are much lower for the carriage of these commodities, even taking into account the value-of-service principle.

These observations confirm the analysis of Chapter 4

and the computer results of Chapter 2. In Chapter 2, our study of agricultural carriers found them less profitable and operating at lower unit costs. Unlike the restriction-protected and rate-bureau-dominated regulated carriers, competition is still alive there. Thus, attempts at monopoly pricing because of a modal locational advantage (*e.g.*, no water or track nearby) are likely to be undercut by competing motor carriers. Nor does inherent cost advantage help, since competing motor carriers have this same advantage. Any advantage that might exist will soon disappear because of low natural barriers to entry. See the striking example of potatoes (Sample 7 below).

Unfortunately, agricultural commodity traffic is the only area where competitive pricing is possible, with the exception of limited bulk carriage by water carriers. Even more unfortunate, the inherent advantage of agricultural commodity transportation does not generally rest with motor carriers, making this one exception of limited competitive effect, although it is a revealing illustration of what could and should be.

There are a number of exceptions to our thesis, particularly among the first eight or nine commodity types, for several reasons. First, there are individual exceptions because of distance discrimination, discussed below. Second, other commodities deviate from our thesis because they have different values in different regions. Thus, bales of cotton mean one thing in the South, but in the East can be priced differently. Third, many of the first commodities have but a 1 to 3 per cent difference in market share between regions. Fourth, there is always somewhat of a lag between market share advantage and rate increase response. Fifth, because of the elimination of private motor carriage from the study (see Appendix 15), and because of the larger commodity statistic sample available from the rail mode, rail market share is consistently from 5 to 15 per cent high, depending on the commodity. The results should be accurate, however, because this effect is shared comparably in all regions. Nevertheless, only about 20 to 25 per cent of the results do not conform to our projected patterns (excluding exempt traffic which should not and does not conform). Each commodity has fifteen to twenty-one regional revenue/cost and market share matchups. On most commodities, the adjustment of from three to six of the rev-

COMMODITY [1] _18_ SOYBEAN CAKE AND BYPRODUCTS (20923)
            no.   name

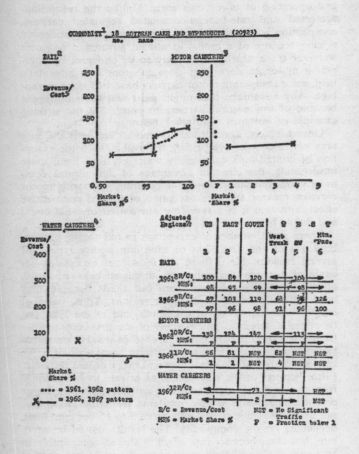

RAIL [2]

MOTOR CARRIERS [3]

WATER CARRIERS [4]

•••• = 1961, 1962 pattern
X,— = 1966, 1967 pattern

Adjusted Regions [7]	US	EAST	SOUTH	W West Trunk	B SW	S Mtn. Pac.
	1	2	3	4	5	6
RAIL						
1961 [8] R/C:	100	89	120	← 10[?] →		
MS%:	98	97	99	← 93 →		
1966 [9] R/C:	97	103	119	68	3	126
MS%:	97	96	98	91	96	100
MOTOR CARRIERS						
1961 [10] R/C:	138	124	147	← 113 →		
MS%:	F	F	F	← F →		
1961 [11] R/C:	56	81	NST	82	NST	NST
MS%:	2	2	NST	4	NST	NST
WATER CARRIERS						
1961 [12] R/C:	←		73			NST
MS%:	←		2			NST

R/C = Revenue/Cost   NST = No Significant
MS% = Market Share %   Traffic
                          F = Fraction below 1

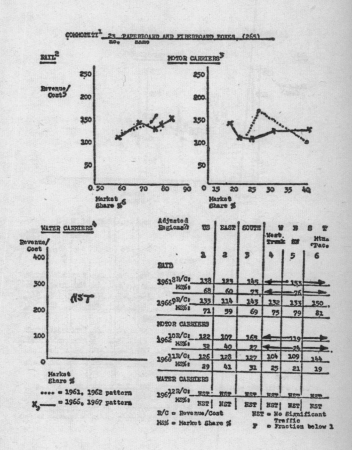

COMMODITY[1] 23. PAPERBOARD AND FIBERBOARD BOXES (265)
no. name

RATE[2]

Revenue/Cost[5]

MOTOR CARRIERS[3]

WATER CARRIERS[4]

Revenue/Cost

NST

Market Share %

•••• = 1961, 1962 pattern
x, ——— = 1966, 1967 pattern

Adjusted Regions[7]	US	EAST	SOUTH	W West Trunk	E MW	T Mtns Pac
	1	2	3	4	5	6
RATE						
1961[8] R/C:	138	123	145	◄———— 151 ———►x		
MS%:	68	60	73	◄—— 26 ——►		
1966[9] R/C:	133	114	143	132	133	150
MS%:	71	59	69	75	79	81
MOTOR CARRIERS						
1962[10] R/C:	122	107	162	◄———— 119 ———►		
MS%:	52	40	27	◄—— 24 ——►		
1960[11] R/C:	126	128	127	104	109	144
MS%:	29	41	31	25	21	19
WATER CARRIERS						
1967[12] R/C:	NST	NST	NST	NST	NST	NST
MS%:	NST	NST	NST	NST	NST	NST

R/C = Revenue/Cost NST = No Significant Traffic
MS% = Market Share % F = Fraction below 1

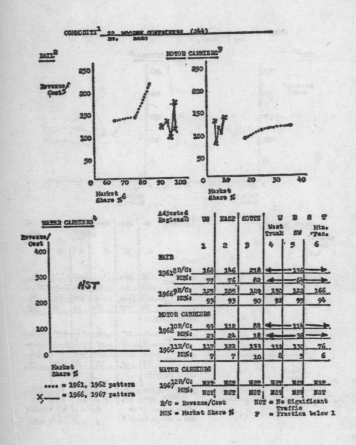

COMMODITY[1] 22 WOODEN CONTAINERS (244)
NO. NAME

RAIL[2]

Revenue/Cost[5]

Market Share %[6]

MOTOR CARRIERS[3]

Market Share %

WATER CARRIERS[4]

Revenue/Cost

Market Share %

NST

•••• = 1961, 1962 pattern
X, = 1966, 1967 pattern

Adjusted Regions[7]	US	EAST	SOUTH	W West Trunk	B SW	T Mtn. Pac.
	1	2	3	4	5	6
RAIL						
1961 R/C:	268	246	218	←	136	→
M%:	77	76	82	←	64	→
1966 R/C:	325	205	329	250	322	166
M%:	93	93	90	92	93	94
MOTOR CARRIERS						
1962 R/C:	99	112	88	←	114	→
M%:	23	24	18	←	36	→
1968 R/C:	137	122	133	112	130	76
M%:	7	7	10	8	5	6
WATER CARRIERS						
1967 R/C:	NST	NST	NST	NST	NST	NST
M%:	NST	NST	NST	NST	NST	NST

R/C = Revenue/Cost   NST = No Significant
M% = Market Share %   Traffic
                       F = Fraction below 1

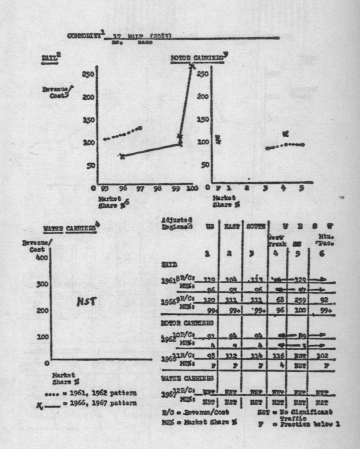

COMMODITY [1] — 17 MALT (2083)

RATE [2]

MOTOR CARRIERS [3]

WATER CARRIERS [4]

NST

Market Share %

.... = 1961, 1962 pattern

X, —— = 1966, 1967 pattern

Adjusted Regions[5]	US	EAST	SOUTH	W	E	S	W
				New Trunk	SE	Nu-Pace
	1	2	3	4	5	6
RATE						
1961 R/C:	119	103	113		129	
MS%:	96	95	96		97	
1966 R/C:	120	112	112	68	259	92
MS%:	99+	99+	99+	96	100	99+
MOTOR CARRIERS						
1962 R/C:	91	94	95		89	
MS%:	4	4	4		3	
1966 R/C:	98	112	114	116	NST	102
MS%:	F	F	F	4	NST	F
WATER CARRIERS						
1967 R/C:	NST	NST	NST	NST	NST	NST
MS%:	NST	NST	NST	NST	NST	NST

R/C = Revenue/Cost   NST = No Significant Traffic
MS% = Market Share %   F = Fraction below 1

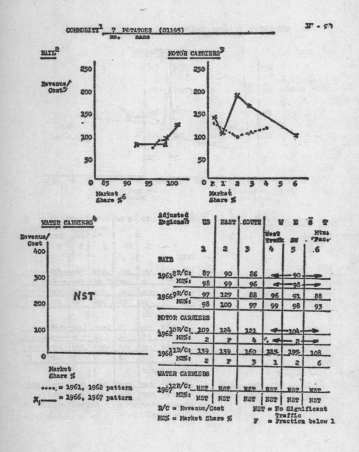

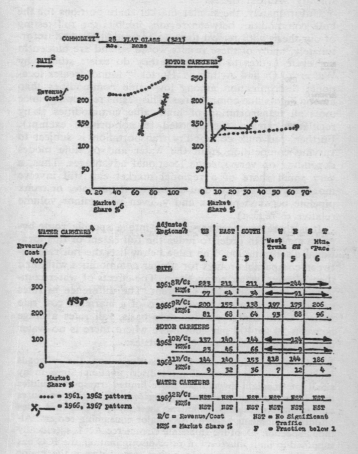

COMMODITY[2] 28 FLAT GLASS (321)
Reg. None

RAIL[2]   MOTOR CARRIERS[3]

WATER CARRIERS[4]

NST

Market
Share %

•••• = 1961, 1962 pattern
X,——— = 1966, 1967 pattern

Adjusted Regions[7]	US	EAST	SOUTH	W West Trunk	B SW	S Mtn. Pace	T
	1	2	3	4	5	6	
RAIL							
1961 R/C:	223	212	211	◄———	244	———►	
MS%:	77	54	34	◄———	91	———►	
1966 R/C:	200	155	138	297	175	206	
MS%:	81	68	64	95	88	96	
MOTOR CARRIERS							
1962 R/C:	137	140	144	◄———	124	———►	
MS%:	23	46	66	◄———	9	———►	
1967 R/C:	144	140	153	218	144	186	
MS%:	9	32	36	7	12	4	
WATER CARRIERS							
1967 R/C:	NST	NST	NST	NST	NST	NST	
MS%:	NST	NST	NST	NST	NST	NST	

R/C = Revenue/Cost   NST = No Significant Traffic
MS% = Market Share %   F = Fraction below 1

enue/cost results would place the pattern into perfect conformity with our thesis.

Unfortunately, the similar market share portions for the bulk commodities between regions inhibits the full testing of our thesis with regard to these commodities. And unfortunately, many of these results would be and are hidden in aggregate figures to the extent they do exist: studies by Walter Y. Oi and Arthur P. Hurter [18] found greater locational discrimination among low-value commodities than among high-value commodities. This seems reasonable since most all transportation of high-value commodities is by regulated carriers (as opposed to non-private exempt). Further, rail bulk commodity transportation is subject to varying competition from the water and pipeline modes depending on very *specific* locational advantages. Thus, a very small share of a regional market can still involve monopoly power (*e.g.*, rail advantage if no water or trunk pipeline between point x and y, even with minor volume relative to region).

It is therefore necessary to go into a specific route-by-route analysis in order to judge the full extent of this locational discrimination. The table below lists the rail rate between comparable routes for similar commodities with, and then without, water competition. The effects of water competition are immediately apparent. The difference in rates cannot be explained away in terms of a marginal cost rate policy. On a center per ton-mile basis, rail rates average between 50 to 400 per cent more where there is no water competition. Ann Friedlaender writes:

In addition to commodity price discrimination, the railroads practice extensive locational price discrimination. Since many small intermediate towns have more limited transport facilities than large consuming and producing centers, market pressures tend to make rates on shipments to these towns higher than rates on larger shipments between two major consuming centers. Although Section 4A of the Interstate Commerce Act is specifically supposed to limit this form of price discrimination, the ICC has generally permitted relatively higher rates between the major centers if the carrier can show the existence of competitive pressures. This is particularly true if the railroad faces water competition.

Locational price discrimination is particularly evident on shipments of bulk commodities. Since the general elasticity of demand for transport on the part of bulk commodities is relatively

Extent of Railroad Price Discrimination Due to Water Competition, Selected United States Routes, 1963

Origin and destination	Distance (miles)	Water competition	Rail rate (dollars per ton)	Rail rate (cents per ton-mile)	Ton-mile rate, long rate as percentage of ton-mile rate, short route	Commodity
New Orleans, La. to Little Rock, Ark.	436	No	12.10	2.78	45	Sugar
New Orleans, La. to Cincinnati, Ohio	834	Yes	10.50	1.25	62	Structural steel
St. Louis, Mo. to Detroit, Mich.	473	No	12.70	2.68		
St. Louis, Mo. to Pittsburgh, Pa.	604	Yes	10.00	1.66	44	Limestone
Baton Rouge, La. to Bauxite, Ark.	346	No	4.39	1.27		
Baton Rouge, La. to Prairie du Rocher, Ill.	735	Yes	2.40	0.33		
Calhoun, Tenn. to Oklahoma City, Okla.	828	No	17.20	2.08	63	Newsprint
Calhoun, Tenn. to Houston, Tex.	834	Yes	11.02	1.31		
St. Louis, Mo. to Jackson, Miss.	505	No	10.01	1.98	63	Iron and steel plates
St. Louis, Mo. to New Orleans, La.	685	Yes	8.89	1.30		
West Va. to Concord, N.H.	722	No	6.04	0.84	60	Coal
West Kentucky to Tampa, Fla.	770	Yes	3.87	0.50		
Bartow, Fla. to Greensboro, N.C.	667	No	7.44	1.12	55	Phosphate rock
Bartow, Fla. to Norfolk, Va.	802	Yes	4.95	0.62		
Riverdale, Ia. to Jones Mills, Ark.	614	No	13.80	2.23	40	Aluminum billets
Riverdale, Ia. to Gregory, Tex.	1,189	Yes	10.69	0.90		
Houston, Tex. to Danville, Ill.	928	No	23.00	2.48	47	Hydrofluoric acid
Houston, Tex. to Chicago, Ill	1,039	Yes	1.21	1.16		
New Orleans, La. to Oklahoma City	673	No	8.00	1.19	63	Wheat for export
New Orleans, La. to St. Louis, Mo.	685	Yes	5.30	0.77		
Amarillo, Tex. to Houston, Tex.	596	No	8.00	1.34	58	Wheat for export
St. Louis, Mo. to New Orleans, La.	685	Yes	5.30	0.77		
West Frankfort, Ill. to Menominee, Mich.	556	No	5.62	1.01	54	Coal
West Frankfort, Ill. to Minneapolis, Minn.	619	Yes	3.37	0.54		
Bartow, Fla. to Montgomery, Ala.	464	No	6.33	1.36	67	Phosphate rock
Bartow, Fla. to Pensacola, Fla.	462	Yes	4.25	0.92		
Bartow, Fla. to Greensboro, N.C.	667	No	7.44	1.12	46	Phosphate rock
Bartow, Fla. to Des Plaines, Ill	1,205	Yes	6.25	0.52		
Bartow, Fla. to Spartanburg, S.C.	559	No	6.91	1.24	50	Phosphate rock
Bartow, Fla. to Norfolk, Va.	802	Yes	4.95	0.62		

Source: Testimony of J. W. Hershey in *Transportation Act—1963*, Hearings before the House Committee on Interstate and Foreign Commerce, 88 Cong. I sess. (1963), pp. 373 ff.

high and the cross elasticity between modes is higher, the existence of water competition should push rates down toward marginal cost. Where competition does not exist, however, the railroads can exercise their monopoly power, subject only to the forces of market competition.[19]

Thesis 2: Inherent Cost Advantage Monopoly Power Pricing. As explained above, aside from locationally-based monopoly power advantage, there is another aspect of intermodal competition which allows *additional* margin for monopoly power pricing: the inherent cost advantage of specific modes. These will not vary by region, and hence were not tested above. In order to test the degree of monopoly power pricing within the range of a mode's inherent cost advantage over competing modes, we must see if profit levels are generally higher for commodities best suited for carriage at high volume over given distances by a given mode.

One way to measure this advantage is to use the same index used for the locational form of monopoly power—market share. A mode with an inherent advantage will certainly tend to capture most of the market.

As they stand, the results show a positive relationship between revenue/cost and market share for four of the five regions. The t values are not high, but since their signs were predicted correctly, on theoretical grounds, in these four regions, a one-tailed test is appropriate. Our results are therefore significant at the 90 per cent confidence level in three of the five regions. In the fourth region with a positive relationship, the t value is significant at the 97½ per cent confidence level. The one region showing a negative relationship between market share and profit level is the Southwest; but the slope is negligible and the t value is insignificant.

Turning to the regression coefficients, the slopes of the relationship by region between profit levels (revenue/cost) and market share are as follows (the first number is the constant term or intercept):

East:	Revenue/cost $= 101 + .38$	(market share)
South:	Revenue/cost $= -39 + 3.27$	(market share)
Western Trunk:	Revenue/cost $= 84 + .7$	(market share)
Southwest:	Revenue/cost not predictable by market share	
Mountain Pacific:	Revenue/cost $= 104 + .48$	(market share)

The slope of the relationship in the South is extremely steep. In other regions, profit levels start at 80 to 105 per cent and rise 1 per cent for each 1–3 per cent rise in market share. The monopoly power pattern is clear.

Discrimination is a matter of general public interest. The present rate structure has evolved slowly, without a massive, sudden dislocative effect resulting in general shipper protests. No one will protest to the ICC (assuming such information were available), because these overall dislocative effects are hidden in the economy. Potential protestants from areas which would be developed in a system of effective competition simply do not exist. Since this non-decision not to locate somewhere precludes a protest, the ICC will not care. And indeed, even if it were to care, even if it were to shift to a cost-oriented policy, it has neither the resources, the proper rate examination mechanism nor the cost-estimating tools to enable it to accomplish the task.

In essence, what is happening here is discrimination of the precise kind the ICC was originally formed to prevent. Not only is the agency not acting to prevent this textbook monopoly power pricing, it is actively concealing and protecting it. While there is little doubt that the market system would create some discrimination (for example, for rail rates based upon the existence of low-cost water carrier service for the transportation of bulk commodities), an intramodal competitive system would set limits on the extent of railroad rate cutting where water carrier competition exists by limiting profits in areas where railroad monopoly power exists. In the absence of this competitive system, it is the responsibility of the ICC to guarantee that discrimination is limited to the extent the market system, efficiency, and the proper allocation of resources would allow. The ICC has completely abdicated this responsibility, allowing excessive rail profits where inherent advantage and monopoly power exist * to subsidize marginal and below marginal cost transportation.

---

* The notion that general market competition will provide sufficient protection from monopoly pricing is rebutted by the fact of present disparities. Earlier, Meyer and his associates wrote: "Nevertheless, one can conclude from the examination of the two kinds of market competition that demand characteristics are insufficient to set an effective ceiling on the rates of noncompeting traffic at a level that precludes monopoly profits." (Meyer, *et al.*, p. 201.)

Discrimination by Distance and Weight

Discrimination based on the distance carried or load weight is a third kind of discrimination superimposed over the two described above: basic value-of-service commodity discrimination, and locational (mode monopoly power) discrimination. This third discrimination is a variation of the inherent advantage discrimination described above. Its basis lies in the ICC policy of allowing or encouraging only one kind of competition—intermodal. ICC policy against intermodal mergers (while allowing monopoly or collusive price fixing within each respective rail, water, and motor carrier mode) results in monopoly pricing by each mode in response to the only competition extant—from the other modes. The levels of this third kind of discrimination will vary since the prevalence and intensity of intermodal competition varies, but overall it exists on a massive scale. Fundamentally, this discrimination involves the use of a mode's inherent cost advantage to gouge shippers where the mode has an advantage and then to lower rates where there is a cost disadvantage.

For example, water carriers have a substantial inherent cost advantage in transporting bulk commodities in heavy loads over long distances, due to low line-haul expense characteristics. Thus, water carriers will charge more, relative to cost, for the longer haul since they have an inherent advantage there and will use the profits to subsidize shorter haul, smaller load transportation than the mode is optimally suited to carry, in order to increase their traffic volume and to drive competing modes out. This discrimination will increase as the inherent advantages of water carriers increases with distance and load weight. Likewise, revenue/cost will decrease as distance and load decreases (as railroad competition increases in intensity).

Railroads and motor carriers behave the same way, creating an interaction of rate setting and market shares which results in each mode carrying large shares of its traffic at inefficient loads and distances, and gouging shippers where it is efficient, to pay for it. The inherent advantage of each respective mode is thus negated, with a misallocation of resources resulting within the transportation industry itself. The impact of this, though hidden, is momentous throughout the economy—increasing general inflationary pressures as inefficiency increases.

According to expert analysis,[20] motor carrier rates substantially discriminate against longer hauls. That is, the rates charged for longer distances are here also more profitable (higher revenue/cost) than for shorter distances. This fact seems quite puzzling at first since the motor carriers' inherent advantage lies with shorter hauls relative to its intermodal competitors. But the reason lies with "an even more discriminatory rail rate system." [21] That is, rail rates discriminate so much against their longer hauls that despite a substantial inherent advantage at hauls of over 200 miles, there is room for profitable motor carrier traffic. In fact, the rail discrimination (revenue/cost) is so great as distance increases that there is room for massive motor carrier transport at these inefficient distances. There is so much room that motor carriers are able to impose, as mentioned above, their own similar rate discrimination—making their inherently inefficient long-haul traffic actually the most profitable (up to a point).

RAIL
1961 Rail Rate Discrimination Ratios
All Commodities

Territorial Movement	Average Haul/Ton (miles)	Revenue/ Out-of-Pocket Cost
S to S	183	120
E to E	257	118
W to W	359	131
E to S & S to E	640	138
S to W & W to S	1204	142
E to W & W to E	1647	132

The statistics presented in the above table reflect other kinds of discrimination as well as that of haul length (*e.g.,* regionally high profits on intra-South traffic) but the general trend is apparent. It indicates that increasing profit (revenue/cost) with distance increases to a distance somewhere just beyond 1200 miles where the discrimination level begins to decline. Specifically, as railroads begin to compete with water carriers at a range where water carriers have enough of an inherent advantage to provide a competitive threat, the rail revenue/cost declines progressively as it becomes more difficult to undercut water carriage and still maintain profits. This turning point will vary with the specific commodity and region, depending upon local conditions. But generally, rail profits will peak lower for *bulk* commodities because water competition for these commodities is more intense due to greater water-inherent advantage for their transportation. Thus, rail revenue/cost should peak at 1000 to 1400 miles for bulk commodities and 1300 to 1700 miles for high-value commodities.

Specific examples from 1961 data will illustrate the increase pattern.

Territorial Movement	Average Haul/Ton (miles)	Revenue/ Out-of-Pocket Cost
Stone Rough NOS		
W to W	80	44
E to E	119	111
S to S	183	144
S to E	845	146
S to W	1003	203
Containers NOS		
E to E	331	120
S to S	389	133
W to W	733	139
E to S & S to E	782	146
S to W & W to S	1108	165
E to W & W to E	1489	176

There are a number of commodities with data more clearly revealing the downward trend once certain peaks have been attained. Dotted lines have been drawn, as with the all commodity charts above, at the point where distance increases seem to cause rate discrimination ratios (revenue/cost) to reverse from increasing with distance increase to decreasing.

Territorial Movement	Average Haul/Ton (miles)	Revenue/ Out-of-Pocket Cost
Hides, Skins, Pelts		
E to E	615	187
W to W	637	206
S to E	1117	218
W to S	1282	278
W to E	1417	216

Territorial Movement	Average Haul/Ton (miles)	Revenue/ Out-of-Pocket Cost
Cabbage		
S to S	938	71
S to E	1214	77
W to W	1373	89
W to E	1857	75
Games and Toys		
E to E	494	133
E to S & S to E	805	148
S to S	918	213
W to W	1398	191
E to W & W to E	2065	151
Clay and Bentonite		
S to S	128	125
E to E	149	130
W to W	632	145
E to S & S to E	907	172 .
S to W & W to S	1275	158
E to W & W to E	1929	123

If two-directional movement is averaged to eliminate direction discrimination, over 70 per cent of the categories of the pre-1964 commodity code conform to this same general pattern. Profits increase markedly with distance increase until haul length reached the 1200 to 1600-mile range, when the profits reverse and begin to decline with additional distance increase.

The computer study using 1966 data further substantiates this thesis. Two typical examples:

Territorial Movement	Average Haul/Ton (miles)	Revenue/ Out-of-Pocket Cost
Livestock		
US to SW	630	79
US to Wtl	855	89
US to E	924	101
US to MtP	1153	107
US to S	1454	161
Soybean Cake and By-products		
US to Wtl	153	68
US to E	352	103
US to SW	384	75
US to S	411	119
US to MtP	1646	126

An example in the motor carrier area is provided by the recent Middle Atlantic and New England Territory Increases, Docket No. 34970,[22] decided February 14, 1969. There the carriers presented evidence revealing weight bracket and distance discrimination as described in the section above.*

OPERATING RATIOS AT ANTICIPATED 1968 LEVEL OF EXPENSES
AT PRESENT AND PROPOSED RATES

Weight bracket	Present	Proposed
Minimums	108.8	103.9
Under 1000	102.5	99.4
1000–1999	88.6	85.6
2000–4999	94.1	90.8
5000 and over	96.9	93.8
All truckload	97.3	94.1
Total—all traffic	98.3	95.0

OPERATING RATIOS AT ANTICIPATED 1968 LEVEL OF EXPENSES
UNDER PRESENT AND PROPOSED CLASS RATES

Mileage block	Present	Proposed
Under 50	110.5	103.9
50–99	100.4	96.2
100–149	95.3	91.4
150–199	94.8	91.0
200–249	91.3	88.0
250–299	95.8	92.5
300–349	94.8	91.9
350–399	98.3	95.2
400 and over	99.0	96.2

The ICC remarked that "The small shipments and the short-haul traffic may not bear their fair share of the carrier costs, either under the present or the proposed rates." But, as with the more recent case mentioned above, ICC disposition did nothing to correct the situation—the increase was merely denied. As above, bureaus will simply exclude these breakdowns from their offers of evidence. Meanwhile, ICC official disapproval enables the agency to maintain its virtuous posture while doing nothing to remedy the condition.

* Motor carrier distance discrimination is analogous to the rail discrimination pattern. Increasing profits by distance operating ratio declines with profit increase until a point is reached where profits begin to decline because of increasing rail competition closer to rail's inherent distance advantage.

The reason for these discrimination patterns has already been suggested by introductory commentary: lack of intramodal competitive checks facilitate monopolistic price discrimination in response to inherent advantage or geographical monopoly power *vis-à-vis* competing modes. The end result is a rate structure which seems grossly to misallocate transportation resources—negating the technological inherent advantages of each mode.

Apart from the obvious consequences of a rail system carrying the wrong kind of freight at inappropriate distances, the system allows adequate room for motor carrier distance discrimination. Thus at the 300- to 1000-mile range, motor carriers carry immense tonnage over routes perfectly serviceable by rail. And the rail discrimination levels are so great through these distances for many commodities, that motor carriers are themselves setting rates which make these runs not only prevalent but up to a point (beyond optimum efficiency) actually the most profitable for motor carriers. And the profits here are partially used to subsidize yet longer haul transportation where rail rate competition finally begins to take effect. Thus, the *average* load x distance statistic for general freight single-line regular route carriers is 4367,[23] approximately twice the maximum load x distance levels most experts believe are optimum for the motor carrier mode.[24] Other more specialized motor carriers are operating at even more inefficient distances. Nor is it a question of motor carriage where rail facilities are unavailable or inappropriate. The extent of the misallocation precludes any such interpretation. One expert put it this way: "Trucks have a clear cost advantage for traffic of less than 100 miles, the rails have a narrow cost advantage at 100 miles, and a clear and increasing cost advantage for traffic moving over 200 miles. . . ." But common carrier trucks conduct an enormous business at 100 plus miles. In fact, Professor Meyer computed, from data gathered in the 1950's, that over 90 per cent of common carrier trucking and over 51.3 per cent of private and exempt intercity trucking are at a distance of over *200* miles.[25] Since that time, average distance has not significantly decreased.

The table below derived from 1961 rail statistics, reveals what appears to be another kind of discrimination. One would expect that generally lower rates (less profit) for

DISCRIMINATION BY DIRECTION AND REGION

ALL COMMODITIES

Direction	Ton-Miles	Tons	Revenue/Out-of-Pocket Cost (profit)
E to S	113,400,000	180,418	152
S to E	238,080,000	371,582	134
E to W	229,162,000	149,118	161
W to E	511,700,000	300,876	115
S to W	96,744,000	83,411	156
W to S	169,740,000	137,950	134

backhaul traffic would be necessary because of the lower demand for backhaul movement and excess capacity. For example, the E to S, S to E traffic levels indicate substantially more tonnage, ton-miles (and carloads) in the S to E direction. Thus, most if not all of the empty backhaul traffic is E to S. The marginal cost of transporting this backhaul traffic is extremely low. The cars must be transported back anyway and the extra cost of the added freight is extremely minimal. Yet rates are not set to attract traffic to these movements. In fact, the rates are set to exact *higher* profit levels on the backhaul (low volume) direction traffic when much lower rates would be necessary to even traffic flow and increase utilization and efficiency. The result would be lower rates, on the average.

Unlike many forms of discrimination, this kind does not enrich carriers at the expense of the public. This discrimination works against the carriers as well as the consumer. It probably exists because of the ICC policy against marginal cost pricing and because of other forms of discrimination. For example, S to E, W to E, and W to S traffic is more likely to be bulk (agricultural or mining) than E to S, E to W, and S to W. This latter traffic is more likely to be manufactured goods. Hence, to some extent, existing value-of-service discrimination exacts this additional price, while ICC policy precludes adjustment.

Related to discrimination by direction is broad geographic discrimination, that is, discrimination which affects traffic patterns between regions of the country and affects rates within regions. There are three aspects to this discrimination: 1. differing revenue/cost levels on interregional traffic patterns which affect a region's export-import levels

and market development; 2 differing revenue/cost levels
for the respective regions on traffic internal to the region
which results in greater region vulnerability to production
in other regions and in higher costs for the consumers in
that region; 3. differing levels of discrimination variation
within different regions, resulting in differing levels of resource misallocation, under-utilization and inefficiency.* All
of these aspects are not separate forms of discrimination,
but are additional visible manifestations of types of described above.

1. DIFFERING INTERREGIONAL PROFIT LEVELS:

	Revenue/Out-of-Pocket Cost
S to E and E to S	140
E to W and W to E	130
S to W and W to S	142

The South, according to the above statistics drawn from
1961 rail commodity statistics, seems to be at a disadvantage. Its commodities, incoming and outgoing, are generally at higher levels than the other two regions.

2. DIFFERING INTRA-REGIONAL PROFIT LEVELS:

	Revenue/Out-of-Pocket Cost
E to E	118
S to S	120
W to W	131

The above table, drawn from the same 1961 report, seems
to indicate that the intra-Western traffic is priced the highest. A close examination of the data reveals that the average length of intraterritorial haul is only 183 miles in the
South but 257 miles in the East and 359 miles in the West,
respectively. The removal of discrimination by distance
would move the southern figure higher relative to the other
two.†

* This third variety involves merely wider gaps between profits of
transporting different commodities in different regions.
† It should be noted that having a great deal of short-haul rail
volume in a region means that the region is being subsidized, therefore the variable is still relevant. In removing it, we merely wish to
examine underlying regional-based discrimination, either the result
of value-of-service pricing or of regional conditions of competition
from other modes.

Further, the southern ratio is greatly influenced by five or six commodities priced well below out-of-pocket cost and transported in great volume: 233,482 tons of pulp-wood at 79 per cent out-of-pocket cost; 12,954 tons of certain agricultural products at 40 per cent; 199,300 tons of crushed stone at 84 per cent; 138,493 tons of gravel and sand at 83 per cent; 206,693 tons of phosphates at 96 per cent; and 273,660 tons of specific forest products at 90 per cent account for 60 per cent of the total volume in the South. These specific commodities are highly subsidized. But what about the rest of the traffic, consisting of a variety of some 200 commodities? Or the 195 commodities moving in East, South, and West intraterritorial traffic (including the commodities above), 61 per cent (120) are priced at highest revenue/out-of-pocket cost in the South, 24 per cent (47) highest in the West, and 15 per cent (28) highest in the East.

Thus, although shorter average hauls and five or six specific low-priced commodities drag southern revenue/cost aggregate figures down, on most commodities they are higher in the South than in any other region. The western figure of 131 per cent is inflated not only by average distance of haul, but by extremely high-priced transportation of wheat. Wheat contributes 48.4 cents per revenue dollar, accounting for over 20 per cent of the total western revenue contribution.[26]

In addition to the varying regional profit levels from the discriminatory system, there are more specific forms of regional discrimination. These aspects have elements of all of the other forms of discrimination, and are in reality techniques for the implementation of discriminatory rate policies. The primary such technique is the grouping by railroads of points of origin or destination for rate-setting purposes.*

The ICC has long recognized the principle that cost per mile generally decreases with increase in distance.[27] This is because terminal and other relatively fixed costs can be spread over more ton-miles. Thus, a non-discriminatory rate structure should encourage rates that will reflect these

---

* In addition, motor carriers use "commercial zones" (areas within which transportation is exempt) to engage in personal and locational discrimination.

cost differences. The railroads, however, have been grouping points of destination, and sometimes points of origin, in order to apply a uniform rate per mile on certain commodities.

To a certain extent, the grouping of points of destination or origin is administratively essential. It would be uneconomical, and a bit silly, to quote a different rate to every address in one city. But to the extent that distance increase appreciably affects reductions in cost, where these cost savings are greater than the resources required to differentiate separate points of origin or destination, the points should be so separated.

The railroads' motivation for grouping widely separated points of destination or points of origin on certain commodities has many possible explanations. Perhaps Section 4 of the Act prevents a railroad from competing with barge competition near a point of origin, and it is possible that at a destination point further along the same run, the railroads have a cost or service advantage. Thus, the railroads want to lower rates on shipments to the closer destination points. But the ICC might require comparable lowering of rates in every instance where water competition presents itself, or might not grant an exemption under Section 4 of the Act. To solve the dilemma, the railroad merely declares the two points within the same destination grouping. In charging the same rate/mile to the two points, it is cutting profit on the more competitive shorter run, relative to the longer run, and charging more per mile than the true cost structure would dictate, for the longer run.

There are other motivations for grouping points of origin or destination. These can involve broad considerations of competitive advantage and affect large areas and significant parts of the nation's economic structure. Perhaps the paradigm case has been the long-standing practice of grouping all points east of Denver as one destination group for shipments of certain commodities from the West Coast.[28] This constitutes a rank form of discrimination against East Coast consignees, who often have little choice but to pay the differential because of the lack of market competition from points east of the Missouri River. Another rather clear example of discrimination involving more than grouping for administrative convenience, is the consolidation of Cali-

fornia and Florida as a single point of origin for the transportation of oranges to New York.[29]

The ICC defense of this practice is rooted in the same
fundamental misinterpretation of its mission that is responsible for the value-of-service policy. The optimum
allocation of economic resources, the efficiency of the overall transportation system in the public interest, are generally
ignored. The ICC sees its function as a sponsor of the
transportation modes it regulates and of the transportation
industry as a whole. Thus, it sees transportation per se as a
desirable end. When the proper allocation of resources and
optimum efficiency requires *less* transportation, as they
often do (since transportation is an item of cost) the ICC
nevertheless seems to stand on the side of more transportation.

The justification for the excessive grouping of at least
points of origin rests with the notion that it encourages
more transportation, since it enables more distant shippers
to compete. One obvious effect is the impact this has on
plant location *vis-à-vis* the distant shippers who are less
likely to develop plant facilities nearer to their own points
of operation and thereby to reduce total transportation and
cost. Professor Turner has recognized a related misallocation:

[The] ICC has given little attention to the possibility that grouping, by depriving better located sellers of their economic advantage of proximity to buyers, may tend to encourage the expansion of resources committed to transport services, thereby
causing misallocation of resources in the economy. Under the
ICC's approach an origin group, for example, becomes too
large only where the group is large relative to the length of
the haul and the nearer shippers are seriously injured by competition from more distant shippers. This standard of injury
required for a violation appears to be much higher than that
applicable to rate relationships other than group rates.

The ICC's favorable attitude toward grouping of rates reaches
far beyond mere permissiveness. It is reluctant to disband
established groups where the more distant enterprises have developed in reliance on group rates. And it has on occasion
required the expansion of groups over carrier opposition.[30]

None of these discrimination patterns, with resulting system inefficiency and cost, would be possible with cost-based
rates (or with intramodal competition). Indeed, the elimi-

nation of intermodal competition,* reversing present ICC policy, would allow intermodal transportation companies to allocate traffic according to cost. They would do this naturally, because efficiency rewards for the company then become identified with efficiency allocation for the transportation system as a whole.

The only competition the ICC allows is contrived and false, and would never be created by the natural market system. It is the least useful of all the kinds of competition possible—and with other ICC policies results in a discriminatory rate system by distance which misallocates transportation resources on a massive scale.

MAXIMUM RATE REGULATION

During the last five years, much attention has shifted from the ICC's minimum rate to its maximum rate policies. The cause has been a wave of rate increases throughout the transportation industry. It should be kept in mind that these rate increases often involve the consideration not only of allowable maximum rate levels, but also of minimum rate levels, since carriers or rate bureaus often accompany rate increase proposals with new minimum charge floors. The raised minimum level is often needed to insure enforcement of higher rates, particularly in the limited areas where competition might exist and there is sufficient margin for competitive undercutting.

It is crucial to understand that not all rate increases are considered by the ICC. Although it has the power to conduct independent, aggressive inquiries into rate increases, it has failed to do so (even when inquiry is informally re-requested by carrier or shipper). It chooses to rely upon formal protests, presumably by those with an economic interest in the matter. Unfortunately, this reliance means that those interests organized to monitor imminent rate actions and to press regularized, professional protests before the Commission have a distinct advantage. With regard to rate increases generally, the larger shippers, with large capital, or with a high stake in minimizing transportation expenses, have permanent representation in Washington. Competing carriers and modes generally welcome rate increases by competitors. It is the small shipper, or the ship-

* Perhaps through the elimination of the current ICC ban on many intermodal mergers.

per to whom transportation is but one of many expenses, who has little opportunity to contest rate increases, unless organized into a powerful trade association. Unfortunately, most of the trade associations active in the transportation area, with several notable exceptions, consist of large shippers. Ironically, the shippers as a group, even the large shippers, are notoriously underrepresented relative to even very small carrier companies.

The rate increase process guarantees the perpetuation of value-of-service discrimination since the transportation of high-value commodities is a less important aspect of their marketing than it is for low-cost or bulk commodities. High-value goods are at least theoretically less likely to be shipped by interests able to organize merely around the transportation thereof. The resulting system also places a premium on bureaucratic skills, access to politically powerful contacts, and willingness to bargain informally (usually to bargain away the interests of others).

Section 216 of the Interstate Commerce Act defines much of the statutory criteria for motor carrier rate setting.*

Starting in 1965, motor carrier rate bureaus accelerated rate increase proposals. Citing inflation and increased labor and equipment costs, various bureaus sought general increases of class and commodity rates. The first requests were based upon primitive evidence, usually little more than a restatement of the previous year's expenses at anticipated wage or equipment expense levels. Information about dealings with affiliates, detailed rate of return analysis, and comparative productivity levels were absent.† Such

---

* 216(g) imposes rate justification on the party proposing a rate change. 216(i) provides that "the Commission shall give due consideration, among other factors, to the inherent advantages of transportation by such carriers; to the effect of rates upon the movement of traffic by carrier or carriers for which the rates are prescribed; to the need, in the public interest, of adequate and efficient transportation service by such carriers at the lowest cost consistent with the furnishing of such service; and to the need of revenues sufficient to enable such carriers, under honest, economical, and efficient management, to provide such service."

† All of this information is essential to an intelligent evaluation of a rate-change proposal. The relevance of dealings with affiliates and rate of return data is discussed in the cost finding section. Productivity levels are crucial, since there is little justification for a rate increase to rely upon a 10 per cent labor wage increase if ton-miles/

fundamental failings, despite the statutory burden of proof, did not much affect the Suspension Board, which has often failed to suspend rate increases, nor the Commission which often approved them.*

In 1967, several changes occurred. First, the railroads began to follow up with broad scale rate increases themselves. Moreover, the strength, both as to argumentative and political power, of the protestants began to increase. The National Industrial Traffic League (the major shippers' trade association) was bolstered by the creation of the Department of Transportation, which began to intervene on behalf of rate increase protestants. These interventions were limited to cases of general importance, and took the form of briefs and evidence before the ICC. For the first time, the shippers were receiving the help they needed. The Department of Transportation demanded that the ICC follow the legal requirements concerning affiliate dealings, that evidence be required on the issues of carrier efficiency, of productivity, of rates of return. Further, the Department took an aggressive role in formulating data to show industry conditions quite disparate from those presented in summary form by the bureaus.

For several years Department of Transportation activity had only marginal effects. The reason for this is a bureaucratic phenomenon which has enraged Department of Transportation officials. Industry rate increases will not always be subject to suspension by the Suspension Board. This is critical, since under the statute there is no recovery for shippers who pay the increased rates if the Commission cancels the increase (for motor carriers). What happens is simple but ludicrous. The industry raises rates, the Suspension Board refuses to suspend them, so they take effect. The matter comes before the ICC. The industry moves for a continuance and begins to stall. Six months pass, then nine months or more. Finally, the ICC is persuaded by overwhelming evidence gathered by the Department of Transportation that the increase is totally *unjusti-*

payroll dollar remains the same. Increased wage or equipment costs would not justify a rate increase if labor or equipment output increased so that cost per unit of revenue producing output (*i.e.*, tonmiles) does not rise.

* Under 50 per cent of all protested motor carrier rates are suspended, despite the lack of refund power if the Commission does not allow the increase.

fiable. The ICC cancels the increase. But unless the ICC specifically so provides, the shippers who have been paying the higher rates for nine months will simply have to swallow their past loss—even though the ICC has determined that the increase has been unjust, unreasonable, arbitrary, or discriminatory. To top it off, the industry can, at this point, declare that wage increases and other "new" costs *now* justify rate hikes, and propose new rates (the same as the rates that were just cancelled, perhaps), that will again take effect when the Suspension Board fails to suspend them.

Although Department of Transportation officials are enraged at the mere mention of ICC policy over these matters, there are at least a few hints of hope in the Commission's most recent decisions of late 1969. First, the Commission is cancelling many of the 1969 rate increase proposals.[31] Second, the ICC is requiring more information and proof from the bureaus than in the past, and is beginning to assume a more aggressive role in examining and criticizing industry-offered evidence. Third, the ICC is at least intimating that the delay tactic described above might be somewhat blunted in the future. For example, Docket No. 34971, Increased Rates and Charges, From, To and Between Middlewest Territory, decided June 5, 1969: "The hearing was postponed to August 19, 1968, by order of April 25, 1968, conditioned upon respondents' compliance with an order to make refunds on shipments after May 20 to the extent increases were not approved." [32] Since the rate schedules took effect April 1, 1968, almost two months of increased rates will be paid even though the increase was ajudged arbitrary and revoked. As unjust as this is, it is a vast improvement over the overcharges of nine months or more possible under previous policy.

Perhaps, the new policy is a response to the brilliant statements of D.O.T.'s Dr. James R. Nelson in opposition to the increases. More likely, it is a combination of changing political forces requiring showcase pro-consumer decisions. Cases in the near future will test the sincerity of these recent gestures. It is certain, however, that even if sincere, they will be of little benefit without either massive changes in the industry's competitive structure and rate making patterns generally, or aggressive agency investigations of more rates on its own initiative and suspensions pending approval, unless emergency conditions require their implementation. The ICC should not rely on occasional Department of Transportation intervention to raise all the issues in every case, nor on a few showcase utterances.

Following the motor carrier lead, the railroads, in 1967, proposed a general and substantial rate increase. They formally estimated that during 1967, due to wages, fringe benefits, and payroll taxes, their increase in operating costs would be $320 million. The actual cost increase, according to the Bureau of Accounts Statement No. M-350, January, 1968, preliminary Report of RR Employment, turned out to be $53.5 million. Similarly, the railroad estimate of 2.25 per cent fewer employees turned out to be far from the eventual figure of 5.25 per cent fewer employees.

The Commission reached a final decision on the railroad's proposal on February 15, 1968. The railroads were required by a Commission order of October 19, 1950, to submit all the cost figures for the previous year by February 14, 1968. The railroads did not submit their reports, and the ICC, in deciding *Ex Parte 256*, relied on the carriers' cost estimates; the estimates turned out to be inflated by a margin of 6.1! It is absolutely inexcusable that the ICC did not compel the submission of the reports by their legal deadline, or, at the very least, delay the proceedings until they were produced.

This failure to comply with Commission proof requirements at least spurred the agency to reassert formally the obligation of the railroads to present minimum cost-accounting evidence in support of general rate increase requests.

. . . while the evidence submitted is here inaccurately explained it is sufficient to justify the increase authorized. We shall expect the petitioning railroads in future general revenue proceedings to make a more complete disclosure of the facts upon which they rely in support of the relief sought.[33]

This was not an oppressive demand; cost accounting has been required in motor carrier rate cases for some years. As a result of this concession, protestants representing the Department of Agriculture were fairly optimistic concerning the outcome of a similar rate battle which ensued the following year, *Ex Parte 259*. This optimism was short-lived.

In order to provide a familiar and comfortable environment for the new rate battle, the ICC selected the same hearing examiner that presided in the *Ex Parte 256* hearing.* The railroads then simply ignored the demand by the Commission for cost-accounting figures, and continued to rely on their own consultants who were easily able to adapt the raw figures to the needs of the carriers. Repeated attempts by the Department of Agriculture to require the railroads to submit the proper cost-accounting figures were held by the ICC to be "prematurely raised." The Commission's final denial, however, was for "insufficient cause." In short, the Commission determined that a party had insufficient cause to demand the information which its adversary had notice would be required of it in any subsequent hearing.

This peculiar series of events aroused the curiosity of Senator Vance Hartke who questioned the Commission about the case in a public hearing. The reply was that the ICC had determined that the railroad estimates had been correct.† A number of questions remain unanswered: 1. Even if the estimates were correct, did they conform to the cost-accounting format which the ICC had said in *Ex Parte 256* would be required in all future hearings of this type? 2. Why hasn't the ICC made public the Bureau of Accounts' corroboration of the railroad figures? Senator Hartke received no comprehensible answer to this latter question, even though the ICC's failure to make this computation part of the public record is a violation of the Administrative Procedure Act.‡

* It is illegal not to rotate hearing examiners, § 11 of the Administrative Procedure Act.

† *Commissioner Murphy:* ". . . we made an independent verification check of the formula that is prescribed for submitting such cost evidence to determine whether it was accurately submitted instead of an independent cost study being made by the Commission, it was a review of the manner in which it was submitted and the figures used." [34]

‡ It appears that the reason why the ICC's "verification" or "analysis" of carrier evidence of cost increases was not included in the record was because "When our cost analysis checks exactly with the figures that the parties are putting in, it would be a duplication of effort and an expenditure of manpower that would serve no useful purpose." [35] In other words, the ICC's figures would merely be the railroad figures. Aside from a check to see if the columns are added properly, what does the ICC do independently? Answer—nothing.

In addition to these questions, there are some indications that these increases may have been improvidently granted, particularly for *Ex Parte 259*, which was rushed through the Commission in almost record time. When asked about the basis for its decisions by Senator Hartke, the Commission merely repeated the industry story—wages have risen, inflation is upon the industry, and it is necessary to have these increases in order to survive.* Indeed, there are indications that mere railroad assertions to this effect are considered sufficient in the ICC to justify massive rate hikes. But an increase in wage levels is irrelevant, by itself, to any need for additional revenues.

In order to justify a need for additional revenue, it is necessary to show increased costs. But increased wage pay scales are not evidence of increased cost. Increasing wages from $2.60 to $2.80 an hour does not add to cost if the same number of ton-miles are carried the next year and the labor force is cut in size so that total payroll costs are reduced. Further, not only can the labor force be reduced in size, but output (ton-miles), can increase, reducing cost/ton-mile even with wage raises.

We have taken total revenue ton-miles for every year since 1962 and divided it by the total payroll. This gives us the relevant figure to consider: revenue ton-mile output for every dollar spent on labor. The figures look like this:

1962: 126
1963: 134
1964: 140
1965: 145
1966: 151
1967: 147
1968: 146 [36]

There is nothing in the record because there is nothing to put in the record.

* The railroads, of course, do go one step further and claim that not only is inflation upon them, but they have been a veritable bulwark against inflation for years by maintaining low rates *vis-à-vis* other costs of production. This impression is created by picking a convenient "base year" for comparison of rail rate stability with general inflation—an ancient statistical trick. This figure would be irrelevant at any rate because if rail costs/unit of output had been falling over this period of rate maintenance, railroads would not be contributing in a real sense to a decrease of inflation. This is what has happened.

The results reveal some support for the increase; output/
dollar spent on labor declined slightly in 1967 and 1968.
But the decline was only after a long and steady increase.
1967 and 1968 levels are still above 1965 figures, a record
high at that time.

The railroads also argued, and the ICC accepted, that the
decline in rail market share had combined with increasing
costs to necessitate rate increases. But market share is as
irrelevant a figure as is increased wage rates or even total
labor costs. It does not matter if rail market share has
plummented from 90–10 per cent, if ton-miles have remained steady or increased. Unless there is some other factor, there is no need for increased rates. Further, a study
by the Department of Transportation estimated the rail
market share has stabilized and that ton-miles, which have
been generally increasing despite market share decline, will
begin to increase at a faster rate.

The final consideration of the ICC—that railroad computed rates of return were low and had fallen to just about
2 per cent—if true, should indeed be a consideration. But
the ICC has made no attempt to determine if in fact it is
true. It is a simple matter to pad a rate base, thus lowering
rates of return, or to hide profits through subsidiaries. Despite supposed controls in these areas, the ICC has shown
little interest in aggressive examination of railroad figures
or in active policing of railroad financial manipulations.

It is altogether likely that, given an investigation into the
railroad rate base and numerous profit-hiding possibilities,
the fact might justify a rate increase similar to the increase
granted in *Ex Parte 256*. The procedures used by the ICC,
however, in failing to demand supposedly required information, in "trusting" the railroad figures, in exhibiting a
lack of sophistication about cost considerations, cast doubt
on the wisdom of their action. The increase in *Ex Parte 259*
is particularly questionable. Now the agency is warmly
receiving new railroad increase requests in 1969.

The ICC has yet to consider several questions. First, the
question raised by James Nelson in his motor carrier increase testimony, as to whether or not it is appropriate to
grant increases based on the figures of a *single year*. Is it
not appropriate to wait three to four years, until a more
definitive trend develops? The supposed disastrous cost increases of 1967, for example, were moderate in 1968.

Second, is there not a responsibility on the part of the ICC to consider more carefully, from the viewpoint of the public interest, the way in which the increase is applied? To be sure, the ICC will deny the application of a specific increase within a general increase proposal, but the basis of this denial is usually a protest by a shipper. Those shippers bothering to protest are those with the most to lose, large shippers. Generally, the interests capable of elaborate protest will be dealt with by the railroads under the table, given less of an increase than those who are small or who cannot afford to organize around the relatively small transportation cost of their enterprise. Those that do protest, usually because of an inability to reach an accommodation under the table, might receive relief from the ICC. Thus, the increases are selectively borne by those groups already discriminated against, small shippers, shippers of high-value commodities, and shippers subject to rail locational monopoly power.

The railroads are not going to be satisfied with rate increases in 1967, 1968 and, most recently, in 1969 (see *Ex Parte 262*, approved by the ICC). They are, in light of the reception given them by the ICC, planning requests for increases for a fourth straight year. All of these general raises, of course, are in addition to numerous specific proposals for the increase of thousands of individual rates over this period. The discriminatory trend of these increases is alluded to by railroads as they write: "The burden of proving specific costs is greater in the selective increase procedure, but in the process they can often reach agreement with shippers on compromise proposals . . ." [37]

The interaction of rail and motor carrier increases, since this limited competition is the major obstacle to completely monopolistic pricing of the already overpriced high-value commodities, is disturbing. The railroads seem to be openly suggesting the possibility of oligopolistic "price leadership" between the modes. They write: "If other modes continue to increase rates, of course, the railroads may well be able to file another general rate increase later in 1969 or early in 1970 . . ." [38]

Perhaps the critical (and the most overlooked) aspect to these rate increases is their impact on inflation. Although often justified in terms of inflating carrier costs, in fact the critical upswing in the price indices occurred just after the first major wave of rate increases in 1965.* Wholesale prices were markedly increased and there has been unabated rise since. There has also been wave after wave of rate increases. Many economists spend much of their time trying to find relationships between inflation and other factors of the economy. One of the leading theories is that steel prices are crucial since steel is so basic to so many different products. It seems clear that the relation between inflation and transportation cost must be highly significant. For not only were inflationary seeds traceable to *wholesale* price indices at almost the precise time of rate increase acceleration (not before), but even more than steel, transportation is a completely pervasive and substantial aspect of our economy. Moreover, transportation cost—as already discussed—is mostly hidden from view, ignored not only by consumers but by the vast majority of shippers and even by a sizable number of economists.

Increasing inefficiency, increasing discrimination, misallocating transportation traffic between the modes, and an increasing misallocative effect directly upon the economy at large—all unquestionably have some impact on inflation. Since inflation may well turn out to be one of the most serious issues America will have to face in the twentieth century, an issue not yet fully faced, transportation should be one of the first industries to be examined. Yet, mysteriously, few have looked here.

Certainly the ICC has given scant thought to the matter. Others had well begin. The price of maintaining an industry which has managed to establish itself as a major independent force, unchecked by competition, might be greater than any of us has imagined. In its blissful and esoteric world of econo-legislative manipulation of those politically too weak or naively unaware to strike an informal accommodation, the surface transportation industry damages our entire economy. Even if action *is* taken, the residual effects of ICC-fostered monopoly, subsidization, and general economic misallocation will be difficult to purge from our economic system.

* See *Economic Report of the President,* January, 1967, p. 72. "The shift away from price stability actually began early in 1965 . . ." See especially Chart 6.

6 / Highway Safety

The trucking industry has changed significantly since it first came under federal regulation in 1935. It was then composed of small, family-owned firms serving compact areas and traveling along local routes. Small staffs of drivers enjoyed close relations with their employers and reasonable working conditions (although low pay). The runs were short and the drivers could live at home with their families. The small compass of the truckers' operations allowed local drivers' unions to bargain for and gain many special advantages. Drivers were treated as ordinary employees, with days off and time-and-one-half for overtime.

The half-completed interstate highway system, among other factors,* has changed all of that for the long-haul driver. Wide expanses of federally-subsidized concrete and asphalt have widened the trucker's horizons. Tractors † are now bigger and more powerful. Trailers † are longer, wider, and heavier, and double tandems † are common sights in many parts of the country. Smaller companies have been steadily merging into larger ones in order to extend territorial reach. As territories grow, the distances between terminals grow, and the drivers' runs become longer and longer. Days and even weeks away from home become the norm for some, as drivers are routed not to a distant terminal and then back, but on circuit routes, including several distant stops. And as trucking goes national, a number of local unions have had to forsake many of their formal

* See Chapter 5 for discussion of rate discrimination patterns and the inefficient allocation of much motor carrier traffic over inappropriate and excessive distances.

† A *tractor* is the propelling unit—where the driver sits and where the power drive is located—of a freight-hauling truck. The *trailer* is the actual freight-hauling unit; and a *tractor trailer* or *trailer truck* is, obviously, the two separate units combined. A *double tandem* is a tractor with two trailer units behind it.

bargaining advantages for the sake of national uniformity.

Perhaps the most important change is that the interstate highway system has led to competition between the trucking industry and the railroads for long-haul transportation of high-value commodities. Fast service is an essential advantage that draws business to the motor carriers—and too many trucking companies emphasize speed at the expense of safety. Cost cutting similarly becomes essential in competition with rails. Spacing out the terminals is one way in which the truckers cut costs; reducing the work force is another. Labor costs account for over 60 per cent of the truckers' expenses, and thus are a prime target of economy measures. This cutting away of manpower has been accompanied by an effort to utilize fully the men who remain. The seventy-hour per eight-day federal *ceiling* has become the frequently exceeded industry *norm*. Manpower cutting has, at the same time, led to reductions in vital back-up personnel such as shop mechanics, who are essential to the proper functioning of the equipment on the road. Skimping on replacement parts has also become common, to the danger of both the driver and the public. While in other fields of employment work hours have lessened and conditions have generally improved, the long-haul truck driver is working longer hours under worse conditions than ever before.

Though the direct enforcement of federal trucking-safety regulations was transferred to the Department of Transportation, the Interstate Commerce Commission still retains a potentially powerful indirect sanction against unsafe practices. As a condition of acquiring and keeping an ICC "operating certificate," a carrier must maintain its "fitness," of which safety is supposed to be one criterion. The Commission can and should check the D.O.T. safety records before granting or extending operating certificates. And it should run periodic checks on the records of carriers already certificated. But according to several ICC bureau chiefs and sources inside D.O.T., the ICC rarely makes such checks. The ICC's abdication of this vital safety-enforcement function is a most serious default of federal authority, because its power to suspend or revoke an operating certificate is the only truly effective enforcement weapon in the federal arsenal. The D.O.T. prosecutions can result only in fines, and these are so small that truckers can profitably run the risk of incurring them.

Sources inside the Federal Department of Transportation disclose that its Washington-based legal staff is actively committed to prosecuting safety violations, but that it is not getting sufficient input from its field inspectors to do the job. The field staff, these sources disclose, is made up of former ICC employees who transferred directly to D.O.T. They have brought with them the ICC's passive, conciliatory attitude, and if they report violations at all, the infractions are minor ones sought out mainly for the sake of fulfilling monthly quotas.

Aside from outright complicity with the truckers at the field staff level, the general chumminess of ICC and D.O.T. officials with the trucking industry is an important explanation of the lax enforcement of federal regulations, and of the failure to advocate—or even to see the need for—more adequate ones. At the lower echelons of federal authority, there is continual interchange between ICC-D.O.T. field staff and trucking company payrolls. More than one dispatcher or terminal manager is a former ICC safety inspector. Drivers report luncheon engagements between ICC-D.O.T. inspection personnel and company officials, even when inspections are currently being made. Chumminess is just as significant, though more subtle and refined, at the upper echelons of regulatory authority, where the power to formulate enforcement policy potentially resides.

The powerful interests that have grown from the vast subsidization of the interstate highway system do not forecast a slackening of the trend toward economization. Rather, they portend a new era of more trucks, more highway utilization, of increased size, speed, and weight, along with cuts in such areas as "labor" and "maintenance" costs. (Appendix 18 includes the recent trends in numbers and truck size. and includes a prediction of future trends, both as to the size and cost cutting, by one of the largest carriers.) At the moment, truckers, through their powerful and well-funded lobbyists, are pressuring in Washington, D.C., and at state capitols for more lenient regulations regarding the lengths, widths, and weights of their trucks, and are soliciting public sympathy through ads in the national press.

The current federal regulations have not kept pace with the industry. The regulations, including the maximum hours of driving, are substantially the same as they were in 1938, when the short-haul, small-scale trucking industry collaborated in writing them. Nor has the number of enforcement officers increased to meet the multiplying volume of trucking. Today, the ratio of federal safety inspectors to registered motor carriers in the United States is approximately one per 170,000 vehicles. Finally, there are indications of official "blinking" at safety violations and of outright complicity with the truckers themselves, so that even the effectiveness of the few officers who are in the field is diminished.

The deputy traffic engineer of the New Jersey Turnpike Authority recently released statistics that are indicative of the safety hazard that trailer trucks pose on the nation's highways. The deputy engineer reported that trucks with three or more axles account for only 12 per cent of the vehicles using the New Jersey Turnpike, but that they are involved in 31.1 per cent of all accidents and in 61.8 per cent of all fatal accidents on that road.

Little research has been done into the causes underlying such "accidents." Usually, attention has been focused on the condition of the road and the drivers, and has gone no further. A survey made of the nation's truck drivers suggests some of the real causes underlying the wreckage in which trailer trucks are increasingly involved. They suggest that to a large extent these often fatal incidents are not "accidents" at all, but are the natural and predictable results of practices alarmingly common in the trucking industry.

Our survey and report were spurred by unsolicited letters from truck drivers reporting unsafe practices for which they could find no redress. The information has been amassed from these letters, from interviews, and from a questionnaire distributed nationally through two truck drivers' publications. Many of the contentions are supported by documentation in the appendices.*

The drivers who reported to this survey are experienced,

---

* In addition to the suggestive documentation contained in the appendices to this Chapter, Supplementary Appendices (available from the Center for Study of Responsive Law upon request) contain over 3000 pages of evidence regarding weight, load, hours, and equipment violations. The evidence includes letters, logs, vehicle-inspection reports, photos, tape recordings, weight slips, carrier memos, etc.

most having spent between ten and thirty-five years behind the wheel. They have jeopardized their positions in their companies and their unions by stepping forward. They have also risked the possibility of tighter controls on maximum hours and thus, in some cases, less pay. That they were willing to take these risks is only one indication of the seriousness of the problem.

Some of the drivers' names and the names of their companies have been explicitly set forth. Others have been omitted at the driver's request. The drivers work for many different companies in all parts of the country, and no contention is made that the companies and officials named are necessarily the only or the worst violators. They are given merely as specific illustrations of what appears to be a national and growing trend. It should be recognized that some trucking concerns are more reckless about their drivers' and the public's safety than are others, and that conditions vary among the different types of hauling. Associated Transport, for example, is a carrier which has allegedly introduced an earnest company "safety" program. That even it would be accused of glaringly unsafe practices (see *infra*), and be the subject of a recent federal prosecution, merely hints at the level of safety in the industry as a whole.

ILLEGAL AND UNSAFE TRUCKING COMPANY POLICIES

MOST FREQUENTLY REPORTED BY DRIVERS
(For a more detailed breakdown of the survey see Appendices 16 and 17)

Allowing drivers only eight hours off duty between fifteen-hour stretches on duty.

Collusion with state and federal law enforcement authorities to violate safety laws.

Collusion with truck drivers' unions to defeat driver protests against unsafe company practices.

Creating conditions of work in which drivers must rely on "pep pills" to stay awake.

Discouraging safe driving by firing, suspending, and otherwise harassing drivers who, by taking safety precautions, delay delivery of freight.

Failing to repair defective equipment that has been reported by drivers.

Failing to report all accidents.

Firing and otherwise harassing drivers who report unsafe practices to authorities.

Knowingly exceeding maximum weights.

Ordering drivers to take routes that avoid weight checks by law enforcement authorities.

Providing inadequate sleeping quarters for drivers.

Requiring drivers to drive defective equipment.

Requiring drivers to drive under hazardous conditions and while ill.

Requiring, encouraging, or making it necessary for drivers to falsify their logs.

Scheduling runs which drivers cannot complete within ten-hour legal maximum.

Scheduling runs which drivers cannot complete without speeding.

Scheduling runs which keep drivers away from home for extended periods of time.

Working drivers beyond ten-hour driving limit and fifteen-hour on-duty limit.

Section 295 of the Motor Carrier Safety Regulations, dealing with maximum hours of driving and on-duty time, was conceived when trucking was a small-company, short-haul industry. Today, although companies have grown from a few vehicles to hundreds, hauls have stretched out from short runs to four and five hundred plus miles, and trucks have become 450 horsepower diesels pulling two forty-foot trailers, similar maximum driving and working hours are in effect. Drivers may be behind the wheel for ten consecutive hours, and may be on duty for fifteen consecutive hours—loading or unloading a trailer, repairing a tire on an icy road—as long as they have eight hours off duty in between. This grueling cycle, fifteen hours on duty, (ten or more of which is driving time), eight hours off, may be repeated *daily*, until the driver has worked a maximum of seventy hours in an eight-day period.

These legal "maximums," outrageous as they are, have become the industry's basis for a "normal" work day and work week. And to cut costs, the carriers are forcing their drivers—by means of schedules which cannot be completed otherwise—regularly to exceed even these limits. In addition, they are encouraging and even forcing the drivers to conceal these violations by falsifying their daily logs. Drivers who call in and report they cannot continue without running over their log are told to "adjust" their log and continue rather than lay over until the next day.

The normal laborer puts in an eight- or ten-hour day, five or six days per week; he can count on regular hours and at least one day off per week. The long-haul truck driver puts in a ten- to fifteen-hour day, often punctuated by only eight hours off duty. Taking into account time to travel from the terminal to the home or motel, time to eat, bathe, and perform various other tasks, the eight hours may provide for only four to five hours of sleep. (The driver who takes a meal with his family may do so at the cost of his eight hours rest.) Yet unlike other workers, the long-haul driver operates a fifty-thousand-pound plus vehicle which poses a potential threat to the hundreds of motorists it passes daily. Any ordinary driver knows the strain of driving a mere auto for seven to eight hours; the long-haul driver requires *more,* not incredibly less, off-duty time than the average worker, to be prepared for his weighty responsibility.

In order to save money and take advantage of the interstate highway system, the carriers are cutting manpower and maximizing labor by stretching out the distances between terminals. Runs over 400 miles are now common and many even exceed 500. To cite some examples: Associated Transport is running drivers 485 miles from Burlington, North Carolina, to Altoona, Pennsylvania; McLean drivers going from Indianapolis to the East Coast take their rest stop at Breezewood, Pennsylvania, 450 miles. Drivers say this run cannot be made in under ten hours under normal conditions. Hemenway drivers are running Winchester, Virginia, to Waynesboro, Virginia, to Bridgeport, Connecticut—555 miles—and are logging it as ten hours or less. And Ellis Trucking of Indianapolis expects its drivers to run a 520-mile Detroit-Cincinnati-Detroit turn, a feat which Ellis drivers say cannot be done in under ten hours.

A recently published ICC study corroborates the drivers' claims that they cannot complete such runs in a time below the legal limit. That study, of transcontinental freight hauling, found the average speed of truck travel to be 40.1 miles per hour.[1] This figure includes the much faster and less congested western runs, along with the hilly and often circuitous eastern runs. How a driver can cover 450 miles or more at under 40.1 MPH in less than ten hours would provide an insoluble problem in mathematics. Of course, to average even 40 MPH on the eastern thruways, with 50–55 MPH maximums, often requires some speeding.

In short, the carrier-scheduled runs are requiring the drivers to speed extensively and to drive well over the ten-hour legal maximum. In our survey 50 per cent of the drivers said it was "fairly common" for them to have to drive for more than ten hours to complete their runs, and over *two-thirds* said that even then speeding was necessary. The necessity to speed is in direct violation of Sections 292.3 and 292.6 of the Motor Carrier Safety Regulations. The latter section specifically states that

no . . . carrier shall schedule . . . the operation of any motor vehicle between points in such a period of time as would necessitate the vehicle being operated at speeds greater than those prescribed by the jurisdictions in or through which the vehicle is being operated.

However, not all the drivers want, or are able, to speed. Many report that company equipment is sometimes so lacking in power, or is so overloaded, that it cannot even reach a speed close to the limit. This inadvertent depressant to speeding is one more reason why the drivers are behind the wheel for more than the legally allotted ten hours.

The carriers' test runs, from which the expected completion time for all drivers is derived for a given route, are carefully conducted under conditions rarely duplicated in actual experience. The carrier takes its best rig, a light load, optimum weather, and light traffic, and runs its best driver over the route. That time becomes the expected norm. Drivers must speed when and where they can in order to come close to the expected time, and then are expected to record any time over ten hours in the "sleep" or "on-duty, not driving" category in the logs.*

It isn't merely the longer single runs that are causing excesses, such as the McLean's Trucking 440-mile Indianapolis to Memphis straight-through run with maximum speed limits of 50 MPH and poor roads through much of Kentucky. The "combinations" runs cause even worse vio-

---

* This, of course, explains why one driver was recently involved in an accident while his log had him recorded as asleep. See *Transport Topics*, May 12, 1969, p. 12.

lations. The carriers are now sending drivers from Cleveland to Columbus to Syracuse, or from Burlington, North Carolina, to New York City to Allentown, Pennsylvania, or from Evansville, Indiana, to Cincinnati, Ohio, and back again. This last trip used to be made without the return and with an eight-hour rest in Cincinnati. It is now run with an immediate return—a distance of some 464 miles. All of these runs, and the many other combinations now being scheduled, cannot possibly be completed, the drivers say, in less than twelve to fifteen hours.

Conditions would not be quite so bad if drivers could plan their schedules so as to be well-rested before beginning their ten hours plus behind the wheel. But drivers never know when they are going to have to start. After their eight-hour rest period they are "on-call" for duty on one-hour notice. Until they have exhausted their maximum seventy hours in seven days, they are on call twenty-four hours a day, seven days a week. "Booking off," or taking a day off, has generally been eliminated. Thus, a driver can be—and often is —up for eight or nine or more hours *before* he starts duty. He could be entertaining company on a Sunday afternoon, have had a few drinks, be just getting ready for bed after a normal thirteen or fourteen hours awake, and *then* be called for ten or more hours of strenuous driving and fifteen or more hours on duty. He may have to spend several hours at the terminal loading heavy freight or waiting for his rig to be loaded, and *then* begin driving. This means over twenty-four hours awake, perhaps thirty-six, during the latter part of which he is handling for a number of hours fifty tons or more of tractor and tandem trailers at high speeds over roads traveled by thousands of motorists. Many drivers in our survey specifically attributed the widespread use of "pep pills" among their associates to uncertainty about when they would be called to work and their consequent inability to plan their rest.

On these impossible schedules it is little wonder that drivers occasionally tire on the road and stop to rest. Both prudence and the federal regulations require them to do so. Section 192.4 reads:

No driver shall drive, or be required or permitted to drive a motor vehicle, while his ability or alertness is so impaired through fatigue, illness, or any other cause as to make it unsafe for him to begin or continue to drive.

Management regards such resting not as a safety precaution but as "delaying the freight." Correspondence submitted by drivers between themselves and their companies reveals that drivers are being suspended for compliance with section 192.4. A terminal manager wrote one such driver, "As you are well aware, an employee is supposed to have sufficient rest prior to departing." How can a driver have "sufficient rest" if the company expects him to be back behind the wheel eight hours immediately after driving for ten or more hours, and after being on duty for fifteen? How can he have "sufficient rest" *prior* to departing when he is given only one hour of notice?

In the absence of a company provision for "booking off" the only way a driver can have more than eight hours at home to rest is to report in as sick. Even drivers who use this excuse legitimately are being disciplined, and a great deal of the correspondence we have received suggests harsh action threatened against drivers who call in sick in order to get more than eight hours off.

Not only do the trucking companies force their drivers to extend driving time beyond the legal limits, they also make the drivers circumvent the fifteen-hour "on-duty" maximum. The practices of Red Star Express of Utica, New York (one of many companies reported for similar practices) mock the letter and spirit of the regulations regarding "on-duty" limits. When a driver pulls into a terminal the dispatcher will tell him in a ritualistic manner: "You are now relieved." The ensuing time is then considered "off-duty" and is therefore excludable from the fifteen-hour maximum, even though the driver is in fact not allowed to leave the terminal but must wait for loading or transfer or repairs. Drivers report waits of from one to eight hours, which they are required to log as "off-duty." A recent Associated Transport instruction to its drivers circumvents the fifteen-hour limit by illegally notifying drivers that they "may" record lunch in transit time as "off-duty" instead of "on-duty, not driving," as the regulations specify.

The lot of the steel hauler is even worse than that of common carrier, general commodity haulers. Steel haulers are *completely* at the mercy of the unpredictable schedules of the steel shippers. When they pull in for a pickup they don't know whether they will have to wait fifteen minutes or eight hours, yet they must be physically present because if they are not at the loading dock their load will go to someone else. After waiting around the loading dock for many long hours, perhaps catching a fifteen-minute cat nap, these drivers must then go on the road for ten hours or more, because the steel is expected to move without delay after loading.

Following is an account, written by a steel hauler, of a typical week. During the seven-day period documented he spent six hours in bed and logged a total of sixteen and one-quarter hours as "sleep." His other "rest" consisted of brief cat naps at the loading docks.

Sunday, 10:00 P.M. Leave home terminal of Detroit, Michigan, with load for Chicago Heights, Illinois. Load was picked up Saturday night and early Sunday morning (9:30 p.m. to 4:30 a.m., home to home).

Monday, 6:00 A.M. Arrive Chicago Heights. Cat nap in truck until 7:00 a.m., when receiving operations begin. Ninth in line to unload. What with loading railroad cars and satisfying production demands, understaffed receiving crew finally unloads truck by 1:30 p.m. Drive back to Gary, Indiana, arriving at 2:30 p.m., turn in bills, logs, and await loading. Sit around terminal until 5:00 p.m., get lucky and am scheduled to load to Cleveland, Ohio, at 8:00 p.m. out of U.S. Steel. Eat supper, hang around some more, arrive in mill at 7:30 p.m. Lots of trucks.

Tuesday, 2:30 A.M. Loaded, billed out, and back at Gary terminal. Clean up, eat. Had planned to sleep after loading, but load broke over Indiana gross by three thousand pounds, so better clear Indiana before daybreak. Leave Gary at 4:00 a.m.; hit Ohio and catch two-and-a-half hours sleep in truck before breakfast at 10:30 a.m. On the way again at 11:30 a.m., arriving at Cleveland consignee's plant at 4:00 p.m. Unloaded by 5:00 p.m., call Cleveland dispatch in time for forced-deadhead to Ironton, Ohio. Get south of Cleveland about seventy miles and have to sleep.

Wednesday, 1:00 A.M. After six hours sleep in truck, wake up, clean up, and eat. On the way by 2:30 a.m. At coffee stop near Columbus, discover low tire and light trouble on trailer. Too busy to repair tire at truck stop, so air it up and commence repairs on trailer lights. Fool around a couple of hours, fixed and ready to go at 5:30 a.m. Arrive Ironton

8:30 a.m. No trucks, no loads. Tear down and repair tire. Hang around terminal until 4:00 p.m. Only truck in, so forced with load of Effingham, Illinois, loading on the 7:00 to 3:00 turn at Armco-Ashland, Kentucky. Clean up, eat, and in mill by 7:00 p.m. Third truck in line, but everybody dogging it tonight; loaded and back at Ironton terminal at 10:30 p.m. Leave then, and make it west of Cincinnati, Ohio, before first coffee stop.

Thursday, 6:00 A.M. Fuel and eat breakfast in Indianapolis, Indiana. Humping for delivery today in Effingham; on the way again by 7:30 a.m. Lose cap off tire on tax-axle coming into Terre Haute, lose half hour replacing it with spare. Just make it in time for delivery at Effingham, catch about forty minutes shuteye waiting to unload. Call Gray, Indiana, for dispatch when empty; he needs equipment. Head out at 4:30 p.m., check into Gary at 10:30 p.m.—too late for loading. Go to hotel.

Friday, 7:00 A.M. After six hours of good rest, woken up by desk clerk—dispatcher wants all drivers out at terminal by 8:00 a.m. Eat breakfast, arrive at terminal at 8:30 a.m. Snag load to Detroit out of McCook, Illinois, immediate loading. Another slow shipper, not load, and back at Gary terminal until 7:00 p.m. Friday night traffic around Chicago very heavy. Scale out load, discover back trailer axle is over limit by twenty-one hundred pounds. Untarp and unchain load, and with help of buddy, have it shifted by 9:30 p.m. Clean up, eat supper and on way by 11:00 p.m.

Saturday, 3:00 A.M. Raining very hard. Just east of Kalamazoo, recently rebuilt generator goes out. Manage to get rig off road into rest area. Can't repair here, so crawl under and remove generator. Catch ride with freight hauler to closest truck stop. He can't repair my generator, but offers to help me chase down another rebuilt if I can wait a couple of hours; in no mood to argue, with the rain and being tired. Hang around garage and restaurant until 7:00 a.m., when great generator hunt commences. Locate right one at fourth stop, and returned to truck stop. Catch ride back to truck with buddy headed west. Still raining, though not so hard. Replace generator and on the way again at 11:30 a.m. Arrive Detroit terminal at 2:30 p.m. Had planned to unload Monday, but Detroit out of empties, and dispatcher arranges for consignee to accept delivery now, so he can load me. Unload and go right to mill for loading, arriving at 7:00 p.m.

Sunday, 1:00 A.M. Home and in bed.*

Men forced to haul the often overweight payloads of bulk steel often operate on schedules like the one above. Their equipment is frequently substandard because as owner-operators they cannot always afford to make repairs right away. And carrier companies often compel their drivers to take improperly loaded shipments to suit the convenience of shippers and consignees. For example, coils of sheet metal are loaded facing front and back, so that they can roll off a flatbed trailer, instead of facing to the side, merely because the front-and-back position facilitiates loading and unloading.

When company drivers must lay over on the road or at distant terminals they often rely on company-provided facilities for rest. Some carriers have contracted with hotels for driver rest facilities which are often described as "filthy noisy holes." At such places the drivers must get their very precious eight hours sleep (or less, counting eating time and time going from and to the terminal.) Their rooms, the drivers disclose, are often above noisy bars or have children screaming and running around in the halls. Many drivers describe their quarters as "brothels." Sometimes drivers are sent to apparently respectable hotels but are given the cheapest and noisiest street-level rooms. Steel haulers, independents, and some company drivers must use the bunk rooms at terminals and truck stops. Some of these are described as "appalling . . . filthy beyond belief." Almost 50 per cent of the drivers surveyed described such unsatisfactory sleeping conditions, and a few even submitted photographs with their questionnaires. The inability to sleep under such conditions is another reason frequently given for the increasing reliance on drugs like benzedrine to stay awake.

To absolutely minimize delays in transit, the trucking companies sometimes put two drivers into tractors with "sleeper berths" so that the payload can move continuously. The wife of one Associated Transport driver based in Tennessee wrote that her husband had less than two hours sleep

* This schedule is taken from a report prepared by Mr. James Leavit.

during a two-thousand-mile haul over rough roads through small towns. The poorly loaded haul was so bumpy the two drivers could not rest. On arrival they requested time to sleep, in compliance with §192.4. Despite their fatigue, they were reloaded and sent out on the return trip immediately. Other drivers report similar experiences. One says that while running solo with a sleeper berth he must keep the motor going for warmth, making it nearly impossible to sleep.

The Red Star Express Company bought a terminal last year in Worcester, Massachusetts. The nearest restaurant was two miles away. The former company had provided transportation to the diner for its drivers, but Red Star abandoned the practice. The drivers were held over for periods of fourteen to twenty-four hours without food. They were booked at a motel where they had to keep their clothes on at night because the heat was turned off. Only three rooms in the whole motel had shades to darken them in the daytime when the drivers frequently must rest. Eighty-six drivers signed and presented to the company a petition protesting these conditions.

To cut the tab per room—often as little as $3.50—still further, many carriers are assigning two drivers to one small room. The most recent schedules now have the second driver coming in after the first has been in the room for four hours. The first driver is awakened or is compelled to rest next to someone who coughs, smokes, snores, or has different sleeping habits. In some of the rooms the beds are attached. The drivers disclosed that many of the just off-duty roommates were "roaring drunk," making sleep in a room with them impossible. Almost one-half the drivers who relied on company-provided accommodations were assigned to rooms with one or more other drivers.

Many of the drivers described in detail a most important and alarming result of these sleep-denying conditions in the trucking industry—the dependence on habit-forming drugs. Almost 80 per cent of the drivers in our survey described the use of such drugs as "widespread." They disclosed that "Hey, you got a pill?" is now a most common question among drivers at truck stops and terminals. Occasionally drivers have prescriptions; more often they get the pills from the black market, from truck stops, and from other drivers. Some use their wife's reducing pills. The plenitude and easy availability of the pills is cited as another reason for their use.

A sense of necessity, certainly not a desire for "kicks," leads most drivers to reliance on drugs. A driver who reluctantly admits having resorted to pills says, "With a family, and kids approaching college age, what else can you do?" To the drivers, who must either stay awake or lose their jobs, the pills are not only an economic necessity, but a safety precaution as well. One writes, "Given a choice between a pill and falling asleep at the wheel, it is safer to take the pill." Writes another, "I'd rather take a pill than kill someone." Most alarming, perhaps, is that a favorite drug is the reflex-warping and habit-forming "bennie." After getting hopped up on pills, some drivers often need liquor to relax in order to sleep. Then, in eight hours, it's back on the road again and more pills.

The use of drugs is especially common among Midwestern steel haulers. The endless waiting at terminals, and the shippers' and consignees' demands for immediate delivery, result in weeks like the one detailed above, where the driver spent six hours in bed. Drugs substitute for sleep for the man caught in this wait-and-haul, wait-and-haul ordeal. One driver reports that all kinds of people approach him for drugs, thinking that he, as a truck driver, must have a source of supply.

With pills or without them, the drivers cannot always stay awake. Dozing over the wheel during the long interstate stretches is common—*almost 80 per cent of the drivers answering admitted to having dozed at the wheel despite pep pills*. A veteran for Red Star Express said that "only the jolt of the wheel when the truck hits the shoulder wakes me up. I see trucks ahead of me weaving back and forth and I know just what they are going through." One can only wonder how many crashes arise from the dulled reflexes of a fatigued driver.

In spite of road-weary drivers and turned-over trucks, the carriers often boast of their "safety" records. To the extent that such records are favorable, they are somewhat deceptive. Much crime on the highways is hidden crime. Since many trucking accidents involve no other vehicles, they receive little publicity and are often not even reported in violation of a regulation. Frequently only the driver, if anyone, is injured. Another factor depressing the trucker's accident statistics is that the motoring public wisely tries to avoid the tractor trailers. A study by Cornell University revealed that the public recognizes trucks and taxicabs as hazards, and thus steers clear. But with more and more truck traffic (Associated Transport now has over 1200 tractors operative) and with the looming possibility of longer, wider, and heavier trailers, it will not be possible to avoid these leviathans for long. Further, the statistics do not at all reveal the number of drivers *forced into* accidents by trailer trucks, while passing or changing lanes. A driver might well concentrate on avoiding a fifty-ton monster in a tight spot and take his chances with whatever else comes along.

Yet the incidents that *are* reported are beginning to stir up some concern. The 1967 Department of Transportation *Accident of Large Carriers of Property* report warns: "Of particular concern is the continuing trend in which commercial truck drivers are involved in single-vehicle accidents. In 1967, 115 (59.6 per cent) of the 193 commercial truck drivers killed were in single-vehicle accidents." [2]

A better index of the threat which trailer trucks pose on our highways is the number of innocent motorists killed in collisions with them. The Keystone-AAA Auto Club has cited statistics comparing the number of fatalities when each of three different kinds of truck collides with a passenger vehicle. The record is especially grim regarding double trailer combinations. When a pickup truck collides with a passenger auto, there are three fatalities per 1000 persons involved; when a trailer truck collides with a passenger car, seventy-one persons are killed per 1000 involved. And when a "double-bottom," or tandem trailer combination, rams a passenger car, *133* persons are killed out of every 1000 involved, or almost *double* the rate of single trailer trucks and almost *fifty times* the rate of pickup trucks.*

* The Pennsylvania Bureau of Traffic Safety has released statistics showing that in 1968, in collisions involving only passenger autos, the ratio between persons killed and incidents was approximately one to 243. But in collisions between trucks and passenger cars the ratio was approximately *one* to *forty-five.*
Another index of the safety record of trucks is the ratio of "accidents to registered vehicles." During the year June, 1968, through June, 1969, in Pennsylvania, this ratio was approximately one to twenty-nine for passenger cars and more than one to ten for trucks. Of course the spread between the ratios of *fatal* incidents to registrations would be much larger.

"The Children Don't See Their Father"

In addition to the problems of insufficient rest, disability, alcoholism, and pep pills, a set of emotional problems and tensions is being created by the carrier policies. Drivers are being sent on runs which keep them away from their wives and families for three to four days in the East and ten to eleven days West of Cleveland. The steel haulers, who chase endlessly from pickup to delivery without any fixed terminals, are frequently away from home for two weeks or more. These practices represent fairly recent changes (except for the home movers) and mean that men with families are for the first time required to stay away from home for long stretches on a regular basis.

The letters we received from truck-drivers' "widows" reflect the stresses the driver's long absences put upon his family and himself. The wife of one Maryland Branch driver wrote to the Branch President,

. . . You keep them out as long as you can until they run out of hours. When they do come home they have to spend their day off resting up getting ready to go back the next day. We don't have any social life together any more. The children don't see their father long enough to talk over their problems either. We have to be both mother and father to them and make all the decisions ourselves . . .

Concern for one's family, the desire to get home as soon as possible, is just one more pressure impelling the driver to push his load and his strength. Some drivers mentioned it specifically as a reason why many resort to pills to stay awake. And as the driver's wife noted, the carriers' policies absolutely minimize the amount of time a driver can be with his family, even when he is at home.

It is deceiving, however, to blame carrier policy alone for the lack of sleep, alcoholism, and drug habits of the drivers. There are indications that even a neutral carrier policy would not lessen current abuses. The drivers themselves are generally in favor of excessive driving and on-duty limits, particularly the younger ones. Long-haul drivers are generally paid by the mile—and more mileage equals more pay. Thus the long-haul driver pay system encourages minimizing sleep—with attendant abuses and speeding. The average long-haul driver is now earning about $13,000 a year, but many actually pull in over $20,000. The union, supporting the drivers who want to earn more than $13,000, arranges mileage pay systems and fails to back those drivers who want time to spend time with their families and who worry about their health. A few drivers are genuinely concerned about public safety, but the vote in our survey was two to one *not* to reduce present driving and on-duty maximum.

"That's the Exam"

The Motor Carrier Safety Regulations require physical examinations for drivers once every three years. The minimum coverage of the examination must include examination for "anemia, limp, tremor, or other form of nervousness such as might be caused by chronic alcoholism. . . . The regulations of the Federal Highway Administration provide that no driver shall be addicted to the use of narcotics or habit-forming drugs, or the excessive use of alcoholic liquors or beverages." Further, a detailed survey of the mouth, throat, thorax, blood pressure, pulse, lungs, abdomen, spine, genito-urinary, reflexes and so on is specifically required in Section 291.11.

The physical exams are frequently described as follows: "The doc asks you as you walk in what the color of his desk is. Then he asks you if you've ever been in the army. If you have been in the army you're ok. That's the exam." One driver reported that the doctor sends the blank forms to the company to fill in.

Alcoholism is perhaps the most widespread undetected malady, but there are probably more obvious problems going unnoticed. A United Van Lines driver who is allegedly blind in one eye and known to have "fits" was reported to the ICC in writing after the company refused to discharge him, with the author volunteering to testify. He received a standard form answer. That was four years ago. The complainant asserts that the man is still driving, "still having fits."

More important, temporary illness, as described below, is generally not considered a valid excuse for a driver's refusal to drive. In at least one company, a driver either takes the load or considers himself as having "quit." Drivers for many companies report suspensions and other forms of harassment—such as being assigned the worst vehicles or the least desirable runs—for declining to drive because of sickness. The presumption is *against* the driver, in spite of federal regulations and common prudence, which call for a presumption *in favor* of the driver (barring a long record of demonstrated malingering and unreliability).

The Wild Ones

Drivers frequently bear the blame for safety violations, such as speeding and operating with defective equipment, which are really attributable to company policies. Nevertheless, drivers sometimes are to blame for recklessness, and Section 291.13 of the Motor Carrier Safety Regulations requires carriers to give "due consideration" in continuing drivers in their service "to the following factors where they exist: (a) Violations of law or regulations governing the operation of motor vehicles of which the driver is guilty, especially as to those violations which tend to establish a disregard for regulatory requirements and for the public safety. (b) The driver's accident record . . . (c) Violations of criminal laws . . ."

The carriers seem to be ignoring the explicit instructions of §291.13. Post-accident investigations by the Department of Transportation have revealed that the drivers had long records of safety violations, but were nonetheless retained by their companies. Our sources could recall many examples of suspensions and dismissals for cautious driving, but few if any for violating safety regulations.

A driver can hardly be blamed, however, for operating defective equipment, when he has reported it to his company and has done all he could to have the defects corrected; or for speeding when that is the only way he can complete an assigned run. Yet many drivers report receiving tickets and even losing their licenses for speeding and for driving defective units which their companies had forced on them.

For this reason, the proposed federal regulations, which would crack down on *drivers* convicted of safety violations, strike at the branch instead of at the trunk. To the extent that safety violations are attributable to company policy, the companies, and not their drivers, should bear the penalties.

THE MAINTENANCE FARCE

Maintenance practices of the carriers are another important factor in making trucking unsafe for both the drivers and for the motoring public. First, the company mechanics, charged with keeping those multi-ton, 450 horsepower freight haulers safe for both driver and public, are regulated by no federal standards—either for their individual qualifications or for the number per vehicle a trucking company must have. Only two and one-half pages of the seventy-one pages of Motor Carrier Safety Regulations are given to inspection and maintenance. According to one driver, the company shops are well equipped but "the mechanics know nothing. They have to take their own cars to a gas station for new points and plugs." After the Red Star Express mechanics "repaired" a tractor on August 4, 1965, the driver got a ticket for the very item supposedly fixed. An Associated Transport driver took out a tractor which had supposedly been inspected in the company shops. It turned out to have no brakes and an air leak at the "quick release valve." When a mechanic was unable to repair the tractor on the road, the terminal dispatcher instructed the driver to continue to the next terminal, but to take a special route to avoid a possible ICC check. The drivers report such occurrences as typical, and almost 50 per cent said they are forced by their company to drive defective equipment. (Others wrote laconically, "they *try* to force me.") The attitude of the company repair shops, they say, is to "get'm out of our territory" with as little work possible. The companies are loath to incur the expense of sending mechanics out onto the highway to repair a crippled truck. As illustrated above, whenever possible they have the truck and driver proceed by a route which will avoid detection by the law.

To meet its schedules, a carrier often sends trucks out onto the road when they should be in repair shops. Even defects *reported* to the company go unrepaired. The Federal Regulations require the drivers to submit daily written safety checks and repair orders. Inspection reports volunteered by aroused and endangered drivers show that potentially lethal defects such as loose steering, lack of power, exhaust fumes entering the cab, and faulty transmissions, are reported two, three, many days in a row without being repaired. And the vehicles are driven hundreds of miles in the meantime. The drivers report being assigned tractors still with safety hazards they themselves reported six months previously. Since they may be assigned a different unit daily, they have no way of knowing what the previous user said about it. Their companies, they disclose, will run a tractor until it either "breaks down or cracks up."

Numerous inspection reports sent to us by drivers showed refusals or failure to repair defective equipment. On one of the reports the driver wrote "Had to use double handful of rags to seal some [of the exhaust leaks into the cab]— it's a wonder someone has not been put to sleep driving this tractor and killed themselves, period." A Youngstown, Ohio, driver wrote in our survey that exhaust leakage into his cab "put me to sleep one time and I turned over."

Such records have not led to increased carrier concern over maintenance—quite the opposite. Manpower accounts for approximately 75 per cent of the trucker's overhead, and when cost-cutting time comes, it is often the mechanics that go. A driver for Associated Transport reports that garage personnel are being laid off even though the hazardous defects reported by the drivers continue to go unrectified.

In order further to cut costs—at the expense of safety— the truckers are also skimping on the replacement of defective parts. Over two-thirds of the drivers said they had run with defective brakes, and one-third said they were forced to do so "often" or more. Defective *trailer* brakes due to worn-out hose connections were singled out by drivers throughout the country as a major cause of concern. In spite of such maintenance, some states entrust the annual inspection of company vehicles to the companies themselves.

Two Michigan drivers of seventy-one years' experience between them submit another example. Their company, Anchor Motor Freight, has its own trick with brake hoses. When a safety investigation turned up worn hoses on its older vehicles, Anchor simply switched these hoses with those on its newer equipment. Anchor similarly "disposed" of 109 unsafe trucks impounded by Michigan authorities by transferring them to its New York and Ohio terminals.

One vehicle hazard which affects the drivers more than the general public is the unsafe bulkheads. The bulkhead, or "headerboard," separates the driver from the load. When the cargo is such that on a sudden stop it might slide through and crush the driver, Federal Regulations require that the headerboard be reinforced. But the carriers frequently ignore this regulation and more than one driver has been "chopped up like hamburger" by steel beams crashing through the rear of his cab. Inland Express is one company which likes to redefine the above regulation to suit its own convenience. According to drivers, Inland has been ignoring the regulation unless the trailer has a "full load." Since at least theoretically there is no such thing as a full load, the regulation never applies (by Inland's standards). Forty thousand pounds of steel pipe is a "partial load," therefore all the protection given the cab and driver is a one-half-inch-thick panel of the resistant strength of cardboard. Such loads are often haphazardly secured. Almost one-half the drivers said they were given loose freight to haul, over one-third said often or more. Special concern was expressed over sheet metal, pipe, and large, heavy coils of metal and paper.

The drivers are particularly worried about the increasing use of multi-trailer rigs. Some states allow two trailers to follow behind a single tractor and there has been talk and test runs of three-trailer "trains." One danger of the two- and three-trailer rigs is the difficulty of getting the rear trailers to properly "track" or follow the leading trailer's wheels. A slightly curved road, a not quite balanced load, or mismatched tires (all of which are common) will cause the rear trailer to "fishtail" or wander back and forth. "If you go any speed at all," says one driver, "they whip all over the highway." A driver with thirty-one years' experience driving semi-trailers and "double bottoms" says the latter are "twice as dangerous as a semi-trailer, because they have twice as many places to bend or jackknife." Trailers "jackknifing" out across the road are a major cause of injury and death on today's highways. Still another driver writes that roads and company tractors cannot handle the trailers the truckers want. He says,

. . . the increase in width is ridiculous. Pulling two trailers (eight feet wide and a total length of sixty-five feet) is too much for the narrow highways and the type of equipment we have to pull them with. They always say they will stick to the four-lane roads when they get these increases but it isn't long until they make us run down every cow path with them.

The public hears only what the truckers say; their drivers know what they *do*. And another reason for the danger of the two-trailer tandems is the practice, cited by over 50 per cent of the drivers, of using worn, treadless and mismatched tires, *especially* on the trailers.

Proper balance between the front and rear trailer is essential if the double bottom is to track properly. A large teamster local in upper New York State has had a continuing dispute with a company which regularly packs its trailers with unbalanced loads. The company has ignored the union's insistence that the weight of the loads be distributed properly. Although the company, Red Star Express, persists in putting the heavy loads in back, it charges the drivers with any accidents its negligent loading causes. A letter from a driver from Kentucky said flatly, "These companies will inevitably load the rear trailer with the heaviest load." Over *two-thirds* of the drivers reported being given unbalanced front and rear trailers, and *50 per cent* said they pulled such rigs "often" or more. Many of the drivers who reported never pulling unbalanced tandems did so because their companies simply had not begun to use double bottoms. Even drivers who were uncritical of their companies' performance on other grounds cited continual carelessness in the balancing of double-bottom loads. Nevertheless, the truckers continue to foist upon the public, through their lobbyists and through ads in *Time* and *U.S. News and World Report,* the dubious claim that the double bottoms are actually "safer" than the shorter, lighter trucks with fewer couplings.

The couplings are yet another factor. Weak couplings have caused many wrecks, and with two or more trailers hooked up behind the cab, the danger is multiplied. Of course, the possibility of an overload increases enormously with the multi-rigs. And even single-trailer rigs are dangerous if the proper precautions regarding couplings, load balancing, tires, and brake hoses are not scrupulously followed.

Running trucks and trailers until they break down or crash is not the only cause of unsafe units on the highways. The trucking companies are not entirely to blame. Highway mile delinquency, trucking style, begins in the manufacture of the equipment. Unlike air and water craft which must pass rigid tests before being certified for use, any truck or trailer can go out on the road if it meets the minimal ICC-D.O.T. and state safety requirements. Thus, drivers report hazardous, ill-designed equipment coming straight from the factories and going right into use. A typical example: a trailer which was overweight on the rear tandems *unloaded*. The drive axles on the connecting tractor did not have enough weight to hold the wheels to the pavement. There are no checks, no safeguards against such trucks and trailers on the road. And investigations of trucking wrecks, like those of auto wrecks, have carefully avoided any inquiry into the basic design (or maintenance) of the vehicle itself. Most inquiry is focused instead upon the road.

The Official Blink

Why don't drivers contest these conditions, or go into other lines of work? As already noted, some like the opportunity for big money. They don't mind the pep pills, or the days and weeks away from home; their $13,000 (and more) a year is more important to them than their own or the public's safety.

Many drivers keep quiet because they need the work. One from Kansas City, Missouri, wrote, "I have two sons in college and have always had my family to support, or I would have quit this business long ago. But I don't know how to do anything else, it seems." To the veteran drivers of over fifteen or twenty years, the trend in driving conditions is only recent, and it is too late in their careers to contemplate a change of work. Wrote one, "I would gladly take less money for less miles traveled and hours worked."

If a driver refuses a run, the dispatcher will just give it to another driver and the next load offered will probably involve the same dangers and violations as the one refused. The companies try to discourage protest by saying, "Well, someone else will take it and you're the only one complaining." More important, in some companies refusal of a load for any reason is considered a resignation. Blackballing is common in the trucking industry, to the extent that companies will check previous employment and refuse to hire drivers dismissed for being concerned about legal safety requirements.

The unions have been of little help to the over-the-road driver. Drivers frequently commented in our questionnaire that their unions had "sold us out," and of all those who sought backing from their unions for refusing to be accomplices to their companies' unsafe practices, less than *one-third* received any support. Most of the drivers said they knew better than to expect such help to begin with, and didn't bother to seek it. Usually, the long-haul drivers are only a small minority within the local and thus exercise little power. The demands and interests of the short-haul and delivery drivers are often very different from those of the long haulers, and the unions probably represent a majority sentiment against any work-practice change which cuts mileage and pay in the interests of long-haul safety. In addition, the union leaders tend to be very "friendly" with trucking management. Less understandable is the failure of the ICC and D.O.T. to respond to a driver's complaint, even when he and others "turn themselves in" to the ICC for safety violations.

Although they are in the minority, some drivers do contest the conditions under which they drive—to their companies, to the unions, to state and federal officials. The unsafe practices that endanger the public endanger these drivers. But the drivers who "make trouble" for the companies are continually harassed. Our survey strongly suggests that the prevalent general company policy of harassing, suspending, and threatening with dismissal drivers who "delay freight" under hazardous conditions in fact acts to *discourage* safe driving. A company will often use the success of its policy as a self-fulfilling justification. That is, Inland will invariably say that a driver who stopped in dense fog after eight hours of driving was wrong because others who were driving the same run at that time did *not* stop. If a driver persists in obeying the regulations, companies will begin to "build a case" against him by issuing letters of warning and suspension for the most trivial things (*e.g.*, failure to sign in on the proper line). Thus, many veteran drivers with spotless records now all of a sudden have two or three letters of warning a month.

Predictably, drivers who have appealed to law enforcement authorities (state, ICC, and D.O.T.) have incurred the wrath of such companies. A recent notice from Branch Motor Express Company, to its drivers makes plain what happens to drivers who reveal the company's delinquency to the authorities: it promises "disciplinary action and possible suspension and/or dismissal" to any man "proven guilty of criticizing this company . . . or any of the labor officials."

NEW YORK, NEWARK, TRENTON
ALLENTOWN, LANCASTER, PHILADELPHIA
READING, YORK, BALTIMORE
BOSTON, FRAMINGHAM, FITCHBURG
SPRINGFIELD, NEW HAVEN, PROVIDENCE

"THE MAIN STEM OF THE INDUSTRIAL EAST"

BRANCH MOTOR EXPRESS CO.

Executive Offices: 114, Fifth Avenue — New York, N.Y. 10011 — 255-7700

Wilkes-Barre Terminal
July 19, 1967

N O T I C E -- TO ALL EMPLOYEES

It has come to the attention of Branch Motor Express that a few drivers who are employed by our Company have been going around to the places they are delivering and criticizing the Company, criticizing other drivers who work for this Company and criticizing the Local Union Officials who represent them in connection with this company.

Branch Motor Express is the means of your livelihood. Branch's progress in this area means security for you and your future. I do not want to dwell on the legal aspects on the conduct of any employee, but I want it made known that there must be strict adherence to the rules of this Company and your Local Union. Any man proven guilty of criticizing this Company, any person employed by this Company (including drivers) or any of the labor officials, will be subject to disciplinary action and possible suspension and/ or dismissal from the employ of Branch Motor Express Company.

I think it is a darn shame when a man will take a paycheck from a company and then go out on the street and criticize the same company, its management, or people who are trying to be fair and do a good job in order to protect this same man's future. I want this criticism to cease immediately. We must all work together for a bigger and better future.

Carl R. Loucks
Carl R. Loucks
Terminal Manager

cc: Local Union 401
    Vince Dagen--NYGO

The ICC, and now the D.O.T., justify their meager inspection and complaint-initiation activities by explaining (as the ICC does in all realms of its regulatory authority), "If there are any violations, somebody will complain." This regulatory wish is highly unrealistic in light of what happens to drivers who *do* complain. And drivers are the only potential complainants. Other companies do not invite official attention to practices of which they may be guilty, shippers and receivers do not complain about speeding and long hours because they result in faster delivery of goods, and few of the general public know where or how such a complaint may be made, nor do they have the resources that might be necessary to make an effective complaint before a regulatory body. As many have discovered, a letter usually elicits a mere form reply, and no more.

Yet even when somebody does complain—usually only drivers who have been fired can afford to—the so-called enforcers have offered little aid. Less than one-third of the drivers who had gone to state or federal authorities about their company's unsafe practices received any assistance or backing, and the ICC's reputation for non-action deterred many more from even trying. Another problem is that the ICC—now D.O.T.—field staff has been reticent about making its presence known. Several drivers commented they *would* have sought assistance, but that they could not locate anybody to go to.

Drivers in upper New York State brought their grievances to a former ICC agent there, now with D.O.T. "We don't get involved with labor" was his reply, these drivers report. But the agent did offer some sage advice: "We don't want to see you getting fired for refusing to violate the law. You are foolish if you refuse. You have wives and families. You stand to lose thousands."

In washing his hands of such "labor" matters—in this case, the firing of a driver for refusal to violate federal law —this agent has reneged on his basic responsibilities. Such failure to enforce the law has been all too present at both federal and state levels. A New York driver with Associated Transport says that in nineteen years on the road a federal inspector has not once checked his log. Over *one-half* the drivers in our survey said their logs had not been checked in transit during the past year. "The companies," the Associated driver says, "hold the ICC and D.O.T. in contempt."

Another says of federal non-vigilance, "The ICC does not seem to care how you log, so long as you have one and it is up to date." That comment was made by a McLean driver from Indiana, but eastern drivers have had similar experiences. New York State is noted by drivers for log checks, but looking at a log and enforcing the law are not always the same. Recently a driver was stopped by a New York State trooper for a check. Accidentally, the driver handed him the wrong log. It was three days in arrears and had another driver's name on it. The trooper looked at it and asked for the driver's license. He examined both carefully, handed them back, and said "OK, go on."

Federal officials and state troopers are the public's only bulwark against unsafe trucks on the highways, but these law enforcement officers appear to be dancing to the industry's tune. The New York State Thruway Authority recently presented a letter to all tandem drivers admonishing them not to jeopardize tandem operations on the Thruway through "carelessness." In its reference to "some groups that would like to cancel tandem operations for their own selfish interests" (*i.e.*, the public concerned about the safety of the tandems), the letter reads as though the Authority considers itself an affiliate or public relations arm of the trucking industry.

Apparently some states have even reneged on their duty to inspect licensed trucks. A Virginia driver writes that the states merely send boxes of inspection stickers to the truckers, instead of requiring inspections at state-approved facilities. The company mechanics then perform the "inspection" and duly attach the stickers. An Illinois driver writes, "State police and ICC very seldom stop us and most of our trucks are unsafe to drive." Another says tersely, "The ICC will not stop these trucks."

Before entering the New York State Thruway trailer trucks are "inspected." Inspection reports are available which show that trucks with broken springs and loose fifth wheels are allowed to pass. Since the same faults reappear on reports on successive days, there evidently has been no intervening effort to repair them. Once a truck driver complained to a trooper about being forced to take overloads. "Look, these guys [the carriers] have to make a living too," the trooper answered. "You drivers shouldn't complain about them. That's our job. You guys should take what you're given and shut up." During a safety check, a driver tried to explain that his fifth wheel was dangerously loose. "Whatsamatta? Get a sour load?" was the reply. The wheel was not looked at. "They're making them that way these days," was what another driver was told when he reported a loose rear wheel during a "safety" check. The Thruway Authority's indifference toward its own safety regulations, even when drivers lay defective equipment at its feet, does not prevent it from blaming the drivers for "accidents" caused by faulty tandems, and issuing notices and warnings to the drivers to this effect.

New York is not the only state which blinks at potentially fatal safety violations. Evidently, some states agree with the truckers that they will not enforce the laws entrusted to them. A memo from Branch Motor Express to its drivers informs them that the listed violations "will no longer be tolerated in the state of Pennsylvania." That the violations will "no longer be tolerated" implies that they previously *were* tolerated. The "crackdown" was announced at a "Truck-Industry—Police Institute." One wonders whether the prior laxity was agreed to at such an "institute," and how many states have such agreements, tacit or overt, in effect.

The carriers have become expert at keeping offenses from the official eye (even though the official eye is likely to blink). Multi-trailer rigs are frequently loaded so that they weigh more than the legal limit. Clever dispatchers know how to avoid weight checks, especially when the scales are permanently located, as in Ohio. When they have an overweight load they simply send it over a route that by-passes the scales.

The truckers have reduced this weight-check avoidance to a fine, if routine art. We have evidence of detailed instructions issued to drivers of Branch for avoiding weighing stations in Pennsylvania and New Jersey.

Branch has good reason to develop such exact law avoidance techniques. Typical company weight slips are available showing overweight loads. These slips signed by the company dispatchers, show the company knowingly and willfully sends overloaded or unbalanced loads out onto the public highways. Branch's overloading and weighing-station avoidance were brought to the attention of the ICC. True to form, the Commission merely acquiesced to the company's explanation that it was routing its drivers over "old" highways "for the purpose of saving the payment of tolls."

The *attitude* of the law enforcement officials is what is most important and disturbing. Either they do not want to do their jobs, or else their hands are greased or politically tied; or all of the above. An Inland Express driver in upper New York State who was suspended for stopping for safety in heavy fog went for aid to a D.O.T. inspector. In ceasing to drive, the man had been complying with the Motor Carrier Safety Regulations §292.14. Inland Express suspended him for excessive stops en route, delay of freight, failure to notify Central Dispatch of any delay of freight, and improper logs—and the D.O.T. inspector seemed to search harder for reasons why he shouldn't assert his authority than for reasons why he could. He interpreted the dispute as a "labor" matter, in which he would not get involved. Many of the drivers in upper New York State are disturbed not only by this agent's reluctance to assert his legal authority, but also by his seeming lack of interest in even meeting or talking with aggrieved drivers.

The agents fail to accept their responsibility even more clearly in another matter. Many carriers have installed what are called "tachographs" in their trucks which record on rotating discs the driving hours, stopping times, and speeds of its drivers. Unlike the logs, the printed tachographs are very difficult to doctor, although the drivers report that the speed calculation on the graphs are consistently five to ten MPH low. Drivers who want the maximum-hours laws enforced have told the D.O.T. inspector about the tachographs (which at least one company keeps carefully locked in the company safe). Yet the inspector refuses to look at them on the grounds that the Interstate Commerce Act does not require that they be kept. He continues to check only the final copies of the logs, which are commonly known to be unreliable.

This abdication of responsibility is in violation of the letter and spirit of the Code of Federal Regulations. Part 1020.1 of Title 49 of the Code requires regulated motor carriers to allow federal agents to

. . . inspect and examine all such lands, buildings, or equipment used in connection with interstate or foreign operations, and all accounts, records, and memoranda, including all documents, papers, and correspondence now or hereafter existing, and *kept or required to be kept.* (Emphasis supplied.)

The authority could be found in this section to inspect the tachographs.

Even when the hours-of-service records are checked in the company's permanent files (by which time in many companies they have been "corrected" to meet the federal regulations), it is only to see if "they cross the t's and dot the i's." The ICC and D.O.T. have been less than avid in prosecuting when safety violations are detected. A driver from Inland Express, Syracuse, New York, asked the local D.O.T. official to make a safety compliance check of his company. To his credit, the official made the inspection, but the company later informed its drivers that its record had been pronounced "good," even though the check had uncovered numerous infractions of the hours-of-driving and hours-on-duty limits. The company, of course, blamed its drivers for the infractions which had occurred, and has subjected the driver who requested the check to continual harassment.

How many infractions of federal law must be stashed away in its files before a regulatory agency will take action against a trucker? D.O.T. had accumulated over five thousand safety violations by Associated Transport over a period of three years, but withheld prosecution until—oddly enough—the eve of this report.

The signs do not presage more vigorous D.O.T. safety enforcement in the future. Spokesman for the highway lobby and foe of highway beautification, Representative William Cramer of Florida, has lobbied for the ouster of Howard Heffron as General Counsel of the Federal Highway Administration. Heffron had begun to light fires under D.O.T. enforcement officials. Among his "sins" was the filing of charges against Safeway Trails Bus Lines for over 6000 safety violations, including working intercity bus drivers up to one hundred hours a week. Heffron has been replaced by David E. Wells, Florida friend of Cramer and a trucking lawyer. For the last three years Wells has represented Redwing Carriers of Tampa, Florida, the largest carrier of dried bulk and liquid commodities in the Southeast. During this time Redwing was classed "unsatisfactory" in safety compliance in 1966 and no better than "marginal" since then. (Redwing's freight includes chemicals, acids, and explosives.) In 1966 Redwing incurred a criminal information charge for twenty-five violations of the Federal Safety Regulations for using faulty equipment. The attorney who represented this company is now the chief attorney in the Department of Transportation—enforcing the motor vehicle safety and motor carrier safety laws. Although there have been indications that the administration of federal safety regulations is to be shifted to another bureau or division, there is little hope of enforcement by D.O.T. on a scale that could deter the continuation of present trends.

Financial sanctions to insure safety are simply not effective, given their present limits. Only the ICC has the truly effective sanction—suspension or revocation of a trucker's certification. With but one exception due to outside pressure, the ICC has not invoked this sanction for the sake of safety. Given the current conditions of the industry and given the ICC's clearly established and stated responsibility to consider safety compliance a criterion for fitness, it has no excuse for its failure. It has not only failed to make a positive effort to judge fitness, but has consistently failed to make the simple phone call to D.O.T. that would yield the recent record of a carrier seeking an extension.

7 / Home Moving

March 10, 1969

Dear Senator Magnuson:

. . . There is a ludicrously wide credibility gap between the charming advertising by the moving industry, and actual performance and ethics. . . . Moving is a difficult enough task without being cheated in the bargain! Whatever Congress can do to force movers to be good Americans will be appreciated by hundreds of thousands of citizens yearly!

Yours sincerely,
Mrs. T . . . E . . . R . . .

Riverside, California
February 21, 1969

Dear Senator Magnuson,

. . . I would like to know who the ICC is protecting. It is a government agency supported by the people, not by any private industry.

The cost of a legal suit for a private citizen between states is prohibitive and that is why moving companies ignore letters and complaints.

I have contacted the ICC and they say they cannot help me.

Very truly yours,
R . . . F . . . E . . .

Orlando, Florida
July 11, 1969

Dear Mr. Nader,

. . . I wrote the ICC and they did nothing about it to this day except to advise me that they are investigating. . . . I believe that ICC is a price-fix monopoly that tells the van lines how much to charge to protect them—no free enterprise and the heck with the consumer. . . . I am sure that you would be the one to wake this situation up, including the ICC.

Sincerely,
S . . . G . . .

Interstate Commerce Commission,
Bureau of Operations
219 South Dearborn St.
Chicago, Illinois
February 17, 1969

Dear Mr. P . . .

. . . This Commission has no jurisdiction over claims for delay, however, and if you are unable to reach a satisfactory agreement with the carrier your recourse is to an appropriate civil court. . . .

Very truly yours,
R . . . M . . .
District Supervisor

Interstate Commerce Commission
Washington, D.C. 20423
February 14, 1969

Dear Senator Magnuson:

. . . The Interstate Commerce Commission does not have jurisdiction to settle loss or damage claims. If the parties fail to reach an amicable settlement, proper recourse is had by filing suit in a court having appropriate jurisdiction. . . .

Sincerely,
Virginia Mae Brown, Chairman

Columbus, Ohio
February 6, 1969

Dear Senator Magnuson,

A year having now passed since my experience with interstate movers . . . I have concluded that:

Government is decidedly pro-industry and contra-citizenry. . . .

The ICC in my case was useless, but they write lovely letters.

Sincerely yours,
D . . . W . . . C . . .

Household moving is a unique service among those under ICC regulation, and the home moving consumer may need even more protection by a public regulatory agency than other consumers in the area of transportation. The individual home owner transferring his earthly belongings to a new city is not a businessman shipping his goods to market, and as a result is at a distinct disadvantage *vis-à-vis* the trucker. His is a one-time move, and he lacks the promise of future business as an incentive for good service and honest billing. He is unfamiliar with trucking and therefore naive about tariffs and industry practices. There are other disadvantages, which he shares with all "small" shippers who need the services of truckers under ICC jurisdiction. His shipment is relatively costly per pound and requires careful handling, but the ICC has been less than eager to supervise the handling and storing of household goods. Perhaps the most important disadvantage of the small shipper is that he lacks legal *bargaining* power, the power to enforce his rights either in the courts or through the ICC. The big trucking company knows this individual cannot afford a private lawsuit. It also knows that he cannot bend the regulatory process to his purpose the way the large shipper or carrier can. He cannot afford, as they can, a staff to sit at the ICC to scrutinize every tariff filed, and protest when it is applicable to himself. He does not read the Federal Register or know when there are Commission proceedings that might concern him. He could not hire a lawyer and enter the proceedings even if he were to have notice. He is a sideline participant, trusting in and needing the protection that must be actively initiated and administered by the ICC.

Individual Americans paying for their own moves comprise roughly one-third of the movers' annual business. Another third is made of "national account" traffic, employee moves paid for by companies with large contracts with the movers. The final third consists of military moves, made under contracts between the D.O.D. and private moving companies. Though these latter two-thirds give rise to their share of complaints, they are not of concern here because in each case the shipper—the large company or D.O.D.*—holds out the prospect of large contracts as an inducement to good service. The Department of Defense, moreover, pays for all damage incurred by military personnel during moves. The individual in such situations moves under the protection of the large company or D.O.D. contract and thus is not as urgently in need of ICC protection as the unaffiliated consumer.

The nation's 183 intercity movers collected $600 million

---

* "Multi-representation," a practice whereby a local mover will become an "agent" of several different moving companies and thereby take advantage of the D.O.D.'s practice of rotating contracts among competing carriers, is beyond the scope of this report.

in 1968, one-third of which came from individual household moves. One in five Americans—40 million—moves
annually. The practices of the movers have stirred thousands of complaints on the local, state, and federal level.
The ICC reports receiving over 5000 complaints per year
—a very high figure considering how unfamiliar the public
is with the ICC. Congressional mail, especially that of Warren Magnuson, Chairman of the Senate Commerce Committee, is increasingly full of complaints as Congress shows
growing interest in consumer affairs. And while the ICC
itself has not devoted much long-range policy planning
attention to the problem, moving consumes more and
more of the agency's staff time. A field agent near the
headquarters of several of the large national movers reports spending 30 per cent of his time on home moving,
although the problem was officially considered to be only 5
per cent of his responsibilities.

The estimate is often the consumer's first step into the
troubled waters of household moving. Although the price
of a move will be determined by the actual weight and distance regardless of the estimate, the moving companies
usually quote the customer a figure he can "expect" to pay.
While the customer is told that the estimate will not be
binding, the industry practice is to induce business by quoting low estimates. Many customers, receiving a low estimate, think that even though the actual weight will ultimately be determinative, they "somehow" might get a
bargain.

The customer does not really feel the crunch of the low
estimate until delivery. Almost without exception, the
movers require full payment in cash or certified check on
delivery. No personal checks are accepted. Thus, if the
estimate was low, and the customer did not provide enough
for the actual charge, he must either get together the
needed cash in a strange city in two hours or else watch
his possessions go off to the storage warehouse.

The experience of S.G. of Orlando, Florida, was typical.
He wrote:

Dear Mr. Nader:

. . . The estimates by Allied Van Lines and Bekins and
Engel Brothers were $600, give or take $50. In fact Bekins was
$590. When they came to Orlando I was called to have a cer-

tified check for $1009. And when I gave him that he demanded another $50 cash and if I didn't pay that he would put the load in storage which would cost $150 more, so I paid him the $50. . . .

I wrote the ICC and they did nothing about it to this day except to advise me that they are investigating.

In part, the estimates problem stems from the structure of the industry. Movers normally operate through local agents, who are not regular company employees. These agents are paid according to the moves they book. Once the move is booked, these agents normally bear no responsibility for its satisfactory completion. Thus, the agent's incentive is to book as many moves as he can, and low estimates are one way to raise the number.

Several solutions have been proposed for the problem of under-estimates. One is to make estimates binding. The industry contends that people would then show the mover only a portion of what they intended to ship. It would seem that an inventory taken at the time of the estimate could solve that problem. The industry also contends, in phrases reminiscent of the Granger movement of the 1880's, that binding estimates would encourage what is known as "rebating"—movers deliberately quoting low estimates to capture business. It is not clear how such price competition would harm consumers, whether it is called "rebating" or anything else. So long as maximum rate levels were enforced, consumers would have everything to gain from a possible discount. A second solution to the problem of low estimates was proposed the last time the ICC reconsidered its regulations for home movers, in 1961. The rule would have required the movers to accept payment of the estimate on delivery, and defer payment of any excess charges for at least ten days.

The Commission rejected this proposal out of sympathy with the industry's contentions. The movers argued that they would not be able to collect many of the deferred payments, and that the amount would, in effect, be lost. Again they used the magic word "rebate." The Commission showed considerably more sympathy with this hardship when coming from the movers than when its analog is voiced by consumers. How the public can collect overcharges or damage claims from the large moving companies, once cash has been paid on delivery, is not even considered a problem by the ICC—which had no consumer representative at its rule-making hearing.*

In short, the Commission had before it evidence of a practice which was subjecting large numbers of American consumers to great hardship. By the Commission's own figures, out of 829,038 moves made in 1960, there were 66,920 over-estimates of 10 per cent or less; 107,402 under-estimates of more than 10 per cent; and 71,753 under-estimates of 20 per cent or more. Yet the Commission decided that deferral of the excess was too harsh on the industry. The movers proposed, and the Commission accepted, an "alternative," whereby the movers would file with the Commission each month a list of all under-estimates of 10 per cent or more. How this industry-proposed "rule" will effectively deter over-estimating is not clear. But unchallenged by public counsel or by an alert Commission, the movers succeeded in having it written into the proposed Code of Federal Regulations provision.

When questioned by the authors about this decision, the Commissioners' answers were predictable. One Commissioner, asked about the possibility of making estimates binding, remarked only that "rebates" might result. Another said that people would cheat and hide encyclopedias under clothes and fill the refrigerator with junk.

Lest there be any possibility that the mover might be legally bound to his estimate, or that the consumer have any bargaining power with regard to price, the Commission has enacted into its regulations (176.10a): "The shipper [customer] shall not be permitted or required to sign the 'Estimated Cost of Service Form.' " (If he did sign it, both parties might be bound by its terms).

HIDE AND SEEK

Many consumers have discovered, too late, that once the loaded van drives off, their possessions have begun an uncharted and untraceable journey. Very possibly the van is headed not out on the road, but back to the local warehouse where the belongings will be stored until another van picks them up. The extra handling and the conditions under

* The bargaining and legal power of a large company to collect an unpaid claim (a normal part of any business) vis-à-vis the power of the average consumer to collect on overcharge seemed lost on the Commission, as did the incredibly high frequency of industry underestimates and overcharges.

which possessions are stored in such unauthorized warehousing are a major cause of loss and damage. The precarious timetables involved in such deposit and pickup arrangements frequently cause substantial delays in delivery. Had a customer been told of such arrangements beforehand he might well have opted for a mover who would carry his load directly. Yet the ICC makes no requirement of disclosure and prescribes no standards for warehousing or handling of shipments en route. Even if a mover does carry the load directly, without warehousing, a family's possessions may have to be transferred from one truck to another in an "interlining" arrangement. Such interlining is often necessary because in the ICC's mode of regulation some carriers are limited in the area in which they can operate. Because of the Commission-imposed fragmentation, the load must be transferred between two or more van lines to get to its destination. Sometimes a load is transferred between vans of the same line when one is going closer to the destination point than the other. Such interlining, along with imposing added costs on the industry and thus on the consumer, is, like warehousing, a major source of loss and damage. It also creates uncertainty as to the location of one's possessions en route. Some families have waited hours, days, even weeks for their possessions to be delivered, and have called the national mover only to discover that the company itself does not know where the shipment is.

Although interlining is a practice which the home owner would like to know about before he engages a company to haul his family possessions, the ICC does not require notice of interlining until immediately before the truck drives away, and then only if the exact arrangements are *known* to the mover.

This regulation, as originally proposed in the 1961 rule-making proceeding, would have required disclosure under *all* circumstances; but the Commission bowed to the industry demand that the phrase "when these are known" be added. Thus a mover need only claim that he did not know in advance what interlining arrangements he would make, and he escapes prosecution under the section. The ICC regulations actually make it advantageous to him *not* to chart carefully a customer's move in advance.

This Commission capitulation is symptomatic of the

ICC's attitude toward the home moving industry. To have required disclosure of interlining arrangements under *all* circumstances would have required the industry to tighten its organization. It would have made the movers prearrange the details of the shipment of a customer's goods, rather than subject the customer to all the vagaries of *ad hoc,* last minute arrangements. Such regulatory pressure would have subjected the movers to the discomfort of change. The ICC was unwilling to apply it.

THE WAITING GAME

Before a family can even confront the damage and delays caused by warehousing, interlining, and careless handling, however, it must first get its possessions onto a van. Very frequently, vans arrive hours or days after the time or date promised. Such delays can be extremely burdensome to the customer. Often a family must vacate a home or apartment by a certain time; it may also have an obligation to arrive at the destination on a particular day. Such obligations aside, it is a trial simply to manage a family when one's appliances, utensils, and household items have been packed away. An obvious alternative would be to call another van line, but it is difficult if not impossible to arrange for a move on such short notice. Although the customer has made no legal commitment to a particular line until the bill of lading is signed, from the time he "books" with a particular company, he has effectively cast his die.

A university professor describes his attempts to communicate by telephone with a national van line, after a van had not arrived to pick up his furniture on any of four days promised:

. . . The dispatcher, harried by my insistence, at last directed that I call Mr. Etheridge at the Chicago terminal, asserting that he was the ultimate authority. . . . I spoke to Mr. Etheridge on the 'phone on the afternoon of Thursday the 16th. Even though everyone in the M . . . organization to whom I spoke implicitly insulted me by their inability or unwillingness to meet their obligation in my regard, only Mr. Etheridge was explicit in his insults. . . . I telephoned Mr. Earl Lewis early Thursday afternoon, first labeling myself "a dissatisfied customer" for your operator and asking her to accept charges. When she declined to do so, I offered to accept the charges and again asked for Mr. Lewis. His secretary informed me that he was busy and asked me to call back. I refused to do so and asked for the name of Mr. Lewis' superior there, and when told that it was Mr. Howard Jackson, I asked to talk with him. But his secretary informed me that he too was busy and asked me to call back. I once more refused to do so and asked for Mr. Jackson's superior. Since Mr. Jackson's secretary, telling me that his superior was you, the president, was loath to allow you to be disturbed by anyone so low and bothersome as a "dissatisfied customer" she found that Mr. Jackson could talk with me after all. . . .

After four days of waiting in vain, when his landlord threatened to have his furniture put into storage, this professor had to rent a truck, load his furniture into it, and drive it 800 miles with his pregnant wife and two children on the seat beside him.

As the movers assert, late pickups are often not their fault, at least not directly. A delay on one pickup or delivery, whether a customer's or the mover's fault, can set back a mover's entire schedule. But mostly pickup delays are a result of overbooking. Business-hustling local agents, paid according to the business they book, take on, free of liability, more customers than their company can realistically serve in the time promised. Another cause of delay to the average customer is the industry practice of rolling out the carpet for "King George." When a van is needed to carry a load paid for by a national account, it will be diverted from "John Smith" even if Mr. Smith placed his order for service far in advance. Affording such special treatment to national accounts would seem a violation of the sections of the Interstate Commerce Act prohibiting preferential treatment, but the Commission has neither passed a regulation against it nor even shown an awareness of the problem.

In 1960 the ICC found in a sample study that movers delivered later than the date promised 30 per cent of the time. Delays of days and weeks are common, and senators have received complaints of delays upwards of one month. Mr. and Mrs. W.D. were assured by a local agent that their possessions would be in Columbus, Ohio, when they themselves arrived. The shipment was a month late and the family had to pay $625 in motel, restaurant, and laundry expenses. Mrs. E.F.S. of Brooklyn, New York, wrote of friends, "The people in question not only suffered the annoyances mentioned, but the expense of one week's motel lodging both in New York and Arizona."

The ICC regulations do not require delivery on the date promised, leaving eager agent-bookers free to make extravagant promises. The regulations require only that the bill of lading note a "preferred delivery date or the period of time within which delivery of the shipment may be expected" (S1056.8). The section is carefully worded to avoid subjecting the movers to legal liability for the promise. The "General Information for Shippers of Household Goods," which movers are required to give to customers, reads, "Unless expedited service is to be rendered . . . the carrier is not obligated to deliver your goods on any particular day, but only to deliver within a reasonable time." More important, the "time within which" clause is often buried in a small space on the bill of lading so that the customer may not even be aware that he has no right to expect delivery on the exact date promised. Furthermore, by slipping a lengthy "time within which" into the small space in the crowded and unintelligible bill of lading, the mover affords himself an easy "out."

The ICC regulations help to immunize the movers from liability for late delivery. As provided by §1056.8 (c), as long as the mover notifies the customer once of any delay in delivery, he has fulfilled his duty under the regulations. Yet mere notification mitigates only a part of the customers grief; the worst hardships—the living expenses, the waiting, the calls to the national headquarters of the movers—must still be borne.

The Commission is remarkably inattentive to the customer's need for an *effective remedy*. Even if the mover does not comply with the Commission's innocuous notice requirements, he is liable to the Commission only. There is no provision in the ICC regulations, such as remission of a part of the transportation cost, which will benefit the customer and actually alleviate his plight. The customer himself does not even have a right of action under the Act. The only present value of the regulations to the customer is their deterrent effect, yet ICC enforcement of the regulations is so infrequent, and the fines for their violation so slight, that a mover might well choose to violate them rather than incur the expense of delivering on time. Lax enforcement denies the customer whatever protection there might be in the deterrent value of the regulations.

The customer's only recourse in such a case is to sue the mover in court. The attorney's fees usually preclude this remedy, and even without the attorney's fees the common law standard is in the mover's favor. Movers are required only to deliver with "reasonable dispatch," usually interpreted as the fastest possible service under the circumstances. A consumer might find it hard indeed to prove that a mover had not done his best under the circumstances, and the expense of assembling sufficient evidence would put the endeavor beyond most people's means.

Early deliveries present similar problems. Often the uncertainties of a mover's schedule result in a load arriving at its destination long before the customer. In such cases, the load is automatically taken to the storage warehouse, where it is subjected to loss and damage, and the customer must incur the cost both of storage and delivery. "Reasonable dispatch" can mean early as well as late, weighted as it is to the mover's, not the customer's convenience. One might think it reasonable that the movers provide free storage when they deliver a load early. As one victim of an early delivery put it, "Whose fault was it that our belongings went into storage?" But here again the movers intone phrases like "rebate" and "unfair advantage" and the ICC nods in agreement.

Mr. and Mrs. R.D.H. of Lansing, Michigan, were handed a $162 storage bill upon arrival from Los Angeles because their possessions had arrived ten days earlier than the Los Angeles agent had promised. The ICC regulations provide no help for people like Mr. and Mrs. H. because, by the grim irony of ICC regulations, a return of the storage fee might be deemed by the Commission an illegal "rebate."

THE SUMMER RUSH

The movers usually blame these service deficiencies— late pickups, late deliveries, warehousing and interlining en route—on the "summer rush." It is true that Americans prefer to move during the summer and, as a result, over 50 per cent of the movers' business falls between May and September. Customers expect good service in the summer months largely because they are promised it by local agents. Perhaps more would move off-season if they were given an honest appraisal of the difficulties of providing satisfactory service in the summer. The movers claim that they lack the equipment to handle this business, but fail to add that they do nothing to alleviate or discourage the summer rush. On the contrary, they encourage it, and they have acted in concert to defeat those among them who would act differently.

In September, 1968, an application by Republic Van and Storage to reduce certain of its off-season rates by 10 per cent was rejected by a three-Commissioner division of the ICC. According to the *Wall Street Journal,* "The request was opposed by most major moving companies, at least some of which, it is understood, would have difficulty offering a similar slack season discount. . . . Republic sought approval of the discount to relieve demands on business in the peak June-September period." Republic appealed the decision and its plan was approved over a year later by the full Commission. The case is but another illustration of an industry attempt, this time unsuccessful, to use the ICC to suppress competitive pressure that might result in better service to the public.

In fact, the inability of the moving industry to handle the summer rush is due mainly to its own structural flaws. Without competition from other kinds of transportation, and protected by the rate bureaus and ICC regulations, the movers have not been subject to pressure to modernize. Routing, for example, is done on an *ad hoc* basis; as shown above, the movers are not sure what will happen to a person's belongings even after they are picked up. Communications between drivers, agents, and central dispatchers and officers are deficient.

Some of the structural weaknesses contributing to summer service deficiencies are actually fostered by "regulation." The parceling out of separate "operating territories" to individual carriers, and the reluctance with which the ICC extends them, creates a need for continual interlining. The lack of coordination between different van lines servicing the same territory means that much excess capacity goes unused, even in the summer months. Often a delayed pickup is not caused by the unavailability of a moving van; the cause is that a van of the particular van line with which the customer booked is not available. Another van line might have a van sitting in the customer's own city, two-thirds full, waiting for another order to carry a full load to the very place the customer is going, but without coordination between the van lines, both customer and the two-thirds loaded van continue to sit. The ICC might reasonably *require* such coordinated service, especially in light of the industry's admissions that it cannot handle the summer surge of business. The requirement could be considered a fair exchange for the antitrust exemption granted to the industry's tariff-making bureaus—thereby making the antitrust exemption work in the customer's behalf as well as in the carrier's.

In spite of the seasonal nature of the moving business, there might be more fancy than substance to the summer rush alibi for service failures. In 1967 the American Mover's Conference did a study of the complaints it received according to month of delivery. It would appear that there is a constant ratio between complaints received and deliveries made. For example, assuming that the movers make roughly half the deliveries in February as they make in July, they receive complaints on an almost identical proportion of the moves for each month.

COMPLAINTS RECEIVED, BY MONTH OF DELIVERY [1] 1967

January	67	July	109
February	51	August	90
March	45	September	83
April	40	October	38
May	49	November	20
June	86	December	08

THE TARIFF MESS

To the typical family man, the tariffs charged by a household mover might have been brewed in a witches' kettle. They are highly complicated, and most people never even see them. Tariffs are documented in tomes on file at the mover's headquarters and in a room on the seventh floor of the ICC headquarters in Washington. Thus, when the typical American is handed a bill in the front yard of his new home, he has no idea what the basic rate structure is, or whether it was fairly applied. The billing process takes place at the national company headquarters, usually hundreds, if not thousands, of miles away.

Unfortunately, billing "errors" are not infrequent. One source close to the industry (a former veteran traffic manager for one of the largest home movers) estimates that of the twelve million Americans who moved in 1969, at least one-half were overcharged and did not know it. During an interview he documented an example: a customer was charged a "stair charge" (an extra assessment for carrying furniture upstairs) of $121, at a rate which applies to business, not household moves. "This guy doesn't know a bill of lading * from a bale of hay or a tariff from a telephone book," was the expert's comment.

Often billing "errors" are merely the inadvertent misapplication of complicated tariffs. Typing, decimal, and addition errors are also common. Errors frequently occur when a clerk multiplies the weight by the mileage instead of by the rate per mile. Along with these clerical errors, there is the "bumping" of weights by the movers themselves. "Bumping" is the trade term for intentionally increasing the scale weight of a shipment. The practice is prohibited by federal regulations, but it occurs nevertheless. For example, different tractors will be used when getting the "tare," or weight before loading, than the weight after loading. Or two loads will be put on the same van, a weight taken, and both customers charged for the combined weight. Two practices expressly forbidden by the federal regulations also occur: getting tare weight with an empty gas tank and filling the tank before getting the loaded weight (which adds up to 600 pounds), and taking the loaded weight with men and equipment in the truck—while these were not on the truck when the tare was taken. Although customers have a right to watch the weighing, few can because of the pressures of moving day. Even if they do, however, they have no way of knowing what was on the van when the tare was taken, before their own possessions were loaded. Such weighing practices are difficult if not impossible to prove after the fact. The industry source says that about 20 per cent of at least one company's weights are bumped.

An ICC field agent, by his own admission not a vigorous enforcer of home moving regulations, says of weight bumping, "There is more of it than I would like to see." †

---

* The contract between home owner and mover.

† Weight bumping was the subject of a study released by the Comptroller General of the United States, in July, 1964. The report was called *Excess Transportation Costs Due to Erroneous Weights On Military Shipments of Household Goods*. The study revealed that

Errors occur in the packing process as well. Some shippers are billed for containers which were not used. Also when the movers do the packing, they sometimes use excess filler material so as to use and charge for more cartons.

Most home owners accept the mover's charges, assured by the ICC certificate number on the side of the truck that the movers are "regulated" and that somebody must therefore be watching them. In fact, nobody is watching over the billing process—moving bills are not audited. As to the scrutability of the tariffs themselves, the ICC has revealed no sensitivity to the individual home owner's needs for a

---

65.5 per cent of the observed shipments weighed less upon reweighing at destination than the carriers had claimed on the weight ticket. The average overcharge was for 365 pounds. Observations of actual weighings revealed the following weight-increasing practices:

1. Drivers and/or crewmen remaining on the vehicle during weighing.
2. Weighing without full fuel tanks. (When the tare—unloaded weight—is taken without full fuel tanks, the tanks can be filled after loading and the weight attributed to the customer's shipment.) The General Accounting Office found that only 35 per cent of the vans observed had full fuel tanks (as required by federal regulations) when the tare weight was taken. Reweighing at destination of vans originally weighed without full fuel tanks revealed that an average overcharge of 542 pounds had been made to the customer—the Government.
3. Improper certification of weights: in some cases drivers were allowed to weigh their own trucks; in other cases, weighmasters signed weight tickets and let the drivers fill in the weight.
4. Using the same tare weight for two different shipments loaded consecutively onto the same vehicle.

As to ICC enforcement of its weighing regulations, the report said:

Information from various sources, including direct observations by GAO of drivers' practices in weighing household goods shipments, shows widespread disregard for weighing procedures prescribed by the ICC. Some of these practices definitely inflated the charges billed to the Government; other practices, although not necessarily causing erroneous charges, demonstrate laxity and carelessness on the part of drivers and carriers in protecting the interests of shippers.

(The report found that D.O.D. was paying $5 million annually in excess shipping charges due to weight bumping, and that although these practices had been studied and reported in 1960, no remedial action had been taken.) The Comptroller General of the United States, Report to Congress of the United States, *Excess transportation Costs Due to Erroneous Weights on Military Shipments of Household Goods*, July, 1964.

more simplified rate schedule than those which only the shipping departments of large businesses can interpret. The Commission, which has the power to initiate complaints, lacks the manpower to do so and has not attempted to acquire that manpower. A section chief at the Commission reveals that with 2,000,000 shipments of all kinds per day, it is impossible for his staff to police this area. Instead, he must rely on complaints. Shippers, he adds, usually do not know when the tariffs have been misapplied, and they do not know enough about the ICC to complain even if they were aware of a misapplication. This section chief goes on to note that the *business* shipper does not complain because he can always pass his increased costs on to his customers. But the homemoving customer has nobody to whom to pass on his expense.

Even if the tariffs were applied as written, however, they are not likely to be "just and reasonable" as required by Section 316 (a) of the Interstate Commerce Act. The movers' rates have never been subjected to the rigorous scrutiny which competition automatically forces upon rates of different carriers. First, contrary to common misconception, the ICC does not set or prescribe movers' rates. It merely requires that rates be published and filed. It has the *power* to challenge the rates, but it never does. Second, again contrary to the common notion and to the movers' communications to their customers, they do not have to charge the same rates. The Commission merely compels them to adhere to the tariffs they file.

The movers are permitted, under special provisions of the Interstate Commerce Act which exempts them from antitrust regulations, to engage in price fixing by belonging to "rate bureaus." Since all, or virtually all, movers belong to the rate bureaus, they will generally not challenge the rates the bureaus file. Further, in home moving there is no competition from other modes of transportation. Thus home movers enjoy virtual freedom from the downward pressure on rates that might be exerted either by competing truckers or by other modes. Their customers, consisting of the unorganized public, lack the awareness and power to protest the rates filed by the moving industry at the ICC.

One of the special exemptions from even minimal ICC scrutiny which the moving industry enjoys has to do with rate increases. Most carriers are required to submit, annually, sufficient economic data to justify the rates they charge. Whatever the shortcomings of the Commission's rate judging formulae, at least the other carriers must meet them. Evidently, however, the movers have convinced the Commission that their rate increases are so infrequent that it would not be worth the expense to file sufficient cost data annually to justify their rates.

A source close to the industry claims that the movers increase their tariffs infrequently only because they jack them up 300 per cent more than necessary each time. Thus they can operate profitably for a long time without changing rates, and they do not undergo annual Commission review. The Commission does not even demand justifying cost figures when the movers *do* up their rates. One high official in the ICC's Bureau of Accounts admits that when the movers filed their last rate increase, they did not bring in enough data to show the boost was needed, but the Commission let them have the increase anyway, demanding only a promise that they would bring in sufficient data at the *next* increase. According to this official, the Cost Section does not make independent investigations of the movers' costs, but relies instead on their own annual reports, which he described as "cursory." *

It is questionable whether moving rates are based in any way on costs. In fact, it is difficult to ascertain *how* the movers arrive at their rates. In part, the movers' rates are straight mileage rates, applicable in any part of the country. Thus, a move between equidistant points in the Rocky Mountains would cost the same as a move over flat southern terrain, even though the labor and trucking costs might be vastly different in each case. It would appear either that the rates for the low-cost moves are subsidizing the high-cost

* Furthermore, there is reason to believe that the real costs in the home-moving industry are largely hidden from view. As the national van-lines companies are set up, the hauling costs are borne largely by the individual operators, who are either local agents, owner-operators working under leasing arrangements, or who are in the cooperative companies (actually the participating owners of the national company itself). It would appear, therefore, that an ICC cost verification analysis could probe no deeper than the first level of reported cost. In other words, the cost figures which the ICC might verify would never include the expenses of the actual operators. But it is within the agent's operations that the real moving costs—the driver and vehicle expense—are buried. He may be grossly inefficient; or he may be getting returns far above his costs and hiding it.

moves or else that reasonable profits are being made on the high-cost moves and exorbitant profits on the low-cost moves. This appears to be the case in a move between Boston, Massachusetts, and Champaign, Illinois, or between Meridian, Mississippi, and Oakly, Kansas. As an expert in moving tariffs has observed, the labor costs would be much lower in the southern move than in the northern, yet the tariffs applied are identical.

It would appear from other indices that ICC regulation is maintaining moving rates at artificially high levels. In some instances, the rates for interstate moves are *more* than those for intrastate moves of equal distance, not under ICC jurisdiction. For example, a tariff expert has pointed out that a home owner moving four thousand pounds of possessions from St. Louis, Missouri, to Kansas City, Missouri—252 miles—pays $5.05 per hundredweight. His neighbor, moving from St. Louis, Missouri, to Kansas City, Kansas—255 miles—pays $6.07 per hundredweight, plus higher packing charges.

So-called "directional" differences are another aspect of the movers' tariffs which invite explanation. The movers' tariffs provide that between certain points it costs more to move in one direction than in another. For example, a family moving four thousand pounds from Chicago to Milwaukee pays $5.00 per hundredweight, or $200 (not including packing and insurance). His Milwaukee counterpart moving to Chicago pays $4.01 per hundredweight, or $160.40.*

The ICC has not questioned whether a backhaul problem exists between two such points at Milwaukee and Chicago, or whether other cost or demand factors justify the differential. And it is not clear that moving vans go back and forth along the same route like railroads or transcontinental truckers. It would seem that instead they crisscross along irregular routes, going where there are loads to carry. In short, the directional differentials found in the home moving

---

* Such directional differentials are not unknown where carriers experience a backhaul problem; that is, where most or all of the available traffic is going in one direction, and only by substantially lowering the rates for the backhaul can a carrier utilize capacity which would otherwise be completely unutilized. The railroads and transcontinental truckers often experience this problem.

industry invite the attention of anyone concerned about carriers' rates, as the ICC purportedly is.

If moving rates merely invite suspicion, the tariffs for packing charges are clearly irrational. Most carriers adhere to two tariffs. One applies between any two points in the United States except points entirely within eleven western States, Canada, and Baja, California; the second applies between points in these latter places, and from these places to the Provinces and El Paso, Texas.

Each of these tariffs has two identical schedules of packing charges. A lengthy analysis of these tariffs reveals evident economic discrimination by the movers resulting from different charges for the same service. The packing bill of a man moving from Klamath Falls, Oregon, to Omaha will be 8.5 per cent lower than that of his next-door neighbor moving by the same agent and van line to Denver, Colorado.

The present tariff structure, based on mileage, encourages the unwarranted manipulation of moving charges. The rates change at intervals of miles, for example every twenty miles. Between Chicago and Washington, one rate applies for from 661 to 680 miles, then a different rate applies between 681 and 700 miles. It is very easy, according to this same expert, for a mover to add or subtract two or three miles on a move which is near the "breakpoint." Such an "error" of only one or two miles can change the rate from ten to twenty cents per hundredweight; an error of ten miles can change it from fifty to seventy-five cents per hundredweight. This is another of the billing "errors" which is nearly impossible for the average customer to discover, and which the ICC refuses to investigate.

C.O.D. ONLY

In most dealings with "unregulated" business, the customer has an ace in the hole against service inadequacies: if he has suffered lost because of poor service, or damage to his possessions, he can simply withhold payment until the damage is adjusted. With the blessings (and sanctions) of the ICC, however, the movers require cash on delivery. Thus the customer does not even have the option of stopping a check once he has paid the movers. No matter how good the individual consumer's credit rating, most moving companies will extend credit only to their national accounts.

The special circumstances of household moving make it impossible to withhold payment in the absence of prior credit agreement. The driver has the owner's goods on his truck. Many drivers will not even open the doors until they have the cash in hand.

Once the van is unloaded, the customer may discover loss or damage to his goods, possibly up to or exceeding the cost of the delivery. The assistant Attorney General for the State of Alabama related such an experience to Senator Magnuson:

> . . . I was also informed that the goods could not be unloaded unless I paid this amount in cash or certified check. At great inconvenience I made arrangements for such payment. When the goods were unloaded . . . numerous items belonging to me, valued at $500, were missing [cost of move—$335.64]. . . . I attempted to have the van line locate my property, but they never did so.

Another customer wrote:

> I hope you realize you are forced to pay in full before they unload your household goods so you have no way to know if there is any damage claim.
>
> If there is, try to collect if you can; they have you at their control.

And another:

> . . . We feel the laws are rigged in favor of the moving companies—bill must be paid on the spot. How much chance does a claim have then?

The consumer is up against a wall. If he balks on payment, his possessions go off to the warehouse where they accumulate storage charges until he changes his mind and decides to pay.

The refusing of credit to individual home owners is simply one more industry practice sanctioned by the Commission regardless of its effect upon the consumer. The ICC-prescribed "Important Notice to Shippers of Household Goods," which the movers must give to customers, reads as though the Commission itself endorsed the practice: "The carrier *will require* payment in cash, money order, or certified check before unloading your goods, unless credit arrangements were made beforehand. Be prepared in case the actual charges demanded at this time are greater than what was estimated." (49CFR§1056-12(a)) While this statement does not say that credit is not allowed, the ICC-prescribed notice gives the C.O.D.-only policy the color of law. Complaint letters to Congressmen indicate that movers often tell their customers that they are not *allowed* to grant credit.

That the movers do grant credit to their national accounts is clearly recognized by the Commission. In sanctioning the systematic denial of credit to individual consumers, the Commission appears to be endorsing discriminatory treatment and preferential service in behalf of the national accounts, in violation of the Interstate Commerce Act.

Even the favored national accounts, however, are considered less important—judging by Commission responses —than the moving companies themselves. In a ruling decided in May, 1969,* some of the national accounts requested that the Commission extend from seven to fifteen days the length of time for which credit could be extended to them. They needed this time, they told the Commission, to coordinate the payment of moving bills with their other bills and to check the bills against the tariffs. The Commission denied the request for an extended credit period. In the same proceeding, however, it granted the movers' request for more time in which to send out bills. The Commission was sympathetic to the movers' bookkeeping problems—that it took them time to amass the billing data from their scattered local agents—but not to the analogous bookkeeping problems of the shippers.

The Commission's policy of sanctioning the denial of credit to individuals represents a policy choice, placing upon the customer the burden of trying to recoup an overcharge or a damage claim from the company, after payment has been made in full. In light of the industry's rusty machinery for responding to such attempts, the burden is considerable. The burden could have been put upon the industry to collect a disputed charge, as it is in most un-"regulated" areas of business. In view of the industry's economic and legal bargaining power advantages over the consumer, one might question if the burdens have been allotted fairly.

* *Ex Parte MC-1* (sub. no. 1).

LOSS AND DAMAGE CLAIMS:
THE CUSTOMER IS ALWAYS WRONG

February 12, 1969

Dear Senator Magnuson,

. . . This shipment was a complete loss. All of the clothing was moth-eaten and unusable. The furniture had been severely damaged—exposed to excessive water and heat. The stuffed pieces—couch, chairs, dinette set and so on had actually been used by someone. . . .

Sincerely,
Mrs. W . . . J . . . D . . .

Of all the consumer problems under ICC jurisdiction, none has caused more grief and loss to the public than the loss and damage to possessions entrusted to household movers. The ICC found in 1960 that over one-half the complaints it received regarding household moving concerned loss and damage. It further found that claims were filed with movers on *one-quarter of the shipments tendered*, and that one-fifth of these claims were never even acknowledged by the movers.[2] (The Commission did not study the adequacy of settlements on claims which were acknowledged.)

The situation has not improved since 1960. Between July 1, 1967, and September 15, 1968, the Commission received, according to then Chairman Paul Tierney, 962 complains within and 4581 complaints not within ICC jurisdiction. Since the Commission regards all loss and damage complaints as "non-jurisdictional," and since no other problem is put to the Commission in such quantity, the overwhelming majority of these "non-jurisdictional" complaints appear to concern loss and damage.

A brief look at industry practices reveals why claims handling engenders so much dissatisfaction. The customer is at a disadvantage from the start, because drivers are assessed the first $50 of every claim. When they inventory a shipment on the bill of lading they describe every piece as "marked," "scratched," "gauged," "chipped." Complaint letters reveal that brand-new furniture has been so described.

One letter related that a brand-new playpen was inventoried "torn, soiled, scratched," and a brand-new coffee table "scratched, top and sides." Another said, "My own bill of lading indicated bad scratches on four pieces of furniture which came through the move completely un-scratched."

The driver's notations are scrawled in code on a cramped inventory list, and during the rush of moving day a harried customer rarely feels he can check the list item by item. Housewives are understandably reluctant to second-guess and antagonize the drivers loading the belongings.*

Thus the customer begins his move with a contract describing his belongings as damaged. The shipment is then subjected to incalculable handling deficiencies en route—warehousing, interlining, crowding, etc. Heavy chests and boxes are put on top of sofas. Foam cushions from couches are used as padding to protect automobiles. †

In order to complete a delivery, a driver will often pick up helpers from a street corner. Such help is cheaper than regular help, and an owner-operator working on a commission can pocket the difference. Local agents bear no responsibility for loss or damage, and are not eager to help. Drivers, though supposedly liable for the first $50, know that their companies are virtually immune from claims. "Well, file a claim," or "Call the company," has been the reply to more than one customer who has complained to the driver of the condition or handling of his wares.

Collection for loss and damage is extremely difficult for the customer because, as a former ICC attorney has pointed out, the roots of the problem lie in the structure of the industry itself. The movers are self-insured, and they handle

---

* A customer who was foreclosed from a claim for loss because the driver had neglected to inventory certain items, described the process: ". . . the men who take the goods out of the home scribble on narrow spaced lines almost illegibly and speedily one's household effects on a small form. They put signs here and there, scribble other notations here and there and to most of us it is so much Greek. . . ."

† Some descriptions of mover handling practices which have come to the Senate Commerce Committee: ". . . I place great importance upon clean bedding so we bought boxes from the mover. . . . We watched them being boxed and *sealed* and placed in the van . . . our things were transferred to another van without our prior knowledge. One mattress is pliable foam rubber, and apparently there wasn't room in the second van for the box so the mattress was taken out of the box and stuffed into a small space in the van. . . . a dish pack of fragile china and crystal was put under a couple of boxes of very heavy books and magazines and a very nice walnut-finished headboard and footboard of a bed was put under a heavy steel playground swingset."

loss and damage claims themselves. But they have never "tooled-up" to handle this part of their business adequately, and there has never been pressure from consumers or from the ICC to compel them to do so. Thus, as complaints document by the hundreds, the movers continue to disregard estimates, demand purchase receipts for items bought years ago, apply outlandish depreciation rates, and contradict their local agents when the latter authorize repairs. None of these practices violate ICC regulations, and most customer claims are too small to justify the expense of suing a moving company.

Had the Commission invested half the energy in devising remedies within its authority that it has spent denying its authority and defending that denial, consumers might find the scales tipped slightly more in their favor. But the Commission has vigorously and continuously denied authority over loss and damage claims. Complaint letters referred to the Commission by Congress are answered with the Chairman's cheery regrets that the Commission "does not have jurisdiction to settle loss and damage claims." In a recent letter to the Senate Commerce Committee, expressing her opinion on a proposed bill, the Chairman used variations of the phrase "the Commission has no power to adjudicate loss and damage claims" three times within one and one-quarter pages.

The Commission rarely seems to consider what it could do or what the complainant really wants it to do. Most of the complaint letters do not ask it to *settle* a claim, but merely to force the mover to settle it. Some letters detail a whole list of grievances of which a damage claim is just one. Yet they all get the same response. It is as though a man staggered into a doctor's office covered with blood, told the doctor he had a gash in his head, a slit down his back, and a broken tooth, and the doctor replied, "Sorry, I don't fix broken teeth."

When questioned about the extent of the Commission's authority over claims-handling practices, Chairman Brown told us that she would have to "investigate" the matter. Her hearing examiner, Richard D. Heironimus, echoed in another interview that the Commission should investigate its authority over claims. Had Chairman Brown merely consulted the Commission's own files, she might have found the answer to this question. In response to the identical query, a recent Chairman sent a letter to a Congressional Committee spelling out with extensive legal precedent the extent of the Commission's authority over claims practices. His letter recognized that the Commission had "consistently held" that it did not have the authority to "determine the merits . . . of *particular* loss and damage claims" (emphasis added) but that the Commission *"does possess the authority to regulate* the carriers' *practices and tariff rules* on the subject." (Emphasis added.) The letter pointed out that the Commission had exerted this authority regarding shipments of grain and eggs. Furthermore, had Chairman Brown read the 1964 household goods rule-making decision, she would have found the Commission announcing publicly that "the examiner was correct in finding that the Commission has the duty to require reasonable practices by the motor carriers in the handling of loss and damage claims."

Home movers, unlike carriers of grain and eggs, are subject to *no* ICC regulations prescribing "reasonable" claims-handling procedures which are clearly unreasonable. The Act does not require that every standard of reasonableness be spelled out in a regulation before the Commission can prosecute. The Commission's authority to determine *fitness* is another enforcement tool which has lain idle. When one-quarter of the annual household moves provoke loss and damage claims, a carrier's procedures for settling these claims might be deemed an important part of his "fitness." But that criterion is never applied to challenge operating authorities.

The Commission has been equally timid in rule making, and so far has applied only the most superficial of remedies to the problem. In the 1964 rule-making decision, it issued a regulation requiring the mover to acknowledge receipt of a damage claim within thirty days, and to make a definite offer of denial within 120 days. Although this regulation does prevent the movers from ignoring damage claims, as they had done 20 per cent of the time,[3] it is only the most meager of beginnings. It merely requires that a customer be told "no" instead of having to infer it from silence. The customer is still without help in achieving a just and reasonable settlement. And as with so many of the Commission's regulations, there is no redress for the consumer even if the mover violates the regulation. A mover prosecuted for not responding to a damage claim at most pays a fine to the government. The customer, the one actually hurt by the practice, gets nothing.

A first step in dealing adequately with the claims problem would be to regulate the practices which give rise to loss and damage claims. The Commission should prohibit such damage-causing practices as warehousing and interlining without the customer's permission, and the hiring of cheap, untrained, temporary labor from street corners. It should set standards for warehousing, and for equipment and padding used on the vans. It should impose more liability on drivers and local agents.

A second step would be to guarantee the customer a fair hearing on his claim. Merely requiring some response to his claim hardly insures the consumer of an adequate settlement. An often mentioned solution would require ICC arbitration of consumer claims. One ICC bureau head objected that binding arbitration would deny the customer of his right to a trial, but individual home owners do not really have this right when they cannot afford to exercise it. Commissioner Kenneth Tuggle objected that the Commission should not become a small claims court.* It is true that the Commission should not plunge any deeper than necessary into a time- and manpower-consuming case-by-case approach, but the Commission itself would not have to be the arbitrator. It would merely have to prescribe standards for arbitration. A possible prototype for such arbitration already exists. In the "un-regulated" New York-New Jersey metropolitan area, loss and damage claims have been entrusted to the arbitration of the Office of Impartial Chairman. According to that Office's director, it receives complaints from customers, investigates the mover's records, holds a hearing, and renders a decision binding and confirmable in the New York State Supreme Court. Most complaints are settled in two weeks, and the service is free to the public. If the Chairman's description is accurate, this office could be a model for a reasonable claims procedure which the ICC might require of the movers under its jurisdiction.

The prescription of reasonable claims procedures, what-

* The Commission seems not to mind massive adjudication of such matters as whether carrier x will be allowed to carry cocoa beans as well as coffee beans between points y and z, however.

ever form it takes, will require imaginative and exploratory use of the ICC's authority. It is even possible that the ICC would need new legislative authority to act effectively in this area—but the Commission has yet to make a gesture toward trying. One wonders whether the much postulated lack of authority is an obstacle or an alibi. Sources on Capitol Hill reveal that the Commission has never asked Congress for added authority in this area. According to the Commission staff, it does not really want it. Congress should look carefully at the ICC's performance with regard to claims procedures, and either give it the authority it may require, or else transfer regulation of the home movers to an agency more responsive to the public need.

WHAT IS TO BE DONE

All tariff floors should be removed in home moving, so that movers could bid even below their published tariffs to attract business. Published tariffs should then become mere maximums, checked by careful regulatory cost analysis, and carriers could quote some customers lower rates than others, as competition required. The Commission demonology would label this practice "preferential" or "discriminatory" pricing, claiming that such pricing would enable certain shippers to gain an unfair market advantage over their competitors by sustaining lower transportation costs. But individual consumers moving their household effects are not like farmers shipping grain to market. Their transportation rate does not represent a cost component of a commodity going to a competitive market. As long as maximum rates are regulated, and standards of service and financial responsibility are maintained, it would appear that an individual consumer would have everything to gain and nothing to lose from the possibility of being offered a lower rate than that published.

The arguments usually used against such a plan are anachronistic. The larger operators, it is said, could take advantage either of their supposed economies of scale or their ability to sustain temporary losses in order to price the smaller operators out of the market. This "destructive competition" argument, which an observer at the D.O.T. has styled the Commission's "argument by catastrophe," has been supported by nothing except piety and faith. The evidence would appear to rebut its applicability to home moving. First, it is not apparent that the larger operators either want to or can price the smaller ones out of business. They have not yet reached the limits of the existing market. There is more demand during the summer months than the movers can meet; and the outer limits of any one mover's share of the market seems not determined by the share taken by other movers, but only by such factors as its own ability to invest in equipment which would lie idle part of the year.

Thus, it is not apparent that there is a monopolizing urge in the household goods industry which only minimum price regulation is keeping in check. Nor is it apparent that the larger movers are so rich that they would be able to undersell their smaller competitors. To the contrary, it has already been noted that the independent movers who do not join the tariff bureaus often undersell the larger national van line companies. Finally, if the industry's own allegations are true, the large movers would probably not have the economic resilience to bear losses long enough to price the smaller operators out of the market. As already discussed, in *Ex Parte MC-1* (sub. no. 1), the movers defeated an attempt by shippers to extend the length of time they would have to pay credited bills, on the grounds that the longer extension of credit would deplete their working capital. If the movers' working capital is so precarious that the extension of credit for an additional week would deplete it, it would seem highly unlikely that they could sustain near or below cost prices long enough to drive their competitors out of business.

But what if the larger operators should somehow use competitive pricing to gain control of the home moving business? As long as reasonable and fair maximum rates, and standards of service, are enforced by a regulatory body, there has been no showing that the public would be harmed. On the contrary, knowledgeable people close to the household moving industry maintain that the key to better service to the consumer lies in the *consolidation* of the industry and the elimination of *fragmentation* of service.

In other words, far from being harmful, the consolidation which might result from the abolition of minimum rates might be a positive good which the ICC might well actively promote. In a statement before the House Special Studies Subcommittee on Government Operations as related to the

Household Goods Moving Industry, the independent-minded president of one of the nation's larger moving companies said that the basic weakness of the household goods moving industry is ". . . the *large number* of carriers offering service to just about anywhere, USA." He added,

It is my studied opinion that the future of the household goods moving and storage industry must be developed around a fewer number of carriers serving the communities of the nation with a large number of affiliated agents who are well organized, experienced, and mindful of both the needs of the American public, the requirements of the regulatory bodies, and the policy of its carrier affiliate.

A former national van line worker agrees, and has proposed that short of industry consolidation, at the very least, "clearing-houses" should be established at the larger urban centers so that customer shipments can be matched with any available van space, regardless of the van line the consumer booked with. (In Seattle, Washington, there is a strong feeling that an oversupply of carriers is contributing to the "small-shipments" problem, and the Seattle Traffic Association is proposing to empower the Washington Public Utilities Commission to compel mergers of motor carriers.)

Not only has the Commission failed to encourage consolidation in the moving industry, but by continuing to grant out bits and pieces of operating authority, it has actively encouraged fragmentation. The last staff study the Commission dared to authorize on the subject of consolidation, in 1942, recommended the deregulation of the trucking industry. A chapter in the more recent Doyle Report is devoted to the problem of eliminating the fragmentation of operating rights. But the Commission has ignored such advice. As a transportation expert who once worked at the Commission has said, the Commission has yet to realize that the question is not *whether* to regulate, but how to regulate. On another occasion this source explained simply, "The Commission is afraid to upset the truckers."

At the very least, it is plain that the present mode of regulation has encouraged stasis in the home moving industry and has insulated it from the need to change. The Commission could have compensated for the absence of competitive pressure by itself imposing high standards of service upon the movers. But instead of prescribing stand-

ards of quality, it has continued to accept industry practice
as the norm.

The broader meaning of ICC acquiescence to current
industry practice, ignoring quality and insulating the industry from the need for change, is illustrated in a recent case
on which an ICC hearing examiner has issued a recommended report.[4] The case involved the application of a large
national moving company for authority to operate in all
forty-eight continental states. Under its present ICC certificate, it is excluded from eleven. In order to gain this authority, it is required by the Interstate Commerce Act to demonstrate a need for proposed service, a "public convenience
and necessity." This moving company, fortunately endowed
with the resources to make such a demonstration, conducted
a telephone survey of movers in a metropolitan area during
the summer. Predictably, the survey revealed that the supply
of service was insufficient to meet the demand for moves to
places this company was seeking authority to serve. It would
seem the company met the Commission on its own terms in
showing that a "public necessity" existed for its services.

The applicant went further. It urged the hearing examiner
to consider the *qualitative* as well as the mere *quantitative*
dimension of "public convenience and necessity." Even if
there existed a sufficiency of service, the applicant argued
that it could introduce a higher *quality* of service. Unlike
most of the larger movers, this company does not disperse
responsibility among local agents. Instead, all of its representatives are company employees. This system, it argued,
reduces or eliminates the abuses of customers which the
agency system fosters. It supported this assertion with the
testimony of institutions which had employed the services
of many moving companies besides itself.

Predictably, the national van lines already empowered
with forty-eight state authority protested the application.
Mustering their formidable collective resources they argued
vigorously that the applicant had not shown an existing
need for more service. The hearing examiner agreed with
the protestants, and rejected the applicant's telephone survey on evidence of technical grounds.

The protestants' argument flatly contradicted their public
statements in other forums. They have vociferously contended that stricter regulation would be counterproductive
because their real problem is their inability to meet the

demand for service in the summer. A recent editorial in a movers' trade journal said that:

. . . the biggest part of the problem is that there is *too much work in a short time period* that causes the big breakdown More rules and more regulations are only going to slow down the available equipment and less of the public will be serviced during the peak season. . . . We must come up with a solution which will spread the work over a larger period of time. . . . All the regulations in the world cannot solve our problems, when there is *more work available than can possibly be serviced*. (Emphasis supplied.) [5]

Despite their admitted inability to meet the existing demand for service, the movers were able to use ICC "due process" to defeat—at least in its initial stages—the entrance of a new competitor.

The ICC's examiner also asserted that the applicant did not really *need* the authority it was requesting. It could already serve the states outside its authority by entering into interlining agreements. This examiner's concept of the applicant's need for additional operating authority typifies the response which proposed service improvements and innovations have met at the Commission. The applicant's argument was that although it could presently serve all forty-eight states, it could provide *better* service if it did not have to subject its customers' belongings to the uncertainties, delays, and loss and damage which result from interlining. But the examiner's primary concern, apparently, was that the *status quo* should be preserved.

One wonders what would happen if a number of potential competitors offering significant service improvements sought ICC certification. One student of the household moving industry sees the introduction of containerization as a solution to the industry's problems. Containerization would enable a shipment to be carried by the fastest and cheapest means available. It could reduce handling costs and loss and damage. Could a potential competitor proposing to offer such an innovation gain entry so long as existing services were deemed "adequate"? Can the Interstate Commerce Act accommodate such an intermodal service? If authority to regulate the movers is kept in the Commission, and the Commission continues in its solicitousness of established methods and entrenched interests, a slow and painful birth is promised such innovations.

It is highly questionable whether the Interstate Commerce Act is the appropriate statute for governing relations between the consumers and suppliers of home moving services. The Motor Carrier section was drafted when trucking was an infant industry in need of protection, and it was constructed primarily with dealings between truckers and commercial shippers in mind. The conclusion is compelling that the ICC is ill suited by statutory authority and certainly by inclination to regulate relations between consumers and home movers. The Commission's whole judicial (some at D.O.T. would add "medieval") apparatus, so amenable to powerful and organized shippers and carriers, is utterly foreign to and beyond the reach of the average individual consumer. The Commercial shipper-carrier context is so indigenous to the Act, and to the Commission's administration of it, that the household moving industry will probably not be fairly and effectively regulated until control over it is vested under another authority. Under another authority, the regulation of household moving might escape the ghosts of 1887 and 1935.

Whether or not the ICC retains jurisdiction over the home movers, the regulatory process must begin to work more in the consumers' behalf. The movers have so far been the beneficiaries of "regulation." They are protected from new competitors and from prosecution for collaborative price fixing. While sheltered from competition on the one hand, they have, on the other, been free from regulatory pressure to modernize, innovate, or even to provide adequate service. They are not required by ICC regulations to meet such basic service obligations as publishing rates which their customers can understand, picking up and delivering at the times promised, providing careful handling, and making fair claims settlements. They have not even had to prove to the Commission that their rates are just and reasonable, as required by the Interstate Commerce Act. Because the movers serve individual consumers, their tariffs and practices have been immune from the pressure which organized and powerful users of other carriers might exert through the formidable ICC procedural maze.

In order to change the nature of ICC regulation so that the home moving public—rather than commercial industry interests—benefits from the agency's protection, the following recommendations are worth serious consideration:

1. Remove the movers' antitrust immunity regarding rates, so that consumers will be able to benefit from price competition, and so that rates will not be artificially maintained to provide profits for the less efficient operators.
2. Reduce or abolish restrictions on routes and lower requirements for entry in the home moving industry, so that
   a. existing demand will be more adequately served;
   b. innovation will be facilitated and encouraged;
   c. better service will be achieved by reducing the need for interlining;
   d. competition will be encouraged.
3. Conduct an annual cost analysis of movers' rates for maximum rate ceilings.
4. Provide public counsel to represent the public in all home moving matters before the Commission.
5. Require the simplification of tariffs, and their publication in a form which customers can understand.
6. Simplify and clarify the bill of lading—the basic contract between mover and customer.
7. Prescribe standards of accountability of local agents to customers, so that there will be less dispersal of responsibility. Encourage the internal simplification of the industry so that authority is more centralized.
8. Reduce wherever possible the need for litigation with regard to customer claims by
   A. Requiring the establishment of a no-fault, administratively-run insurance system to replace the present system of litigating claims. Make recovery rest only upon a prima facie showing of loss or damage (including loss due to *delay*). At the very least, prescribe reasonable claims-handling procedures for the movers, possibly arbitration. Congress should provide the ICC with whatever legislative authority it may need to act effectively in this area.
   B. Revising the regulations so that penalties for violation directly benefit the customer. (For example, provide a return of a percentage of the charges if delivery is late.)
9. As a less desirable alternative to 8 B, enact legislation to allow for recovery of reasonable attorney's

fees in successful actions for loss or damage (including loss or damage due to delay). Such legislation would discourage litigation in the long run by encouraging movers both to provide more careful handling, and to offer more reasonable settlements.

10. Require the extension of credit to customers meeting prescribed requirements.

11. Require the extension of credit on all amounts exceeding the estimate by 10 per cent.

12. Require the mover to meet the promised pickup and delivery dates, allowing for a reasonable leeway provided customer is informed in advance of this leeway. As in 8 B, require mover to forfeit part of charge to customer for failure to meet promised date.

13. Require the prior consent of the customer to any warehousing or interlining of his shipment en route.

14. Prescribe standards for
    a. Packing, handling, and warehousing;
    b. Equipment and padding used on vans;
    c. Drivers and helpers (eliminate picking up help at street corners);
    d. Handling of complaints and relations with public (eliminate such practices as evasion of long-distance inquiries from customers).

15. Provide stricter enforcement of ICC weighing regulations.

16. Require the movers to provide industry-wide "clearing-houses" at population centers, so that if one company cannot meet a promised pickup date, the customer might locate a van of another company which can accommodate him.

8 / The Failure of Enforcement

Favoritism

The Elkins Act (see Appendix 1) was designed to outlaw personal discrimination or favoritism for a given shipper by a carrier. Theoretically, there must be some cost or value or competitive distinction to justify a rate differential between two similar services. However, regulatory definitions of similar ("like") services are so narrow, and matters of "competition" and "value" can be so easily manipulated, that a great deal of personal discrimination exists throughout the rate system in spite of Elkins Act provisions. The effect of much of this ignored rate discrimination is to enhance the advantages of shippers with bargaining power—which unfair advantages gave rise to the Act in the first place. Rate discrimination is perfectly legal under ICC interpretation. Even tariff footnotes that grant rate discounts or describe special circumstances of service for the benefit of favored shippers have not been deemed illegal by the ICC.

Thus, certain kinds of favoritism are "legally" sanctioned through a discriminatory rate system, yet there are other practices which the ICC does categorize as illegal under the Elkins Act. Crude violations of the Act exist in the form of direct financial kickbacks and easily observable favors, but most illegal "concessions and rebates" today are subtle, esoteric, and complex. Many of these concessions are far more massive and significant than the direct kickback of the nineteenth century. The enforcers of the Elkins Act— a small group of special agents in the Bureau of Operations —recognize the fact that "shippers and carriers are resorting to more ingenious and devious schemes to circumvent the law than was formerly the case"; [1] but despite this recognition of the changing nature of Elkins Act violations, the ICC has ignored these practices and allowed them to continue. It often refuses to proceed with prosecution against violations which are complicated or innovative, preferring an easy, cut-and-dried prosecution that adds another number to the annual-report table on enforcement activity.

Some of the current practices which discriminate against the smaller shipper are the following:

Assigned Pool Cars   In the big railroad yards as many as two to four thousand railroad cars are kept aside for major shippers and are not available for other customers, despite Commission orders to make cars available as soon as possible, and despite common carrier obligations. Some of the favored shippers are Archer Daniels, Midland, Whirlpool, General Motors, Ford, and General Foods. Coincidentally, these companies never complain about a shortage of cars.* A few large freight forwarders receive the same advantage.

Specially Equipped Cars   Many of the "assigned" cars are specially equipped for use by the big shippers. For example, boxcars and flatcars are often provided with extensive racks for the carriage not simply of a commodity type, but of a shipper's *specific* commodity. Often these racks are expensive and difficult to remove. This practice not only represents preferred treatment, but it also, along with assigned pool cars, limits the number of cars available to shippers generally, since specially equipped cars can only carry certain freight. There is little doubt that racks are sometimes necessary to increase capacity, but the shippers who benefit are not paying the full cost.

Failure to Charge for Return Empty Traffic   Certain cars are exclusively devoted to large shippers, and at the end of a delivery are immediately returned to the plant of the large shippers (often big car manufacturers) *at no cost*. For example, railroad cars, after dropping off auto equipment, are sent immediately back to Dearborn, Michigan, *at no charge;* yet a small shipper can wait for months before getting a car he has repeatedly asked for. This discriminatory service provides a free source of cars at no cost, and 50 per cent of the transportation (the return

* See Chapter 9 below for full discussion of the car shortage problem.

trip) is provided free. The problem falls under the jurisdiction of Commissioner Murphy, who documents all such violations and is supposedly "clamping down" with fines. However, the fines are so small that the violations pay.

Failure to Charge Required Expenses in Transit Large shippers are afforded unlimited intraplant and interplant switch services *at no cost*. Such practices are difficult to detect and once again are of great benefit to the automobile manufacturers at most of their plants.

Failure to Charge Demurrage (see Chapter 9) Large shippers may avoid having to pay demurrage charges (fines for the detention of boxcars beyond the time allowed for loading, unloading, etc.), because the demurrage clerk at the railroad is often paid off. The ICC's car service agent can only detect these violations by scrutinizing the records of the demurrage clerk, which of course are only as accurate as the clerk allows them to be.

Credit Extensions Most extension of credit is done legally, but it still favors the big shipper because he is afforded a number of delays in the billing process that in effect extend his period of credit. Though the carrier has the responsibility for preparing the shipping order, the large shipper usually furnishes it himself, and may delay in getting it "cut" (typed). This shipping order, which includes the rate, consists of several documents: * the bill of lading and the way bill—which contains the car number, the commodity, the consignee, and specific instructions. Often on the way bill of a large shipper there are instructions for "weight charges to follow": when the rail carrier receives the shipping order, it has a great backlog and does not get around to drawing up a memo way bill during the interim before the necessary weight information is received. The carrier cannot issue the revenue way bill, and therefore can't issue the freight bill—and obviously the shipper cannot pay until he has received the bill.

Normally, according to ICC regulations, a shipper has 120 hours (five work days) following the first midnight after presentation of the freight bill to pay his debt. (Since a weekend invariably intervenes, the shipper actually gets

---

* Large shippers with large traffic departments have the resources to delve into each shipment's circumstances to insure getting the lowest possible rate. Smaller shippers, with perhaps a one-man traffic department, are not always aware of the lowest applicable rate.

seven days.) But because of the delays involved in the above billing and weighing procedures, the period of credit extension is considerably longer.* At the other extreme, a freight forwarder collects its money from the small shippers *before the transportation service is performed*. Small shippers clearly do not get the substantial benefits from the delays discussed above.

Commodity Misrepresentation Traffic managers, or freight salesmen, will misdescribe items in order to get lower freight rates. Some examples: 1. A shipper throws in a shoelace with a shipment of coal, which he then labels "miscellaneous." 2. An apple is added to 40,000 pounds of potatoes, and the shipment is labeled "mixed groceries." 3. One tire is put into a shipment of one type of auto part and the shipment is labeled "mixed parts." Such misrepresentation is widespread, blatant, and obviously a violation of the ICA. Furthermore, according to Mr. Meyer, Chief of ICC Rail Enforcement, such violations are undetectable since the ICC does not have the power to "break the seal" on boxcars.† During 1969 only three violations of this nature were prosecuted. Despite the lack of concern, Director of the Bureau of Operations, Robert Pfahler, says it's "not a big problem because there have been few complaints." ‡

Special Weight Agreements (*Stipulations*) Instead of an entire shipment being weighed, often the unit of the commodity is weighed and the total weight is arrived at by multiplying unit weight by number of units. The "standard" weight per unit is determined at one of several railroad inspection bureaus, which are sponsored by the railroads, and are not part of the ICC machinery. The unit-multiplication practice is legal, but often absurd. The shipper ships more than the number of units he lists on the contract, or he ships some or all of a different commodity than the one listed. The former, of course, weighs more per unit than the latter.

Both small and large shippers can secure these weight

* It should be especially noted in this regard that large shippers with centralized accounting systems can't possibly pay their bills within seven days since it takes five days to get the bill to the central office.

† It does have the power to break the seal on trucks.

‡ An irrelevant excuse, since the parties most likely to know of this practice are benefitting from it, and would hardly complain.

agreements, but the large shipper, because of volume, is in a much better position to benefit from the abuse. The biggest violations often occur in piggyback shipments.

Circuitous Routing Shipments of large shippers are sent on highly indirect routes until the commodity being transported is sold. Upon sale a diversion order is sent out for a small charge and the shipment is rerouted directly to the buyers. Indirect routing provides the shipper with free storage space and ties up boxcars (an important abuse in view of the boxcar shortage—Chapter 9). The pricipal benefactors of circuitous routing are the lumber and potato industries.

These practices represent only a sample of the ongoing discrimination by rail carriers in favor of large shippers, which is precisely what the Elkins Act was initially designed to eliminate. It is important to realize that these violations and contraventions of the Act are undetectable by competing carriers or shippers. The ICC policy of relying on complaints as a major part of its policing process, therefore, is totally unjustified in this area. At the same time, the ICC itself is incapable of discovering violations, and unwilling to prosecute on the rare occasion that these practices are brought to its attention.

Mechanisms of Enforcement

It may well be that the ICC, given the resources it deploys, is unable effectively to police any violations of the Interstate Commerce Act. The Commission's field force consists of three of its bureaus: operations, accounts, and enforcement. The first two have the task of detecting violations, while the third is charged with seeing that the violations are corrected, penalized, and/or not repeated.

The job of the Bureau of Operations is to police motor carriers, rail carriers, freight forwarders, and water carriers. "No one polices pipelines," says Director Pfahler, "at least I don't know who does." Yet pipelines, a rapidly expanding form of transportation, are within the jurisdiction of the ICC. (Gas pipelines are within the jurisdiction of the Federal Power Commission.)

In the Bureau of Operations, there are 127 District Supervisors, *i.e.*, investigators, located in about eighty area offices, who are assigned the task of policing motor carrier activity. Twenty-five of these men are designated as roving supervisors. Many of the investigators, who are supposed to spend 100 per cent of their time in the field, do not do so, according to Assistant Director Harris; more than half of their time is taken up by administrative office work, which includes processing complaints and applications for temporary authority.

When the total of less than 127 investigators is compared with the number of carriers—100,000 (17,000 regulated and approximately 83,000 unregulated or unauthorized, according to Assistant Director Harris)—the situation seems ludicrous, and so conceded Commissioner Bush in an interview.

The policing of motor carriers is not only limited by the number of investigators but also by the methods employed: compliance surveys, road checks, and follow-up complaints.

"A compliance survey consists of a complete examination of the motor carrier's compliance with the Interstate Commerce Act, and the Commission's Rules and Regulations." Though tautological and completely uninformative, this "description" represents *in toto* the official Bureau of Operations' response to the formal request for a description of the nature of the ICC's compliance survey. Actually, Assistant Director Harris told us that the surveys are carried on by the District Supervisors (investigators) without notification. (This is not completely true, since all carriers know about and immediately recognize the black or gray car all ICC investigators drive.) The investigator examines the records, bills of lading, freight bills, C.O.D. registers, and routings of the carrier. Assistant Director Harris admits that compliance surveys cannot detect certain violations: commodity mislabeling, and failure to conform to commodity and route restrictions are two prominent categories of undetectable violations.

The planned frequency schedule of the Bureau of Operations call for compliance surveys to be conducted on Class I carriers every three years and Class II carriers every five years.[2] This schedule may vary in accordance with complaints received. For example, a crash program may be instituted, with many investigators descending on a particular area where complaints indicate a high concentration of violations.

The frequency schedule, an investigation once every

three to five years, certainly undermines any effectiveness which a compliance survey might have. The intervals between an investigation of any one carrier permits that carrier to operate for a long period of time, either knowingly or unknowingly, in violation of the ICA or ICC regulations. The lengthy interval removes the deterrent effects of an ICC investigation and thus fosters carrier circumvention.

The argument here is not that the compliance surveys are conducted poorly, but simply that not enough resources are devoted to them to make them effective. In 1966, 1967, 1968 the number of surveys conducted were rate and general compliance surveys, 711, 776, 887 respectively; and compliance surveys covering economic regulation, 2155, 2178, 2764 respectively.[3] The performance, in terms of man-hours and per cent of all man-hours of the Bureau of Operations, represents for 1966: 17,208 man-hours equal to 6.9 per cent; for 1967: 42,800 man-hours equal to 14.4 per cent; and for 1968: 23,192 man-hours equal to 12.7 per cent.

The ICC has neither quantitative nor qualitative statistics measuring the effectiveness of the compliance surveys; nor has it any inclination to derive any. Thus, the only way an outsider can assess the efficacy of the compliance survey investigative technique is to draw inferences from the comparison of the task to be done with the amount of resources devoted to that task. Since the magnitude of the former so dramatically overshadows that of the latter (800 surveys per year for 17,000 regulated and 83,000 unregulated carrier companies), it appears that the efficacy of compliance surveys is limited. This argument does not condemn the Bureau of Operations' disposition of its manpower, but simply shows that under the present regulatory system, ICC-initiated policing is inadequate, and that more resources must be devoted to the compliance survey method to make it adequate; *i.e.*, the cost of regulation should be recognized as high.

The road check involves the inspection of stopped vehicles for violations. Until the second quarter of 1967, when jurisdiction over safety was transferred to the Department of Transportation, safety violations were a main concern of the ICC road check. Up to that time, "A road check [consisted of] one man checking at least twelve vehicles during an eight-hour period—hardly very massive coverage." [4] At present, road checks are directed solely at economic violations. States also conduct road checks, to detect violations of the ICA and ICC regulations as well as violations of state laws and regulations. However, according to Assistant Director Pfahler, the ICC does not receive records of the results of state road checks. Despite the fact that the ICC relies heavily on these checks, state reports are sent directly to state directors who take action as they see fit. Violations are *sometimes* passed on to the ICC. Yet the lack of coordination between these two systems of road checks results in duplicated and inefficient effort. D.O.T. road checks for safety violations are similarly uncoordinated with the ICC's Bureau of Operations.

The average length of time per road check is eight hours. The average inspection time per vehicle is twenty to thirty minutes.[5] The Bureau of Operations does not know the average or total number of vehicles checked. Over one-half of the truck drivers responding to our questionnaire (see Chapter 6) reported that they had *never* been checked.

The resources involved in road checking in terms of man-hours and per cent of total man-hours of the Bureau of Operations are for 1966: 173 man-hours representing .06 per cent; 1967: 118 man-hours representing .03 per cent; 1968: 302 man-hours representing .16 per cent.[6] These statistics are even more striking than those for compliance surveys, because there are well over 250,000 regulated intercity tractor trailers and trucks to be stopped and checked.[7] And there are additional, practical limitations on the road check technique. The ICC does not have, nor does it seek, power to stop moving vehicles. The Bureau of Operations investigators must rely on state police to aid them in stopping vehicles, or they must set up the road check at a point where the vehicles stop—*e.g.*, a toll both. The flexibility of the road check is therefore severely limited, and drivers who spot the road check relay word back to other drivers, who can then take routes which avoid the check. In addition, only a few vehicles can be inspected at one time. When all the investigators at a road check are occupied, vehicles are passed through. An average eight hours per road check means that any particular road check's effectiveness will diminish as the eight hours progress. Thus not only will very few violations be turned up by the road checks, but what little man-power is used, is being used ineffectively. By the fourth hour the word will be out and the road check will become useless. It is quite normal, therefore, for a truck driver to drive for ten years and never be inspected at a road check.

Road checks *are the only self-initiated ICC means of detecting gray area violations,* and the amount of resources devoted to them is woefully small. It is no wonder that gray area traffic continues to flourish.

Follow-up of complaints comprise the great bulk of Bureau of Operations' policing activities. The resources devoted to this technique in terms of man-hours and per cent of total man-hours are as follows:

	Man-hours: Compliance Survey Follow-ups	% of Total Man-hours of Bureau of Operations	Man-hours: Road checks and Compliance Surveys	% of Total Man-hours of Bureau of Operations
1966	154,929	62.4%	17,381	7.4%
1967	128,517	43 %	42,918	14.7%
1968	125,948	69.4%	23,494	12.9% [8]

As has been pointed out above, heavy ICC reliance on complaints to police the trucking industry is unjustified for two reasons: 1. Those in a position to know about violations do not always find it in their best interests to report them to the Commission; and 2. those whose interests lie in having the violations corrected are often not in a position to discover or detect violations or cannot bear the expense of litigation before the ICC.

The policing of railroad transport is considerably easier than the policing of truckers, because tracks don't move, operating authority is not a preoccupying factor, and there are only seventy-five major railroad carriers.

Because of the last consideration and because railroad lines extend through several regions, investigation of railroad facilities is centralized in Washington, D.C. (Motor carrier investigations are decentralized according to region.)

Eighteen special investigators, under the direction of the

Chief Rail Investigation in the Section of Railroads of the Bureau of Operations, Joel E. Burns, are responsible for policing railroads to insure rail compliance with the ICA and ICC rules and regulations. Though they are primarily concerned with the investigation of railroads, up to 25 per cent of their time may be spent overseeing water and motor carriers.[9] Ten to 15 per cent of their work is routine compliance surveys, with the rest being special investigations. In addition to these men, there are fifty car service agents whose sole job is to maintain adequate car movement.

There are 3646 railroad terminals and yards which warrant inspection. In addition, there are 114,012 miles of yard tracks, sidings, and passing tracks which also must be considered since 100 freight cars can be stored (hidden) on one mile of track.[10]

According to Merrell J. Oaks, Assistant Chief of the Section of Railroads in the Bureau of Operation, it would take seventy-five *fully qualified* agents just to determine accurately where boxcars are in the country at any moment.[11] Thus, while at first it may seem as if the ratio of the magnitude of the task of investigating railroads to the resources deployed is not as disproportionate as it is in the investigation of motor carriers, a reappraisal reveals the difficulties that the Bureau of Operations faces with respect to policing railroad compliance.* It is also important to remember that the ICC does not have, nor has it ever sought, the power to open boxcars (though it can break the seal on trucks), and is thus unable to detect any violations (see Chapter 6).

The Bureau of Operations polices water carriers through compliance surveys and follow-up of complaints at ports and carrier places of business. It conducts no river checks. Investigators rely on carrier records to detect most violations. Again, wrongful labeling of commodities cannot be detected by ICC-initiated investigative techniques. Particularly important in the water carrier area is avoidance of the barge mixing rules. There is virtually no policing of freight forwarders and literally no policing of non-gas pipelines.

---

* Three special agents, for example, are responsible for seven large states: Illinois, Michigan, Wisconsin, Indiana, Minnesota, and the Dakotas. There are no special agents in the entire Pacific Northwest.

Perhaps more important than the lack of Commission manpower for enforcement is the entire agency philosophy behind its program of violation detection. The Commission makes no attempt to set priorities according to the social importance of a violation type or the potential deterrent value of a given prosecution.

The special agents in the field are given very little guidance. One special agent has received no more than three to six case assignments from Washington a year for each of the past three years. Agents are generally left to their own devices. The clearest instruction is a reminder to ask "what, why, when, where, etc.," an instruction one special agent noted was taken from Kipling's "Just So" stories. The only communications received from Washington regarding priority considerations consist of explicit urgings to ignore considerations of priority. These urgings take two forms.

First, Bureau of Operations upper staff generally refuse to prosecute matters which are important simply because important matters generally take more time, involve higher stakes, offend more powerful interests, and are more complex. The special agent finds that his reports on important or innovative violations are ignored.[12] Often, a special agent will be explicitly told to stop turning in compliance surveys in these areas.[13]

Second, agents are constantly reminded that the only important task is to achieve a greater number of completed investigations than in previous months and years so that annual report comparisons will show improvement. This emphasis necessarily results in a reversal of proper priority standards, since it encourages prosecution of trivial offenses which can be investigated and processed quickly. Some special agents are known simply to enter the offices of industry weighing and inspection bureaus and reword or reproduce their records of trivial violations.[14]

ICC preoccupation with the maintenance of a quota system in order to insure increasing numbers of investigations is evident in several documents that the ICC would rather not see released. Although the agency denies the existence of a quota system, it includes a "regional objective" column on the monthly report of field activities form. A more direct expression of this phenomenon is expressed in a memorandum to all special agents from the Bureau of

Enforcement. Note the dearth of concern for importance of violation as Mr. Murphy urges special agents to make every effort "consistent with quality to increase your pace so that the totals for the entire year will equal or exceed last year." The specific reminder of the recipient special agent's performance in terms of number of investigations as compared to average levels further emphasizes the intended message.

Although the Director of the Bureau of Enforcement, Bernard Gould, makes the final decision on prosecution of a violation of the ICA, regional directors have the discretion to settle an investigation through "administrative handling." In effect, this informal procedure relies on voluntary assurances of future compliance by the carrier once the carrier has been informed that the violation has been detected. The procedure merely involves a phone call or letter to the carrier, who agrees to correct the violation. On the face of it, the expediting of investigations is indeed worthwhile—and may even be necessary—when the carrier is unaware that the violation is taking place. However, the Bureau of Operations has no follow-up procedures to assess the performance of the administrative handling technique; nor are there any follow-up investigations to insure correction of the violation, unless there are later complaints.

BUREAU OF ENFORCEMENT
WASHINGTON, D. C.

January 16, 1969

MEMORANDUM TO SPECIAL AGENT ———

Subject: Field Evaluation of Work Performance.

Recently, after consolidating regional reports for the first quarter of Fiscal 1967, the Managing Director called our attention to the fact that the number of investigations concluded by special agents was less than for the same period of Fiscal 1966. We explained that the decrease probably was due to the fact that some agents were occupied by difficult and time-consuming investigations of substance which had hurt our statistics for that period. We predicted, however, that the full year's performance would show an improvement. Since we have just passed the midway point in Fiscal 1967, the following information will inform each of you to see just how we stand statistically at December 30, 1966, and enable you to see at a glance what we need to do during the last 6 months to equal, or hopefully, to exceed our performance during Fiscal 1966.

	Investigations Completed	
		(6 months)
	Fiscal 1966	*Fiscal 1967*
All Agents	708 (18 agents)	347 (17 agents)
General Average Per Agent	39.3	20.4
Individual Monthly Average Per Agent	3.3	3.4

So that you may compare your particular performance against the bureau average, there is shown below a comparison of your figures for the 12 months of Fiscal 1966 with the first 6 months of Fiscal 1967.

	(12 months)	*(First 6 months)*
	Fiscal 1966	*Fiscal 1967*
Number Investigations (Including Compliance Surveys) Completed by You.	19	12
Your Monthly Average	—	—

Where your Fiscal 1967 performance was at a lesser rate than Fiscal 1966 due to involvement in time-consuming investigations beyond your control, or for other reasons, every effort should be made, consistent with quality, to increase your pace so that the totals for the entire year will equal or exceed last year.

Murphy

Finally, there are no figures as to how carriers are dealt with who fail to live up to their promises to comply.

ICC failure to evaluate the effectiveness of its voluntary compliance procedures in the field is exacerbated by its misuse of the sanctions that could potentially have a deterrent effect. The use of deterrence is particularly appropriate for the control of relatively rational entities like corporations when there are difficulties of detection and limited enforcement resources. Setting enforcement priorities with regard to use of formal sanctions is the responsibility of the Bureau of Enforcement. Proper use of these sanctions can give teeth to the warnings of the system of voluntary compliance.

The principal sanctions at the disposal of the Bureau of Enforcement are criminal (fine and imprisonment), civil forfeiture suits (brought under 2461 FRCP), settlement under the Federal Claims Collection Act, civil instruction, and the Commission's power to issue cease and desist orders. In addition, insured carriers may bring damage and civil injunction suits against violators; and the ICC has the power to suspend, modify, or revoke the certificate of a carrier.

Civil penalties and forfeitures are more commonly imposed on violators than criminal sanctions.[15] Knowingly failing or neglecting to obey an order the ICC has made under Sections 3, 13, or 15, of Part I of ICA or under the Panama Canal Act 49 USC 51 provides a $5000 forfeiture penalty for each day of the contrivance of the offense. Otherwise, the civil forfeiture penalties are $100–$500 per offense per day. The fact that the fines accumulate for each offense and each day of the offense makes large fines theoretically possible. The fines imposed by the criminal sanctions are also imposed *on each offense.* The penalties imposed under Section 10 (1), which provides criminal penalties for violations of parts of the Act for which no penalty is otherwise provided, are 1. fines up to $5000 for each offense and 2. liability for up to two years imprisonment if the offense involves unlawful discrimination in rates, fares, or charges. These penalties are representative of the range of fines and imprisonment which can be imposed under the criminal provisions of the ICA.

The Elkins Act (49 USC 41), discussed earlier in this chapter, is one of several supplementary criminal statutes: it provides for fines of $1000–$20,000 per offense and/or imprisonment up to two years.

Fines are thus the basic weapon of ICC enforcement policy. It has often been charged that industry considers fines to be merely a business expense. The fines are so small that often a carrier can make money through violations—*i.e.,* the revenue derived from the violation far exceeds the amount of the fine. An analysis of ICC press releases * from January, 1969, to August, 1969, demonstrates the low levels of ICC fines. Of the twenty-six fines levied against railroads, eighteen were less than $10,000. The fines against motor carriers and their shippers were even less imposing: 115 were between 0–$2000; sixteen were between $2000–$5000; two were between $5000–$10,000; and three over $10,000. At those prices, violating the law pays.

In addition, it is quite possible that a fine may never be

* According to Director Gould, this is a comprehensive indicator.

imposed, or at least not for a very long time. The ICC may choose to handle the violation through administrative channels, or by seeking an injunction. An injunction is simply a slap on the wrist: a court order telling a carrier not to do something that it was illegal for him to do in the first place. Of course, an injunction invokes the "knowingly and willfully" requirement of several violation provisions, but the benefit from injunctions in no way alters the fact that the carrier is profiting from a violation of the law until the injunction is ordered by the court.

One reason why fines are so small is that the ICC avoids the Elkins Act as much as possible. The Act carries the $1000 to $20,000 fine range per charge count and the possibility of a jail sentence,* so the Commission opts for the civil penalties—with a low range of fines and no chance of imprisonment. Since fines do not appear to be stiff enough to compel compliance, harsher sanctions must be resorted to—and are available.†

Violations could result more often in imprisonment. A wealthy businessman who would not flinch at a $20,000 fine would certainly shy away from possible imprisonment. Yet at the present time only one person is in jail for violation of the ICA or Elkins Act.[16]

Another most effective sanction available to the ICC is its ability to revoke a carrier's certificate, stripping it of its authority to engage in the transportation business. About 100 revocation proceedings are started each year, but all are resolved without resort to revocation. The procedure begins with a hearing, initiated by the ICC, at which time the hearing examiner reviews the evidence of the fitness of the carrier. If he finds a violation, he will issue a cease and desist order to the carrier. In order to get a revocation, the Bureau of Enforcement must prove that the carrier will-

---

* Courts are reluctant to impose criminal penalties on corporations and particularly on businessmen, because of the stigma attached; yet there are at present no comparable civil penalties to be imposed. As Assistant Director O'Brien points out, the Bureau of Enforcements prosecution program could be significantly advantaged if there were alternative corresponding civil penalties for many violations. Yet no one has ever proposed that Congress provide these additional sanctions to the ICC.

† Of course the court makes the final determination of the sanction to be imposed, but it is the duty of the Bureau of Enforcement to argue for and obtain the appropriate penalty.

fully violated the hearing examiner's order. The process is long and involved, and usually stops at the cease and desist order stage.

The "willful" requirement imposes a high burden of proof on the Bureau of Enforcement, but that burden is not insurmountable. Indeed, there are cases of flagrantly willful violations, and many unfit carriers.

In any event, a high burden of proof alone cannot account for the fact that since the inception of Part II of the Act, which imposed regulations on motor carriers, *only three certificates have been revoked*. The ICC's Bureau of Enforcement is failing to take advantage of a sanction which is at its disposal and which has an extremely powerful deterrent effect.

In addition to its policing functions, the Bureau of Enforcement is in the rare (within the ICC) position of having a direct role in protecting the public. It intervenes to develop the record in fitness cases and also in important cases such as mergers or general rate increases.

Concerning intervention for the public interest in cases of general importance, the complete description provided by Director Gould of Bureau of Enforcement activities for the past three years up to July, 1969, consists of briefs and oral arguments. 1. *Briefs filed in ICC proceedings*. In 1967 there were 140 briefs filed in motor carrier cases, nine in rail cases; in 1968, 147 and twenty-seven respectively; in 1969, 140 and seventeen respectively. 2. *Oral arguments*. In the last three years the Bureau of Enforcement has participated in a. *one* merger case arguing five minutes; b. *Ex Parte 252* (incentive per diem charges), fifteen minutes; c. *Ex Parte 242* (express company terminal areas), thirty-five minutes; d. Docket No. 3666 (government transportation of explosives and other dangerous articles), forty-five minutes; e. MCC 4937 (Keller Industries, Inc.), twenty minutes; f. MCC 4367 (G. Arrendondo Transfer Co., Inc.), thirty minutes; g. Docket No. 34013 (rules governing assembling and presentation of cost evidence), thirty minutes; and h. MCC 4455 (Kingpack, Inc. investigation of operations and practices), thirty minutes. Thus, in three years the Bureau of Enforcement has orally argued for two hours on behalf of the public interest.

The Bureau of Enforcement's general effectiveness can be evaluated by an examination of the types and extent of its prosecutions. The press releases of the ICC from January, 1969, to August, 1969, reveal that there were prosecutions for a. ten car service order violations; b. 0 insurance violations; c. six household moving violations; d. 0 small shipment violations; e. five abuses of exemption violations (agricultural and commercial zone) by motor carriers; and f. eight credit extension violations, all against railroads. In addition, there were prosecutions for fifteen rebate, rate, or concession violations under the Elkins Act —seven against rail carriers and eight against shippers. On the other hand, there were 180 prosecutions for violations by motor carriers, either for operating outside the scope of granted authority or without authority.

This prosecutional mix is a function of how the ICC views its regulatory task. That view is further reflected in the Commissioners' adjudicatory workload—75 per cent of ICC cases, occupying 50 per cent of Commission time, are operating authority cases. Despite massive discrimination, violation of the Elkins Act, car shortages, home moving fraud, violations of safety regulations, inefficiency, *et al.*, the ICC concentrates its enforcement activities on the protection of existing violators from competition and challenge. Protection of entry barriers and certificate restrictions dominates the Bureau's activity.

9 / Boxcar Shortage

The problem of boxcar shortages, which has been a matter of some concern to such knowledgeable legislators as Senator Warren G. Magnuson for thirty years, is about as tangible as shadows dancing on the walls of a cave. Neither the Commission nor its critics have the sort of hard facts that could define the magnitude of the shortage.

Nevertheless, what few facts there are indicate that the "problem" has become a crisis. There are simply not enough plain unequipped forty-foot narrow-door boxcars. On January 1, 1958, there were 685,276 such boxcars; on March 1, 1969, there were only 401,864. Moreover, that was a drop of nearly 2000 from the count of the previous month (February 1, 1969—403,241). Perhaps more relevant is the number of serviceable boxcars, which on January 1, 1958 was 653,060 and on March 1, 1969 was 374,459—and that figure was down nearly 1500 from the previous month (February 1, 1969—376,007).[1]

The victim of this shortage is invariably the small grain and lumber shipper, who may even have to dump his produce because he can't find a boxcar to transport it to market. Statistics on the shippers' losses resulting from the shortage are not kept by the ICC. It should be remembered, however, that the chronically erratic availability of boxcars means economic loss for the shipper whether or not the shortage reaches acute proportions during a particular year.

In the first place, the farmer may have to borrow money for storage and overhead expenses. He pays his creditors once his produce has been marketed. A long wait for a boxcar may mean the difference between profit and loss in extra interest on borrowed money and storage costs.

Second, the difficulty of estimating the exact date of a shipment's arrival, due to the unpredictabliity of boxcar speed, creates a critical problem for the farmer. Rather than miss an important connection due to late delivery, he may choose to load his produce at the earliest possible date and take the risk of incurring a demurrage fine.* The farmer's constant fear that his produce may never reach the market is an unpleasant and important side effect of the boxcar problem. Paul Reider, the ICC Railroad Division Chief, does not think that the farmers actually load up early very often, but his division has studied neither the frequency of this practice nor its cost to the farmer. Until such studies are conducted, the economic loss resulting from the boxcar crisis will remain a matter of conjecture based on the few individual complaints that might be recorded.

The figures that *are* available (and cited above) on the shortage have been "graciously" (in the words of one official) provided to the Commission by the Association of American Railroads. The A.A.R. identifies boxcars as simply plain or equipped; it would be easier to understand the nature of the shortage if the cars were classified as to restricted use or non-restricted use. If cars were classified according to use, it would be possible to determine what critics have long suspected—that there is no shortage of cars for automobile parts manufacturers, and that the crisis affects primarily the small grain and lumber shippers.

An itemized record of complaints also would help determine who is really affected by the crisis, but of course the ICC keeps no such records. It does not even record the number of complaints each year. Other significant factors, such as which producers and what areas have had to bear the brunt of the shortage, have not been assessed by the ICC.† The Commission relies almost entirely on the industry it is supposed to regulate for figures regarding the dimensions of the shortage. Predictably, the presentation of

* A demurrage fine is an ICC-regulated charge that a shipper pays to a railroad for allowing ready-to-use rail cars stand unused for a shipper's convenience. The charge increases with the length of time the car remains idle: if the car is not moved for ten days, the shipper pays the maximum demurrage fine of $50.

† If the ICC had such information, it could make a better case to Congress for funding to increase manpower or authority to deal with the boxcar problems.

these figures is so vague that the Commission is unable to make any useful formulations.

To aid the ICC in boxcar regulation, the A.A.R. provides the Commission with a weekly form entitled CS 44-C which does show shortages by railroad, region, and kind of car. In the interest of what one A.A.R. official described as "intermodal equity" (it would be "unfair" for the truck and water competitors of the railroads to have access to figures documenting railroad failure to provide boxcars), the Commission will not allow anyone to see these figures. There is no evidence to indicate that this solemn pledge has ever been broken. Even the Department of Transportation considers the figures sacrosanct and has respected the ICC's position by not requesting the records to implement the study it is presently compiling on the boxcar shortage.

There is no explanation for these procedures, other than the ICC's willingness to sacrifice the public interest to that of an industry it is supposed to regulate. The notion that it is unfair to require information from the railroads that is not required from truckers or water carriers seems disingenuous. The latter modes are not as blatantly guilty of car shortages. If they were as guilty, the solution is not to exempt the railroads but to require the information from all modes that are forsaking their legal obligation to provide adequate service on demand.*

Even though figures are lacking on the true dimensions and economic effects of the boxcar shortage, it is known that the ICC has permitted certain practices to contribute to the crisis. One of these practices is the use of boxcars by the Department of Defense.

In a speech delivered on June 24, 1969, Senator James Pearson (R-Kans.) provided a vivid description of the D.O.D.'s appropriation of boxcars. Various military installations, the Senator discovered, had been using the boxcars for storage, and had been paying large demurrage fees. His findings indicated that demurrage charges amounted to almost one-half million dollars a year for certain military ordnance operations:

. . . In 1967 the Louisiana Army ammunition plant in Doyline, Louisiana, paid $360,000 in demurrage charges alone. The

---

* Note that the same excuse is used to justify suppression of railroad rate and detailed profit data.

same plant paid $246,000 in 1968. The ammunition export point at Sunny Point, North Carolina, incurred similar excessive charges of $395,000 and $256,000 in 1967 and 1968 respectively. The naval ordnance plant, Thorne, Nevada, in 1968, paid, out of the Federal Treasury, $312,000 for demurrage charges.

Senator Pearson further observed that:

. . . the Department of Defense is paying out on the order of tens of millions of dollars and possibly $100 million for what I view as railway parking fines.

In concluding his remarks, Senator Pearson thanked the ICC for assisting him in securing the information.

In this case, although the ICC was aware of the situation, it took no action of its own besides providing Senator Pearson with information.

Another factor contributing to the shortage is favoritism and preferential treatment for major shippers. A Chicago area ICC special agent has estimated that as many as 3000 to 6000 cars are kept quietly aside for major shippers and not counted. Some of the favored shippers are Archer Daniels, Midland, Whirlpool, General Motors, Ford, and General Foods. These cars are unavailable to fill the needs of smaller shippers, and are often unused for substantial periods of time by the major shippers.

The ICC inspectors are required to send their Washington, D.C., office a form detailing complaints about such favoritism by type and region. One agent told us that once the reports have been filed, "It is as if they drop off the end of the earth." Actually, these reports appear to be relegated to the status of non-reports. Mr. Reider, Chief of the Railroad Division, denied that there were any records of assigned cars, or, as railroad special agents sometimes euphemistically refer to them, "dedicated cars." In light of the fact that the ICC keeps no itemized record of complaints, it is interesting that Mr. Reider observed that few complaints about car shortage had come from auto parts manufacturers, the usual beneficiary of assigned cars.

The ICC's ingenuity in behalf of the large shipper is not limited to "dedicating" cars. Demurrage charges do not begin until a car is ready to unload, and the fines for favored shippers may be lowered or avoided altogether by a "liberal" determination of when a car is ready for unloading.[2]

Demurrage is a difficult area for the railroad car service agents to police. An agent must rely on the word of the railroad yard demurrage clerks as to when the cars arrived and when they are ready to be unloaded. The only real way to catch violations is to know when all the trains come in and go out of the yard. That would require constant surveillance of each yard, and would probably be impossible even if the number of car service agents were to be increased.

Large shippers take advantage of this limited surveillance to avoid demurrage charges by sending more cars than can be unloaded. For example, while ten cars are being unloaded, they send four more. These cars are supposed to be CP—constructively placed for loading—which means that they are ready to be unloaded, and demurrage charges will begin to run after a specified period of time. According to a railroad service agent, demurrage clerks do not always CP the cars of large shippers with the same vigilance as is accorded to small shippers. Furthermore, demurrage clerks never CP a car that arrives on the weekend, and will sometimes list big shippers' cars which have come in on the weekend as arriving at 7:30 a.m. Monday morning. The result is that the favored shipper gets Monday free because demurrage is assessed only from the first day the car has been in the yard at 7:00 a.m.

For longer periods of time, there are other ways to avoid demurrage payments. A boxcar need not travel by the most direct route. An elaborate itinerary can be carefully planned to give the commodities a scenic journey and to guarantee the shipper that his products will be sold as soon as they reach their destination. A careful examination of the wood on certain boxcars reveals that the cars have been traveling around the country for an extended period of time without being unloaded.

Frequently, demurrage fines are lower than the cost of storage for a comparable period, especially since the demurrage bill need only be paid when the company is caught. In the case of the large shipper, getting caught is a rare enough occurrence to justify the risk of illegal delay.

The collection of demurrage penalties is one of the major shams of ICC policy. Invariably, the Commission will cite large fines to prove that it is doing its job, when, in fact, these fines represent only a small percentage of the total violations and are an acceptable price for the large shipper to pay for the benefits of cheap storage. At the same time, the small farmer may be hurt by a demurrage fine that he has to pay because he couldn't predict when his produce would arrive at the marketplace.

Yet another factor in the shortage is the slow motion of empty cars. Unless compelled to do so by the ICC (under the authority of service order 1009), the railroads have no incentive to move empty cars at the same rate as full ones. The ICC has issued such orders in fifteen cases since the passage of the rule on October 7, 1968.[3] According to Mr. Reider, there have been "thousands of requests" for ICC action under the service order (though the exact number, as with other boxcar figures, is not tabulated by the ICC). The ratio of requests for emergency rulings under service order 1009 to actual orders granted indicates that the ICC does practically nothing to force railroads to move their empty cars quickly. Again, the ICC refuses to use a remedy at its disposal to alleviate the boxcar shortage.

There is also evidence from a Chicago area special agent demonstrating that all empty cars do not move at the same speed. The so-called "assigned pool cars," previously mentioned, are often returned immediately to a large shipper at no charge. Although there is a fine for preferential treatment of empty cars, the fine is small, and so rarely enforced that the risk is justified. This kind of discrimination in favor of large shippers is exactly what the ICC was established to prevent.

It should surprise no one that the Commission does have certain means at its disposal to cope with the crisis but has thus far refused to take decisive action. It has generally assumed that higher demurrage penalties will deter illegal use of boxcars and will produce a more efficient system of utilization. The failure of this assumption is quite obvious, and the Commission's deterrent policy must be re-evaluated in light of the shortage's beneficiaries and its victims.

The only other enforcement tool used by the ICC is the per diem charge. This charge is the amount one railroad pays to another for the use of its freight cars. Higher per diem charges would serve as an incentive for railroads to invest in freight cars and to keep cars as long as doing so is cheaper than purchasing their own.

The ICC does not seem to think, however, that per diem charges could contribute to a solution. Despite the fact that Congress, on May 26, 1966, amended the Interstate Commerce Act * and recognized "the important influence exerted by daily rental or per diem charges on the adequacy of the national car supply," and "directs the ICC to fix per diem charges . . . upon a basis which will encourage the acquisition and maintenance by the railroads of a car supply adequate to meet the needs of commerce and the national defense," [4] the per diem charges established on January 1, 1964, were still in effect in April of 1969. In a public letter dated April 7, 1969, Senators Magnuson, Hartke, and Pearson wrote Chairman Brown:

. . . The events of the past year indicate quite clearly, we think, that the situation will continue to deteriorate unless the ICC implements without delay the authority delegated by Public Law 89-430 concerning the revision of per diem charges.[5]

Chairman Brown responded to the criticism in the Magnuson, Hartke, and Pearson letter with the following statement before the Senate Committee on Commerce:

. . . As the Committee is aware, the Commission initially attempted to implement this law in 1966 with the institution of *Ex Parte 252* through the establishment of an interim incentive per diem rate to apply pending a further study and investigation. Following hearings in which 189 railroads, the Commission's Bureau of Enforcement, and other interested parties participated, the Commission determined in a report decided October 3, 1967, that it lacked sufficient information upon which to establish any incentive per diem rate.[6]

The Commission's disregard of the Congressional mandate was not unanimous. Commissioners Stafford and Murphy both dissented vigorously. Commissioner Murphy noted:

. . . In passing Public Law 89-430 Congress presented the Commission with a mandate to insure the adequacy of the national railroad freight car supply. The majority, in face of recurring chronic freight car shortages, declines to follow this mandate when it fails to put to use the means made available to alleviate the situation.[7]

* Public Law 89-430, amending Section 1 (14) (a) of the ICA.

Since the first study in 1967, an additional survey, *Ex Parte 252*, sub. 1, has been authorized and completed by the Commission, though to date no higher incentive per diem charge has been recommended.

The Commission's response to the Congressional mandate to increase per diem charges is a classic example of bureaucratic inertia. The ICC is simply not doing its job. It is unlikely that the Commission will ever obtain "sufficient information upon which to establish any incentive per diem rate." Surveys are expensive, time consuming, and always open to attack as lacking sufficient information. In a petition for reopening of the per diem question, the attorneys for the Chicago, Burlington and Quincy Railroad stated:

. . . The amount of an incentive per diem charge, necessary to make boxcar ownership a more attractive investment, must be based in the final analysis upon the Commission's best judgment. It is simply not susceptible to mathematical proof. The Commission could hold hearings on this issue for months, and the record thus made would contain nothing more than a series of individual guesses and judgments. The amount of the incentive charge necessarily must rest in the sound discretion of the Commission.[8]

So high a regard for its own discretion the Commission did not have, and consequently, more than three years after obtaining a Congressional mandate for action to remedy a deteriorating situation, the Commission has not taken action.

Like all bureaucracies, the ICC sees a solution, or at least an amelioration, in increased manpower. In a report to the Senate Commerce Committee, the Commission proposed the establishment of a Permanent Railroad Service Board "which will be such as to enable them to devote full time and attention to service order problems as emergencies or crises arise in the car service area." [9] Presumably, this would be a review board of officials comparable to hearing examiners who would enforce ICC regulations such as service order 1009. Furthermore, the Commission observes, "to afford an adequate coverage in the field, the present ceiling of forty-nine agents should be restored to the former level of seventy-two." [10]

There is little question that this is an area in which the

ICC could use a larger staff. One service agent is often faced with the impossible task of policing vast areas. Yet, as has already been said, the Commission has shown no sign of acting quickly (or in some cases, at all) on the reports submitted by its investigators. In the words of one embittered agent, a report to Washington is "like a belch in a church, a resounding noise that doesn't occur."

In the ordinary world, the additional agents would be a necessary improvement, but in the netherworld of the ICC, additional manpower may simply result in a larger volume of reports filed and forgotten.

To solve the boxcar problem the ICC will have to do more than ask for additional manpower. They must use that manpower to obtain the information that will help them solve the crisis. Otherwise, the analogy of one ICC official —who privately compared the request for more agents to a housewife solving a plumbing leak in the basement by hiring another four people to mop rather than repair the leak—will become even more fitting than it is now. If the Commission kept an itemized record as to the nature and source of complaints, it would be possible to pinpoint the areas in which concentration is actually needed. Although the number of boxcars has declined dramatically in the last decade, it is possible that the problem is also one of ineffective utilization and distribution of boxcars, as well as scarcity.

Furthermore, the Commission should allow consumer groups access to the highly secret CS-44C forms which give detailed information as to the weekly shortages of all railroads in each region of the country. What the Commission has called the "interests of intermodal equity" should be abandoned in favor of an approach that would allow the shipper the privilege of knowing in advance whether there are any cars to haul his commodities.

To obtain information of this sort the Department of Transportation has recently undertaken a survey to estimate the "Economic Effects of the Freight Car Shortages." Such a survey might have been given an effective start by an itemized record of complaints from victims of the shortage, had the Commission kept records of such timely subjects.

In order that railroads be encouraged to purchase new boxcars, and to keep an adequate supply of cars on the line, the Commission should prescribe an increase of at least 50 per cent in the existing per diem charges on plain boxcars—over 90 per cent of such cars are currently subject to not more than a charge of $3.58 per day.[11] In fact, most of these cars pay $2.79 or less.

If raising per diem rates fails to provide the incentive to railroads to purchase plain boxcars, the Commission should ask Congress for a mandate to compel the purchase of plain unequipped boxcars. If such a remedy is unpalatable, Congress may have to develop a subsidy system.

Faster and more predictable service is a necessity for more efficient utilization of boxcars. According to the Association of American Railroads, the average speed of a moving boxcar in 1968 was 43.9 mph which was an increase from the 1958 figure of 43.6.[12] However, when one considers that the average time of boxcar movement is only about two hours per day,[13] these figures are somewhat less than impressive. Moreover, unless compelled to do so under the authority of service order 1009, empty boxcars move at a slower rate than full ones. The ICC has the machinery to order the faster movement of empty cars, and must exercise this authority aggressively.

The ICC should also provide shippers and carriers with an incentive to utilize boxcars more efficiently. For example, shippers and carriers might find it profitable to share the cost of a new sampling procedure marketed by the International Stanley Corporation. Whereas in the past, grain inspection has been accomplished through hand samples and a two to three day delay, the new machinery siphons off a random sample of grain that can be tested before it leaves the inspection site. This sampling device, however, is expensive, and considerable prodding may be necessary before shippers and carriers will be willing to make the necessary investment to insure its widespread adoption.

The ICC could encourage shippers and carriers to adopt this new procedure by means of public support, industry-wide education, and, if necessary, a subsidization program to help finance its cost. Thus far the ICC has done none of these, and the Commission is skeptical about the benefits and cost of the new sampling procedure.

Finally, the Commission must make some attempt to supervise boxcar movement for the country at large. At present, only one company—the Commodity Credit Corporation—provides the ICC with statistics as to its boxcar needs; it does so only one week in advance, and as a courtesy to the Commission. The ICC makes no attempt to elicit raw data about anticipated demand from the shippers. It has no information of this sort pertaining to the boxcar demand and movement in the Midwest during the automobile model change period. To use the available cars efficiently, the Commission should be operating along the lines of a traffic control center, seeking and acquiring enough information to be able to regulate the movement and flow of commerce, which, after all, is one of its most important functions. Instead, the Commission has chosen to act in a ponderous quasi-judicial fashion, which, in the regulation of freight car movement, is to say that it has not acted at all.

10 / Passenger Trains: Planned Obsolescence

In the 82nd Annual Report of the Interstate Commerce Commission (1968), the ICC begins its discussion of railroad passenger service with a recitation of the decline of intercity rail passenger service since 1958:

The number of regular intercity trains has declined more than 60 per cent from the 1448 trains operated in 1958. (By summer, 1969, the number was down to less than 500, with fifty more ready to be removed if approved by the ICC.)

Fourteen railroads have abandoned all intercity service, and six have only one pair of trains left.

Intercity service over 36 per cent of the 1958 routes has been completely eliminated.

Non-commutation passengers have decreased 40 per cent and first-class passengers have dropped 70 per cent.

Rail investment in new equipment for intercity service has nearly ground to a halt, and the quality of service has deteriorated in a number of instances.

These facts describe the decline of railroad passenger service in the United States since the enactment in 1958 of Section 13a of the Interstate Commerce Act. It is ironic that these words come from the federal regulatory agency charged with the promotion of a balanced transportation system, for since being endowed with the power under Section 13a to approve the discontinuances of individual passenger trains, the ICC has watched the demise of the passenger train and has done little to halt it. It has exercised its regulatory powers with timidity and a lack of imagination. What is more, while constantly protesting that its powers over railroad passenger service are limited, until very recently it has failed to request that Congress vest it with greater or more meaningful authority, and has consciously acted to keep its discretionary powers to a bare minimum.

"The ICC gets away with what it does because it hopes that no one is watching," says an ICC practitioner, formerly an ICC attorney. Since 1968, with the enactment of Section 13a, the ICC has gotten away with a great deal, and in so doing has contributed to the decline of the nation's passenger train service.

Section 13a (1) states that the ICC must allow a discontinuance unless it finds that the train is "required by the public convenience and necessity." 13a (1) was a railroad-sponsored statute aimed at enabling the railroads to discontinue unprofitable trains without the approval of the states in which the trains operated. It was not meant as a conclusive answer to the overall question of rail service to the nation's passengers. It ignores the fact that there may be a great public need for a particular passenger train even if passenger revenues do not make the train profitable.

The extent of ICC jurisdiction over rail passenger service is unclear. The Commission recently ruled that it could not prescribe standards of service for passenger trains, although it appears to have the authority to do so from a reasonable reading of the Interstate Commerce Act.* As the ICC sees it, its only authority in the area is to approve or disapprove railroad discontinuance petitions under Section 13a of the ICA, and informally to process individual complaints from the general public.

Between 1958 and May, 1969, 1060 different trains were discontinued by the railroads with the approval of the ICC.[1] As of May 1, 1969, over fifty more trains were being considered for discontinuance.[2] Railroads that want to discontinue passenger service are almost always allowed to do so, and the Commission has never challenged the two major excuses they use to justify discontinuances. The railroads claim that they are losing a great deal of money carrying passengers; and the reason for the decline of passenger

* See Appendix 20 for a full discussion of this ruling, *Adequacies —Passenger—Southern Pacific Company Between California and Louisiana*, 335 ICC 415 (1969).

service is that passengers have deserted the trains for other modes of transportation because of a general preference for the inherent advantages of air or automobile travel.

It appears that the railroads have in fact exaggerated the costs of railroad passenger service maintenance, and have purposefully downgraded their facilities in an attempt to show that both their profits and the public's interest in railroad travel are declining. The railroads want to discontinue passenger service because they are capable of making a greater profit on the transportation of freight. Since competition from other modes of transportation is the major force that inhibits complete monopoly pricing by the railroads, profits are directly related to the lack of intermodal competition on various kinds of traffic. In the transportation of freight—as already discussed—the railroads possess substantial (although varying) monopoly power. Such is not the case with passenger transportation, however. The evolution of the automobile and the development of air travel have created a situation of widespread and vigorous intermodal competition. Thus, although it might be possible for the railroads to achieve profits from passenger service, it will necessarily be less profitable than freight transportation, where monopoly power is more prevalent.

It is impossible for the ICC to tell whether the railroads do or could make money on passenger service, because the Commission relies almost entirely on figures provided by the railroads. We interviewed Commissioner Kenneth H. Tuggle about the rail passenger situation, asking whether the cost figures submitted to the ICC by the railroads were ever checked for their accuracy or honesty by the Commission. Tuggle has been for many years a permanent fixture on the ICC's Division 3—the division responsible for making decisions about passenger discontinuances under Section 13a of the Interstate Commerce Act. Tuggle, as the chairman of Division 3, has assumed the role of "expert" on the rail passenger situation within the ICC. He answered our inquiry by saying that the Commission—far from considering comprehensive audits—contends that even the imposition of occasional spot checks on the railroad accounts would be impractical. When asked how the ICC knew whether the railroads were submitting accurate, honest figures about the cost of equipment, maintenance, etc., in order to justify their claims that they are losing millions of dollars on rail passenger service, Commissioner Tuggle responded simply, "We *assume* so."

The result of this Commission assumption is that the railroads have never been subject to a comprehensive, professional, independent audit. There has been no sophisticated attempt, despite the importance of the cost issue and the obvious fact that the railroads have a vested interest in inflating expense and decreasing revenue estimates, to utilize modern statistical techniques in order to evaluate railroad passenger cost estimates intelligently. Although regression analysis is ideal for the detailed study of alternatives for assigning joint and common costs, the ICC refuses to take advantage of it.

Rail passenger service should not be discontinued, even though alternate forms of transportation are available, because in some areas of the country the railroad is the only means of transportation available between cities. The passenger train also has several key advantages over other forms of transportation: its excellent track location brings passengers directly into the middle of big cities, near business areas; it is unaffected by almost all adverse weather conditions; it does not pollute the air and the environment through its propulsion alone; * it does not share its right-of-way with other passenger modes, and thus is unaffected by traffic jams; it has an extremely low marginal cost per passenger (additional passengers can be transported on extra train units for far less relative cost than for airline and bus passengers); and it provides excellent comfort to passengers if service is properly maintained.

The only possible natural liability of the passenger train is its relative lack of speed, and even this problem must be viewed with the following things in mind. First, with the highway and airport congestion getting worse, the time saved in the air between cities approximately 200 miles away is almost entirely lost in airport and highway tie-ups. Second, the development of fast trains, which is just beginning, may reduce or even transcend the advantage now held by the airplane at these intermediate distances. As for

---

* But see Appendix 21 for a description of how the railroads have negligently polluted the environment through the dumping of raw human waste onto tracks and rights-of-way.

the intercity bus, the train is potentially faster because of its own natural speed, and because of its freedom from traffic jams which can paralyze a bus system.

The Department of Transportation's Federal Railroad Administration has recognized the public's need for passenger service by proposing a new Comsat-like corporation called "RailPax" to take over railroad passenger service and develop new, fast trains to serve highly-populated "corridors" between the nation's major cities. This particular proposal, which must survive the Budget Bureau and Congress to reach fruition, is one of several that proponents of rail passenger service could be happy with. The significance of this proposal lies in the federal government's recognition that there is a market and a need for high-quality rail passenger service.[3]

Although the railroads and the ICC continue to talk about declining demand for rail passenger service between cities, there are surveys to indicate that the demand is there —if only decent service is offered to the public. For example, a recent survey of Milwaukee businessmen showed that 94 per cent of the respondents believe that frequent, reliable, clean, fast, and modern train service between Chicago and Milwaukee would produce greater patronage. Fifty-five per cent said that they would use the train more if such service were offered. Obviously, people do not want to take dirty, slow, and ancient trains, but they will support decent rail service if it is offered.[4]

The development and success of the Penn-Central's "Metroliner" between New York City and Washington, D.C., is a good example of the potential success of high-speed "corridor" trains all over the country. In its first year, 700,000 people took the Metroliner, which still is not as fast a train as could be developed. This was a 46 per cent increase in the number of rail passengers between the two cities from the previous year. The Metroliner's powerful competition, the Eastern Airlines shuttle, showed practically no increase in its passenger total over the previous year, despite the fact that its previous growth rate had been between 3 per cent and 15 per cent. The director of the demonstration projects in the Department of Transportation Office of High Speed Ground Transportation, Robert Smith, was quoted on the first anniversary of the

Metroliner: "There's no doubt that it has been, for the most part, a big success with the public; the statistics on passenger traffic are pretty good proof of this." [5]

One of the most significant set of statistics about the first year of Metroliner operation describes the age and affluence of the Metroliner passengers. In the words of the Penn-Central Company's "Metroliner Facts," (Penn-Central Press Release, Philadelphia, Pa., January 16, 1970) issued on the first anniversary of the inauguration of this service, "Metroliner passengers are active, affluent. A U.S. Department of Transportation survey disclosed that one-third are between twenty-one and thirty-five, another third between thirty-six and fifty. Sixty-five per cent have family incomes over $15,000, and 34 per cent over $25,000."

These facts should destroy the thesis offered by a leading apologist for the railroad industry, Professor George W. Hilton of UCLA, that only the poor and the aged will ever take the passenger train. Professor Hilton's thesis is stated in his book, *The Transportation Act of 1958* (Indiana University Press, 1969):

Only low-income people, persons with an irrational fear of flying, or aged persons whose alternative uses of time are negligible are likely to opt for rail. The higher a man's income becomes the more likely he is to convert from rail to air. Consequently, the regular increase of income of low-income persons, like deaths among the aged, tends to shrink the market for rail passenger travel.

Professor Hilton's dire predictions for the passenger trains are based on the belief that the state of railroad technology will remain at its current level forever. The Metroliner proves that people can be induced to ride on a fairly fast, comfortable train, and thereby take advantage of the considerable inherent advantages of the mode described above. And, according to Penn-Central's statistics on the Metroliner, the new generation of rail passengers will not be limited to the poor and the aged.*

* The success of the Metroliner is significant because of built-in difficulties with ticket operations: passengers have been required to pick up tickets at the station before the trip in order to get a confirmed seat, and no phone reservations were taken. Nonetheless, the Metroliners ran at a consistent 80 per cent capacity their first year. As for the "TurboTrain" between Boston and New York, it ran at 65–70 per cent capacity despite three handicaps: 1. only one trip

The fact is that even without fast, new trains, 92,070,639 people took non-commuter trains in 1968; 295,617,840 people took non-commuter and commuter trains—constituting a large market to abandon. As summarized by the editor of *Trains* magazine:

On the face of it, a passenger instrument which can propel 200 to 300 people at eighty miles an hour with only 1500 horsepower and a crew of three or four men is not bound for the museum for the same reason that the stage coach landed there. Man has yet to invent an overland passenger mode of transport with the train's unique combination of speed, safety, comfort, dependability, and economy.[6]

The need for the passenger train clearly exists—the question is how to finance it. Freight subsidies seem to be an illogical method in the long run, since it makes little sense to require shippers to bear the burden of providing passenger service. Subsidization of passenger operations by non-railroad income of the railroad companies would seem to be at least a more realistic alternative. In view of the common carrier responsibilities of the railroads, and in view of the neglect of those responsibilities for the higher returns from freight service, and the even higher returns from real estate, mining, and assorted other holdings, it would seem just to require the giant corporations which operate passenger trains for the "public convenience" to finance passenger operations from the other vast resources of their corporations. The Penn-Central Company, as already demonstrated, is perhaps the largest single private landholder in the United States; other railroads are owned by parent corporations with comparably lucrative non-railroad holdings.[7]

However, the politics of railroading make it highly unlikely that passenger service will be financed entirely from non-railroad income. That leaves the government subsidy as the only alternative to the abandonment of passenger service entirely.

For ten years after the 1959 *Passenger Train Deficit* case, the ICC sat idly by and watched the number of passenger trains dwindle toward extinction, without recommending

---

each way daily; 2. schedules were made available only on request; 3. the Penn-Central failed to advertise the new Boston-New York train service.

that the federal government consider subsidizing the passenger trains. The Commission's chief "clients," the Association of American Railroads and the individual carriers, were strictly against government subsidies. They did not want anybody to disturb them in their systematic exit from the passenger business. The Commission, accordingly, never recommended subsidy when it went to Congress with legislative recommendations in other areas. But in 1969, political pressures finally began to build up, as the public realized the end was near and as railroads began to escalate downgrading practices. Thus in January, 1969, the A.A.R. officially endorsed, for the first time, the concept of government operational subsidies; six months later, the ICC followed suit in its report to Senator Magnuson on the costs of intercity passenger service.[8]

Congress now has before it several proposals to provide relief to the nation's rail passengers. The Commission's years of silence, in the face of crying need for Congressional action, are particularly damning when it is remembered that in 1961 the Doyle Report said that it was the ICC's responsibility to suggest necessary changes in federal policy to Congress.[9]

The railroads have demonstrated little interest in maintaining rail passenger service beyond that level which is politically necessary. They have stated their case via several media. First, they published a pamphlet called "The Case of the Vanishing Passenger Train," distributed by the Association of American Railroads. Second, they attempted to influence public opinion through a canned editorial service called the Industrial News Service, which Senator Lee Metcalf of Montana called "one of this country's principal prefabricators of public opinion." [10] Industrial News Service was created as a "national utility propaganda service" by Samuel Insull forty years ago. It was used by the American Medical Association to forestall Medicare, and has also been utilized by private power companies.[11] The following editorial was sent by INS to more than 11,000 subscribing newspapers in 1968:

A recent analysis of newspaper editorials by the Association of American Railroads showed a remarkably broad grasp of railroad problems by the public—with but one exception. That had to do with discontinuance of rail passenger trains. Apparently, the public has failed to understand its own changing transportation preferences and the ensuing economic stress that has been placed on the rails.

The A.A.R. has released a pamphlet entitled "The Case of the Vanishing Passenger Train." In it, the story is told of why passenger trains are disappearing. People have simply chosen other forms of transport and not because of declining service. Shortly after World War II, the railroads and the Pullman Company spent over $500 million for new, modernized passenger equipment. This equipment included ultramodern chair cars, plush sleeping cars with showers, valet service, radio-telephones, dining cars with full course meals, lounge cars with coffee shops and bar service, vista-dome observation cars, air conditioning and other conveniences and luxuries. In spite of these innovations, passenger traffic declined. If the rails were still running as many trains as they ran in 1957, passenger deficits in 1967 would have been about $1.5 billion—more than the industry's total net operating income from freight service. In 1959, the ICC conducted a long investigation of the passenger train crisis. It reported railroads have "conscientiously endeavored to improve their standards of service" and "generally have not discontinued trains without serious efforts—sometimes prolonged—to make them pay and only after sympathetic consideration of public convenience."

The U.S. will depend more and more on the rails for the hauling of freight. To meet this transport challenge, every available rail investment dollar must go for the continuation of a modernization program which is reshaping the railroad industry from the ground up to the benefit of the entire nation.[10]

Thus the railroads assert that the reason for decline of intercity passenger service is entirely that "People have simply chosen other forms of transport, and not because of declining service." This viewpoint, incidentally, is supported fully by Commissioner Tuggle, who in an interview stated that there is absolutely no question that the people deserted the railroads, and that not even to some degree have the railroads deserted the people.*

That there is, however, at least some doubt as to the correctness of that conclusion is expressed by Senator Lee Metcalf on the floor of the Senate:

This opinion is in sharp contrast to the feelings of my constituents, who, in writing to me, have expressed their sincere and vital need for the train for business and recreational purposes.[12]

* Tuggle's opinion conflicts directly with several recent 13a cases in which the ICC has refused to allow a discontinuance where it

In fact, the railroads' policy of purposefully downgrading their facilities has made the passenger train unpalatable. And fewer passengers take the train today than they did ten years ago simply because of the drastic decline in the number of trains operating. A big city like Dallas, Texas, has no train service—it is the largest city in the world without rail passenger service.

In his 1966 book, *Megalopolis Unbound: The Supercity and the Transportation of Tomorrow*, Rhode Island Senator Claiborne Pell comments on the state of passenger service by focusing on the role of railroad management in its decline:

U.S. railroads more often than not seem to have deliberately run passenger services on a non-competitive, unprofitable basis. . . . As a result, rail passenger service, organizationally speaking, is treated as the stepchild of the freight service. The Doyle Report found that only three or four railroads in this country had vice presidents assigned to passenger service, and most of them gave it no separate, high-level attention. Bookkeeping and operations have been hopelessly intertwined with freight service in so many cases, so that there is no clear executive responsibility for making a profit on passenger service, and no clear line of authority for making the decisions necessary in order to trim costs and exploit public demand where it still exists.[13]

The railroads' explanation is further disputed by a man who attempted to purchase a ticket on the Rock Island-Southern Pacific "Golden State" from Los Angeles to Chicago, and reported the following experience to the ICC:

I do not believe that two railroads, such as Rock Island and Southern Pacific, have a right to discontinue train service when they deliberately discourage people from riding their trains. Upon my arrival in Los Angeles, I went to the Southern Pacific ticket office at the Union Station to purchase a roomette from Los Angeles to Chicago. When I asked the ticket salesman for the space, he said, "Are you sure you don't want to go by plane? It is much faster and more comfortable." I said no, and again asked for a reservation. Once more he tried to convince me to go by plane, but I refused. Finally after much arguing, he sold me the room. He did this to several other people and

found that the railroad had deliberately downgraded its service in order to build a deficit.

was able to convince them to go by plane, which they did. That is one reason why the "Golden State" loses money.[14]

When the railroads realized that they could make more money hauling freight than passengers, they decided to let their passenger obligations slip toward a hoped-for oblivion. As a matter of fact, many of them did more than *let* their passenger service deteriorate. We have reliable information from a source in the railroad industry that many railroads, including the Chicago, Burlington & Quincy, have special teams of employees whose corporate task is to devise ways of discouraging passengers from taking the train!

What every passenger on a train knows is that most cars are old and dirty. A 1959 study for the Subcommittee on Transportation of the House Committee on Armed Services on the age of passenger train cars revealed the following statistics: [15]

	Over 30 years	*26–30 years*	*21–25 years*	*16–20 years*	*11–15 years*	*6–10 years*	*1–5 years*
Coach	56.31%	12.52%	5.05%	5.17%	5.83%	8.10%	7.02%
Coach and Combination	65.54%	14.81%	3.38%	4.19%	3.70%	4.19%	4.19%
Dining	36.76%	10.73%	4.35%	10.65%	9.23%	25.58%	2.70%

This study indicates that after 1932 very little capital investment was made by the railroads in passenger cars, except for a brief period in the 1950's. Of the coaches in service on Class I railroads in 1958, 68.83 per cent were over twenty-six years old—more than half were over thirty years old. The seeds of discontent over poor passenger equipment were apparently planted long before the passenger train began losing customers to jet airplanes and superhighways.

Ten years after the above study, the ICC's *Investigation of the Costs of Intercity Rail Passenger Service* published an inventory of passenger cars as of December 31, 1968. It is not a study of all Class I railroads, but is limited to eight carriers, thus excluding such carriers as the Penn-Central, the Southern Pacific, and the Chicago, Burlington and Quincy. The figures here indicate the average age of passenger cars for the eight railroads.[16]

Carrier	"Headend"	Coaches	Other	Total
Santa Fe	17 years	17 years	21 years	17
Chesapeake and Ohio and Baltimore and Ohio	27 years	25 years	18 years	24
Great Northern	23 years	18 years	20 years	22
Illinois Central	42 years	34 years	19 years	33
Missouri Pacific	6 years	20 years	19 years	10
Seaboard Coast Line	33 years	28 years	21 years	29
Southern	31 years	30 years	26 years	30
Union Pacific	10 years	15 years	15 years	12
TOTAL	23	23	19	22

The railroads have obviously failed to provide the capital efforts necessary to keep their equipment modern and appealing. The *average* Illinois Central coach is now thirty-five years old. The Illinois Central is now owned by Illinois Central Industries, which owns close to $300 million in property, and which has been selling Loop property in Chicago that ultimately will bring in close to $1 billion in sales to developers. To replace the current fleet of I.C. coaches within ten years, cash payments of only $3,161,000 would be required by the tenth year.[17] The burden of building a new fleet of coaches is, of course, lessened by the depreciation deductions allowable by the Internal Revenue Code. The standard price of a passenger coach in 1968 was only $200,000. To say that a giant corporation like Illinois Central Industries cannot afford such relatively minor expenditures is to blink at the obvious.

One result of the ancient state of passenger coaches is that maintenance costs have risen dramatically. According to one train executive quoted in the May 17, 1965, issue of *Railway Age,* a new coach would require *one-sixth* the yearly maintenance that present coaches require. In the ICC's *Investigation of Costs of Intercity Rail Passenger Service,* avoidable expenses for repairs of passenger cars for the eight railroads studied amounted to $28,889,135. One-sixth of this sum is $4,814,855, and the resulting savings of $24,074,280 would have *reduced the avoidable costs of the carriers 21 per cent.* After taxes, if the one-sixth figure is accurate, the avoidable costs of the railroads would have been reduced from $74.9 million to $60,221,559. This would be a far cry from the $118.1 million figure publicized by the ICC.

In the area of basic management structure, the railroads have been deficient for decades. The problem, according to the Doyle Report, was that even those roads which went so far as to elevate passenger officials to vice presidential stature, failed to vest in these officials the *authority* to make passenger service work.[18] To this day, the railroads themselves refuse to treat their passenger responsibilities as anything more than a nuisance which, by the grace of the ICC, will someday disappear.

According to the authoritative *Pocket List of Railroad Officials*, as of August, 1969, of twenty major Class I railroads with substantial intercity passenger traffic, only *two* had vice presidents in charge of passenger service. These vice presidents are surrounded by extremely small staffs, and are clearly subordinate to comparable freight officials. The Southern Pacific Company, for example, has a chairman, a president, two senior vice presidents, and ten vice presidents, as well as a general counsel. Whatever authority there is over passenger service is vested in the Traffic Department, headed by a vice president. He has an assistant vice president and two assistants to the vice president, as well as a general freight traffic manager. Below *them* is a passenger traffic manager with one assistant. Such low-level placement of responsibility is not an exception. The following is a partial list of the other railroads, and the position of the passenger man in the hierarchy of each company:

1. *Santa Fe:* General Passenger Traffic Manager, in Traffic Department, under Assistant Vice President and Vice President.
2. *Baltimore and Ohio:* Director, Passenger Services, in "Administrative Group," under Vice President and General Staff Officer. Parallel "Groups" include Merchandise Freight (Vice President), Coal Business (Vice President), Labor Relations & Personnel (Vice President), and Law Department (Vice President).
3. *Chicago and North Western:* Director of Commuter Passenger Service, in Sales & Marketing Department, under Vice President for Sales & Marketing.
4. *Chicago, Burlington, and Quincy:* General Passenger Traffic Manager under Vice President of Traffic

Department, below Assistant Vice President of Traffic for Sales and Service of Freight.

5. *Great Northern:* Passenger Traffic Manager, under Vice President of Marketing Department.

6. *Illinois Central:* Vice President of Passenger Services Department.

7. *Norfolk and Western:* General Passenger Sales Manager, under Vice President of Traffic Department, and below Assistant Vice Presidents for Merchandise Sales.

8. *Northern Pacific:* Passenger Traffic Manager, under Vice President of Traffic Department, and below Assistant Vice President for Freight Sales and Service.

9. *Penn-Central:* Assistant Vice President of Passenger Service Department, below Vice Presidents of various freight sections.

10. *Seaboard Coast Line:* Vice President for Passenger Traffic.

11. *Southern:* Director, Passenger Sales, under Vice President of Traffic Department.[19]

In addition, the Association of American Railroads, the industry's trade association located in Washington, D.C., has no division or department with responsibility for promoting passenger service. According to *The Pocket List of Railroad Officials,* there is not a single A.A.R. officer whose responsibilities are listed as dealing with passenger service alone.

The extent of advertising and promotion suggest the value attributed by industry to a given product or service. In 1946, the "Passenger Traffic" Study of the Railroad Committee for the Study of Transportation suggested that the railroads' passenger service difficulties were due to ineffective coordination between sales and promotion, insignificant advertising sums, and inadequate sales training. The expenditures of each common carrier passenger mode for advertising in 1943 per $100 of revenue were: [20]

A.A.R. public relations expenditures	$ .012
Railroad expenditures	$ .139
Motor truck lines	$ .270
Motorbus lines	$ .742
Domestic airlines	$3.624

Between 1950 and 1957, aviation advertising in magazines grew by 125 per cent while railroad advertising dropped 24 per cent. "If the industry had earmarked only 1 per cent of every $1 of gross for advertising last year, it would have had a budget of $100 mililon . . . for national institutional advertising of any or all phases of railroading," according to a 1958 trade magazine.[21]

In an important 1966 case involving the proposal of the then New Haven Railroad to drop all its passenger service, Commissioner William Tucker (now head of the New Haven Region of the Penn-Central) stated: "To fully meet its obligation as a 'common carrier' of passengers, the railroad must accord to promotion of its economically viable passenger service the same *reasonable effort* it would accord to promotion of its basic freight services, as, for example, when the latter were threatened by competitive forces."[22] Despite this statement, however, the number of dollars spent by the major railroads in promoting their passenger trains remains extremely small. The railroads have simply not tried to promote rail passenger service to compete with the airlines.

In 1967, the year with the latest available official ICC figures, twenty-three selected railroads around the country,[23] all with a substantial amount of passenger revenue, spent an average of 0.067 of 1 per cent (0.00067) of their total revenue on passenger service advertising.

The real disparity appears when promotional expenses by the major airlines are compared with those for passenger service by the railroads. Nine key airlines[24] spent an average of 3.48 per cent of their total revenues on promotional expenses.

A simple glance at any metropolitan daily would show how great an effort the airlines have made to seek passengers. When one competitor outspends another by approximately 5000 per cent,* it is highly doubtful that the outspent competitor has made a "reasonable effort" when "threatened by competitive forces." The inescapable conclusion is that the railroads have done their best to be noncompetitive.

---

* The railroad passenger advertising commitment is a larger percentage of its purely passenger revenues, but is still a small proportion (less than one-tenth) of the comparable air carrier commitment.

When a railroad *does* attempt to promote its passenger service, it gets results. A commuter railroad in Boston, the Boston & Maine, recently started putting money into radio and newspaper advertisement, and within a few weeks showed a 5 per cent increase in passenger fares.[25] One can only speculate what effect similar efforts, on a larger scale, would have had on the railroad industry.

The railroads' purposeful downgrading of passenger service has also been reflected in sales and marketing techniques. The railroads have been anything but aggressive in their marketing efforts, even with the popular Metroliner. The passenger who wants to take a coach seat cannot make a telephone reservation. The only way to get a coach seat on this train is to be at the station in advance. (The airlines' allow phone reservations for one year in advance for coach seats.) No commission is made to travel agents for the purchase of Metroliner seats, and not all travel agents have Metroliner seats available. In fact, only Pullman seats are reserved on a commission basis from travel agents. (All airline seats are available from travel agencies, and the airlines actively "push" travel agency sales by paying travel agents 5–6 per cent of each sale in commission. American Airlines in Boston estimates that between 25–30 per cent of their passenger sales revenue comes from travel agencies they have actively sought out.[26])

One study in the 1950's showed the potentially beneficial effects that aggressive marketing could have on the railroads. An incentive program for passenger ticket sellers was set up, whereby those sellers surpassing a per-set quota received awards. The results: Pullman sales above quota; first-class revenues up 10 per cent; coach sales also increased. On the basis of 1955 figures, the revenue increase from this technique would have been $49.1 million nationwide, without any additional men or equipment. But the railroad industry turned down the plan when it was proposed for nationwide installation.[27]

Lately, on a number of occasions, the Commission has found as a matter of legal fact that individual carriers purposefully downgraded their passenger service in order to chase away passengers and justify their discontinuance of the "deserted" train.[28] These cases have generally been decided by the entire Commission, and not by Division 3, headed by Commissioner Tuggle. On such occasions, the

ICC has rightfully refused to allow the discontinuance for a year because of the downgrading.

The famous "Adequacies" * case posed the issue of downgrading in a broader context than a single discontinuance case. Five states petitioned the ICC to investigate the downgrading of the Southern Pacific's "Sunset Limited." In the recommended report by hearing Examiner John Messer, it was found that the Southern Pacific had consistently sought to downgrade the quality of Sunset Limited service between New Orleans and Los Angeles, by, among other things, removing the sleeper service on the 1177-mile leg between New Orleans and El Paso, Texas. Messer found that the "service presently available on the Southern Pacific's Sunset Limited is inadequate to meet the reasonable needs of the public, in violation of Section 1 (4) of the Interstate Commerce Act." [29] The ICC Hearing Examiner wrote an expansive report, touching not only on the "Sunset Limited" but also on the rail passenger situation in general. He found that: [30]

The surest way for the railroads to disseminate information to buyers or potential buyers is to operate good, clean, well-maintained passenger trains at a speed equal to that of their expedited freight trains, on schedule and with adequate creature comforts. Such a happening would be more newsworthy than a man biting a dog and the press coverage would no doubt be substantial. . . . If the defeatist attitude of the rail carriers could be overcome and reasonable efforts be made to improve the passenger service, a considerable portion of the lost patronage could be recovered. . . . The evidence reflected in this record, as well as in numerous other reports of this Commission, justifies the conclusion that the S.P., and other railroads, has (sic) downgraded its passenger train service and that this has contributed materially to the decline in patronage.

After the case languished within the ICC for forty-one months, the Commission asked Congress to give it power over standards of service, announcing that it thought it lacked the power to enforce standards of service. In September, 1969, the ICC decided the "Adequacies" case against the State of California.

In an address before the Railroad Transportation Institute's Fall Transportation Seminar in Denver in October, 1968, Commissioner George Stafford—new Temporary Per-

* See Appendix 20 for a full discussion of the "Adequacies" case.

manent Chairman of the ICC—spoke eloquently about the tactics used by the railroads to discourage passengers from taking the train:

At present, even feeble efforts to secure passenger traffic are a thing of the past. At a time when airlines emphasize pretty girls whose only duty is to soothe each passenger's cares and serve drinks and food, the railroads continue the tradition of requiring their passengers to suffer at the hands of conductors, a group in general terms as insensitive to the needs of today's traveling public as a computer to a newborn baby. At a time when such slogans as "Leave the driving to us" and "Up, up and away" are hammered into the mind of the public by TV, radio, magazine and newspaper advertising, there is almost no indication by the railroads that they have *one* passenger train let alone nearly 600.

Too often these days in discontinuance proceedings, we hear reports of busy telephone lines at rail terminals, the failure to give information about trains or supply timetables, and the refusal to take reservations when space is in fact available. In one recent case, we heard of a call to a station that was simply terminated in the middle of the conversation because the hour of closing had arrived.

Despite its professed concern over the condition of rail passenger service in this country, the ICC very often fails to take the steps within its power to require the railroads to maintain even minimum standards of service. The failure of the Commission to act is clear in another case against Southern Pacific made by various western states. In April, 1968, the S.P. filed a traffic change, whereby it discontinued almost entirely the transportation of checked baggage, human remains, newspapers, and other traffic generally handled by passenger service. California, New Mexico, and Oregon formally requested, under Section 15 (7) of the ICA, that the Commission suspend and investigate the tariff change. California contended that the full baggage service was required by the public, and that the discontinuance of this service would deter passenger traffic from the Southern Pacific and other railroads interlining with the S.P. California also contended that the commercial users of this service would be disadvantaged, and that the general effect of the action by the S.P. would be to lower passenger revenues and further downgrade the S.P.'s trains in the eyes of the traveling public. Oregon similarly alleged these deleterious effects, and also stated that the discontinuance of the human remains transportation service would affect the transportation of corpses from Vietnam through San Francisco to Oregon and Washington.

The ICC decided not to suspend the tariff change, meaning that if the states protesting the tariff change wished to continue their protest, they would have to bear the burden of pressing their case. If the ICC had simply decided to suspend the tariff, the burden would have rested with the carrier to prove that full baggage service was *not* required by the public convenience and necessity. Nevertheless, the states proceeded with their formal complaints.

After June 17, 1968, the State of California did not hear from the Interstate Commerce Commission. The Southern Pacific has handled no through baggage since June 1, 1968, except for two trains between Ogden, Utah, and San Francisco. The ICC has not been completely silent on the question of baggage service: in 1969, it would not allow the Penn-Central to discontinue *its* baggage service. Evidently, the Commission saw no legal or practical obstacle to that decision, yet it has not even scheduled hearings on the complaint against the Southern Pacific.

We contacted the Interstate Commerce Commission about the case, Docket No. 34997. It was revealed that in January, 1970, California asked the ICC about the case, and the Commission finally began to arrange for disposition of the case. We asked the Assistant Chief Hearing Examiner why there had been an eighteen-month delay since the S.P. ceased its full baggage service. He replied that the Commission was at that time considering the "Adequacies" case, and that it wanted to wait for the disposition of that case so as not to waste its (the ICC's) meager resources.

The two cases are not procedurally interconnected since one was a state request for an investigation of railroad downgrading, and the other was a state request for a routine tariff suspension and investigation. The Commission handles thousands of such requests in the freight area every year. Further, the ICC did find the time and resources in 1969 to take action regarding the Penn-Central on the very same issue of baggage service. Why did the Commission fail to consolidate the two cases at that time if it was worried about wasting its resources on mere passenger service problems?

The fact is that the ICC showed no intention of ever taking this case up, until reminded by the State of Cali-

fornia in January, 1970, that it had not acted. In delaying
in cases like this, and in construing its own authority as
narrowly as possible in the "Adequacies" case, the Interstate Commerce Commission belies that concern over the
decline in rail passenger service which it professes in report
after report to Congress.

Whatever doubt ever existed about whether the American railroads really care about their passengers' comfort
and convenience was destroyed on August 14, 1969. On
that day, a trainload of passengers en route from Omaha
to Billings, Montana, on a C, B & Q train were treated to
unusually speedy railroad service. The result for the railroad
was a federal prosecution and a $2500 fine.

The train was en route from Omaha to Billings at around
8:30 a.m., when the railroad was informed that a federal
court in Wyoming had upheld the ICC's discontinuance of
Trains 41 and 42 of that route. With uncharacteristic speed,
the train, by pre-set plan, raced to and halted at the next
stop, Hemingford, Nebraska, in the western part of the
state (population 904). There the passengers and the mail
were unceremoniously dumped. An unscheduled bus took
them to available transportation.

The object of the abrupt halt was to best the Washington
attorney handling the opposition to the ICC discontinuance
order in his attempt to get the U.S. Supreme Court to issue
a temporary restraining order to prevent the railroad from
stopping the train. The railroad won the race, but lost the
war. What it did not know was that a member of the House
Committee on Interstate and Foreign Commerce (which
oversees the ICC), Glenn C. Cunningham of Nebraska,
was vacationing in Fort Robinson, west of Hemingford,
and was waiting for the Billings-Omaha leg of the discontinued train. ICC officials in Washington were as ashamed
of the incident as the C, B & Q should have been, especially since initial press reports had it that Congressman
Cunningham was actually on the train which was halted in
Hemingford.

The country will forever be involved in the chicken-and-
egg controversy about who killed the passenger train until
the railroads' claim that there is no significant need for
passenger service in this country is tested. For this reason,
the ICC has been suggesting for several years that a major

study of the nation's passenger trains needs be conducted with federal monies. There is now no federal policy for the surface transportation system of this country. Section 13a is addressed only to the problem of the nation's railroads being forced to carry so-called "milk" trains through the slowness of state regulatory agencies. It does not, as some railroad economists have maintained,[31] state a Congressional intent to allow *all* railroads to get rid of *all* trains running at a loss. That interpretation would contradict other federal policies which are intended to provide as much of a choice to the traveler as possible under the National Transportation Policy, and to provide a basic ground transportation system for the National Defense.[32]

Thus, a major study as to public needs for surface transportation in this country is urgently needed. While it is being conducted, there ought to be a moratorium on passenger train discontinuances by the ICC, so that when the report is released and the need for passenger trains perhaps established, there will be some existing trains left to begin to meet that need. There are less than 500 trains left, and the railroads can push discontinuances through the ICC very quickly, as each case must be decided within four months. Soon rail passenger service may not exist.

The study should not be limited to the need for passenger trains alone, but should investigate the need for ground transportation services in general. The ICC fails to support a comprehensive study, insisting instead on the narrower study of railroad services it has been advocating for three years.[33] The question of who should conduct this study is extremely important. Attention ought to be focused on recruiting "experts" who have open minds about the question to be studied. No "expert" who has regularly been on one side of the issue should be connected with this study.[34]

The ICC did conduct an *Investigation of Costs of Intercity Rail Passenger Service,* released in 1969, but it does not fulfill the need for a study of future demand for various forms of ground transportation. Rather, it projects how much money eight particular carriers would save if they got rid of their passenger service as of December 31, 1968. The ICC came up with a figure of $118.1 million for the eight carriers. The correct figure is actually closer to $74.9 million (37 per cent less than the one quoted by the Commission), taking into account the income tax savings resulting from higher gross income after dissolution of passenger service.

The publicizing of the pre-tax figure constitutes somewhat of a violation of the ICC's own case law. In recent 13a cases, the Commission has announced that the tax consequences of reduced losses cannot be ignored, reporting that it is unrealistic "to ignore the heavy tax impact that frequently accompanies the savings in a train discontinuance, an impact which would eliminate a material amount out of every dollar supposedly saved." [35]

The Cost Investigation found that the railroads themselves were making an even greater exaggeration of the costs of rail passenger service than the Commission did: they were measuring the cost in terms of the "full deficit" of all their services ($214.2 million) rather than in terms of actual "avoidable costs" ($74.9 million). The latter "avoidable costs" measures the amount of money that could be saved if passenger services were halted. The former includes both "avoidable" expenses, and expenses shared between freight and passenger service, expenses which could not be eliminated with the elimination of passenger operations. Such shared costs include equipment and structures which would have to be retained by the railroad to continue its freight operations.

The practical significance of the use of the full deficit to estimate how much the railroads could save if they got out of the passenger business is enormous. In the words of the ICC study: [36]

Use of the ICC full deficit, which was $214.3 million in 1968 for the eight carriers, to approximate the savings that could have been made by eliminating intercity passenger service, results in a major overstatement of those savings. Even if all data were wholly accurate and all rules were uniformly applied, it is apparent that neither solely related nor full expense costing would indicate the trends or size of the burden of intercity passenger service.

The Cost Investigation was an admirable attempt by the ICC to approach a particular problem from a "task force" point of view. It was limited by time and resources, but the staff work done, headed by Richard E. Briggs, was at least headed in the right direction. Several cautionary statements must be made about the study, however. First, as mentioned above, the figures used in this report were figures submitted by the railroads to the ICC. They are inherently suspect, since it is in the interest of the railroads to inflate expenses and deflate revenues, in order to justify their claims about losses from passenger operations. In fact, the ICC found significant errors in the carriers' estimates of their avoidable expenses and in their annual reports. The total errors in their estimated avoidable expenses amounted to $17,078,-762, for a net *decrease* in net avoidable expenses of $13,-061,078.[37] As for errors in their annual reports to the ICC, the net passenger losses of the eight railrads were overstated by $4,418,292.[38]

Even after discovering these errors, the ICC issued its own warnings hidden away on page 27 of the report: [39]

Although all reported expenses were tested to determine if they would have been avoidable, most of the expenses not found avoidable were not checked for accuracy of reporting in the carriers' annual reports. *Thus, the total amount of error in the data reported to the Commission is not known. It should not be assumed that all unexamined expenses are without some error.* (Emphasis supplied.)

As long as the ICC continues to reply on figures submitted to it by the railroads, it cannot adequately judge the burden of passenger service in dollars and cents.

And although the ICC formally gave up *its* "full deficit" as a way of stating how much the railroads could save if they diverted themselves of rail passenger service, it reverted to its usual timidity when faced with having to rap the knuckles of the railroad industry, by announcing that it was retaining the "full deficit" reporting method until Congress acted in the area of rail passenger service.

This action should be reversed, and the carriers required *now* to use the avoidable cost method because, first, the ICC has no business considering the time and money of the railroads more important than the public's interest in knowing at least a reasonably accurate version of how much the railroads are losing carrying passengers. Second, the decision to wait for Congressional action is too open-ended, with no definite time within which the railroads must begin to use the new method. Third, the ICC engages here in the common but discouraging practice of passing the buck to Congress, when the resulting harm in inaccurate reporting far outweighs the possible burdens placed on the carriers.

Whatever the reason for the decline of intercity rail passenger service—and it seems clear that the railroads themselves have been responsible for a great deal of the decline—strong federal action is needed now in order to preserve a national asset which will, with proper management, undoubtedly be of great importance to the nation's passengers in the years ahead. Certain changes should have been made a decade ago, when the ICC reported the dangers ahead in its *Passenger Train Deficit* case. The changes in federal policy will cost money, but, as Commissioner Tuggle admitted in an address in October, 1969, not nearly so much as comparable changes would cost in airline and highway policies.

These changes will be of great benefit to the American people and the American economy. The costs of pollution from automobiles and buses are obvious. Airlines have been recognized as a major cause of air pollution. Delays in the air are costly, both to the airlines and the air passengers; one study estimated that the total "cost of effectiveness" of the air-support system will be nearly $3 billion a year in 1975.[40]

A prerequisite for these changes must be the development of a more positive attitude both in the ICC and in the railroad industry. In the atmosphere of gloom and resignation that has reigned for so long, the belief that there is absolutely no future in the rail passenger business has become an accepted truth. As stated in a 1959 report to the Secretary of Commerce by a transportation consultant,[41]

Concentration on the fact that there is a deficit in the passenger service as a whole can have paralyzing effects on railroad management and labor because of the negative viewpoint and psychological pressures created by the idea that the whole function is a burden. *Even if portions of the whole are profitable, they may be lost or ignored because of a total climate of despair or frustration.*

Aside from this important attitudinal change, various concrete steps should be taken now, not to save the passenger train as it is—dirty and slow for the most part—but to lay the groundwork for the re-invigoration of the passenger train system.

First of all, a comprehensive study must be made in conjunction with D.O.T., by an independent consultant not connected with the railroad industry, of the needs for ground passenger transportation systems in this country for the next thirty years. Such a study was called for by the Doyle Report in 1961. It will take D.O.T. about one year and $2 million to complete—a necessary and worthwhile investment.

Second, pending completion of such a study, an immediate moratorium on passenger train discontinuances must be ordered for the ICC, to insure that there are some trains left when the study is completed.

Third, Congress must pass a strong Standards of Service bill, such as the one proposed by Representative Brock Adams, so that the ICC can begin to put the railroad passenger train in order. Such a law was requested by the ICC in its "Adequacies" decision. This request should be granted, and the ICC given strong authority, so that there are no further excuses for inaction.

Fourth, some decision must be made on how passenger service is going to be financed. It is possible for Congress to require the railroad companies to recognize their common carrier responsibilities and divest some of their vast non-railroad income to finance their passenger operations. The ICC has recognized the dangers to passenger service from excessive diversification into non-railroad holdings,[42] and Congress could meet that recognition by requiring the ICC to consider non-railroad income in 13a cases.

Montana Senator Lee Metcalf insists that Congress should consider non-railroad income of carriers if it decides to inaugurate operational subsidies. Metcalf said in September, 1969, before the ICC: "The question of a carrier's non-rail income as part of its entire total financial position is pertinent to any discussion of our government's transportation policy, and more particularly so if the carrier happens also to be a conglomerate." [43] The railroads do not deserve a federal operational subsidy without any requirement that they shoulder more than a small part of the burden they helped so much to create.

With a federal operational subsidy, the railroads should be forced to bear more than 20 per cent of the deficit arising from passenger operations. It is up to Congress to arrive at a precise allocation of this burden: when it is remembered that the railroads failed to try to make passenger service popular, and when account is taken of the other urgent needs in this country, Congress might be willing to place a larger share of the burden where it belongs—not on the taxpayers, but on the railroad companies.

The above steps must be taken now, but they alone will not solve the basic problems in rail passenger service. Long-range solutions are needed as well.

Congress now has before it several proposals for the revitalization of the nation's railroad passenger service. The current method of moving passengers by rail has obviously failed, and any solution *must* take into account the narrow interests of private industry, capital, and competition, and the need for a concerted governmental policy. Disagreements over the particular plan for the revitalization of rail passenger service should not and cannot prevent Congress from reaching a comprehensive solution in the 91st Congress. In fact, one program could be adopted without excluding others, for Congress could decide to adopt an immediate system of capital subsidies, and then phase in a national rail passenger corporation within a few years. If Congress does not take whatever steps are necessary to correct the errors and deficiencies of the past immediately, the railroads and the Interstate Commerce Commission will dissipate whatever passenger trains remain, and 100 million passengers will be left without rail transportation.

11 / Findings and Recommendations

Findings

THE COMMISSION (1)
Commision appointments have been made almost solely on the basis of political considerations, resulting in a Commission that is unqualified and weak.

> Every Commissioner has a political sponsor. The position, despite its critical importance, has become a political payoff, an elephant's graveyard for political hacks.
>
> The only three Commissioners with any experience received their experience from the industry side.
>
> There is no evidence that any of the Commissioners are even capable of developing that "sharpness" between regulators and regulated which is a prerequisite to regulation in the public interest.

The ICC is now primarily a forum at which private transportation interests settle their disputes.

> The ICC chooses to define policy through its massive caseload, asserting itself directly only through a mere dozen or so rule-making proceedings each year.
>
> Only if the settlement of special interest disputes over the allocation of the transportation market compliments the needs of the public, is the public interest served.
>
> Costs of making and presenting a case (aside from ICC filing fees) are substantial—even for the minor expansion of operating authority—and thus prohibitive for the public and for small businesses.

As a passive forum, the ICC has failed to provide for any useful mechanism for the representation of the public interest in the development of the record.

D.O.T. has intervened on several occasions, but has made it clear that regular intervention will not be forthcoming.

The ICC has asked its own Bureau of Enforcement to enter cases to "develop the facts" in this regard, but Bureau participation has been limited in comparison to that of private interests. Further, the Bureau is not structured to represent the public interest on an *ad hoc* basis.

The Commission's upper staff has a collective personality of extreme conservatism, with all policy recommendations made from within the framework of conditions extant in the 1930's.

The average tenure in the ICC of Bureau Directors is thirty-one years.

Any suggestion to encourage some competition is met with stock answers: "The result would be chaos," or "We remember the 1930's."

Further precluding the possibility of a public interest perspective is the Commission's relationship with industry—which can be generously described as "intimate."

Two hundred twenty trips by Commissioners in three years. According to one Commissioner, 25 per cent of expenses paid by industry.

Pleasure cruises, with industry jets standing by for the Commissioner's use.

An incredible waste of time with 1 million words in three years of speeches written for industry by ICC staff, and extensive travel to meet with industry executives (all well represented in Washington) in the surface transportation meccas of Puerto Rico, Hawaii, and the Bahamas.

The ICC has numerous advisory groups to help set policy at the initial, formative stages within the agency—including not one consumer or consumer representative.

Job interchange levels between the ICC and industry have grown, with "deferred bribes" becoming the norm.

Many officials admit they receive job offers from industry while in government employ.

In the past decade all but one Commissioner who has left the agency has ended up working for a carrier or a carrier association directly, or indirectly as an ICC Practitioner. Many of these men are unqualified in the field and have been chosen because of their connections back in the agency, or as a reward.

A high rate of job interchange at the middle and lower staff levels is more understandable than at the top levels, since most young attorneys view the ICC as a training ground for later transportation industry practice.

Congressional oversight has not affected agency policy.

Hearings are considered "part of the game," and hostile questions are a necessary part of the hearing process.

Congressional oversight committees are understaffed.

Transportation industry investment in the campaigns of Congressmen, particularly on the House side, is substantial.

Much legislation recommended by the ICC originates with industry.

Relations between the public and the ICC have been nonexistent.

The ICC does not discourage esoteric annual reports, news releases, etc., which only the transportation industry can understand.

The ICC's information disclosure policies reflect its extreme solicitousness for industry.

There is evidence of deep corruption at the ICC, beyond "politics" and favoritism.

THE INDUSTRY (2)

The rail and pipeline modes have particularly unique cost structures, with high natural barriers to entry and a potential excess capacity problem.

The ICC's cost analysis tools are out of date and crude.

There is no efficiency advantage in large-size trucking, water, or railroad operations.

A few firms increasingly dominate the entire transportation market under ICC regulation.

There is a great deal of unexplained variation in the efficiency of carriers.

Variation increases where fewer firms are in competition and where ICC regulation is more extensive and specific.

Other studies indicate low utilization of facilities relative to potential for all modes.

Low-cost, low-efficiency carriers are protected by the rate bureaus and restrictions.

Intermodal competition is highly variable and severely limited because of locational advantages and because each mode has a distinct cost advantage for the carriage of specific types of commodities given distances at given loads.

The ICC has not analyzed the full nature and extent of intermodal competition, but relies on it alone to prevent excessive monopoly power pricing.

THE CORPORATE CONGLOMERATE:
CONSOLIDATED MENACE (3)

Rail mergers are motivated, at least in part, by the railroad's desires to expand in size and volume, to limit further price and service competition from other railroads, to combine assets to invest greater resources in diversified interests, and to improve efficiency.

The last wave of rail mergers, beginning in 1959, has created substantial monopoly power for certain carriers within the rail mode.

The ICC has failed to consider the impart of major rail mergers on the shipping public, despite the legal requirement to do so, and has generally rubber-stamped merger requests.

The ICC has failed to consider the interconnecting nature of rail mergers or their virtual permanence once accomplished.

The ICC has failed to develop any kind of plan for rail ownership, or any consistent criteria for merger approval.

Mergers appear to be creating carriers of a size which exceed optimum efficiency and indicate economic disadvantages.

Studies have suggested that promised cost savings of mergers do not occur, but the ICC continues to lend full and unquestioning credence to railroad claims of improved efficiency.

Analysis reveals that most alleged savings are quite possible without merger.

The ICC merger process does not allow for critical examination of merger proposals or for adequate representation of non-carrier interests.

Carrier estimates and data are not carefully checked by the ICC.

Hearing examiners are overwhelmed by the voluminous and technical records, and are not provided with adequate assistance.

Despite interventions by the Department of Justice, and more recently by the cities and the ICC's own Bureau of Enforcement, general economic considerations are not fully explored or considered.

Other possible protestants, such as labor, are sometimes indirectly satisfied under the table to the detriment of the general public interest.

The ICC has no idea who owns the railroads.

Although an essential piece of information in ownership and merger policy, the ICC has refused to fulfill its basic responsibility to acquire these basic data.

There is substantial ownership of railroad stock through Swiss bank accounts and the "street names" of various brokerage houses. Yet another layer of anonymity exists as large investment banks hold stock for individuals through the street names. The ICC refused to look further, and has not pursued the matter.

The failure to determine who owns the railroads is exacerbated by the fact that one-third of the nation's Class I railroads are each owned in whole by less than fifty mysterious persons; past history indicates substantial common ownership is possible and effective in influencing carrier policy.

The ICC has refused to fulfill its responsibility to regulate interlocking directorates.

Many in the ICC did not even know that approval was necessary.

Approval is granted routinely.

The ICC has also routinely approved motor carrier mergers, despite the lack of natural economies of scale for the mode.

The ICC has done virtually nothing about the development of holding companies for the purpose of diversification, despite potential dangers.

Diversification is already extensive.

The commodities clause is avoided.

Capital is drained from transportation facilites.

The ICC has not enforced Section 10 of the Clayton Act.

It has not kept track of subsidiary ownership and dealings and has ignored reports sent in from the field.

Reports of competitive bidding, required by the Act, are not carefully collected and scrutinized.

THE PROTECTION RACKET (4)

The ICC has constructed substantial barriers to entry into the transportation industry, barriers which protect the inefficient.

Carriers are not granted certification so long as existing carriers are potentially able to carry the traffic.

Offering more efficient, faster service, more responsive to the needs of shippers, is not considered relevant to certification.

The offer of lower rates to shippers cannot be considered as a factor in determining the adequacy of existing service under present ICC procedure.

The ICC's barriers to entry stand as *de facto* obstacles to black entrepreneurship.

The ICC has refused to grant authority for blacks, even, in one case, with shipper support and a loan commitment from another federal agency.

Subdivision of operating authority grants to specific carrier types, routes, and commodities has created an infinite number of markets in which carriers can exercise monopoly power.

Authority limitations are extensive and detailed, with some carriers possessing clusters of authority grants.

The great bulk of the ICC's caseload consists of requests by carriers for the privilege of expanding their respective ICC-protected markets into new commodities and along new routes.

ICC justifications for providing entry protection for each carrier have no basis in fact.

Common carrier service is not enhanced by the system.

Assured profits have not resulted in technological progress.

Fly-by-night operations have not been avoided.

Excess capacity has not been eliminated.

All available evidence indicates that with regard to every one of these justifications, excessive regulation and entry protection has resulted in worse conditions: the decline of common carriage, technological stagnation, thriving and growing gypsy operations, increasing excess capacity.

ICC regulatory policies have in fact increased concentration, made intramodal collusive pricing easier, reduced incentives for increased efficiency, facilitated rate discrimination, and lessened service competition.

Most evidence and studies indicate the desirability of a deregulated market system.

THE RATE RAPE (5)

Rate bureaus are not carefully regulated.

Little information is required in rate bureau annual reports.

Although the right of individual carriers to set their own rates is guaranteed by law, the rate bureaus are able to enforce collusive monopoly rates by subjecting independents who undercut bureau rates to expensive litigation within the ICC.

Statistics and interviews indicate that rate bureaus are able to enforce monopolistic prices for each mode.

The ICC's minimum rate powers are used to protect inefficient carriers and modes from competition.

The ICC allows a low rate floor in intermodal disputes when an unregulated carrier or mode or a mode regulated by another agency is involved, but then uses a higher rate floor when an ICC regulated mode is involved.

The ICC has failed to allow railroads to engage in marginal cost pricing, even where there is excess capacity.

The ICC continues to allow commodity discrimination although the historical reason for the system no longer exists.

The discrimination pattern adds to excess capacity and the misallocation of resources between the modes, increasing overall transportation inefficiency and cost.

This discrimination also has pervasive effects through-out the economy. It affects plant location, moving plants miles closer to points of distribution. This has added to the highly dense nature of our urban centers and has directly contributed to urbanization, congestion, and pollution.

The economic effect of the misallocation of resources within the transportation system itself and within the economy at large has been greater overall inefficiency, higher costs, and inflation.

There is also reason to believe that this discriminatory system leads to the over-utilization of natural resources, to our ecological detriment.

The ICC has conducted no study to measure the consequences of this system within the past decade.

After presiding over the destruction of intramodal competition, the ICC has allowed massive rate discrimination on the basis of each mode's monopoly power *vis-à-vis* competing modes.

The ICC does not effectively police or judge rates on its own initiative, relying on protests which neither protect the public interest nor effectively limit damaging discrimination.

Since each mode has different locational and inherent cost advantages, each has a substantial margin for monopoly pricing.

Our own studies, and other evidence, indicate massive discrimination by location, distance, area, *et al.*, as each mode collusively prices well above cost (sometimes five or six times cost) where it has a monopoly advantage and at or below cost where it does not. The result is not only the misallocation of resources between the modes (resulting in carriage at inefficient loads and distances for each mode at higher overall cost), but in discrimination by shipper and by location, further misallocating resources throughout the economy.

The ICC has purposefully suppressed important statistical evidence which indicates the nature and extent of this discrimination.

In addition to the above, the ICC allows "personal" discrimination, the most explicitly outlawed variety and the basis for the ICA in the late nineteenth century.

The ICC has generally failed to limit carrier and bureau requests for rate increases, despite monopoly power by each mode.

There are indications that the modes are now engaging in "price leadership" between themselves as rates are dramatically increased.

The massive rate increases began within months of the most recent acceleration of inflation.

With the exception of several recent motor carrier rate increase cases (partially due to D.O.T. intervention), the ICC has failed to question seriously, much less verify, industry-submitted data; has failed to consider carefully cost increases allegedly justifying rate hikes *vis-à-vis* increased productivity; has not closely examined rates of return; and has allowed a single year of expense rise to justify rate increases.

With regard to motor carrier rate increasese, the ICC has allowed the Suspension Board to increase rates even though there is no provision for refund if the Commission finds the increase unreasonable. Shippers pay until and even if the Commission finds rates unreasonable.

With regard to rail increases, the Commission has completely abdicated its responsibilities. It has allowed the carriers continually to avoid complying with ICC cost evidence requirements, despite Department of Agriculture protest and despite the fact that insufficiently documented "estimates" of expense increases turned out to be inflated by a factor of 6 to 1.

Cost checks are virtually non-existent, and what little is done by way of carrier expense verification is done in secret, in spite of due process requirements.

HIGHWAY SAFETY (6)
According to extensive interviews, research, and a survey of over 1300 truck drivers throughout the country, and substantial documentation produced therefrom, there is massive violation of truck safety regulations.

50 per cent of the drivers were commonly forced to exceed maximum driving limits of ten hours.

48 per cent were on duty for more than the maximum seventy hours in an eight-day period.

78 per cent of the drivers admitted that they had drowsed at the wheel.

56 per cent said that taking pep pills was "common in their industry."

74 per cent had to exceed speed limits to meet company deadlines.

36 per cent said they were forced to drive rigs with inadequate brakes often or more.

41 per cent said they were forced to drive with exhaust leakage into the cab often or more.

42 per cent said they were forced to drive with unsafe loads often or more.

Although the ICC has a potent sanction against carriers who violate these regulations—revocation of authority—it rarely is used.

The ICC even fails to make the simple call to D.O.T. to determine the safety violation record of a carrier whose "fitness" they are considering, although it has explicitly been given that obligation.

Despite current conditions, no carrier, with possibly one exception, has had its authority revoked in recent years because of safety violations.

HOME MOVING (7)

Home movers make estimates which are not binding and which almost invariably underestimate the final bill, then demand full payment in cash on delivery.

Personal checks are not accepted.

Failure to pay within two hours, despite low estimates or no open banks, means that belongings are not delivered, but carted off to a warehouse.

Over one-half of America's moving consumers are overcharged and few know it.

There are numerous tricks for overcharging, including weight bumping, distance manipulation, etc.

Home moving tariffs make no sense, but are never examined by the ICC, despite the obvious lack of opportunity for shipper protest.

Promised dates of departure or arrival often are not adhered to.

Ignorance of any given truck's location adds to uncertainty about pickup and delivery.

Many carriers deliberately overlook and cannot meet their own deadlines.

Interlining and warehousing, often unknown to customers result in numerous incidents of damage, pilfering, etc.

Claims collection is almost impossible.

The ICC has responded to over 5000 complaints per year from victimized home movers by rushing into conference with home moving representatives to formulate a set of rules which serve only to improve the Commission's public image.

The ICC fails to require carriers to keep approximate track of their trucks.

The ICC fails to enforce weight regulation.

The ICC fails to examine tariffs.

The ICC fails to allow higher tariffs for summer rush traffic or lower barriers to entry.

The ICC refuses to shift the collection burden from the customer to the more powerful carrier.

The ICC fails to consider service abuses in extensions of operating authority and fails to suspend or revoke the authority of carriers.

The ICC responds to most complaints with form letters professing "no jurisdiction."

THE FAILURE OF ENFORCEMENT (8)

There is massive violation of the Elkins Act.

The ICC has failed to respond to modern schemes for providing concessions and rebates to large shippers.

Assigned pool cars, specially equipped cars, failure to charge for return empty traffic, failure to charge required expenses in transit, failure to charge demurrage, credit extensions, commodity misrepresentation, special weight agreements, abuse of transit privilege, circuitous routing, *et al.*, are largely ignored by the ICC, to the detriment of small farmers and small businesses.

The ICC's Bureau of Enforcement manpower is allocated very poorly.

Many sections are under-rated; salary and status levels are too low for work performed.

There are so few enforcement personnel given the industry regulated, that compliance with the law is an open joke.

Many truck drivers have never had their logs checked.
Enforcement procedures are extremely inefficient.

Priorities are non-existent, with explicit instructions from
Washington to "increase numbers" so annual report tables
can show greater activity.

Some agents merely go to industry weighing and inspection bureaus and reproduce their records of trivial
violations.

Sanctions are virtually unused.

Despite the lack of manpower, the ICC refuses to
maximize deterrent effect by utilizing its sanctions.

Criminal sanctions are rarely used, despite the severity
of many violations.

Civil penalties are generally very slight.

Operating authority revocation or suspension, perhaps
the most effective sanction, is not used.

BOXCAR SHORTAGE(9)
The ICC has failed to solve the boxcar shortage problem
which plagues small farmers each year.

This is one of the major problems the agency was
created to solve; after eighty-three years the problem
still exists.

The ICC contends that the dimensions of the problem
are currently minimal, but has made no study to substantiate that contention.

The ICC refuses to reveal what statistics it does have
about the efficiency of particular railroads in meeting
common carrier service requirements, because of what
it terms "intermodal equity."

Despite lack of data, there are known industry practices
which add to the shortage problem and which the ICC
has done virtually nothing to change.

The Department of Defense uses boxcars for storage,
generously preferring to pay the demurrage. Other large
shippers less willing to pay the fines are provided boxcar
availability and not charged demurrage through a variety
of dodges.

Generally, even if paid, demurrage fines are accepted
as a part of the business by large corporations. Meanwhile, they hurt the small farmer who might have to pay

demurrage to be sure there is a car available for the brief period when he must have it available.

The ICC has refused to utilize full Service Order 1009 authorizing it to force carriers to move empty cars at the same speed as full cars to satisfy a need. The ICC has used this authority only fifteen times in the past one and one-half years in response to thousands of complaints.

The ICC has refused to revise per diem rates upward, which would increase boxcar supply, despite a clear Congressional mandate to do so.

PASSENGER TRAINS (10)

Although there is a great need and a great demand for passenger trains, the passenger train is disappearing, with less than 500 now left.

With increasing air and road congestion, trains can equal car and plane speeds in the up to 200-mile range.

Trains go right into the center of most cities.

Train propulsion systems pollute less than alternative modes.

Trains have a potential cost advantage at short to intermediate distances.

Trains are not subject to weather or congestion impediments.

Polls and recent train improvement experiments indicate tremendous demand for train travel.

The railroads have caused the decline of the passenger train because of greater profits on freight traffic.

The railroads have caused the decline of the passenger train because of greater profits on freight traffic.

Railroads seek to allocate resources to freight handling facilities because there are at present only minor limits on their monopoly power with regard to freight. With passenger auto and air travel, the railroads' potential monopoly power is not as great in the passenger area as it is in freight. ICC permissiveness and less competition for freight carriage make it more profitable.

The railroads are purposefully downgrading passenger service and are harassing passengers in order to show falling demand to justify discontinuance of trains.

Passenger train management has been given a low priority in rail carrier executive hierarchy.

Cars have not been upgraded or replaced.

No effort is made to encourage sales, with virtually no advertising, no reservation arrangements, no incentive plans for sales, no travel service agreements.

Some railroads have teams which purposefully find ways to harass and discourage potential passengers.

The ICC has done virtually nothing but preside over the funeral.

The agency has refused to regulate service, construing its own authority as narrowly as possible.

It has failed to suggest concrete alternatives.

It has accepted rail figures about revenue loss from passenger operation without question, despite their doubtfulness.

Most recently, the Commission has conferred privately with carrier management about the discontinuance of a large portion of the passenger trains remaining.

Recommendations

Specific recommendations are contained in the body of this report, and others are implicit from criticisms made. The following are our broader recommendations.

The ICC should be abolished in its present form.

Because there has been much reliance on misguided ICC policies, change must come through planned stages. There is a need for some of the functions the ICC should be providing.

A transportation regulatory agency should be created from the ground up.

The new agency should remove overly restrictive barriers to entry and encourage competition within the various modes of transportation.

Unrestricted certificates should be liberally granted and liberally revoked.

Insurance, safety, and common carrier obligations must be enforced, and violation should be grounds for certificate revocation.

Rate bureaus and agreements should be outlawed, and antitrust laws applied and vigorously enforced.

The new agency should concentrate on the policing of rate discrimination and on maximum rate regulation, particularly where monopoly power may be inevitable, as with railroads.

Sophisticated formulas based on modern statistical technique should be used to computerize verification and analysis techniques.

It is necessary gradually and rationally to reduce discrimination in stages, since plants have been inefficiently constructed at less than optimum locations in reliance on the present system.

It is necessary to fully utilize the market where feasible, to see that rates are set at proper levels, and to carefully regulate rates where monopoly power exists.

Rates should be based on cost, with marginal cost pricing allowed where there is excess capacity.

Aftermath

The ICC's official response to the 1200-page report was to refuse comment. The agency openly stated that it would not only refuse to answer the allegations of the report, but would say nothing at all unless Congress required it to do so. One high official expressed the agency's attitude to a *Time* correspondent: "Don't panic. If it just dies down, forget it."

Appendices

APPENDIX 1 Summary of the Interstate Commerce Act *

I. OBLIGATIONS AND RIGHTS OF CARRIERS

A. Before instituting interstate transportation for hire not exempted by some statutory provisions, all regulated carriers must now obtain proper authority from the Commission, either in the form of a certificate of public convenience and necessity required for common carriers, or in the form of a permit required for contract carriers and freight forwarders.

B. All regulated carriers are obligated to institute and provide for-hire transportation, subject to limitations or conditions specified in the authority granted by the Commission. Carriers' services must be available upon request (up to the limits of their facilities), equally to all shippers. Carriers are excused from this duty only when the Commission, acting in the interests of national emergency, declares an embargo or issues car distribution directions or other orders for the movement of traffic (Sections 1(15) and 420 of the Interstate Commerce Act). This power of the Commission has been affirmed by the courts. (See *U.S. v. Michigan Portland Cement Co.*, 270 US 521; *Froehling Supply Co. v. U.S.*, 194 F 2d 637; *U.S. v. Southern Ry. Co.*, 364 F. 2d 86; *U.S. v. Southern Ry. Co.*, 380 F. 2d 49.) The courts have also held that the Commission's orders issued under emergency powers are equally applicable to intrastate traffic. (See *Chicago, M., St. P. & P. R. Co. v. McCree & Co.*, 91 F. Supp. 57.)

C. To insure equality in treatment and charges, carriers must publish and file with the Commission their tariffs or schedules of charges for all services offered by them; they may not charge, demand, collect or receive a greater, lesser or different compensation than the rates or charges specified in the lawfully published tariffs in effect at that time (Sections 6(7), 217(6), 218(a), 306(c), (d) and (e), and 405(c) and (e)).

* The source of this summary is a memo on shipper and carrier compliance by Bernard Gould, Director of the Bureau of Enforcement, ICC. Due to the reduction of this 1200-page report into book form, as noted earlier, the appendices have been abbreviated. Additional documentation of most contentions within the body of the report, and further appendix material, are available upon request. The full report as originally issued may be purchased for $30 from the Center for Study of Responsive Law, Washington, D.C. In addition, some 5000 pages of supplementary appendices are available from Robert Fellmeth, c/o Grossman Publishers, Inc., 125A East 19th Street, New York, N.Y. 10003.

D. Carriers are required to collect their charges promptly and, without some regulatory permission, may not relinquish possession of any freight at destination until all tariff rates and charges are fully paid. (Sections 3(2), 223, 318 and 414 of the Interstate Commerce Act.) In *U.S. v. Hocking Valley Ry. Co.*, 194 Fed 234, aff'd 210 Fed. 755, cert. den. 254 US 757, it was held that unauthorized extension of credit for transportation charges was tantamount to granting the concessions and punishable by law.

E. In relaxing the above strict requirements of prompt payment, an amendment to the original legislation provided that transportation charges may also be collected in accordance with rules and regulations prescribed by the Commission to govern the settlement of rates and charges and to prevent unjust discrimination. Such rules and regulations have been prescribed by the Commission with regard to each particular mode of transportation and published in the Code of Federal Regulations (See 49 CFR 1320 for rail carriers and 49 CFR 1322 for motor carriers; 49 CFR 1323 for water carriers; and 49 CFR 1324 for freight forwarders). In essence, these regulations provided that a carrier, upon taking the necessary precautions, may (but is not required to) grant credit to a shipper in respect to payment of the transportation charges for a period not to exceed the limits prescribed by the regulations.

F. Carriers must comply with the provisions of the Interstate Commerce Act and related acts, as well as with the rules, regulations and orders of the Commission. In addition, all carriers must strictly observe their own tariffs which, upon being properly published, have the binding force of a statute (See *Pennsylvania R.R. Co. v. International Coal Mining Co.*, 238 US 184; *Davis v. Portland Seed Co.*, 264 US 403.)

G. In performing their transportation services, carriers are entitled to protection from unfair or destructive competition.

H. With the exceptions specifically provided in certain instances, carriers are permitted to consolidate or merge their properties or to acquire control of each other, provided it is done with the approval and authorization of the Commission, and upon the terms and conditions prescribed by the Commission's order.

II. OBLIGATIONS AND RIGHTS OF SHIPPERS

Generally speaking, the obligations and rights of shippers correspond respectively to the rights and obligations of carriers. In particular, these duties and rights may be summarized as follows:

a. Shippers have a duty to utilize only properly certificated carriers when certification is required.

b. Shippers must pay lawfully established transportation charges and are protected from excessive rates and charges. Payments must be made either upon delivery of the freight or within the credit periods established by the Commission's regulations.

c. Shippers are entitled to obtain the quantum and quality of service on equal terms with other shippers similarly situated, and may not seek preferential treatment with respect to either service or charges.

d. Shippers must observe the provisions of the Interstate Commerce Act and other related acts, and comply with the Commission's orders directed against them.

III. ENFORCEMENT OF OBLIGATIONS AND RIGHTS OF CARRIERS

   A. *Punitive ex post facto remedies*

The remedies dealing with violations already committed may be classified as follows: criminal prosecution; civil forfeiture suits; and non-litigative settlements in lieu of forfeiture suits. They are described in that order.

   1. *Criminal prosecution*

The provisions authorizing criminal prosecution are found in the Interstate Commerce Act, Elkins Act, Clayton Antitrust Act, and in Title 18 of the United States Code (Crimes and Criminal Procedure). A brief summary of these provisions is given below.

   a. Paragraph (1) of Section 10 of the *Interstate Commerce Act* provides the criminal penalties for violations of the provisions of Part I of the Act for which no penalty is otherwise provided. The fine is not to exceed $5000 for each offense. Additionally, if the offense for which a person is convicted involves unlawful discrimination in rates, fares, or charges, the person, in addition to the above fine, is liable to imprisonment in the penitentiary for a term of not exceeding two years. Penalty provisions for similar violations of Parts II, III, and IV of the Act are to be found for motor carriers in Section 222(a), for water carriers in Section 317(a), and for freight forwarders in Section 421(a).

Paragraph (2) of Section 10 provides identical penalties as in paragraph (1) against common carriers for giving or permitting transportation at less than published rates through false billing, false classification, false weight, false claims, or by other devices or means. Comparable provisions (although different as to the extent of the sanction) are to be found for motor carriers in Section 222(c), for water carriers in Section 317(b) and for freight forwarders in Section 421(b).

   b. Paragraph 1 of Section 5 makes it unlawful for common carriers without Commission approval to enter into pooling agreements involving traffic, service, or earnings. Violations are subject to the penalty provisions of Section 10(1) of the Act.

Paragraphs 2, 3 and 4 of Section 5 deal with unlawful control, consolidation and mergers of common carriers, and unlawful acquisitions of trackage rights without Commission approval. Criminal penalties for such violations are those provided in Section 10(1) of the Act.

   c. Section 20(7)(b) makes it unlawful for any person to make false entries in any reports, accounts, records, etc., or to destroy, mutilate, alter or falsify any such records, reports, accounts, etc., of common carriers. Violations subject carriers to fines of not more than $5000 or imprisonment for not more than two years, or both. Comparable provisions are to be found as to motor carriers in Section 222(g), as to water carriers in Section 317(d), and as to freight forwarders in Section 421(d).

   d. Under Section 1(20) the construction, operation or abandonment of a rail line is made unlawful unless approved by the Commission, and persons convicted of such violation are subject to a fine of not more than $5000 or by imprisonment for not more than three years, or both.

   e. Section 3(2) authorizes the Commission to issue credit regulations governing the settlement of rail transportation charges. Although no penalty is specifically provided for violating this section, prosecutions for severe violations have been prosecuted under Sections 10 and 16(8) of the Interstate Commerce Act, and Section 1 of the Elkins Act. Comparable provisions for motor carriage are to be found in Section 223, for water carriers in Section 318, and for freight forwarders in Section 414 of the Interstate Commerce Act.

f. Section 15(8) which gives the rail shipper the right to route his shipment when there are two or more through routes and through rates applicable to his shipment and which requires the common carrier railroad to observe such route, subjects the carrier to the criminal penalties provided in Section 10(1) for willful failure to observe such route.

g. Section 15(11) makes it unlawful for a common carrier to disclose information to persons other than the shipper of consignees concerning the nature, kind, quantity, destination, consignee, or routing of any interstate shipment, which information may be used to the detriment of prejudice of such shipper or consignee, or which may disclose his business transactions to a competitor. Any person or carrier who violates these provisions would be subject, under paragraph 12 of Section 15, to a fine of not more than $1000. Comparable provisions are to be found as to motor carriers in Section 222(e) and (f), as to water carriers in Section 317(f), and as to freight forwarders in Section 421(f).

h. Under Section 1(7) any common carrier who issues a free pass or free transportation to any person not authorized to receive free transportation is subject to a fine of not less than $100 nor more than $2000. Provisions of this section have been made applicable to motor carriers under Section 217(b) and to water carriers under Section 306(c).

i. Section 20a provides for a fine of not less than $1000 nor more than $10,000, or for imprisonment for not less than one year nor for more than three years, or both, upon conviction of any director, officer, attorney, or agent of a carrier who knowingly assents to or concurs in any issue of securities or assumption of obligations without Commission approval, or any sale or other disposition of securities contrary to a Commission order. Provisions of Section 20a (2 to 11) have been made applicable to motor carriers under Section 214.

This Section also provides the same penalties against any person who holds the position of officer or director of more than one carrier without Commission approval or for any officer or director to receive for his own benefit any money or other thing of value in connection with sale of securities by the carrier or to share in any proceeds thereof, or to declare dividends from any funds properly included in a carrier's capital account.

j. Section 4 makes it unlawful for a carrier to charge more for a shorter haul than for a longer haul over the same route, or to charge greater compensation as a through rate than the aggregate of the intermediate rates unless specific authorization to do so is granted by the Commission. Violations of this section are subject to the penalties provided in Section 10(1).

k. Section 1(17)(b) makes it unlawful for a carrier agent or employee of a railroad to solicit, accept, or receive money property, or any bribe, with intent to be influenced thereby in his decision or action with respect to supply, distribution, or movement of cars. Violations are punishable by a fine of not more than $1000, or imprisonment in the penitentiary for not more than two years, or both. Section 420 makes this provision applicable to freight forwarders.

1. Section 1(8) provides that violations of the "commodities clause" under which it is unlawful for a railroad to transport any commodity, other than timber or products thereof, in which it has any interest, direct or indirect, except such commodities as may be necessary and intended for its use in the conduct of its business as a common carrier, subject a carrier to the penalties provided for in Section 10(1) of the Act. The "commodities" provision is applicable only to rail carriers.

m. Section 22(1) provides for criminal penalties under Section 10(1) for a carrier which unlawfully charges greater or less compensation than specified in its published tariff with respect to joint interchange mileage tickets or baggage. This provision has been made applicable to motor carriers by Section 217(b), to water carriers by Section 306(c), and to freight forwarders by Section 405(c).

n. The Elkins Act (49 USC 41) was enacted on February 19, 1903, as supplementary legislation to the Interstate Commerce Act, for the purpose of providing effective enforcement means in the field of transportation, or, as stated by the U.S. Supreme Court on several occasions, to cut up by the roots every form of discrimination, favoritism, and inequality. (See *Armour Packing Co. v. U.S.* 209 US 56; *Louisville & Nashville R.R. v. Mottley,* 219 US 467; *U.S. v. Koenig Coal Co.,* 270 US 512.) The Court has also held that the Elkins Act "in its measure of fine and punishment is a terror to evildoers." (See *Penna. R.R. Co. v. International Coal Co.,* 230 US 184.)

With respect to carriers, the Elkins Act provides that willful failure on the part of a carrier subject to the Act to regulate commerce and the acts amendatory thereof to strictly observe its published tariffs is punishable by a fine of not less than $1000 and not more than $20,000 for each offense; the same penalty is imposed if such carriers offer, grant, or give rebates, concessions, or discriminations in respect to the transportation of any property in interstate or foreign commerce; in addition, the individuals convicted of these offenses may also be liable to imprisonment for a term of not exceeding two years. The Elkins Act specifically affirms that the act, omission, or failure of any officer, agent, or other person acting for or employed by the carrier or shipper shall be deemed to be the act, omission, or fatilure of such carrier or shipper as well as that of the person involved, and that the rates published and filed by a carrier shall be deemed to be legal rates, conclusively binding upon such carrier, its officers and agent.

o. Section 10 of the *Clayton Antitrust Act* (49 USC 53) prohibits common carriers from any dealings in securities, supplies or other articles of commerce to the extent of $50,000 in any one year with another corporation, firm, etc., when there are common officers, agents, or directors, or if they have any substantial interest in such other corporation, unless such dealings or purchases are made under competitive bidding. Any common carrier which violates this section is made subject to a fine not to exceed $25,000, and every director, agent, manager, or officer of such carrier who aids or abets such violation is subject to a fine of not to exceed $5000, or a jail sentence not to exceed one year, or both.

p. Under Title 18, Section 660 of the United States Code, the embezzlement, theft, and misapplication of common carrier funds, securities, property or assets by a president, director, officer, or management of a carrier subjects the violator to a fine of not more than $5000 or imprisonment of not more than ten years, or both.

2. *Civil Forfeiture Suits*

Civil fines, penalties, and civil forfeiture suits have also been provided by Congress as an important means of remedying violation by carriers of specific sections of the applicable statutes. Such civil proceedings, when not specifically covered by other statutory provisions, are brought in accordance with Section 2461 of the Federal Rules of Civil Procedure. The more important statutory provisions are as follows:

a. Section 1(17)(a) of the Interstate Commerce Act authorizes the Commission to bring civil actions against carriers for violations of Commission service orders or directions with respect to car service. For violations, penalties of not less than $100 nor more than $500 for each offense, and $50 for each and every day of continuance of the offense are authorized. These provisions are made applicable to freight forwarders by Section 420 of the Act.

b. Sections 20(7)(a) of the Act provides a forfeiture penalty of $500 for each offense and for each day such offense continues with regard to the failure or refusal of a common carrier to keep accounts, records, etc., in the form and manner prescribed by the Commission, and for failure or refusal to submit accounts, records, correspondence, and other documents to authorized Commission agents, examiners, and accountants for inspection and copying. Comparable penal provisions with regard to motor carriers (also covering unauthorized operations) are contained in Section 222(h), and with regard to water carriers in Section 317(d).

c. Section 20(7)(c) provides a forfeiture penalty of $100 for each day that a carrier is in default with regard to filing of annual or other required reports within the time allotted by the Commission. Comparable provisions are made with regard to motor carriers in Section 222(h).

d. Under Section 1(21) the Commission may order an extension of a line of a railroad, and failure to obey such order subjects the railroad to a forfeiture penalty of $100 for each day during which the refusal or neglect to obey the order continues.

e. Section 20(7)(d) provides a forfeiture penalty of $100 for each day that a common carrier fails to accord to special agents, accountants, or examiners of the ICC access to, and opportunity for inspection and examination of lands, buildings, or equipment of the carrier.

f. Section 16(8) subjects any common carrier or its agents to a forfeiture penalty of $5000 for each offense for knowingly failing or neglecting to obey any order of the Commission made under the provisions of Sections 3, 13, or 15 of Part I of the Act. In case of a continuing violation, each day is deemed a separate offense.

g. Section 6(10), which deals with failure or refusal of any carrier to comply with the terms of any regulation or order issued by the Commission under the section concerned with tariff circular rules, subjects the carrier to a forfeiture penalty of $500 for each offense and $25 for each day of the continuance of the offense. (Violations of similar nature on the part of motor carriers, water carriers, and freight forwarders are dealt with under the respective criminal provisions of Section 222(a), Section 317(a), and Section 421(a).)

h. For knowing or willful neglect or failure by a carrier to obey Commission orders issued under Section 51 of the Panama Canal Act (49 USC 51), provision for civil forfeiture penalties of $5000 for each offense and for each day of the continuance of the offense are applicable under Section 16(8) of the Interstate Commerce Act.

i. Section 19 a(k) of the Interstate Commerce Act, which concerns the valuation of property of carriers, provides a forfeiture penalty of $500 for each offense and for each day of its continuance for failure or refusal of a common carrier to comply with requirements of Section 19(a).

j. Section 1(12) declares to be unlawful the failure or refusal of a railroad serving coal mines to maintain and apply, during a period when there is a shortage of coal cars, just and reasonable ratings of such mines and to count each and every car furnished to or used by such mines for transportation of coal against such mine. Each car not so counted is deemed a separate offense and the offending carrier is made subject to a forfeiture penalty of $100 for each offense.

(See *United States v. Fruit Growers' Express Co.*, Pa. 1929, 49 S.Ct. 374, 279 US 363, 73 L. Ed. 739; *United States v. Clyde S.S. Co.*, C.C.A. N.Y. 1929, 36 F. 2d 691, cert. denied 50 S. Ct. 350, 281 US 744, 74 L. Ed. 1157; and *United States v. Western Pacific R. Co.*, C.A. Utah 1967, 385 F 2d 161, cert. denied 88 S. Ct. 1805, 391 US 919, 20 L. Ed. 2d 656.)

3. *Non-Litigative Settlements*

Since July 19, 1966, the Commission has been enabled by Congress significantly to reduce the amount of time and money consumed in litigation under the Interstate Commerce Act and supplementary legislation through use of the provisions of the Federal Claims Collection Act of 1966 (31 USC 952).) Under this legislation, the Commission may enter into Settlement Agreements with parties who might otherwise be put through the ordeal of protracted legal proceedings, to compromise and collect civil claims not to exceed $20,000 each. Such authority may not be exercised as to claims bearing indications of fraud, presentations of false claim, misrepresentation, or violation of the antitrust laws. A compromise effected under this provision is final and conclusively binding on the parties and the government as to the right to institute civil forfeiture proceedings for the same claims.

B. *Compulsion As To Future Behaviour of Carriers*

The Commission is also empowered under specific provisions of the Interstate Commerce Act and the Elkins Act, and for the particular purposes set forth therein, to take steps toward the regulation of the prospective behaviour of carriers as to the future.

1. *Civil Injunction Actions By ICC*

Many provisions of the Interstate Commerce Act and supplementary legislation authorize the ICC to request the Attorney General's Office to institute proceedings in the federal courts to have carriers enjoined from particular illegal actions in which they are engaged or may engage in the future. The Commission may thus proceed to have civil injunctions obtained against carriers in connection with abandonments of service; violation of antitrust laws; enforced furnishing of cars; operation without proper authority; unauthorized consolidation, merger or acquisition of control; practice of discriminations; or violations of Commission orders. Moreover, in case of the violation by motor carriers of any statutory provision, rule, regulation, requirement, or order, the Commission may apply directly to the federal district courts under Section 222(b)(1) for issuance of a writ of injunction or other process to restrain further violations. Statutory provisions providing for injuctive relief are as follows:

a. Section 3 of the Elkins Act authorizes the ICC to request the Attorney General to institute proceedings to enjoin a common carrier from engaging in carriage at less than the published rates on file or from committing unlawful discriminations.

b. Section 5(8) authorizes the Commission to apply to the federal district courts for writs of injunction or other process, mandatory or otherwise, to restrain carriers from violation of the consolidation, merger and control provisions of Section 5. Comparable provisions are to be found as to freight forwarders in Section 411(e).

c. Under Section 1(20), the ICC may sue in the federal courts to enjoin the unauthorized and unlawful construction, operation, or abandonment of a railroad line.

d. Section 16(12) authorizes the Commission to apply to any district court for the enforcement by injunction of any order of the Commission other than for the payment of money, because of the failure of any carrier to obey such order. Comparable provisions are to be found in Section 222(b) as to motor carriers, in Section 316(b) as to water carriers, and in Section 417(b) as to freight forwarders.

e. Under Section 20(9) the Commission may request the Attorney General to apply to the federal courts for issuance of writs of mandamus to compel common carriers to comply with the provisions of applicable statutes. Similar provisions are to be found as to motor carriers, water carriers, and freight forwarders, in Sections 222(b), 316(b), and 417(b), respectively.

f. Injunctive relief for the enforcement of Commission orders issued under Section 51 of the Panama Canal Act, 49 USC 51, may be had under Section 16(12) of the Interstate Commerce Act.

g. The Commission may enforce its order under Section 1(9) for a railroad to provide a switch connection by applying to the federal courts under Section 16(12) for mandatory injunction.

2. *Civil Injunction Actions By Carriers*

In addition to the statutory provisions which authorize the ICC to take initial steps toward having suits for injunction initiated in the federal courts, there is provision made in Sections 222(b)(2) and 417(b)(2) for any person, including a competing carrier, injured by another's operation in clear and patent violation of the terms of section 203(c), 206, 209, 211 or 410 (relating to requirements that for-hire motor carriers, freight forwarders, or brokers may operate only in accordance with the terms of certificates, permits, or licenses issued by the ICC), or any rules, regulations, requirements, or orders issued thereunder, to apply directly to the federal district courts for enforcement of such provisions by writ of injunction or other process to restrain the parties from further violations. The Commission, represented by the Bureau of Enforcement, is authorized to appear as of right in any such civil action brought by the allegedly injured person.

(See *Baggett Transp. Co. v. Hughes Transp. Inc.* (CA 8, 1968, 393 F. 2d 710, cert. denied 393 US 936, 89 S. Ct. 297).)

3. *Revocation or Suspension of Operating Rights*

Upon complaint or on its initiative, the Commission may institute an investigation proceeding against a regulated carrier. If it is found that the carrier willfully failed to comply with the provisions of the Interstate Commerce Act, or with any lawful order, rule, or regulation of the Commission, or failed to observe the terms, conditions, or limitations imposed by the Commission in granting the operating rights, then the Commission may suspend, modify, or revoke the certificate or permit issued to such carrier (Sections 212, 312(a) and 410 of the Interstate Commerce Act).

4. *Cease and Desist Orders of the Commission*

The Commission may also, upon a complaint or on its own initiative, institute an investigation into the practices of a carrier, and if it is found that a violation has been committed or an unauthorized operation has been conducted, the Commission may order corrective measures or issue cease and desist orders for discontinuance of unlawful practices (Sections 15, 216, 218, 307, 315 and 406 of the Interstate Commerce Act). Pursuant to Section 2 of the Elkins Act (49 USC 42), such orders may be issued not only against a carrier, but also against other persons (including shippers) which are "interested in or affected by" the practice under consideration. (See, for example, *Empire Truck U-Drive-It, Inc.,—Investigation*, 96 M.C.C. 29.)

IV. ENFORCEMENT OF OBLIGATIONS AND RIGHTS OF SHIPPERS

The Interstate Commerce Act and supplementary legislation make provision for the enforcement of the rights and obligations of shippers, in addition to those of carriers previously mentioned. Enforcement here is also had by means of punitive measures as through use of compulsion as to future actions.

A. *Punitive Remedies*

Enforcement of penal provisions may involve direct prosecution of shippers, their joinder in criminal prosecution of carriers, joinder as parties in interest in civil forfeiture suits, and involvement in claims settlement transactions.

1. *Direct Prosecutions*

Shippers and other persons may be the subject of direct prosecutions for criminal violations in accordance with several provisions, most notably Section 1 of the Elkins Act. The more important criminal prosecution provisions are as follows:

a. Section 10(3) provides that any person or company, or employee thereof, who delivers property to a common carrier for transportation and who knowingly and willfully obtains or attempts to obtain transportation at less than the established rates by means of false billing, false classification, false weighing, false representation as to contents, false statement, or by any other device is made subject to a fine for each offense not to exceed $5000, or imprisonment for a term not exceeding two years, or both. Comparable provisions are to be applied as to motor carriers under Section 222(c), to water carriers under Section 317(c) and to freight forwarders under Section 421(C).

b. Section 15(8), previously mentioned with regard to the duty of carriers, gives shippers the right to route their shipments when there are two or more through routes and through rates applicable to their shipments, and the common carrier railroads are obliged to observe such routes. Any carrier who willfully fails to observe the shipper's routing subjects himself to the general criminal provisions to be applied under Section 10(1) of the Act.

c. Sections 1(17(b) makes it unlawful for any person to offer or give any money, property, or thing of value or a bribe to any person acting for or employed by a railroad, with intent to influence his decision with respect to supply, distribution, or movement of cars. The penalty for violation of this provision is a fine of not more than $1000 for each offense, or imprisonment for not more than two years, or both. This section is made applicable to freight forwarders by Section 420 of the Act.

d. Section 222(c) subjects any shipper who knowingly solicits, accepts or receives a rebate, concession, or unlawful discrimination or who knowingly and willfully assists any persons to obtain transportation for less than the applicable rates by means of false statements or any other device, to a fine of not less than $200 nor more than $500 for the first offense and not less than $250 nor more than $2000 for any subsequent offense. Comparable provisions are made applicable to dealings with rail carriers under Section 10(3), with water carriers under Section 317(c), and with freight forwarders under Section 421(c).

e. Section 1 of the Elkins Act makes it unlawful for any person or corporation to offer or give any rebate, concession, or discrimination in respect to the transportation of any property by a common carrier whereby such property is transported at a less rate than that named in the published tariffs, or whereby any other advantage is given or discrimination is practiced. Any shipper who knowingly violates this section is made subject to a fine of not less than $1000 or more than $20,000. Any person or employee who is convicted of such violation is additionally made liable to imprisonment for a term not exceeding two years, or to both such fine and imprisonment.

2. *Joinder as Aider and Abettor*

Shippers and associated persons may also face criminal prosecution for unlawfully aiding and abetting or assisting carriers in illegal practices. (Title 18, USC Section 2).

a. Under Section 10(4) any person who aids or abets a common carrier in an unjust discrimination is made subject to a fine or imprisonment, or both, and such person is also made liable, jointly and severally with the carrier, in an action brought by the consignor or consignee discriminated against for all damages suffered.

b. Section 1(3) of the Elkins Act provides that any shipper who knowingly, directly or indirectly, by any means or device whatsoever, receives or accepts a rebate or offset against the regular transportation charges from a common carrier, is made liable, in addition to any penalty provided, to forfeiture of an amount of money equal to three times the value of the consideration so received or accepted by the shipper within a period of six years prior to commencement of the action, may be included in the calculation of the amount of the treble forfeiture.

3. *Joinder in Civil Forfeiture Suits*

Shippers and their employees may be subjected to or joined in civil forfeiture proceedings and suits to enforce civil fines and penalties for violation of the provisions of the Interstate Commerce Act and supplementary legislation. Under applicable provisions they are also made liable for repayment of civil damages suffered by other persons such as competing shippers and carriers.

a. Under Section 10(4), any shipper or employee who, by payment of money or other thing of value, by solicitation or otherwise, induces or attempts to induce a common carrier to discriminate unjustly in his favor as against any other consignor or consignee or aids or abets a carrier in such act, is, together with the common carrier, made jointly and severally liable for all resulting damages, in an action to be brought by any consignor or consignee discriminated against.

b. Under Section 16(4), all parties in whose favor the Commission has made an award for damages by means of a single order issued in accordance with the complaint provisions of Section 13, including shippers claiming for damages suffered as a result of violations of the Act by carrier defendants, may be joined as plaintiffs in a civil action wherein all joint plaintiffs are maintaining a suit against all joint carrier defendants. An identical provision as to shippers who have claims against freight forwarders may be found in Section 308(g).

c. Section 2 of the Elkins Act provides that, in any proceeding brought to enforce the statutes relating to interstate commerce, whether before the Commission itself or the federal course, it is lawful to include as parties, in addition to the carrier, all persons interested in or affected by the rate, regulation or practice under consideration, and that orders and decrees may be made with reference to and against such additional parties to the same extent as they are authorized with respect to carriers.

4. *Non-Litigative Claims Settlements*

With regard to shippers, as with carriers, the Commission was authorized under the Federal Claims Collection Act of 1966 (31 USC 952) to avoid the necessity of prolonged litigation by utilization of Settlement Agreements to collect civil claims for violation of statutory provisions. Use of this procedure by the Commission is again limited to claims not exceeding $20,000 each and only for circumscribed situations.

B. *Compulsion as to Future Behaviour of Shippers*

The Commission has been provided with certain powers and duties to take steps to compel shippers to comply in the future with statutory provisions and Commission orders applicable to them.

1. *Civil Injunction Actions Under Section 222(b) of the Interstate Commerce Act*

Under the provisions of Section 222(b), a shipper acting in concert or participating with a carrier may be joined in civil injunction proceedings brought by the Commission and may be made subject to injunction or other process, including mandamus, to restrain him or any of his employees or representatives from further violations.

2. *Joinder Under Section 2 of the Elkins Act*

Under Section 2 of the Elkins Act, it is made lawful, in any proceeding for the enforcement of the statutes relating to interstate commerce, whether such proceeding is instituted before the Commission or in the federal courts, to include and join as parties in interest all persons interested in or affected by the rate, regulation, or practice under consideration, including shippers and related persons, and to make inquiries, investigations, orders, and decrees with reference to and against such parties to the same extent as with respect to carriers.

3. *Complaints for Inadequacy of Service or Other Reasons*

Any shipper dissatisfied with the rates and charges, the service rendered, or with prejudicial or discriminatory treatment, is entitled to file a complaint with the Commission. Upon receiving the carrier's answer, or upon full investigation of the complaint if it appears necessary, the Commission may grant the necessary relief and, in particular, may issue orders to remove the prejudice or discrimination or to correct the service inadequacy (Sections 13, 15, 204, 216, 218, 304, 307, 315, 403 and 406 of the Interstate Commerce Act).

4. *Complaints for Recovery of Reparations or Overcharges*

Whenever a shipper believes that the rates charged by the carrier were unjust and unreasonable, or unjustly discriminatory, unduly preferential or prejudicial, it may file a complaint for reparations, requesting that just and reasonable rates be determined by the Commission and an award of reparations be made. Similarly, if a carrier has assessed and collected transportation charges in excess of the lawfully applicable rates, the shipper may file a complaint for recovery of overcharges. The Commission's findings in this connection may be used as prima facie evidence in suits brought in courts for recovery of the damages or the aggrieved party may first institute an action for the determination and enforcement of such claims in court which would refer the matter to the Commission for the determination of the lawful and applicable rates (Sections 13, 16, 204(a), 216(c), 308(c) and (d), 406(b) and 406(a) of the Interstate Commerce Act).

The Commission's General Rules of Practice prescribe that where the Interstate Commerce Act provides for an award of damages and the carrier involved is willing to pay them, a petition for authority to pay may be filed by the carrier on the special docket in the form prescribed by the Commission. If the petition is granted, the Commission will enter an order authorizing the payment (Rule 25).

APPENDIX 2 Commissioners' Trips

Following is a list of the trips that each Commissioner who held office in September, 1969, took during the past three years. None of the Commissioners ever visited a meeting purely of consumers.

Mrs. Virginia Mae Brown (1966–1969): 48
  6 local traffic clubs
  3 general transportation associations
  3 railroad industry groups
  5 motor carrier industry groups
  1 water industry group
  1 freight rate bureau
  4 transportation seminars
  5 ICC business
  1 ICC Practitioners Association
  1 Motor Carrier Lawyers Association
  5 miscellaneous political
  5 miscellaneous civic
  6 miscellaneous industry

George Stafford (1967–1969): 34
  2 general transportation associations
  2 railroad industry groups
  7 motor carrier industry groups
  1 home movers' groups
  5 shippers' groups
 10 ICC business, government business
  3 ICC Practitioners Association
  1 miscellaneous political
  1 miscellaneous civic
  1 miscellaneous industry
  1 transportation seminar

Dale Hardin (1967–1969): 24
  1 general transportation association
  1 railroad industry group
  1 motor carrier industry group
  2 shippers' groups
  5 transportation seminars
  6 ICC business and government business
  5 ICC Practitioners Association
  1 miscellaneous civic
  1 M.C.L.A.
  1 miscellaneous industry

Donald Jackson (1969): 4
  1 miscellaneous civic
  3 miscellaneous industry

Willard Deason (1966–1969): 9
  1 motor carrier industry group
  2 home movers' groups
  1 transportation seminar
  1 ICC business
  1 ICC Practitioners Association
  2 miscellaneous political
  1 miscellaneous industry

John Bush (1966–1969): 32
- 2 local traffic clubs
- 3 general transportation associations
- 2 railroad industry groups
- 10 motor carrier industry groups
- 1 shippers' group
- 3 transportation seminars
- 4 ICC business
- 1 bus industry group
- 2 ICC Practitioners Association
- 2 M.C.L.A.
- 1 miscellaneous political
- 1 miscellaneous civic

Kenneth Tuggle (1965–1969): 9
- 1 general transportation association
- 3 railroad industry groups
- 1 motor carrier industry group
- 1 shippers' group
- 1 transportation seminar
- 1 ICC Practitioners Association
- 1 miscellaneous industry

Paul J. Tierney (1966–1969): 33
- 2 railroad industry groups
- 7 motor carrier industry groups
- 5 shippers' groups
- 1 bus industry group
- 7 transportation seminars
- 3 ICC business, government business
- 1 general transportation association
- 4 ICC Practitioners Association
- 1 M.C.L.A.
- 1 miscellaneous political
- 1 miscellaneous civic

Robert Murphy (1966–1969): 39
- 5 general transportation associations
- 2 railroad industry groups
- 4 motor carrier industry groups
- 1 bus industry group
- 1 home movers' industry group
- 10 shippers' groups
- 3 transportation seminars
- 9 ICC business, government business
- 4 miscellaneous industry

Laurence K. Walrath (1966–1969): 19
- 1 local traffic club
- 1 railroad industry group
- 3 motor carrier industry groups
- 3 shippers' groups
- 6 ICC government business
- 1 general transportation seminar
- 1 ICC Practitioners Association
- 1 M.C.L.A.
- 2 miscellaneous industry

APPENDIX 3 Commissioners' Itineraries

The itineraries of Commissioners Bush and Tierney from 1966–1969, reproduced here, are typical of commission sojourns. Rarely is a visit made to an educational transportation seminar, and never—as stated above—to a *bona fide* consumers' group.

COMMISSIONER JOHN BUSH (Ohio)

Date	City	Purpose
1/12/66	New York City	Member of Roundtable Discussion at National Transportation Institute.
1/24/66	New York City	New Haven hearing.
2/17/66	Palm Springs, California	Speaker, Meeting of Board of Governors of the Regular Common Carrier Conference, American Trucking, Inc.
3/8/66	Miami, Florida	Speaker, 18th Annual Meeting of Common Carrier Conference, Irregular Route, American Trucking Associations, Inc.
4/18/66	Honolulu, Hawaii	Speaker, 20th Annual Membership Meeting, Western Highway Institute.
5/12/66	Chicago, Illinois	Moderator of panel discussion, 37th Annual Meeting of Association of Interstate Commerce Commission Practitioners.
5/19/66	Philadelphia, Pennsylvania	Speaker, 29th Annual Conference, Motor Carrier Lawyers Association.
6/13/66	Hot Springs, Virginia	Speaker, 36th Annual Convention of Virginia Highway Users Association.
8/7/66	New York City	Visit to New York field office.
9/12/66	Asheville, North Carolina	Speaker, 37th Annual Convention of North Carolina Motor Carriers Association, Inc.
10/18/66	Nashville, Tennessee	Attended Congressman Joe L. Evins Day; invited by Harold Sims, Chairman.
11/3/66	Phoenix, Arizona	Speaker, 37th Annual Meeting of the National Association of Motor Bus Owners.
12/9/66	Chicago, Illinois	Speaker, Joint Meeting of the Chicago Regional Chapter of the Association of Interstate Commerce Commission Practitioners and the Traffic Club of Chicago.

Date	City	Purpose
2/17/67	Toledo, Ohio	Speaker, Institute on National Transportation Policies, Toledo Area Chamber of Commerce.
3/30–4/2/67	Palm Springs, California	Participated in the 30th Annual Conference of Motor Carrier Lawyers Association.
4/10/67	Phoenix, Arizona	Speaker, 21st Annual Membership Meeting of the Western Highway Institute.
4/21/67	Biloxi, Mississippi	Speaker, Annual Meeting of Alabama Trucking Association, Inc.
6/21–30/67	Geneva, Switzerland	Meeting of the United Nations Committee of Experts on the Transportation of Dangerous Goods.
8/30/67	Little Rock, Arkansas	Participated in the signing of the Cooperative Enforcement Agreement between the Arkansas Commerce Commission and the Interstate Commerce Commission in accordance with Public Law 89-170.
9/24–26/67	Fayetteville, North Carolina	Attended the North Carolina Motor Carriers Association, Inc.'s Convention.
10/12/67	Chicago, Illinois	Speaker, Railroad Transportation Institute's Fall Seminar.
3/5/68	Dallas, Texas	Speaker, Oil Field Carriers Conference and Shippers Oil Field Traffic Association and Oil and Gas Well Supply Traffic Association.
5/3/68	Roanoke, Virginia	Speaker, combined meeting of the Roanoke Valley Traffic and Transportation Club and the Delta Nu Alpha Transportation Fraternity.
5/14/68	Columbus, Ohio	Speaker, combined meeting of the Columbus Chapter of National Defense Transportation Association and the Delta Nu Alpha Transportation Fraternity.
7/26–28/68	Boston, Massachusetts	Attended the Transportation Seminar sponsored by the New England Council and the New England Regional Commission.
9/22–24/68	Chicago, Illinois	Attended Association of American Railroads Data System

Date	City	Purpose
		Division's Annual Meeting.
5/13/69	New Orleans, Louisiana	Speaker, 21st Annual Convention and Tank Truck Equipment Show of National Tank Truck Carriers, Inc.
6/10/69	Hot Springs, Arkansas	Speaker, Midwest Association of Railroad and Utilities Commissioners' 1969 Convention.
6/28/69	Portsmouth, Ohio	Speaker, Annual Meeting of the Scioto County Bar Association and guest lawyers from the central-southern Ohio area.

COMMISSIONER PAUL TIERNEY (Maryland)

Date	City	Purpose
3/23–25/66	Palm Springs, California	Panel discussion, Annual Meeting of the Western Forest Industries Association.
5/3–5/66	Dallas, Texas	Speaker, 7th Annual Mid-Year Meeting of the ATA Private Carrier Conference.
5/11–13/66	Chicago, Illinois	Speaker, ICC Practitioners Association.
9/21–22/66	St. Louis, Missouri	Panel discussion, FBI Convention of Society of Former Special Agents.
2/24–25/67	Atlanta, Georgia	Speaker, 65th Annual Meeting of the Atlanta Freight Bureau.
3/29–30/67	College Station, Texas	Speaker, 9th Annual Transportation Conference of Texas A&M University.
5/2–4/67	Detroit, Michigan and Chicago, Illinois	Speaker, Annual Meeting of the National Conference of State Transportation Specialists; inspected ICC regional office, Chicago.
6/21–26/67	San Francisco, California and Portland, Oregon	Speaker, 38th Annual Meeting of the Association of Interstate Commerce Commission Practitioners; attended ICC Region 6 Staff Conference, S.F.; inspected Southern Pacific Company plant.
8/3–4/67	Boston, Massachusetts	Transportation panel discussion, Joint Meeting of the Transportation Management Club of Boston and District No. 1 Association of ICC Practitioners.

Date	City	Purpose
9/12–13/67	New York City	Speaker, Purchasing Agents Association of New York First Fall Dinner Meeting.
9/21/67	New York City	Attended the Hayden, Stone Transportation Forum Panel Discussion.
11/1–2/67	Louisville, Kentucky	Speaker, Louisville Chapter, Association of ICC Practitioners.
12/2/67	Baltimore, Maryland	Speaker, Workshop Seminar sponsored by the Baltimore Chamber of Commerce.
12/8–9/67	Pittsburgh, Pennsylvania	Speaker, Community Relations Committee of the Pittsburgh Railroads.
2/7–9/68	Los Angeles, California	Attended funeral of Commissioner Grant Syphers.
2/13–16/68	Palm Springs, California	Speaker, Board of Governors, Regular Common Carrier Conference.
3/7–8/68	Des Moines, Iowa	Speaker, Annual Meeting of the Centerville Chamber of Commerce.
3/11–14/68	Miami, Florida	Speaker, Annual Meeting of the Irregular Route Common Carrier Conference.
4/18/68	Providence, Rhode Island	Speaker, Signing of the Cooperative Agreement between the ICC and the State of Rhode Island.
4/20–7/68	Honolulu, Hawaii	Speaker, Annual Meeting of the Western Highway Institute.
5/2–3/68	Detroit, Michigan	Speaker, Motor Carrier Lawyers Association Conference.
6/2–3/68	White Sulphur Springs, West Virginia	Speaker, National Freight Traffic Association Spring Meeting.
6/19–22/68	Minneapolis, Minnesota	Speaker, Annual Meeting of the Association of ICC Practitioners.
7/25–26/68	Boston, Massachusetts	Speaker, Special Transportation Seminar Sponsored by the New England Council and the New England Regional Commission.
8/21–23/68	Denver, Colorado	Speaker, Transportation Law Seminar on Practice and Procedure before the ICC, presented by the Motor Carrier Lawyers Association and University of Denver Law College.

Date	City	Purpose
9/10–13/68	Chicago, Illinois	Speaker, Annual Meeting of the National Association of Motor Bus Owners.
9/18–25/68	Yukon Territory, Canada	Speaker, Annual Convention of the Alaska Carriers Association, Inc.; inspection trip from Fairbanks to Anchorage; discussions with members of Alaska Public Utilities Commission.
10/17/68	Wilmington, Delaware	Speaker, 5th Annual Delaware Valley Transportation Conference.
11/12/68	Chicago, Illinois	Speaker, 80th Annual Convention, National Association of Regulatory Utility Commissioners.
11/19–21/68	Miami, Florida	Speaker, Board of Directors, American Trucking Associations, Inc.
11/25–26/68	Toronto, Canada	Speaker, 42nd Annual Convention of the Automotive Transport Association of Ontario.
1/14/69	Chicago, Illinois	Speaker, Transportation Association of American Board of Directors, special luncheon honoring Dr. George P. Baker.
4/9–13/69	Minneapolis, Minnesota	Speaker, Minneapolis Traffic Club.
5/27/69	Pittsburgh, Pennsylvania	Speaker, luncheon to commemorate Trailer Train's 50,000th car going into service.
7/1/69	Hartford, Connecticut	Attended funeral of Commissioner Wallace Burke.

APPENDIX 4 Formal Contacts Between the ICC and Industry

INDUSTRY, PROFESSIONAL, AND PRIVATE ADVISORY AND LIAISON GROUPS
IN WHICH THE ICC PARTICIPATES, AS OF MARCH, 1969

Name of committee, group, or liaison activity	Purpose	Sponsoring and/or participating outside organizations	ICC bureaus and offices participating
1. American Institute of Certified Public Accountants (AICPA)—ICC Liaison Committee	To discuss important accounting matters of mutual interest and innovations of accounting concepts to determine their effects on accounting rules and interpretations prescribed by the ICC for all modes of transportation.	Members of CPA firms selected by AICPA to serve on the committee	Bureau of Accounts
2. American Railroad Engineering Associations	To keep abreast of new developments and techniques in railroad engineering as relates to equipment, tract, bridges, and other way structures.	American Railroad Engineering Association	Bureau of Operations—Section of Railroads
(a) Committee Eleven—Engineering and Valuation	To keep abreast with the current regulations, orders, and reporting requirements of regulatory bodies, agencies, and courts. To make the most efficient use of automatic data processing equipment with respect to engineering, accounting, and depreciation records.	Representatives of the railroad industry who are members of the American Railway Engineering Association	Bureau of Accounts
3. American Trucking Associations, Inc. (a) National Accounting and Finance Council	To keep abreast of technical changes and advances in the industry; discuss and exchange views on proposed and suggested changes in accounting and reporting requirements to insure uniform-	American Trucking Associations, Inc.	Bureau of Accounts

	ity of treatment. These meetings are attended by either departmental or field employees. Upon request the Bureau arranges for its personnel to address the various committees.		
(b) American Trucking Assn.: General; Accounting and Finance Council; National Classification Board; and Research and Transport Economics Department	The Bureau maintains active, informal liaison, generally with ATA and especially with the various listed areas of responsibility within ATA for the purpose of obtaining economic and related information, defining, developing, and coordinating economic data requirements; and the coordination of reporting requirements.	Officials of the ATA and representatives of motor carriers	Bureau of Economics
4. Association of American Railroads (a) Executive Committee; Cost and Statistics; Disbursements; and Internal Audit Committees	To keep abreast of technical changes and advances in the industry; discuss and exchange views on proposed and suggested changes in accounting and reporting requirements to insure uniformity of treatment. These meetings are attended by either departmental or field employees. Upon request the Bureau arranges for its personnel to address the various committees.	Accounting Division of AAR composed of representatives of various railroads	Bureau of Accounts
(b) Finance & Accounting Department; Railroad Accounting Officers General Committee;	The Bureau maintains active informal liaison with the various areas of responsibility within the AAR for the purpose of obtaining economic and related information, defining, developing, and	Officials of the AAR and representatives of railroads serving on Committees	Bureau of Economics

Name of committee, group, or liaison activity	Purpose	Sponsoring and/or participating outside organizations	ICC bureaus and offices participating
Costs and Statistics Committee; Bureau of Railroad Economics; Data Systems Division; Car Service Division; and Public Relations Department	coordinating economic data requirements, working out details of special studies involving railroad participation; coordination of reporting requirements.		
(c) Car Service Division	To determine data on car service, car supply, car distribution, etc.	Association of American Railroads	Bureau of Operations— Section of Railroads
(d) Operations-Transportation Division	To ascertain data on per diem and multi-level value of equipment; demurrage; storage.	Association of American Railroads	Bureau of Operations— Section of Railroads
5. Common Carrier Conference of Domestic Water Carriers-Accounting Committee	To keep abreast of technical changes and advances in the industry; discuss and exchange views on proposed and suggested changes in accounting and reporting requirements to insure uniformity of treatment. These meetings are attended by either departmental or field employees. Upon request the Bureau arranges for its personnel to address the various committees.	Various water carriers and barge lines	Bureau of Accounts
6. Transport Facts Advisory Committee (TAA)	To review, advise, and improve on data in TAA Fact Book.	TAA	Bureau of Economics

7. Highway Research Board—Intercity Highway Freight Transportation—Indirect Effects of Highway Improvement	To promote study of and solutions to highway and general transportation problems, and discussion thereof.	Sponsored by National Academy of Sciences. National Research Council and participants are government agencies interested in transportation, university and private groups interested in transportation (air lines, research groups, etc.)	Bureau of Economics
8. National Shippers Advisory Board	These regional boards hold quarterly meetings at which representatives of the Commission attend and actively participate in discussions.	Railroads and Shippers	Bureau of Operations
9. 13 Regional Shippers Advisory Boards (field)	These regional boards hold quarterly meetings at which representatives of the Commission attend and actively participate in discussions.	Railroads and Shippers	Bureau of Operations
10. Eastern, Western, and Pacific Demurrage Bureaus	To give interpretations and informal opinions on applicability of demurrage and storage charges, as well as interpretations of service orders affecting these charges.	Railroad Industry	Bureau of Operations
11. National Coal Association	Discuss the loadings of bituminous and anthracite coal.	National Coal Association	Bureau of Operations— Section of Railroads
12. American Short Line Railroad Association	Discuss car service to member lines.	American Short Line Association	Bureau of Operations— Section of Railroads

APPENDIX 5 Tenure of Top Commission Staff

Name	Title	Years with ICC
James C. Cheseldine	Chief Hearing Examiner	42
Alvin L. Corbin	Deputy Director, Office of Proceedings	30
Edward H. Cox	Director, Bureau of Traffic	43
Howard L. Domingus	Assistant Director, Bureau of Accounts	34
Thaddeus W. Forbes	Deputy Director, Office of Proceedings	34
H. Neil Garson	Secretary	21
Robert W. Ginnane	General Counsel	15
Bernard A. Gould	Director, Bureau of Enforcement	34
Edward Margolin	Director, Bureau of Economics	11
Robert Newell	Assistant Director, Bureau of Traffic	34
John H. O'Brien	Assistant Director, Bureau of Enforcement	14
Matthew Paolo	Director, Bureau of Accounts	32
Robert Pfahler	Director, Bureau of Operations	23
Robert G. Rhodes	Assistant Director, Bureau of Economics	11
Sheldon Silverman	Deputy Director, Office of Proceedings	23
Bertram Stilwell	Director, Office of Proceedings	44

POLICY MAKERS (excluding Secretary, General Counsel)
1. All: 29 years (average)
2. Director level: 31 years (average)

APPENDIX 6 Investigation Breakdown

Railroads Line Haul—Code 10
Class I
    Annual Revenues over $25 million:

Not subject to C.P.A. certification	1 year
Subject to C.P.A. certification	2 years
Annual Revenues between $5 and $25 million	2 years

Class II

Annual Revenues between $500,000 and $5 million	3 years
Annual Revenues under $500,000	5 years

Switching and Terminal Companies—Not Jointly
    Used—Code 11

Annual Revenues over $5 million	2 years
Annual Revenues under $5 million	5 years

Switching and Terminal Companies—Jointly Used—
    Code 12

Annual Revenues over $5 million	3 years
Annual Revenues under $5 million	6 years

Electric Railways—Code 13

Port Authority–Trans-Hudson Corporation	*As desired
Annual Revenues over $500,000	3 years
Annual Revenues under $500,000	6 years

Express Companies—Code 20

Railway Express Company	1 year

Freight Forwarders—Code 21

Annual Revenues over $1 million	3 years
Annual Revenues under $1 million	6 years

Holding Companies—Code 22

Rail	3 years
Motor	*As desired

Protective Service Companies—Code 23	3 years
Sleeping Car Company—Code 24	3 years
Stockyard Companies—Code 25	*As desired
Pipeline Companies—Code 40	3 years

Water Carriers—Inland and Coastal—Code 50

Annual Revenues over $3 million	2 years
Annual Revenues between $500,000 and $3 million	3 years
Annual Revenues under $500,000	6 years

Maritime Carriers—Code 51	6 years

General Commodity—Code 30 (A-1)
    Annual Revenues over $1 million

Not Subject to C.P.A. certification	1 year
Subject to C.P.A. certification	2 years
Carriers not subject to instruction 27 (requirements with regard to reporting)	2 years

* Examined on a need basis. Motor carrier holding companies not subject to accounting but reporting requirements. Also, stock yard companies.

Annual Revenues between $500,000 and $1 million	2 years
Annual Revenues under $500,000	3 years
Household Goods—Code 31 (A-2)	
Annual Revenues over $1 million	2 years
Annual Revenues under $1 million	4 years
Petroleum—Code 32 (A-4)	
Annual Revenues over $1 million	2 years
Annual Revenues under $1 million	4 years
Others—Codes 33–36 (including local)	
Annual Revenues over $1 million	3 years
Annual Revenues under $1 million	6 years
Undetermined—New Class II's—Code 37	As soon as possible
Passenger—Code 38	
Annual Revenues over $1 million	3 years
Annual Revenues under $1 million	6 years
Passenger and Property—Code 39	3 years

APPENDIX 7 Distribution by Docket Type of Oral Hearings and Cases Heard

FISCAL YEARS 1966, 1967, AND 1968

	Finance Cases			Operating Rights Cases			Rates and Practices Cases		
	1966	1967	1968	1966	1967	1968	1966	1967	1968
Rail Finance Cases	200	389	453						
Motor Carrier Finance Cases	130	133	140						
Motor Carrier Operating Authority Cases				3953	3883	2803			
Formal Docket Cases (Rate Complaints and Investigations)							76	39	30
Investigations and Suspension Cases							18	12	27
All Other Cases				82	91	98	25	9	7
Total Cases Involved in Hearings	330	522	593	4035	3974	2901	119	60	64
Total Hearings Held	259	282	440	2033	1841	1753	80	56	49
Consolidated Hearing Ratio	1.3	1.8	1.3	1.9	2.2	1.7	1.5	1.1	1.3

APPENDIX 8 Blacks Within the ICC

The ICC Manual states in its section on "Equal Employment Opportunity": "Executive Order 11246 of September 24, 1965, established and reaffirmed Government policy for exclusion and prohibition of discrimination against any employee or applicant for employment in the Federal Government because of race, creed, color, or national origin. . . . The Commission will provide equal opportunity in employment for all qualified persons." [1]

If one counts the number of blacks employed at the ICC, there appears to be no "problem" of minority—chiefly black—employment at the Interstate Commerce Commission. The level of black employment in the ICC is relatively high and all the laws are there to protect black employees against job discrimination. Yet, beneath the surface of official policies and apparently benign employment totals lies a racial situation which is every bit as troubled as the society at large.

In the U.S. Civil Service Commission "Evaluation of Personnel Management, Interstate Commerce Commission" (1963), attention was focused on the issue of equal employment opportunity for minority groups. "The prevailing attitude toward this public policy program has been that no problem regarding discrimination or the employment of minority groups exists in the agency, and that therefore little more needs to be done in this area." This official attitude was belied by statements of supervisory personnel indicating the kind of prejudice existing in the ICC: "Every time a Negro is to be considered there is maneuvering here; they don't want Negroes in the Bureau and have very few." "I have none and never have had; some of my employees would not like it, and I try to keep them happy." And, ironically, "It's the Negroes who talk about discrimination who are causing all the trouble, stirring things up." Further findings of the 1963 study included the statement that "There appears to be evidence that a number of organizational segments of the Commission will not and do not give consideration to Negro applicants." [2]

While the official posture of the Commission has improved considerably since the 1963 study—and, as the study indicates, virtually *any* effort to education of the ICC staff on an equal employment policy would have been an improvement—the Civil Service Commission's criticisms of racial prejudice and discrimination affecting the employment status of blacks have evidently not been recognized by all the supervisory personnel in the ICC.

Black morale at the Interstate Commerce Commission is extremely low. Black employees interviewed at the Commission stated that the level of prejudice against blacks is more intense than at other governmental agencies. They point to "pockets" of blacks in certain operations at the Interstate Commerce Commission that make the Commission look like a segregated society. Many blacks tell of their difficulty in getting promotions as rapidly as whites with comparable educational and employment backgrounds. Others speak bitterly about whole offices of blacks being "kept down" as units. Others talk about the sparcity of blacks above the first floor at the ICC—the floor on which generally menial work is performed by offices that are predominantly black.

When asked to pinpoint the apparent reason for the atmosphere of prejudice that confronts black employees at the ICC, some blacks blame the personnel management of the Commission for the problem, despite the fact that the ICC upper management has at least gone through the steps required by the Civil Service Commission, issuing policy statements against racial discrimination and the like. Many point to the method by which promotions are made at the ICC, and center on the role of the supervisor, usually the white supervisor, in deciding whether an individual employee gets advanced or not. "The problem," says Bruce Gordon, Chief of the Mail Room of the Commission, "is largely that of the white supervisors acting out their personal prejudices against black employees."

As of December, 1968, there were 324 "minority" employees at the Interstate Commerce Commission.* [3] This was a slight increase from the 318 minority employees in 1967,[4] and represented an increase of 0.3 per cent in the percentage of minority employees out of all employees. This represented a higher percentage of minority employees than exists overall in the federal government.[5] But the ICC's percentage of minority employees in the lower levels of federal employment—GS 1-4—which are filled by non-professionally-trained and inexperienced employees, is much higher than in the rest of the federal government. The latest figures available for the entire government, for 1967, show that minority group members occupied 51.5 per cent of GS 1-4 jobs in the ICC compares to 20.5 per cent for the entire government.[6] For 1968, the percentage had dropped to 49.4 per cent, but is still an extremely high proportion, especially when compared to the very low percentage of minority group members in higher levels of employment. For GS 5-8 jobs, which in 1969 at the Commission ranged from $6600 to $8753 on the average, minority group members held 18.4 per cent of jobs in 1967, and 21.1 per cent of jobs in 1968. This compared with 11.6 per cent in the federal government as a whole in 1967. For GS 9-11 jobs, which included attorneys and other beginning professionals, the percentage of minority group members in 1967 was 1.3 per cent, while in the government as a whole it was 4.3 per cent. By 1968, the ICC percentage increased to 2.5 per cent (from four blacks to eight). GS 9-11 jobs in 1969 paid on the average between $9232 to $11,000. For GS 12-18 jobs, which ranged in average salary from $13,667 to $30,239 at the ICC in 1969, minority group members held 0.4 of 1 per cent of the jobs in 1967 and 1968. This compared to 1.8 per cent for the entire federal government in 1967. There are no minority group members above GS-14 in the ICC, and only three above GS-12. That means there are no hearing examiners and very few attorneys, administrators, accountants, statisticians, economists, or investigators who are member of minority groups.[7]

The figures speak for themselves—the percentage of blacks "on the first floor" is far greater than in the rest of the federal government, and the number of upper-level and even middle-level policy jobs is extremely small, even lower in percentage than in the rest of the U.S. Government. The reasons are many, and some of them are, of course, beyond the control of the ICC. First, the number of

* The federal government figures are for "minority group" members. In the ICC, this means blacks. The authors use the terms interchangeably, however, referring to the former when describing government statistics.

blacks with the educational background to qualify for the higher level positions is relatively small. Second, there are many agencies that present more exciting possibilities than transportation regulation for blacks with adequate educational achievements: OEO, the Justice Department, HUD, and HEW, for example. In fact, officials of the Personnel Office use the probable higher attractiveness of these other agencies as a partial excuse for the relatively low percentage of blacks in the higher levels of the Commission. Nonetheless, that percentage is still very low.

The core of the problem for blacks within the ICC is the way promotions are handled in the Commission and throughout the federal government. The so-called "Merit Promotion Plan" in essence promotes people not on their merit but on their ability to get good recommendations from their supervisors. Under the ICC Merit Promotion Plan announced July 1, 1969, when a vacancy occurs, the Personnel Office selects certain "qualification standards," under Civil Service Handbook X-118, that describe the vacant job. Personnel then reviews the "Qualification Inventory Record" filled out by ICC employees to indicate their educational and job skills and selects a certain number of "highly qualified" employees, usually from three to five, but no more than ten, whose educational and job skills meet the "qualification standards," and whose "Performance Appraisal for Promotion" is favorable. From this list, the "selecting official" (the supervisor of the vacant job), after interviews, chooses one employee to fill the vacancy.

Involved in this process are four separate points where discretion is allowed. First the Personnel Office has a certain amount of discretion in selecting the "qualification standards" for the particular vacancy. Second, the immediate supervisors have wide discretion in filling out the "Performance Appraisal for Promotion" for their subordinates and, to the employee's disadvantage, these appraisals are *not* available for inspection. Racial prejudice here can effectively be cloaked in broad terms of disapproval of the particular employee. Employees need good promotion potential ratings in order to get ahead, and their careers can be sabotaged by the prejudices of one supervisor. Third, the Personnel Office has a great deal of discretion in selecting those employees it considers "highly qualified" for a particular vacancy. It can exclude employees at will, and can find enough immaterial reasons to cloak otherwise arbitrary exclusions. Fourth, the "selecting official" can simply exercise his own discretion by not accepting an employee on racial grounds, yet professing to make a choice on "objective" standards.* [8]

Thus, individual employees can effectively be eliminated from consideration for promotions at several levels. Blacks at the ICC freely volunteer stories of blacks and whites with identical educational and employment backgrounds getting different promotional treatment. Many such incidents illustrate how blacks with higher objective qualifications were passed over for apparently less-qualified white employees.

Proving discrimination against blacks is difficult because of the murky nature of the promotion process. But the story of one black

---

* Of course, these wide areas of discretion afford the opportunity for promotions to be made on non-racial but equally arbitrary grounds—favoritism, "rocking the boat," etc.

man is instructive: going for an interview for a job for which he was qualified and placed on the "selection roster," he was told by the "selecting official" that he would not be given this job because it was apparent to this "official" that the black man simply wanted this job for his own advancement! [9] As it is difficult to understand how any reasonable man could object to an employee's seeking a promotion for his own advancement, this incident appears to illustrate white prejudice on the part of individual supervisors who block the legitimate progress of individual black federal employees. Despite his anger over having been prevented from getting ahead, the black man who had this experience was aware of the difficulty of proving any discrimination in the case.

Another way in which official procedures tend to weigh against the black employee is in the area of job classifications. Each job has a formal "job description," which is the official identification of the work being done by the person holding the job. Sometimes, however, the actual work being done is either far more difficult or far less difficult than the official description indicates. But the official description is the basis upon which promotion possibilities are based: a group of employees placed in a certain job description can be effectively kept from further advancement because of the official "dead-end" nature of the job description. The job description may recognize only limited educational and skill requirements, while in fact the job requires—and the employee has—enough education and skill to qualify for promotion.

One group of employees hurt by the official classification procedures were those in the Process-Serving Branch in the Sections of Records and Services. Prior to 1961, the clerks in that office were classified as "Legal Instrument Examiners," and the code designation given them was #963. In 1961, the designation was changed to #301, "Docket Clerks." This change did not result in a changed job description—the content of these employees' jobs remained the same —but when they attempted to be considered for promotions at a higher grade, they were told that they were ineligible for promotions because they were no longer classified as "963's." They were told that with their educational backgrounds and experience, there were no higher jobs in the 301 category for which they were qualified. Of course, in the old 963 category, they would have been eligible for higher pay. All of these "963's-turned 301's" were black. The office responsible for the change was the ICC Personnel Office. No one can be sure why, but the solution to these employees' problems is clear: they should be reclassified as "963's" and put back on the promotion trail.

Another basic complaint of the black employees at the ICC is that people who are unaware of job vacancies can be passed over by the ICC without their ever knowing it. The posting of job openings around the ICC building was finally begun on July 1, 1969, so this complaint has to some degree been answered. Although the "selecting official's" decision is not appealable, the selection of the three to ten employees for consideration for promotions *is* appealable. But employees must know of the vacancy in order to appeal their exclusion from the "highly qualified" group. Prior to July 1, 1969, therefore, jobs were filled in a vacuum, allowing blacks and others to be discriminated against without their knowing it. This procedure rankled with every single black the authors spoke with, and quite a few white employees as well. The Personnel Director, however, in response to a question from the authors as to why job openings had not been posted prior to July 1, 1969, asked, "Why should they have been?" [10]

A recent incident at the ICC further illustrates the problems faced by blacks within the ICC. When asked to discuss the details of this case, the Personnel Director, Mr. Adams, refused on the grounds that he would not discuss the details of a particular employee's record, even though he was told that the employees involved had voluntarily discussed the case with the authors at some length.*

The office involved is the Composing Unit of the Section of Administrative Services. There are ten women employees in the office, all black, and seven of the ten have been together for about a decade. For two years they tried to bring their pay scale up to the levels earned by comparable employees in other governmental agencies. Their Unit sets type for all ICC printed reports. The basic equipment involved is the cold-type automatic composing machine, in which operators sit at a console and key-punch the type. A Type Foundry ("ATF") equipment was installed in 1965. This equipment demanded extra skills for the workers, and Mrs. Dorothy Wheeler, the supervisor, was sent to New Jersey to learn to train workers on this new equipment. Since employees are given pay scales based partly on the equipment they operate, the Unit contended, upon installation of this new equipment, that operating it entitled them to higher pay. What followed is the story of a lonely battle against the powers that be in the Interstate Commerce Commission.

In September, 1967, Mrs. Wheeler sent Mrs. Agatha Mergenovich, her immediate supervisor, a formal memorandum requesting that her Unit be transferred from their current pay scale, at which no employee was higher than a GS-5, to "Wage Board," a separate and higher pay scale for certain governmental printing employees. The Composing Unit contended that the addition of the ATF equipment made them eligible, according to C.S.C. standards, for Wage Board. Mrs. Merganovich, located two doors away from Mrs. Wheeler's Unit, responded by asking for more information. Mrs. Wheeler then began a one-year information-gathering effort in her spare time, vacations, and evenings, and eventually gathered a file on the subject nearly two inches thick, in which she established that comparable units in other federal agencies received salaries consistently higher than those received by the ICC Composing Unit. In September, 1968, she sent Mrs. Mergenovich a second memorandum, setting out her Unit's case in full. The matter was sent to the Personnel Office, where it was decided that the addition of the ATF equipment did not qualify the Unit for pay scale advancement, since it was just an addition to the basic equipment used, the Justowriter. Frustrated by the action, the Unit's employees threatened to take their case to the Civil Service Commission, but Mrs. Mergenovich and the Personnel Office themselves went to Civil Service, and early in 1969 received an authorization from Civil Service to classify this Unit as Wage Board.

* One wonders whose interests Mr. Adams believes he is protecting.

Mrs. Wheeler then presented to her supervisor, Mrs. Mergenovich, their suggestions for a pay plan for the ten employees. The Unit waited for an answer. Finally, some of the employees could wait no longer for an answer, and on June 30, 1969, they addressed to Managing Director Bernard F. Schmid, under whose authority are both the Section of Administrative Services and the Personnel Office, a request to give this matter his immediate attention. Three days later, Mrs. Mergenovich submitted to the Composing Unit their proposed standards of pay. With the general pay increase for federal employees taking place on July 1, the proposed pay increase for the Unit would have resulted in practically no increases at all for the individual employees. One employee, the Assistant Supervisor, would actually receive the same amount of money under the Wage Board scale as she would have received anyway under the old GS rating pro-rated under the general pay increase. For the members of the Composing Unit, it was a meager reward for two years of conscientious work; as one of them said, "There must be some reason for this."

There must in fact be some reason for the ICC's treatment of these ten employees in this manner. There must be some reason for their decision to pay the Supervisor of a Unit with a uniformly high attendance record and an unusually high degree of employee morale, less money than the Assistant Supervisor of Composing Units with ATF equipment in other governmental agencies.

The matter now rests with the Civil Service Commission. The members of the Composing Unit appealed to the C.S.C. after the rejection of their appeal to the Personnel Office of the small or nonexistent pay increase offer. The members of the Composing Unit and their supervisor believe that they will win out on their pay increase. They recall the many mornings they came in early to get needed work out on time, the extra work they have done over the years to compensate for the often shoddy work sent to them by other Units in the ICC, and the two years of research done on their behalf by Mrs. Wheeler to try to convince the people who make the decisions at the ICC that their Unit deserved a pay increase to match the skills and work they perform on a daily basis.[11]

They had to go their route alone, never aided, often hindered, by the Section of Administrative Services and the Personnel Office of the ICC. Since the Personnel Director has refused to discuss this matter, it is not known whether an independent research was done by his Office in deciding initially not to grant the Unit Wage Board status, or on what basis the decision was made. The extensive cross-agency research done by the Supervisor of this Unit *should* have been done by the responsible officials at the ICC. When these employees made their initial request for the pay increase, it must be noted, the employees were asked by the managerial level of the ICC to gather further additional information on their own. It is a testament to the integrity of the individuals concerned that they did not simply walk out of the ICC to gain employment in a federal agency with a different attitude toward the aspirations of the individual employees.

The black employees of the ICC believe that they do not have the same opportunities as whites. They feel that they are underpaid, that they are generally discriminated against in promotions. The blacks expressing these beliefs are aware of the difficulty of proving actual discrimination, and, because of the general structure of the society, they are not surprised to encounter racism at the ICC. In the words of one black woman with considerable experience at the ICC, "When you continually get passed over for promotions, when whites just off the street get promotions, and the blacks are left behind, when you continually get the run-around, you begin to say, 'Why bother?' " [12]

Some believe that a full airing and resolution must come from within the ICC. In a letter to the ICC, one former employee stated: "It should be noted that I feel that the entire Personnel Practices of the Interstate Commerce Commission leave much to be desired. Perhaps at a later date, some disinterested investigative unit of the Federal Government can survey the Personnel Practices of the Agency and prove my contention." [13]

It is the authors' view that an independent investigation of this subject is in order.

APPENDIX 9 Cost Structure Study

The cost structure of each mode is relevant to a proper understanding of the effects of ICC policies toward competition on the structure of the industry. For a mode in which fixed costs are a substantial portion of the expense of transportation, marginal cost * is likely to be well below the average cost of transportation.† Economists refer to this pattern as indicative of a "declining cost industry." A mode with marginal costs well below average costs is more able to undercut a competing mode in cutthroat fashion for long periods of time in order to attain monopoly power.

To the extent that the fixed costs are threshold costs, or sunk costs,‡ they constitute natural barriers to entry into the mode. To the extent that fixed costs are not adjustable to changes in traffic volume over short periods of time, the mode is particularly subject to problems of excess capacity. Both of these characteristics are extremely important in assessing the impact of ICC competition (and rate) policies. High natural barriers to entry mean that even without regulatory barriers (*e.g.*, without limiting grants of operating authority), a carrier has the opportunity to exploit its monopoly power without fear of competitors from within the mode which might be attracted because of the excessive profits of the monopolistic carrier. Ease of entry tends to inhibit the lengthy exercise of monopoly power pricing. Competition, whether direct or through potential entry, drives rates (prices) toward cost. §

Although not treated in detail, our study contains the basic data, or suggests the appropriate tools, for the more precise determination of the cost structure of each mode. Our study in this regard merely involves the application of multiple regression ** technique in order to ascertain, according to recent data, the rate of cost change with increases in traffic volume †† by analyzing a cross section of carriers in each mode. The variability of cost with increases in volume for a mode is relevant to all of the cost considerations mentioned above. High variation with low threshold cost indicates low entry barriers, little excess capacity problem, and marginal costs close to average costs. If the relationship between fixed and variable costs is affected by plant size, utilization or density measures, or other operational characteristics, then we are able to tell with greater precision the circumstances under which excess capacity, or natural entry barriers, are likely to affect an individual carrier within a mode.

* Marginal cost can be defined in the case of railroads, for example, as the expense directly associated with the transportation of one more car of widgets.

† Average cost is total cost divided by total units of operation (*e.g.*, ton miles).

‡ Threshold costs are usually defined as the fixed costs necessary to attain a given level of output. Sunk costs are usually defined as the threshold cost necessary to operate at *any* level of output.

§ The problem of excess capacity, relevant to the need for the full utilization of constructed facilities, is important to ICC merger policy (*e.g.*, the need for rail mergers in order to abandon under-utilized facilities) and to rate regulation policy (*e.g.*, marginal cost pricing, see Chapter 5).

** Multiple regression is a statistical technique which analyzes the nature of the relationship between sets of numbers. It is usually necessary to conduct this analysis by computer.

†† The study is from a cross section sampling of carriers from 1967 or 1968 data. The same analysis can be applied to a time series study of individual carriers.

APPENDIX 10 Intermodal Freight Competition

PERCENTAGE DISTRIBUTION OF TON MILES OF FEDERALLY REGULATED AND UNREGULATED INTERCITY FREIGHT TRAFFIC IN THE UNITED STATES, BY MODE OF TRANSPORT, 1939–67 *

Year	Airways	Rail-roads	Inland waterways			Motor carriers			Oil pipelines		
			Total	Reg-ulated	Unreg-ulated	Total	Reg-ulated	Unreg-ulated	Total	Reg-ulated	Unreg-ulated
1939		62.4	17.7	n.a.	n.a.	9.7	3.6	6.1	10.2	n.a.	n.a.
1940		61.3	19.1	n.a.	n.a.	10.0	3.3	6.7	9.6	n.a.	n.a.
1941		62.4	18.2	n.a.	n.a.	10.5	3.5	7.0	8.9	n.a.	n.a.
1942		69.5	16.0	n.a.	n.a.	6.4	3.0	3.4	8.1	n.a.	n.a.
1943		71.2	13.7	n.a.	n.a.	5.5	2.8	2.8	9.5	n.a.	n.a.
1944		68.6	13.8	n.a.	n.a.	5.4	2.5	2.9	12.2	n.a.	n.a.
1945		67.3	13.9	n.a.	n.a.	6.5	2.7	3.8	12.3	n.a.	n.a.
1946		66.8	13.8	0.8	13.0	9.1	3.4	5.7	10.3	8.1	2.2
1947		65.3	14.4	0.9	13.5	10.0	3.7	6.3	10.2	8.1	2.1
1948		62.6	14.6	0.9	13.7	11.2	4.5	6.7	11.6	9.1	2.5
1949		58.4	15.2	0.9	14.3	13.8	5.2	8.6	12.5	10.0	2.5
1950		56.2	15.4	0.9	14.5	16.3	6.2	10.1	12.2	9.6	2.6
1951		55.6	15.5	0.9	14.6	16.0	6.1	9.9	12.9	10.2	2.7
1952		54.5	14.7	0.9	13.8	17.0	6.2	10.8	13.8	10.9	2.9
1953		51.0	16.8	1.0	15.8	18.0	6.4	11.6	14.1	11.1	3.0
1954		49.5	15.4	0.9	14.5	19.1	6.4	12.7	15.9	12.6	3.3

Year											
1955		49.4	16.9	1.0	15.9	17.7	6.5	11.2	15.9	12.6	3.3
1956		48.2	16.2	1.0	15.2	18.7	6.1	12.6	16.9	13.2	3.7
1957		47.2	17.5	1.0	16.5	18.5	5.9	12.6	16.8	13.1	3.7
1958		46.3	15.7	0.9	14.8	20.5	6.6	13.9	17.5	13.9	3.6
1959	0.1	45.6	15.3	n.a.	n.a.	21.5	n.a.	n.a.	17.6	n.a.	n.a.
1960	0.1	44.1	16.8	n.a.	n.a.	21.7	n.a.	n.a.	17.4	n.a.	n.a.
1961	0.1	43.4	16.0	n.a.	n.a.	22.7	n.a.	n.a.	17.8	n.a.	n.a.
1962	0.1	43.8	16.3	n.a.	n.a.	22.6	8.2	14.4	17.3	15.0	2.3
1963	0.1	43.4	16.2	n.a.	n.a.	22.9	8.3	14.6	17.5	15.0	2.5
1964	0.1	43.4	16.3	n.a.	n.a.	22.8	8.1	14.6	17.5	14.9	2.6
1965	0.1	42.5	15.7	n.a.	n.a.	23.3	8.4	14.9	18.4	15.8	2.6
1966	0.1	43.0	16.1	n.a.	n.a.	21.8	n.a.	n.a.	19.1	16.4	2.7
1967	0.1	41.6	15.6	n.a.	n.a.	22.1	n.a.	n.a.	20.5	n.a.	n.a.

* Friedlaender, *op. cit.*, p. 206.

INTERCITY FREIGHT TRAFFIC IN THE UNITED STATES, BY MODE OF TRANSPORT AND BY PERCENTAGE FEDERALLY REGULATED, 1939-67 *

(In billions of ton miles)

Year	Airways	Railroads	Inland waterways			Motor carriers			Oil pipelines		
			Total	Regulated Total	Regulated Percentage	Total	Regulated Total	Regulated Percentage	Total	Regulated Total	Regulated Percentage
1939	0.012	338.9	96.2	n.a.	n.a.	52.8	19.6	37.1	55.6	n.a.	n.a.
1940	0.014	379.2	118.1	n.a.	n.a.	62.0	20.7	33.4	59.3	n.a.	n.a.
1941	0.019	481.8	140.5	n.a.	n.a.	81.4	26.8	32.9	68.4	n.a.	n.a.
1942	0.034	645.4	148.6	n.a.	n.a.	59.9	28.1	46.9	75.1	n.a.	n.a.
1943	0.053	734.8	141.7	n.a.	n.a.	56.8	28.8	50.7	97.9	n.a.	n.a.
1944	0.071	746.9	150.2	n.a.	n.a.	58.3	27.3	46.8	132.9	n.a.	n.a.
1945	0.091	690.8	142.7	n.a.	n.a.	66.9	27.3	40.8	126.5	n.a.	n.a.
1946	0.093	602.1	124.0	7.4	6.0	82.0	30.4	37.1	92.5	73.1	79.0
1947	0.158	664.4	146.7	8.8	6.0	102.1	37.7	36.9	104.2	82.3	79.0
1948	0.223	647.3	150.5	9.0	6.0	116.1	46.7	40.2	119.6	94.5	79.0
1949	0.235	534.7	139.4	8.4	6.0	126.6	47.9	37.8	114.9	91.4	79.5
1950	0.318	596.9	163.3	9.8	6.0	172.9	65.6	37.9	129.2	102.1	79.0
1951	0.379	655.4	182.2	10.9	6.0	188.0	72.3	38.5	152.1	120.2	79.0
1952	0.415	623.4	168.4	10.1	6.0	194.6	70.8	36.4	157.5	124.4	79.0
1953	0.413	614.2	202.4	12.1	6.0	217.2	76.5	35.2	169.9	134.2	79.0
1954	0.397	556.6	173.7	10.4	6.0	214.6	72.3	33.7	179.2	141.6	79.0

1955	0.481	631.4	216.5	13.0	6.0	226.2	82.9	36.6	203.2	160.6	79.0
1956	0.563	655.9	220.0	13.2	6.0	253.8	83.0	32.7	230.0	179.8	78.0
1957	0.572	626.2	231.8	13.9	6.0	244.9	78.3	32.0	222.7	173.7	78.0
1958	0.579	558.7	189.0	11.3	6.0	247.0	79.1	32.0	211.3	167.8	78.0
1959	0.739	582.0	195.0	n.a.	n.a.	275.0	n.a.	n.a.	225.0	n.a.	n.a.
1960	0.778	579.1	220.3	n.a.	n.a.	285.5	n.a.	n.a.	228.6	n.a.	n.a.
1961	0.895	567.0	209.7	n.a.	n.a.	296.5	n.a.	n.a.	233.1	n.a.	n.a.
1962	1.289	600.0	223.1	n.a.	n.a.	309.4	111.9	33.8	237.7	205.4	86.4
1963	1.296	629.3	234.2	n.a.	n.a.	331.8	120.6	36.3	253.4	217.2	85.7
1964	1.504	666.2	250.2	n.a.	n.a.	349.8	125.1	35.8	268.7	229.5	85.4
1965	1.910	708.7	262.4	n.a.	n.a.	388.4	140.3	36.1	306.4	263.5	86.0
1966	2.252	750.8	280.5	n.a.	n.a.	380.9	n.a.	n.a.	332.9	285.9	85.9
1967	2.592	731.2	274.0	n.a.	n.a.	388.5	n.a.	n.a.	361.0	n.a.	n.a.

* Friedlander, *op. cit.*, p. 204.

APPENDIX 11 Intermodal Passenger Competition

PERSON-NIGHTS—DISTRIBUTIONS BY TYPE OF TRANSPORT AND TRAVEL
AND HOUSEHOLD CHARACTERISTICS: 1967 *

Distribution by Type of Transport

	Person-nights		Percent distribution by type of transport					
Travel and household characteristics	Millions	Percent	Auto	Bus	Train	Commercial air	Ship or boat	Combinations and other
Distance (One-Way Straight-Line Miles)								
Less than 50 miles	108.0	100.0	92.8	4.1	.7	.5	1.5	.4
50 to 99 miles	196.6	100.0	94.0	3.8	.9	.5	.3	.5
100 to 199 miles	274.6	100.0	91.4	3.9	1.8	1.6	.1	1.2
200 to 499 miles	326.1	100.0	81.2	5.0	2.4	8.9	.1	2.4
500 to 999 miles	230.2	100.0	67.0	3.2	5.9	19.4	—	4.5
1000 miles and more	283.1	100.0	55.2	1.9	5.0	32.3	.2	5.4
Outside United States	155.7	100.0	40.4	2.2	.6	40.8	7.8	8.2
No answer	5.6	(¹)	(¹)	(¹)	(¹)	(¹)	(¹)	(¹)
Family Income Level								
Less than $4000	232.6	100.0	69.9	9.5	5.9	9.8	.2	4.7
$4000 to $5999	218.2	100.0	79.4	3.8	3.6	11.5	.2	1.5
$6000 to $7499	206.9	100.0	82.0	2.6	2.0	10.4	.5	2.5
$7500 to $9999	284.1	100.0	79.7	2.2	2.2	13.3	.4	2.2
$10,000 to $14,999	295.2	100.0	73.8	2.0	1.3	17.2	1.8	3.9
$15,000 and more	166.5	100.0	60.7	1.8	2.1	28.9	2.8	3.7
No answer	166.4	100.0	73.6	2.5	2.6	15.4	1.3	4.6

Occupation of Household Head							
Professional and managerial workers	548.8	100.0	72.4	2.2	1.9	18.9	1.3	3.3
Clerical and sales workers	179.6	100.0	74.3	3.4	2.4	16.2	.8	2.9
Craftsmen, operatives, and laborers	450.0	100.0	81.6	3.5	2.7	9.6	.9	1.7
Service and private workers	61.8	100.0	74.0	7.1	5.5	10.6	.4	2.4
Other [2]	339.7	100.0	69.4	4.9	4.1	15.3	.9	5.4
Education of Household Head							
No school or elementary only	233.9	100.0	73.5	8.2	5.4	8.4	.4	4.0
High school	673.7	100.0	78.4	3.2	2.5	12.2	.6	3.1
College	656.6	100.0	71.5	2.1	2.0	19.6	1.6	3.2
No answer	15.7	(1)	(1)	(1)	(1)	(1)	(1)	(1)
Area of Origin							
In SMSA—in central city	446.5	100.0	67.0	5.1	3.4	19.9	1.5	3.1
In SMSA—outside central city	602.8	100.0	75.1	2.1	1.9	16.7	.8	3.4
Non-SMSA	530.6	100.0	80.6	3.7	3.3	8.5	.8	3.1
Total person-nights	1,579.9	100.0	74.7	3.5	2.8	14.9	1.0	3.1
Purpose of Trip							
Business and conventions	207.5	100.0	60.4	2.2	1.8	30.1	.5	5.0
Visits to friends and relatives	663.7	100.0	74.1	4.4	4.7	14.1	—	2.7
Outdoor recreation	268.6	100.0	91.8	2.9	.3	2.6	1.3	1.1
Entertainment and sightseeing	188.7	100.0	66.8	2.4	1.1	18.9	5.1	5.7
Other pleasure	160.5	100.0	72.3	5.3	3.6	14.0	.1	4.7
Personal and family affairs	87.1	100.0	80.4	.8	.7	15.3	1.1	1.7
No answer	3.8	(1)	(1)	(1)	(1)	(1)	(1)	(1)

— Represents zero.

1 Not distributed.

2 Includes unemployed, retired, and those whose occupations were not reported, as well as household heads in the Armed Forces who took trips while *not* under military orders.

* *Passenger Travel Census*, Bureau of the Census, 1967.

Travel and household characteristics	Person-nights		Percent distribution by type of transport					
	Millions	Percent	Auto	Bus	Train	Commercial air	Ship or boat	Combinations and other
Vacation Travel								
Vacation	970.3	100.0	75.7	3.1	2.9	13.8	1.4	3.1
Not a vacation	520.0	100.0	74.3	3.6	2.1	16.4	.2	3.4
No answer	89.6	100.0	65.1	6.8	5.9	17.4	.6	4.2
Size of Party								
1 person	421.5	100.0	52.3	8.4	4.5	28.2	.8	5.8
2 persons	455.8	100.0	72.3	3.1	3.5	16.5	2.1	2.5
3 and 4 persons	411.1	100.0	86.9	1.1	1.8	7.6	.4	2.2
5 persons and more	291.5	100.0	93.3	.4	.6	3.4	.4	1.9
Time Duration								
1 day	89.7	100.0	92.4	1.7	.9	—	.3	.7
1 night	188.1	100.0	90.8	2.2	.8	4.0	.2	.9
2 nights	279.3	100.0	82.7	3.3	1.7	5.1	.2	1.5
3 to 5 nights	248.4	100.0	80.0	3.4	1.9	10.6	.6	2.1
6 to 9 nights	251.5	100.0	73.1	3.8	3.6	12.0	.9	2.6
10 to 15 nights	78.9	100.0	64.9	3.6	5.7	16.0	1.4	2.8
16 to 20 nights		100.0				21.6		
21 nights and more	444.0	100.0	58.8	4.4	4.1	23.6	2.1	7.0

— Represents zero.

¹ Not distributed.

² Includes unemployed, retired, and those whose occupations were not reported, as well as household heads in the Armed Forces who took trips while *not* under military orders.

* *Passenger Travel Census,* Bureau of the Census, 1967.

PERSON-TRIPS FOR REGION OF ORIGIN—DISTRIBUTIONS BY TYPE OF TRANSPORT AND PURPOSE OF TRIP: 1967 *

Characteristic	Millions of person-trips					Percent distribution by characteristic				
	United States	North-east	North Central	South	West	United States	North-east	North Central	South	West
Total	361.2	72.1	112.2	100.7	76.2	100.0	100.0	100.0	100.0	100.0
Type of transport										
Auto	310.8	59.5	99.4	87.5	64.4	86.1	82.5	88.6	86.9	84.6
Bus	9.4	2.6	1.9	2.9	2.0	2.6	3.6	1.7	2.9	2.8
Train	5.2	1.4	2.2	1.0	.6	1.4	1.9	1.9	1.0	.8
Commercial air	28.9	7.4	6.8	7.6	7.1	8.0	10.3	6.1	7.5	9.2
Other	6.6	1.1	1.8	1.6	2.1	1.8	1.7	1.7	1.7	2.6
No answer	.3	.1	.1	.1	—	.1	—	—	—	—

PERSON-TRIPS FOR REGION OF DESTINATION—DISTRIBUTIONS BY TYPE OF TRANSPORT AND PURPOSE OF TRIP: 1967 †

Characteristic	Millions of person-trips						Percent distribution by characteristic					
	Total	North-east	North Central	South	West	Outside U.S.	Total	North-east	North Central	South	West	Outside U.S.
Total	361.2	65.8	97.3	108.5	74.7	14.9	100.0	100.0	100.0	100.0	100.0	100.0
Type of transport												
Auto	310.8	56.4	86.9	95.3	62.7	9.5	86.1	85.7	89.5	87.8	83.9	63.8
Bus	9.4	2.3	1.7	2.7	2.1	.6	2.6	3.5	1.7	2.5	2.9	3.9
Train	5.2	1.3	1.7	1.2	.9	.1	1.4	2.0	1.7	1.1	1.2	.6
Commercial air	28.9	4.8	5.6	7.6	7.5	3.4	8.0	7.3	5.7	7.0	10.0	22.8
Other	6.6	.9	1.3	1.6	1.5	1.3	1.8	1.4	1.3	1.5	2.0	8.9
No answer	.3	.1	.1	.1	—	—	.1	.1	.1	.1	—	—

* *Passenger Travel Census*, Bureau of the Census, 1961.
† *Id.*

DOMESTIC INTERCITY PASSENGER MILES*

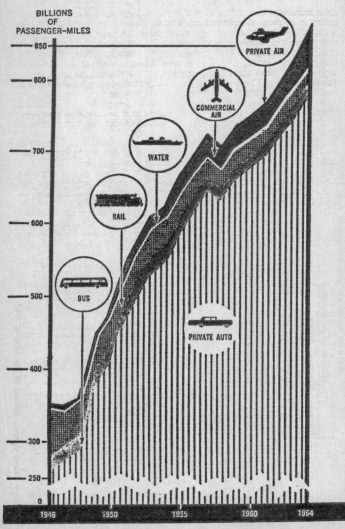

BILLINGS
OF
PASSENGER—MILES

850
800
700
600
500
400
300
250
0

PRIVATE AIR

COMMERCIAL
AIR

WATER

RAIL

BUS

PRIVATE AUTO

1946   1950   1955   1960   1964

* R. L. Banks and Associates, *Intermodal Competition*, Washington, D. C., 1966, Vol. 2, Part III.

APPENDIX 12 Control of Entry: *De facto* Discrimination

One important side effect of the Commission's rigid control-of-entry policy is *de facto* discrimination. The application for certification, on which all potential new truckers must show that their operations serve the "public convenience and necessity," is a standard format. It is difficult to distinguish between any two of these applications, and the Commission's actual choice as to who receives authorization is, to a large extent, determined by the pressures and protests of local trucking monopolies. These truckers invariably challenge the granting of a new license by asserting that it does not in fact serve the "public convenience and necessity," and the Commission generally supports them. Thus the standard of "public convenience and necessity" actually insures the *status quo*—a *status quo* in which blacks have no economic role.

The effects of the ICC's restrictive entry policies on prospective small trucking interests are clear in the case of Joe Jones. In November, 1965, Jones, a black trucker in Atlanta who had obtained a Small Business Administration loan of $25,000, was denied a motor carrier license because he could not show "real and urgent need for his services." Jones seemingly had met the formal public convenience and necessity standard: he had testimonials from the Mayo Chemical Company and the Sophie Mae Candy Company that only he could provide the service they need, and that if he was not granted a license they would be forced to purchase their own trucks. Nevertheless, the Commission argued that Jones had not shown that a real and urgent need for his services existed.

The battle was joined on November 15, 1965, with Commission Chairman Webb making the opening statement for the ICC: "The fact that one government agency loans money to a person to go into the trucking business carries no implications that another government agency will grant the person motor carrier authority." On the contrary—the ICC has insisted upon the power to scrutinize all applications carefully. The ostensible reason for this power is to regulate the industry so as to allow entry only to those truckers who do not compete "unreasonably" in areas where authority has already been granted to other companies.

Jones was not without resources in the ensuing two-year and seven-hearing battle with the ICC bureaucracy. A veteran with a 50 per cent disability, he had been in the trucking business as a driver for over twenty years. He was an articulate entrepreneur, capable of mobilizing public and Congressional support in his fight against the bureaucrats. On March 31, 1967, in a condescending opinion, the Commission reluctantly approved Jones's seventh attempt to obtain a license.

> . . . Since this Commission has been directed by Congress to consider the effect which denial of the permit would have upon the applicant, we cannot disregard the fact that by the action of one agency of the federal government, applicant has assumed a large debt which, in the absence of favorable action by *this* agency, cannot be repaid.
>
> (MC 127681 sub. 1)

However, the Commission gave public warning that the Jones case would not be a precedent for future opinions.

Not long after the Commission's decision, Jones was driven out of business. He is reluctant to discuss his case, but one can imagine that the expense of two years and seven hearings before the ICC, and the hostility of the local monopolies that opposed his entry, were important factors in the failure of his trucking operation.

Like Jones, Leamon McCoy, a black trucker from New Jersey, has come up against the ICC wall. McCoy had a unique operation hauling low-grade cargo to and from docks in New Jersey. U.S. Steel and other large concerns backed him with impressive testimony. He met the ICC standards and was granted a thirty-day license, but in May, 1969, the temporary license was allowed by the Commission to expire.

Throughout the summer McCoy fought back. The expense, however, of remaining in business so that he would be ready to start work immediately if his license were approved took its toll. McCoy did not know how long he could last; if the interminable delay to which Joe Jones was subject was also to be his fate, he would probably go bankrupt. The ICC policy of granting probationary approval prior to granting a final license places the small businessman at a particular disadvantage: he can ill afford the delay that may ensue between the thirty-day approval and the final grant of operating authority.

McCoy was not especially bitter about the ICC, although he did feel that "the ICC is too impressed with the value of a certificate. They spent twenty minutes telling me how much the license was worth." At the end of the summer in 1969 McCoy had not been granted a license.

Black people, deprived of opportunity by centuries of direct and *de facto* discrimination, are not able to improve their position in this critical area because of the restrictive standards that bar entry to anyone who might pose a threat to existing carriers. The only way to improve chances for black entrepreneurship is to improve opportunities for all small concerns, black and white, by abandoning the entry restriction policy.

APPENDIX 13 The Use of the Interstate Highway System *

The Interstate Commerce Act contemplates two types of motor carriers, irregular and regular route carriers. It leaves up to the ICC the elucidation of criteria defining each. For our purposes, regular route carriers "are restricted territorially and limited to the use of specified highways."

The development of the National System of Interstate and Defense Highways scheduled for completion in the late 1970's marks a radical change in surface motor transportation. "Commercial users of the Interstate System will enjoy savings in operating costs, time costs, and accident costs. Improved highway and traffic conditions decrease costs of fuel and oil consumption, tire wear, maintenance, and depreciation." It is estimated that by 1975 commercial users will decrease costs of operation by two billion, 969 million. Use of these superhighways clearly results in a competitive advantage.

Naturally, carriers have not waited the eleven years since the enactment of the Interstate and Defense Highway Act until the ICC Interim Report in 1968 to take advantage of the economies offered by superhighway use. The Commission's Deviation Rules, revised in 1957, have allowed some use (as "uncertified alternate routes") of the superhighways as sections have been completed. The purpose of the 1968 rule making was to formulate a policy allowing for reasonable and efficient use of these roads.

All of the usual interests participated in the hearings. The bus lobby suggested that "a passenger carrier holding certificated regular route authority to operate between two points . . . be allowed to utilize any other highway *provided that this use would not materially change the competitive situation existing between such carriers and any others.*" (Emphasis added.) A carrier would further be allowed to service intermediate points on superhighways with the usual showing of public convenience and necessity. In sum, the bus lobby would allow full use of the new roads with appropriate restrictions to prevent a material change in the existing competitive situation.

The motor carriers of property lobby—the Regular Common Carrier Conference (RCCC)—put forth its own proposal. It would allow a general commodity carrier operating over a route between designated terminals, upon application, to operate over the interstate highway system extending in the same direction where the distance over such segment of the "interstate highway system between the points of departure from and return to its present service route is not less than 85 per cent of the distance over its present route." If the carrier already had authority to operate over an alternate route, it could operate on the interstate highway as another alternate route "provided that the mileage over such segment is not less than 90 per cent of the mileage over the authorized . . . alternate route." In certain circumstances a carrier would be allowed to serve intermediate points on the proposed superhighway route. However, this application would be subject to protest by a carrier already holding such authority. The RCCC offered a proviso that applications involving use of an interstate segment *less* than 85 per cent of the regular authorized route would be subject to full protest by competing regular route motor carriers with the burden on the applicant to prove that the "*com-

* All quotes are from the leading case of 107 M.C.C. 108–117.

*petitive relationship between itself and the protesting carriers would
not be materially changed. . . ."* (Emphasis added.)

The Department of Transportation put forth a proposal not so
insistent on preserving the existing competitive relationships. A motor
carrier operating over a regular route would, upon application, receive authorization to use that segment of an interstate highway extending in the same direction. "Where the carrier is authorized to
serve intermediate points on its present route it would be authorized
. . . to serve all intermediate points on the" superhighway except if
specifically excluded on its original route. "Where the carrier proposes to serve new points on the interstate route, the application,
insofar as it seeks authority to serve such points, shall be subject to
protest by those carriers already holding such authority."

In certain areas where the superhighway is accessible to use of all
carriers operating in such areas, the D.O.T. would allow that authorization be given to all if doing so will not substantially change the
competitive relationship among them. Applicants not serving areas
subtending the interstate system would be authorized to sue the system unless existing carriers in the area show that they are not handling all of the traffic which they are able and willing to transport.
Finally, where service proposed over the system would materially
alter the competitive relationship obtaining between applicant and
other regular-route carriers authorized to serve between the designated termini, such other carriers may file applications for and receive interim certificates authorizing use of the appropriate segments
of the . . . interstate system." Note that changing the competitive
situation would not be grounds for disproval of application for superhighway use.

Naturally, the bus and property motor carrier people opposed the
D.O.T. proposal as "unduly disruptive of existing competitive relationships." The D.O.T. opposed the former's plans as "unduly
emphasiz(ing) the maintenance of existing competitive relationships."
Other interests tried to protect their competitive positions.

The ICC hearing examiner's report, characterized by the D.O.T.
as "an unwarranted distrust and fear of competition . . . that would
negate the advantages of the Interstate System through imposition
of a complex administrative machinery upon the regular-route carrier's use of that system," would allow for motor carrier (both
passenger and property) use of superhighway segments, provided
that the reduction in mileage over the proposed route from the point
of departure from, to the point of return to, the original route does
not exced 15 per cent in the case of property carriers. Where
authority was sought to use a superhighway as an alternate to an
existing certified alternate route, authorization would be granted if
mileage reduction over the superhighway did not exceed 10 per cent.

"The examiner's report indicates that approval of such applications as are described above will hinge upon consideration of the
following dominant criteria: (a) the effect of the proposed change
in a carrier's method of operations on competing carriers, and
(b) the effect of such change on shippers and communities previously served by the carrier, but for which no provision is made in
the contemplated operating change." The examiner called for case-
by-case application consisting of extensive detailed information. Provision was made for the filing of protests by interested parties.

Carriers must maintain adequate service over their current routes and "no service would be authorized at intermediate points on the superhighway unless such points are 10 miles or less from the appurtenant service route." The examiner's report was attacked by the motor interests on the grounds that it was too restrictive in its authorization of use of the superhighways, in its allowance of protests by competing carriers, and in its requirement of great detailing of all affect routes. In addition to its aforementioned criticism, the D.O.T. suggested that all regular route motor carriers having authority to operate between two terminals be given authority to use any portion of the interstate system. This would place the "burden on protesting carriers to challenge the free use of the interstate system and to demonstrate by substantial evidence why a particular carrier should not be allowed to use that system." All carriers, motor and railroad, reject the D.O.T. proposal as "leading to the disruption of the present competitive situation in the regular-route motor carrier industry."

The Commission reached its own conclusion. It decided to consider passenger motor carriers separately from property motor carriers because (a) with passenger carriage, a small time reduction, resulting from superhighway use, can materially affect the competitive situation while the competitive effect is less substantial with property carriers, and (b) property carriers are too numerous to deal with on a case-by-case basis while passenger carriers are not so numerous as to be unworkable. Therefore, a general rule is applicable to property carriers, while passenger carriers are individually certified.

Passenger Carrier Certification: Common carriers will be authorized to use the superhighways, with adequate opportunity for protests by competitors, if applicants show "that use of such superhighway route will not materially change the competitive situation betwen such carriêr and any other carrier or carriers." Criteria for determining whether such a change is likely are (a) "the mileage over the proposed superhighway route." If the mileage is not less than 90 per cent of the original route that is prima facie evidence that a material change in competitive situations will not result; (b) "the extent to which the proposed superhighway route parallels or extends in the same direction as the authorized service route"; (c) a comparison of running times of applicant and competitors in regard to original and superhighway routes; (d) length of time and fequency of operation of carrier upon original route; (a) volume of local traffic to be convenienced by new route. Detailed applications describing all routes concerned are required.

Property Carrier Certification: A certified regular route common carrier is authorized to use the superhighways provided that either "(a) the superhighway route . . . is wholly within twenty-five air-line miles of the carrier's authorized regular service route . . . or (b) any segment of superhighway used is not less than 85 per cent of the distance between such points over the carrier's authorized regular service route . . ." Some limited service of intermediate points on the superhighway route is authorized. Interested parties may file objections to the operations of any particular motor carrier.

We can make at least two broad generalizations about the ICC's decision. First, the ICC would oversee the use of the interstate system in intimate detail, including approval of each and every new routing, if not for its budgetary and manpower limitations. The administrative and carrier expense that will be required in application, consideration, and approval of merely passenger carrier use of the interstate system will be substantial. Those resources should be utilized for far more important purposes. Second, while it is assumed that the ICC desires motor carriers to take advantage of the economies inherent in superhighway use and pass these savings on to the consumer, the ICC would rather forego these economies than materially change the competitive situation. This is a striking example of how the ICC sacrifices the interest of an efficient transportation system in favor of protecting entrenched transportation interests. It would seem obvious that the use of the interstate system would provide economies that would materially change the competitive situations insofar as certain carriers, for innumerable reasons, would save more money from the system's use than would others. And equally obvious is the policy consideration that those carriers who, for one reason or another, including the use of superhighways, do gain economic advantages *should* have this advantage translated into a competitive advantage which will materially affect the competitive situation. The alternative is a static situation in which the advantages of reduced costs and heightened efficiencies are negated. The ICC should attempt to maximize economies, thus lowering the total cost of national transportation. When certain carriers, as a result of superhighway use, have lower costs and more efficient service, they can charge lower rates, and thus attract shippers and passengers at the expense of other competing carriers who are less efficient. Healthy competition should drive out the inefficient in favor of the efficient. Maximum use of the interstate highway system is inconsistent with maintaining the existing competitive situation. The ICC must permit change in the latter if it is to effect the former as Congressional intent and sound transportation policy would have it. Specifically, we sympathize with the D.O.T. proposals in questioning (1) the necessity for such close ICC administrative scrutiny of superhighway use by individual passenger carriers; (2) the criterion for passenger carrier approval of maintaining the existing competitive situation; (3) the mileage limit—90 per cent for passenger service, 85 per cent for property carriers—as a consideration in superhighway service approval (one would think that the greater the mileage saving in superhighway use, the greater the economies involved and the cheaper the cost of transportation, and the more the ICC should encourage its use); (4) the distance from regular route to furthest point on superhighway (the mere fact that a superhighway is at points more than twenty-five airline miles from the authorized regular service route ought not prevent carrier use of the highway if such use will result in economies); and (5) the restrictions on intermediate point service.

APPENDIX 14 Blacks Within the Industry

A careful look at the employee levels of the industry reveals that the ICC has not been willing to make the conscious policy decisions that would provide equal opportunities for black workers within the transportation industry, and has not exercised its Congressional mandate to make racial hiring policies a test of motor carrier fitness.

On May 2, 1968, the Justice Department filed suit in the U.S. District Court in Ohio seeking relief for violations of Title VII of the Civil Rights Act of 1964 (78 Stat. 253-266), 42 USC 2000e-2000e-15. The complaint alleged that Roadway Express, a large carrier with United States mail contracts and terminals in twenty-four states, "has pursued and continues to pursue policies and practices that discriminate against Negroes and which deprive or tend to deprive them of employment opportunities or adversely affect their status as employees because of their race." The Justice Department complaint charged that Roadways "employs no Negroes among its approximately 2110 line haul (over-the-road) drivers, or its approximately 1334 officers and managers, or its approximately 232 professional, technical, and sales personnel; of approximately 1143 office and clerical employees, two are Negro. The balance of Roadways' Negro employees are garage workers, pickup and delivery drivers, dock workers, checkers, and service workers." [1]

A suit similar to the Roadways lawsuit was filed by the Equal Employment Opportunity Commission on behalf of interested parties against Leeway Motor Freight, Inc. in a U.S. District Court in Oklahoma on March 13, 1968. [2] As in the case of Roadways, Leeway was a party to mail contracts with the Post Office Department of the federal government and had only recently been approved for its federal contracts at a compliance review. Leeway responded to the allegations by stating that it had "no way of knowing how many Negroes have applied for employment or for what job classification such applications may have been made." [3]

The key to both cases was the non-existent number of blacks who were over-the-road or long-haul drivers. In the past, companies refused to hire blacks for over-the-road driving for very pragmatic reasons—nearly all of the trucking stops excluded blacks. As far as can be ascertained, the ICC has never made a study of truck stops which denied admission to blacks. This was an inexcusable abdication of authority. Today, however, the predominance of these truck stops is not the major reason for the exclusion of blacks.

In most cases, blacks are excluded by a complicated seniority system which forces them to forfeit whatever benefits they may have worked hard to achieve in order to become over-the-road drivers. Although the seniority system also makes it difficult for whites to transfer from city to over-the-road positions, whites are usually allowed to begin working as over-the-road drivers if they have had prior experience with other firms, while blacks are told that they must gain experience with the company as city drivers first. In a random sample of twenty major companies, an EEOC computer study revealed what staff attorney David Copus described as a "consistent historical pattern of exclusion of Negroes from over-the-road driving positions," a pattern which has been of no concern to the ICC.

One wonders why it has been necessary for the Justice Department and the EEOC to go to court when the ICC could have compelled these large trucking companies to comply with Title VII of the 1964 Civil Rights Act. The ICC could have made the Bureau of Enforcement a party to any license hearing, and the Bureau could have raised the violation of the 1964 Civil Rights Act as relevant in determining the fitness of the carrier. If the ICC felt that it lacked this authority (which it does not), it should have asked Congress for a mandate to enforce the Civil Rights Act.

In the final analysis, the racism which is pervasive in the trucking industry is a matter of no apparent concern to the ICC. Moreover, ICC inaction in this field should make the public wonder whether its officials are even aware of the racist practices of an industry it is supposed to regulate.

APPENDIX 15 Rate Regulation Study

By taking the thirty market share and revenue/cost figures of the 1966 rail results and running regressions by region, the authors removed the factor of regional variation. There are several reasons why the 1966 rail group was selected for this testing. First, much of the information was in convenient form since the calculations were all made by computer for this group. Second, data on another eleven commodities which could not be used for the overall study because of the lack of matchable data.

The 201 regional market share figures and 201 revenue/cost figures were separated by region. This eliminated one form of interference, but it meant that discrimination by commodity would interfere with the results. Further, since rail alone was being tested, this commodity or value-of-service interference would tend to be against us. That is, rail market share would generally be higher for the relatively subsidized bulk commodities which are priced at lower revenue/cost general commodity discrimination pattern because the rail mode has an inherent advantage in the transportation of these commodities over the intermediate distance spread.

Further work is being done to refine the model and eliminate a number of possible biases. Refinements may increase or decrease the significance of the results as reported here.

EXPLANATORY NOTES TO GRAPHS ON PAGES 160–165

[1] Thirty commodity categories were selected for the rate pattern computer study. Commodities were selected from among all major commodity types: grains and agricultural commodities, livestock, ores, lumber and forest products, manufactured items. In addition, the broad categories of "farm products," "livestock and livestock products," "lumber and wood products" have been included.

The selection of commodities was governed by three considerations: 1. Since the study is designed to explore the relationship between a mode's monopoly power (as measured by market share) and price setting (as measured by profits or revenue/cost), all the modes carrying that commodity in substantial volume must be included in the study. Otherwise, the market share of a mode included in the study might be far less, or more significantly, vary in a different manner from region to region, than the results would indicate. Thus, since air and pipeline transportation have not been included in the study, it was necessary to limit our commodity selections to those not carried in a relatively substantial volume by these two modes. This was relatively easy since air freight transport is as yet an insignificant percentage of total volume for most any commodity type and pipeline transportation is still quite specialized. 2. Since mileage figures for the motor carrier statistics rest on regional, aggregate averages, commodities were selected which generally travel in significant volume and generally from a variety of points of origin to a variety of destinations. This makes individual variations from the regional mileage averages less likely and less significant. Further, since truckload increments are governed by certain specified limitations, it was necessary to pick most commodities with a minimum requisite density. 3. Since a further purpose of the study was to compare recent patterns with those from 1961–1962, it was necessary to choose commodities for which there are comparable data. This need was complicated by a commodity classification scheme change as of 1964 (actually adopted on September 13, 1963). However, many commodities survived the scheme change intact; others could be approximated by combining two pre-1964 categories to compare with one post-1964 category, or vice versa.

The post-1964 scheme is the end result of a Bureau of the Budget code "Commodity Classification for Transportation Statistics" in turn adapted from the Bureau of the Census "Standard Industrial Classification." It is commonly termed the "Standard Transportation Commodity Code" (STCC).

The commodities chosen, together with the appropriate designation numbers, are listed below. They represent about 20 per cent of the categories with measurable traffic which can be traced through the 1964 change.

No.	Pre-1964 Designation	Post-1964 Designation	Commodity
1	900	01	Farm Products
2	33	01121	Cotton in Bales
3	3	01132	Corn
4	5	01136	Sorghum Grains
5	1	01137	Wheat
6	43	01144	Soybeans
7	85	01195	Potatoes
8	910	014	Livestock & Livestock Products
9	203	01411	Cattle
10	313	102	Copper Ores
11	315 & 317	103	Lead & Zinc Ores
12	311	105	Aluminum Ores
13	343	14714	Phosphate Rock
14	215	2011	Meat
15	231	2025	Cheese
16	759	206	Sugar
17	749	2083	Malt
18	45	20923	Soybean Cake & By-products
19	930	24	Lumber & Wood Products
20	411	242	Lumber & Dimension Stock
21	415	243	Millwork, Veneer, etc.
22	781	244	Wooden Containers
23	783	265	Paper & Fiberboard Boxes
24	533	28123	Sodium Compounds
25	769	284	Soaps, Detergents, etc.
26	501	29111	Gasoline
27	549	307	Plastic Products
28	693	321	Flat Glass
29	685	36	Electrical Machinery
30	615	37112	Assembled Freight Vehicles

[2] The rail mode data includes commodity statistics for all railroads having $3 million or more average operating revenues from 1963 to

1966. The precise data is projected from the ICC's 1 per cent waybill sample of these carriers.*

[3] The motor carriers submitting commodity volume and revenue data include all Class I common and contract motor carriers subject to the ICC order of December 9, 1966.† Certain specific types are excluded (dump trucks, retail delivery, household goods, *et al.*). Further, it should be kept in mind that the motor carrier mode carries a substantially greater market share than our data will indicate through expanding traffic via private carriage. However, this carriage does not compete on the same direct basis with rail and water carriage for common carriage traffic and is properly excluded from our market share calculations.

[4] The water carriers include all of the Class A carriers as defined by the ICC.‡ As with rail, and to a lesser extent motor carriage, all but a small proportion of the mode's traffic volume is by the largest class of carriers.

[5] The revenue/cost statistic, or profit level, or rate discrimination ratio, is computed for each region for each commodity. Out-of-pocket cost is the cost basis of this index for all three modes. For this reason, somewhat differing levels of revenue/cost are appropriate between the modes if one wishes to compare long-run fully-distributed costs. See below for full discussion of methodology.

[6] Market share, a standard index of monopoly power, is figured on the basis of traffic volume, or ton miles for a given commodity in a given region. It is computed simply by taking the total traffic volume in ton miles for all three modes.

Note that the 1961–1962 rail and motor carrier market shares will not always add up to 100 per cent because water carriage market share is here presented only for 1967. It was impossible to get the revenue/cost information for water carriers before 1966 because of ICC data gathering inadequacies.

[7] Regions are matched between the modes with some difficulty and with a measure of complexity because of the agency's varying regional schemes. Fortunately, the Bureau of Economics decided to further divide the West into Southwest, Western Trunk Line, and Mountain Pacific regions in arranging the 1966 rail way bill raw data. This means a more detailed breakdown for 1966–1967 analysis than for 1961–1962. Motor carrier regions were matched with the New England, Central and Middle Atlantic regions coinciding with the rail Official or Eastern region. The rail South was matched with the motor carrier region of the same name. The rail Southwest was matched with the motor carrier region of the same name. The rail Western Trunk Line was matched with the Mid and Northwest motor carrier regions. Finally, the rail Mountain Pacfic region was matched with the motor carrier Rocky Mountain and Pacific regions.

* Before 1956, the ICC classified railroads, as well as terminal companies, *et al.*, into three categories: Classes I, II, or III. As of 1956, railroads were classified as either Class I or Class II. The line distinguishing Class I was placed at $3 million in annual operating revenues. In 1965, this line was raised to $5 million.

† A class I motor carrier receives more than $1 million in annual operating revenues from property motor carrier activity.

‡ Class A water carriers have average operating revenues exceeding $500,000.

The water carriers presented a more difficult problem because their location was not as easily amenable to complementary division. They failed to match closely the boundaries of the rail regions, as did the motor carrier regions, in the Mississippi and the Great Lakes. It was therefore necessary to allocate this traffic according to average volume to the five main 1966 rail regions. Thus, the Mississippi River traffic was allocated between the Southwest, East, South, and Western Trunk Line according to average volumes thereto. Exceptions were made for commodities with ascertainable deviations. Great Lake and Atlantic Coast traffic was similarly allocated to the appropriate rail regions. Pacific traffic presented no difficulty since it was all allocated to the Mountain Pacific region.

All data were computed by region according to points of destination. That is, we computed total U.S. to x region market share and revenue/cost.

[8] The 1961 revenue/cost statistics are derived from the ICC's 1961 burden chart," *Distribution of the Rail Revenue Contribution by Commodity Groups—1961*, by the Bureau of Accounts. In order to ascertain U.S. to x region, so the results could be fairly matched to other results, we have averaged revenue/cost by volume for the various traffics to x region.*

The 1961 rail market share has been computed on the same basis, with rail traffic volume computed from total ton-miles transported to the region involved.

[9] The 1966 revenue/cost statistics were more difficult to obtain. Since the 1961 chart, above, the ICC has acceded to industry pressure and refused to convert the raw data into meaningful form. However, the Bureau of Economics, for the first time, quietly compiled the raw data in a little known compendium called *Territorial Distribution Traffic and Revenue by Commodity Classes—One Percent Sample of Terminations in the Year 1966*. The data includes some simple divisions (*e.g.*, total tons divided by total carloads to give us tons/car) but no revenue/cost information. Therefore, despite the existence of an ICC program capable of easily transforming the raw data, it was necessary for us to write our own program or go through a twenty-step formula to get one profit statistic for one commodity traveling to one region. We chose the former course.

The program uses the same formula used in the 1961 computed results. The way train average mileage is ascertained by multiplying average way train mileage for the region involved (found in a Bureau of Accounts publication, *Rail Carload Cost Scales by Territories*, pp. 6–7) times total carloads and total tonnage. Through train car miles and ton-miles are then computed by subtracting the regional average way train car miles and ton-miles computed above from total car miles and total ton-miles found in the Bureau of Economics' *One Percent Sample—1966* publication, above. Each regional movement is broken down by percentage of volume carried by various car types (*e.g.*, gondola, boxcar, covered hopper, *et al.*) from the ICC Bureau of Economics other way-bill based publications (see *Distribution of Traffic for Selected Commodity Classes by Type of Car*).

We have, therefore, broken down the carload and tonnage amounts

* 1961 data, unlike 1966 rail raw data, does not include the aggregate U.S. to x region statistics, but merely lists East to x, South to x and West to x.

of each commodity to relate to terminal cost rates according to the car types and region involved. In addition, the car mile and ton-mile line-haul costs are separately computed according to their cost rates by region and car type. In addition, the car miles and ton-miles are further divided between through train and way train traffic (as explained above) and these are separately related to the varying cost rates involved, both for through train car miles and through train ton-miles and for way train car miles and way train ton-miles.

The cost rates involved for the terminal costs by carload and ton and for the line-haul costs for through train and way train car miles and ton-miles by region and by car type, are drawn from the 1965 table published by the Bureau of Accounts in *Procedures of Developing Rail Revenue Contribution by Commodity and Territory—Year 1965*. Since the rest of the data is from 1966 or 1967, the cost rates may have increased 3–4 per cent, but not enough to make a significant difference in the final output.

Finally, loss and damage costs are added in accordance to the average cost in cents per ton by commodity. This information was obtained from the Bureau of Accounts' *Rail Carload Cost Scales by Territories*.

Revenue statistics were obtained from the *Territorial Distribution Traffic and Revenue by Commodity Classes* by the ICC Bureau of Economics.

The 1966 market share data (ton-miles) was obtained from the same source.

[10] Motor carrier 1962 revenue/cost calculations are not as precisely broken down as the rail data above, but motor carrier costs do not require the precise differentiation demanded by the complexity of the rail industry cost structure. Truckloads and tonnage were computed for traffic terminated for the nine motor carrier regions by the then Bureau of Transport Economics and Statistics in a publication titled *Motor Carrier Freight Commodity Statistics*. The sample upon which this data is based, the region matchup scheme with the rail regions and measures taken to minimize ICC ambiguous "truckload" definitional instructions are mentioned above.

The truckload amounts for each commodity arriving at each region are divided into the tonnage to ascertain the approximate average load. ICC regional average cost studies for motor carriers from 1964 to 1966 are consulted, and out-of-pocket cost rates are computed from tables therein according to the average load for this traffic, ascertained above, at average distances for traffic in that region. The tonnage figure above is then multiplied by twenty to get total cwt. units. The cost rate (expressed in $\not{e}$/cwt.) is multiplied by this figure. The resulting total cost figure is divided into the revenue statistic, which is also derived from the *Motor Carrier Freight Commodity Statistics* document. Resulting ratios are then averaged according to traffic volume where two or more motor carrier regions must be combined for rail matching purposes.

Market share calculations for the motor carrier portion are made by multiplying total tonnage of a commodity to a region by the average haul statistics for the region as computed from the ICC's average cost studies. Ton-miles are added together where two or more regions must be combined to approximate one of the rail regions (see 7. above).

[11] The 1966 motor carrier results are computed in the same manner as for 1962 above. The source of the operational and revenue data, however, is the 1966 *Freight Commodity Statistics*, now published by the ICC Bureau of Accounts. As mentioned above, the average cost tables are from nine separate regional cost studies from the years between the 1962 and 1966 revenue data. Costs may have varied slightly before and after these studies, but the one to three years involved is not likely to be very significant.

With both 1962 and 1966 motor carrier results, we are confronted with the possibility of variation from regional load averages, relied upon in the cost rate and market share calculations. All that can be said is that commodities were selected to minimize these problems, as well as truckload definition difficulties as much as possible. Generally, dense, high-volume commodities were selected with numerous small shippers involved so as to closely relate to the truckload data and average regional distance figures.

[12] The water carriage figures were, perhaps, the most difficult of all to compute. The ICC does not compile any water carrier commodity data. Further, there is no mileage data or cost data whatsoever anywhere, even in the annual reports required by the ICC, only "expense" figures. However, the ICC does require a Form KA, Schedule 541, of freight carried during the year by Class A and B inland and coastal water carriers.* This schedule contains tonnage and revenue information by commodity. Fortunately, separate compilations for each individual carrier was not too insurmountable an obstacle since there are few major water carriers of freight in any one region or area. It was possible to duplicate these forms for thirty of these carriers, which covered over 95 per cent of the tonnage carried in any of the water carrier regions.

These forms were then compiled by us into the appropriate regional categories. Later, they were adjusted by formula to different categories in order to match the rail regions (see 7. above).

The cost data presented particular problems because of the lack of mileage and cost rate data. As a result, annual reports were surveyed and cost rates were computed according to vehicle types operated and areas of activity (see Chapter 3 for discussion of cost rate). These rates were updated for rising labor costs, but were differentially assigned to different commodities depending upon the nature of the vehicle involved (*e.g.*, river barge, package freighter). Costs varied generally from between two to five mills per revenue ton mile. Mileage was computed laboriously from the ports and volumes contained in the annual report and Schedule 541. Mileage was used to apply ton-miles to the cost rate and to compute the ton-miles for market share purposes.

* For maritime carriers, this is called Form M, Schedule 5000, "Domestic Freight Carried During Year."

APPENDIX 16 The Truck Driver Safety Survey

A number of measures were taken to minimize bias in the results of the truck driver safety survey.

1. Truck drivers from the Northeast and Midwest were consulted in the wording of the questionnaire, which generally followed the provisions of current safety regulations supposedly in force, in order to assure a proper understanding by the drivers of the intent of the question.

2. The questionnaires mailed to us were surveyed for accuracy on several bases. First, postmarks were examined to be sure that one source was not submitting a great number of questionnaires in order to influence the results. Second, the carriers named as employers were checked to be sure they existed. Third, doctrinaire answers, either completely positive or completely negative, were isolated for separate verification. Interestingly, there were few of these, as the answers were highly selective in nature.

3. A number of the drivers were called and requested to send verification, if available, of complaints made in the forms. Most of them not only expressed a willingness to do so, but subsequently submitted various forms of documentary evidence.

DRIVERS — PLEASE FILL OUT THIS FORM—then tear it out neatly, fold it, staple or tape at the top and drop it in the mail. Only the answers will be used in a summary report, outlining current safety regulation violations. This summary report will be forwarded to the appropriate Congressional Committee. YOUR NAME WILL NOT BE USED!

The questions below are for the use of a team of investigators looking into the safety and physical condition of trucks and their drivers. The survey is part of a general inquiry into the ICC and Department of Transportation being conducted in association with safety advocate RALPH NADER. It is in your interest to answer these questions fully and honestly.

NAME_____ COMPANY _____

PHONE_____ ADDRESS_____

CITY_____ STATE_____ ZIP_____

YEARS DRIVING_____ LOCAL DELIVERY_____ OVER THE ROAD_____

AVERAGE NUMBER OF MILES YOU DRIVE IN A YEAR _____ MILES.

THE ONLY TRUE ANSWERS WILL HAVE TO COME FROM THE REAL EXPERT ON TRUCKING SAFETY—You, the driver!

———————————————————— (fold here) ————————————————————

ANSWERS ARE IN PERCENT

1. Should the 15 hour on duty limit be reduced to 12 hours and the 10 hour driving time limit reduced to 8 hours? Yes34No66

2. a. Is it fairly common in the industry that you have to exceed the 10 hour driving limit after your 8 hours or more of rest? a/ Yes51No49
   b. How long are your longer runs, including combination runs? b/_____MILES
   c. From where to where? c/_____to_____to_____
   d. How long does it take, on the average, to make these longer runs? d/_____HRS.
   e. Is it ever necessary to exceed the speed limits in order to make runs in expected times? e/ Yes71No 29

3. a. Are the conditions of your job such that it is necessary for you to stay "on duty" for more than 15 hours? a/ Yes46No54
   b. If yes to above, Why? b/_____
   c. Have you ever had to stay "on duty" for more than 70 hours in one 8 day period? c/ Yes48No52
   d. If yes to above, Why? d/_____
   e. Are you ever required to mark driving time as merely "on duty—not driving" time? e/ Yes30No70.
   f. Is it a company policy to record lunch stops as "off-duty?" f/ Yes67No23.
   g. Is pressure ever brought to bear on you to falsify your log? g/ Yes40No60.
   h. Does your company use Tach-O-Graphs? h/ Yes___No___.

4. a. Are you satisfied with company-provided sleeping accomodations (if you use them)? a/ Yes 53 No 47

    b. Are you able to sleep easily? b/ Yes 36 No 64

    c. Are other persons assigned to your room while you are still in it? c/ Yes 46 No 54

5. a. How long, on the average, are you awake before you're called to go on duty? a/ 5 HOURS (average)

    b. How long have you been awake when you complete a run, on the average? b/ 18 HOURS (average)

    c. What has been your longest period awake at the end of a run, on the average? b/____ HOURS

    d. Have you ever drowsed at the wheel? d/ Yes 80 No 20

6. a. In your opinion is the use of "pep pills" widespread in the industry? a/ Yes 61 No 39

    b. If yes to above, why? b/

7. a. Are complaints about defective equipment corrected immediately? a/ Yes 50 No 50

    b. How long does it take, on the average, to start repairs? b/

    c. How often have you driven a rig which: "OFTEN — OCCASIONALLY — NEVER"

        c1. Had inadequate brakes? c1/ 40 -- 40 -- 20

        c2. Had exhaust leakage into the cab? c2/ 32 -- 41 -- 27

        c3. Had an imbalanced load between front and rear trailers? c3/ 40 -- 26 -- 34

        c4. Held unsecured or loose freight. c4/ 33 -- 30 -- 37

        c5. Contained steel without a reinforced bulkhead? c5/ 25 -- 25 -- 50

        c6. Had weak or broken springs? c6/ 26 -- 44 -- 30

        c7. Had a loose fifth wheel? c7/ 34 -- 22 -- 44

        c8. Ran on treadless tires? c8/ 36 -- 24 -- 40

        c9. Ran on re-grooved front tires? c9/ 3 -- 8 -- 89

        c10. Was more than the maximum legal weight? c10/ 38 -- 36 -- 26

        c11. Had defective or inadequate lights or reflectors? c11/ 32 -- 32 -- 36

        c12. Other: c12/

    d. Has your company ever reprimanded you for refusal to drive defective equipment? d/ Yes 30 No 70

8. a. Are you satisfied with federal safety enforcement? a/ Yes 19 No 81

    b. Are you satisfied with state enforcement? b/ Yes 34 No 66

    c. How many times, during the past year, have you been stopped for speeding? c/____ TIMES

    d. How many times, during the past year, has your log been checked in transit? d/ 0 TIMES = 52%

    e. How many times, during the past year, has your company warned you for delay or for your refusal to drive because of sickness, hazardous conditions, etc.? e/____ TIMES

    f. How many times has your company suspended you for the above? f/____ TIMES

    g. How many times has your company attempted to dismiss you for the above? g/____ TIMES

    h. Are all accidents reported? h/ Yes 79 No 21

    i. How many accidents that you know about have not been reported? i/

9. a. Does your company see to it that you receive a periodic physical exam at least once every three years? a/ Yes 87 No 13

    b. Does the physical include careful examination of eyes, including an eye test, as well as ears, mouth, throat, chest, pulse, blood pressure? b/ Yes 84 No 16

    c. Which of the above is not examined? c/

10. a. Who is responsible for the safety of the vehicle? a/ Driver____ Company____

    b. Does the company ever force you to drive a defective piece of equipment? b/ Yes 48 No 52

    c. Does the company ever force you to haul what in your opinion is an "unsafe" load? b/ Yes 42 No 58

11. a. Have you ever sought assistance from a state or federal agency about defective equipment or unsafe loads? a/ Yes 32 No 68

    b. Did you receive assistance? b/ Yes 32 No 68

    c. Have you ever sought support from the union about defective equipment or unsafe loads? c/ Yes 45 No 55

    d. Did you receive support? d/ Yes 31 No 69

12. a. In which capacity are you presently employed Company Driver ☐ Owner Operator ☐ (If O-O how many pieces of equipment do you own?__)

    b. Which of the following do you normally haul?

        1/ Freight ☐ 2/ Steel ☐ 3/ Auto ☐

        4/ Tankers ☐ 5/ Household ☐ 6/ Produce ☐

        7/ Refrigerated ☐ 8/ Other ☐ (Specify)

HAZARDOUS VEHICLE CONDITIONS MOST
FREQUENTLY REPORTED BY DRIVERS

Direct Hazards to Public
  Defective and inadequate lights and reflectors
  Defective trailer hitches
  No "chuck blocks"
  No drive-wheel fenders
  Overloads
  Partial loads of petroleum without baffles
  Powerless equipment
  Unbalanced loads
  Unsecured and loose loads

Direct Hazards to Driver
  Broken speedometer
  No reinforced bulkhead when carrying steel loads
  Cracked and pitted windshield
  Defective or no shock absorbers
  Defective or no windshield wipers
  Deficient defrosters
  Deficient seats
  Excessive holes in fire walls
  Exhaust leakage into cab
  Loose doors
  No "blind-spot" mirrors
  Leaking grease seals

Other Hazardouts Defects
  Wheels and Brakes
    Bad front end—front end "play"
    Brakes too weak for loads and equipment
    Defective brake cables to trailers
    Defective or no hand brakes
    Defective trailer brakes
    Frozen brake cams
    Inferior "wedge-type" brakes
    Treadless, regrooved, and mismated tires
    Worn steering linkage—defective steering
  Other
    Bent and broken frame
    Loose air connections
    Loose and cracked fifth wheels
    Weak and broken springs
    Weak cabs—cabs chained to frame
    Worn and broken fifth wheel pin

APPENDIX 17 Some Typical Excerpts from Letters Regarding Trucking Safety

"We have runs which are . . . 400 to 543 miles one way with two to three pedal stops. Company expects you to make the same time with a 220 horsepower engine as a 335 horsepower—if you can't make it in ten hours then falsify your logs. . . . instead of getting better and safer, working conditions are getting worse. I could tell you things about this company that would make your hair stand up. Most drivers feel the ICC is bought . . ." —RC

"I drove tractor #.... from Pitts. to Richmond, Va. where the tractor brakes had been completely backed off. . . . Many vehicle condition reports disappear." —GT

"Driving times are commonly violated. . . . Fast driving, loading and unloading quickly, short time to eat, and result tired driver to drive home yet. Spend an hour with your family awake and zip to bed for a quick five to six hours sleep and back to reloading. Now, if you don't run like this you're picked on by the company for cargo damages, no matter how slight, coming in a few minutes late. Steward is afraid of company. Agent (what a laugh) is never there and won't come." —MB

"Many times you cannot rest at daytime in hotels with no airconditioning. . . . Also, 3–4 hours after you are in bed they will put another driver in the same room (separate bed) that you have never seen before. Many times it takes 1½–2 hours to arrive at hotel from the time relieved from duty, by the time you eat and shower, up to 3 hours have elapsed, then if you are awakened 2–3 hours later by another driver coming into your room and they call you for a 400 mile run 8 hours from time last relieved from duty, you can imagine how much rest you get." —AC

"One week I went 42 hours without so much as a nap. The drivers there must unload and they show off duty for all this unloading time. After unloading they will drive to the next destination without any rest." —RK

"My average on duty time is 30 hours on duty plus my 8 hours off duty. . . . Our trailers are as close as possible in order to give us as much length as possible, therefore broken air lines are quite common." —CN

"The American Trucking Association's claim that twin-trailers are as safe as a semi-trailer is strictly false. Ask any driver who has a choice. Also these companies will inevitably load the rear trailer with the heaviest load. It may also interest you to know the daily ICC condition report of equipment is neglected by many of these companies and with a shortage of good mechanics much of this repair work is 'penciled' and not repaired at all." —CM

"Many of the drivers still are willing to do whatever they have to—

to work all the time simply for the money. Even if it means taking drugs, etc. . . . the rest stay drunk until they go out again. . . ."

—FP

"I put a 429 mile run in the questionnaire because this is a turn around run from Winchester to Phila., Pa. and return. The speed limits are mostly 25 to 45 MPH, except on the Interstate. These roads are jammed with traffic and the best I could ever do on this run was 10 hours driving; driving as hard as I could drive with a load. Then after getting there they usually hold you one to three hours getting your load ready for the *return trip*."

—CL

". . . you would do well to clean up your own nest first. By this I mean clean up your colleges and return their management to responsible people not long haired rabble-rousers. . . . All you people in Boston are looking for is an easy buck and if you have to be spoilers to get it why not? . . . find out how safe they are (drivers) if they don't shell out from $20–$45 to load or unload in your fair city. . . ."

—CK

"The whole business of the drivers filling out logs is phoney. I personally don't know of any company who says "you must run and log illegally" but—you are to log every day so that it appears legal."—RT

". . . the drivers are so money hungry that they themselves are breaking down conditions. . . ."

—JL

"We are forced to drive tractors daily that are so loud we have to stuff our ears with cotton. The 5th wheels on all our Co. tractors are too far forward making it impossible to hold in event of a blow out and very hard to hold on any type of roadway due to the excessive weight this 5th wheel lets them place on the steering axle."

—JS

"From Burlington N.C. to Brooklyn N.Y. is 11¼ to 12¼ hours . . . you have to run wide open all the time."

—JL

"I have weight tickets, defective equipment reports—where repairs were refused when the steering arm was ready to fall off. This caused two of our drivers to be killed but the truck was cut up in pieces before we could prove it. Then reported the driver went to sleep. . . . Drivers forced to operate defective equipment or be fired. . . ."—RC

"I think pep pills are in widespread use for two reasons: 1—Because scheduled runs are so demanding and that a man under normal conditions can't make these schedules. 2—There are many drivers who believe it is an absolutely necessity. . . ."

—WS

"In many cases I have been on duty for more than 72 hours consecutive."

—BO

"I have seen more than twenty drivers come and go. Reasons were assorted, but all agreed on one thing. UNSAFE EQUIPMENT! . . . I myself came close to killing a family of four because of no brakes. . . . The driver is always blamed. . . . I can recall driving a stretch of road known as blood alley, between San Francisco and San Jose—US 101—with all my trailer brakes plugged off and one diaphragm on the tractor leaking badly! I was told to drive it all night and it would be fixed the next day—I drove it that way for a week. Equipment was a 1962 GMC Semi—7100 gallons of gas!! I was told myself in front of three other drivers that I would never turn another wheel for anyone again if I complained once more about the equipment not being safe."   —RJ

MOTOR TRUCK REGISTRATIONS
IN THE UNITED STATES

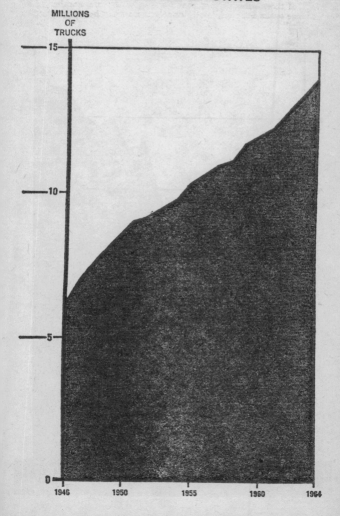

MILLIONS
OF
TRUCKS

15 —

10 —

5 —

0

1946   1950   1955   1960   1964

THE INCREASING PROPORTION OF HEAVY TRUCKS

TRUCKS 50,000 LBS. AND OVER AS A PERCENTAGE OF ALL TRUCKS OPERATING ON MAIN RURAL ROADS

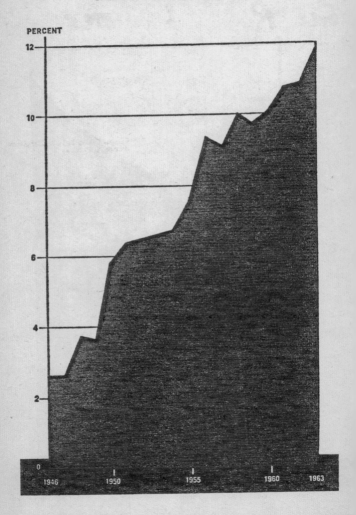

ALL ROAD DRIVERS

INTER-OFFICE CORRESPONDENCE

Lancaster, Penna.

Date: 2/24/66

From the desk of: E. F. Oettel

To: Irwin Levin
cc: Lou Czehosky

Re: Penna. State Police Institute
Hershey, Penna.

On February 17, 1966, I was present at the Truck Industry-Police Institute, at the Police Academy in Hershey, Penna.

We have been advised at this meeting that the following violations will no longer be tolerated in the state of Penna.

#1 - TAILGATING 500 FT.

#2 - SPEEDING 70

#3 - ENTERING PASSING LANE WITHOUT PROPER CLEARANCE

#4 - NO BODY LIGHTS   Protect

#5 - ~~RUNNING OVERLOADS ON TURNPIKE TO AVOID SCALES.~~
~~(WEIGH DETAIL WILL OPERATE ON TURNPIKE)~~

As you can see this could be very costly to our drivers as well as to Branch Motor Express Co.

Please advise all Terminal Managers, Dispatchers and Drivers of this crackdown in the State of Penna. and on the Penna. Turnpike.

Thanks.

E. F. Oettel

APPENDIX 20 The "Adequacies" Case: How the ICC Abdicated Its Responsibility

> The Interstate Commerce Commission announced today that it will ask Congress to preempt from the States, and assign to the Commission, jurisdiction over the quality and adequacy of railroad passenger service.
> —*lead paragraph in ICC press release of September 12, 1969, announcing ICC decision in "Adequacies" case.*

> The Interstate Commerce Commission, ruling that its hands are tied, today asked Congress to give it broad authority to regulate the quality of the nation's fast-fading railroad passenger service.
> —*lead paragraph in U.P.I. story of September 12, 1969.*

The image of the ICC presented to the public by the two sentences quoted above is a false one. It might appear that the Interstate Commerce Commission is a progressive administrative agency, doing its utmost with the meager powers allotted to it by a stingy Congress, and boldly requesting that Congress "assign" it powers necessary to combat the problems of "the nation's fast-fading railroad passenger service."

The truth is quite the opposite. The Commission's decision of September 10, 1969, that it lacked the authority to regulate the quality and adequacy of the nation's rail passenger service, is a prime example of administrative cowardliness, a misreading of administrative law, and, above all, a severe blow to the public interest the ICC was created to protect.[1]

Responsibility for the writing of this unsigned decision belongs to Commissioner Kenneth H. Tuggle, reputedly the closest friend of the railroads within the ICC. Contrary to its policy in important decisions, and, of course, to the policy of courts of law, the ICC issued its decision in this extremely important case without a designated author. It has positively been ascertained, from sources within the ICC, however, that the report was written by Commissioner Tuggle, with the assistance of his attorney advisor, Robert Brooks.

The "Adequacies" case was pending for 880 days when it was decided by the Interstate Commerce Commission. Three western states came to the Commission on April 15, 1966, and filed a petition asking the ICC to institute an investigation, under three sections of the Interstate Commerce Act, into the quality of service provided by the Southern Pacific Railroad Company in its New Orleans-Los Angeles "Sunset Limited."

The substantive charges leveled against the Southern Pacific were that it had removed sleeper facilities between El Paso and New Orleans, a traveling distance of 1177 miles, and had removed dining car facilities for first-class passengers. In general, the states charged that "S.P. has, over a number of years, consistently downgraded, discouraged the use of, and eroded the quality of its common carrier passenger train service."[2]

Almost from the day of the filing of the petition by the three states —California, Arizona, and Louisiana—the ICC pursued a policy which, when considered as a whole, deserves to be called little more than a fraud on the American public.

The case will be appealed by the State of California and other intervening parties, and they will have the courtroom to argue their case fully and openly.[3] It would be sufficient, therefore, to substantiate specifically the general charges made above, in chronological order, and to provide an outline of the logical legal arguments against the ICC's decision.

To begin with, the Commission delayed the expediting of this case for such a long period of time that one might make an argument that the due process rights of the parties have been violated by the Commission. While the average ICC case lasts only 18.1 months,[4] from petition to decision, in this case, there was an elapsed time of an incredible forty-one months between the time of the petition and the time of the decision. Admittedly, this was not an "average" case, yet it is clear that here delays were of an inordinate nature.

During that time there were 189 separate petitions for passenger train discontinuance. Of these 189 petitions, the Commission has already approved 100, while thirty cases were pending at the time the "Adequacies" case was decided. This represented a total loss to the nation's passengers of 249 trains, while the fate of sixty-four trains was undecided at the time of the "Adequacies" case decision. Thus, while the Commission sat on the case, they were themselves presiding over the ever-increasing pace of railroad discontinuance, so much so that if they had waited any longer to decide the case, there may have been little left for them to regulate.* The Commission seemed to be doing its very best for months at a time to avoid having to hear the case, and, once heard, to avoid reaching a decision on the case. In fact, oral arguments were held almost one full year—eleven months and three weeks—before the decision of the Commission was made public. The following is the chronology of the "Adequacies" case, in itself a case study of how a federal regulatory agency can quietly defeat the public interest by allowing it to be drowned in delay:

Total Time	Elapsed Time	Event
—	—	4/15/66: California, Louisiana, Arizona file petitions for investigation. S.P. replies, claiming no jurisdiction for ICC.
2 months	2 months	6/21/66: ICC issues order for investigation.
3½ months	1½ months	8/4/66: ICC issues order setting forth "special procedure" requiring petitioners to file verified testimony by 9/26/66; Southern Pacific, by 10/24/66.

* In an editorial entitled "Waiting for the Funeral?," *The Evening Star* (Washington, D.C.) commented on the delays in the "Adequacies" case six weeks before the decision was finally announced. The editorial stated that the ICC was "content that it has done its job by telling Congress what to do," but that "while Congress deliberates, and the ICC waits, more trains make their final trips, and those still running are downgraded. Eventually, as things are going, the railroads will kill all of their remaining service. Then, of course, there will be no need to rule in the Messer case because there will be no more trains. But the ICC could always say, 'well, we tried—we told Congress it ought to act.' "[5]

Total Time	Elapsed Time	Event
4½ months	1 month	9/8/66: Time for petitioners' testimony extended to 1/16/67.
8½ months	4 months	1/3/67: Time for petitioners' testimony extended to 2/27/67.
10½ months	2 months	2/27/67: Petitioners file testimony 5 months after initially scheduled. S.P. has until 3/20/67.
11 months	½ month	3/9/67: Time for S.P. testimony extended to 4/20/67.
12 months	1 month	4/13/67: Time for S.P. testimony extended to 6/20/67.
14 months	2 months	6/20/67: S.P. files testimony 8 months after initially scheduled.
17½ months	3½ months	9/25/67: Hearings set for 11/25/67.
19½ months	2 months	11/25/67: Hearings begin, lasting through mid-January, in major cities along the route of the "Sunset Limited."
24 months	4½ months	4/22/68: Hearing examiner John Messer issues recommended report and proposals, asserting (a) ICC has jurisdiction, and (b) S.P. downgraded service, and proposing national standards for rail passenger service.
27 months	3 months	May–July, 1968: Parties file exceptions and replies thereto.
29 months	—	7/22/68: Oral argument set for 9/18/68.
40 months	11 months	8/7/69: "Because of the widespread interest in the so-called 'Passenger Adequacies' case now pending, ICC announces decision will come before 'mid-September.' "
41 months	1 month	9/10/69: ICC decides case, asserting that it lacks authority to enforce standards, requests Congress to grant it the authority it claims it lacks.
41 months	—	9/12/69: ICC announces decision.

Much of the delay in the forty-one-month odyssey of F.D. 34733 (the case number assigned it by the Commission) was requested by one or another of the parties. But the fact remains that the ICC had to approve every delay requested. And, once the case was heard by the entire Commission, it was not until one of the parties threatened the ICC with a writ of mandamus that the ICC announced that the Commission would have a decision by the first anniversary of the oral hearing.

The Commission, in its very first procedural decision in the case, on June 21, 1966, set the stage for its later claimed lack of authority by refusing to institute an investigation under the section of the Interstate Commerce Act giving the agency its broadest authority and discretion. While California petitioned the ICC under Sections 12(1) and 13(2), the Commission turned its back on its usual practice of instituting investigations under Section 13, and chose to institute the investigation under 12(1).

The significance of this decision not to investigate the states' charges under both Sections 12(1) and 13(2) is that by failing to use the powers afforded it under the latter section, the Commission was able to seek the umbrage of an old Supreme Court case which allegedly showed that 12(1) did not give the Commission the authority to enforce Section 1(4) of the Act in the area of rail passenger service. No such authority exists for Section 13(2), however; thus, if the ICC had simply decided to honor the petition of California under *both* sections, it would have had to confront the substantive charges leveled against the railroad—that service on the "Sunset Limited" was below a standard which should be required of an interstate common carrier. Since granting the petition under both sections of the Interstate Commerce Act would have been a routine act, nothing but some rationale known only to the ICC prevented them from doing it—except, perhaps, an unwillingness under any circumstances to confront the charges of downgrading being made against the Southern Pacific.*

On April 22, 1968, hearing examiner John Messer issued his recommended report to the Commission, in which he made two major decisions: 1. that the Commission had the requisite jurisdiction to tackle the problem of inadequate service on the nation's passenger trains; 2. that the Southern Pacific must restore the diner car and sleeper between El Paso and New Orleans on the "Sunset Limited." Messer also recommended that the Commission enact industry-wide standards for the maintenance of passenger service. These recommendations were made after or shortly before the ICC had recognized in several cases that railroads were following the conscious policy of downgrading their passenger service, in order to turn away passengers and justify discontinuance.[7] In fact, Southern Pacific, in a case separate from the "Adequacies" case, was found to have wilfully downgraded the "Sunset Limited" itself, and a petition for discontinuance of the train was turned down.[8]

The "Messer Report," as it came to be known, burst upon the railroad scene like a bombshell, because it reversed the ICC's long-standing view that it did not have the jurisdiction to enforce standards for rail passenger service. The standards set up by Messer, if approved by the entire Commission, would also have gone a long way toward protecting the rights of railroad passengers at the hands of the railroad industry. In an understatement, one Washington business reporter stated in April, 1969: "The Messer report has been the source of serious concern to the railroad industry since it was issued." [9]

After the oral hearing of the case before the Commission in September, 1968, the Commission as a whole began the ponderous deci-

---

* When questioned by letter about the failure of the Commission to institute the investigation under both Sections 12(1) and 13, the Secretary's office of the Commission replied: "The Commission's action in granting petitioners' request for an investigation under the provision of Section 12(1) of the Act as reflected in the minutes of the Commission vote dated June 21, 1966, made it unnecessary for the Commission to reach the ancillary petitions under Section 13(2)." This conclusion, that a decision as to Section 13(2) was made unnecessary by the decision as to 12(1), is wrong, as the above discussion makes clear.

sional process that culminated in the September, 1969, decision against jurisdiction. One incident during the long wait for the ICC's decision in this important case deserves mention. On April 8, 1969, Washington *Evening Star* reporter Stephen Aug, who covers the ICC on a regular basis, wrote a story in which he predicted the votes of the individual Commissioners at that time. Instead of quickly coming to a decision at the time of the article in *The Evening Star*, and thus squelching rumors that heavy politicking was taking place among the Commissioners on the vote, the Commission instead instituted an investigation of the circumstances leading to the *Star* article. They searched high and low, in and out of the Commission, for the "leak." While it is true that the decisional process of the agency ought to be kept secret until the actual announcement of a vote, the verve with which the Commission searched for the culprit is in marked contrast with the lack of verve with which it pursued the decisional process.

On August 7, 1969, the Interstate Commerce Commission announced that "(b)ecause of the widespread interest in the so-called 'Passenger Adequacies' case now pending," the Commission would reach a decision in the case by "mid-September." Apparently, the words "widespread interest" were a severe understatement, for it was reported that the Commission was acting so "quickly" only because the attorney for one of the parties supporting the states threatened to go to federal court to seek a writ of mandamus to force the Commission to reach a decision.[10]

Finally, on September 12, 1969, the Interstate Commerce Commission announced its decision: by a 7–2 vote, it had found that it lacked jurisdiction over the quality and adequacy of interstate railroad passenger service. Because the courts are apparently going to hear an appeal from this decision, there is no need here to engage in lengthy legal arguments with reference to this decision. Many of the strong arguments against the decision are made in a lengthy dissent by former Chairman Paul J. Tierney. Virginia Mae Brown also dissented in the case. She stated: "(T)he majority has expressed in this report only those legalistic concepts which serve its purpose. . . ."[11]

That seems to be a fair description of the majority decision. It appears to be nothing more than a political decision in search for a legal rationale.

The Commission found that it had no jurisdiction despite the wording of Sections 1(4) and 12(1) of the Interstate Commerce Act:

1(4): It shall be the duty of every common carrier subject to this part [Part I of the Act] to provide and furnish transportation upon reasonable request therefore, . . . [and] . . . to establish . . . just and reasonable fares.*

12(1): The Commission is hereby authorized and required to execute and enforce the provisions of this part.

* Section 1(4) established the basic common carrier responsibilities of the railroads. The Supreme Court in 1958 ruled that Section 1(4) "not only authorize(s) the railroads to take all reasonable and proper steps for the transfer of persons and property between their connecting lines, but imposes affirmative obligations on them in this respect." (See *AT & SF Ry. Co. v. Chicago*, 357 US 77 (1958).)

The wording of Section 12(1)—"authorized and required to execute and enforce"—appears to be sufficiently clear and unambiguous to vest the Commission with the requisite authority. Instead, the Commission searched far and wide for ways to avoid this clear statutory duty. They came up with five reasons not to read Section 12(1) the way it apparently was written:

> . . . other parts of this same statute, which lead to a different conclusion; the United States Supreme Court's interpretation of these same two provisions; findings of Congressional committees dealing with the same subject matter and actions of Congress thereon; the decision and practice of this Commission; and the laws and practices of the States with regard to passenger trains.[12]

None of these five reasons, upon examination of the decision, justify the ICC's decision. Some are illogical, others simply a misstatement of the relevant law.

1. *Statutory construction:* Contrary to the Commission's correct statement of the law that the "whole statute together" must be considered, the majority instead cited one section 1(18), completely out of context, "solely as an example—to show that not all questions regarding Part I enforcement are answered by the above-quoted excerpts." (Sections 1(4) and 12(1) above.) [13] This is a curious bit of illogic: because one section *can* be construed differently than the obvious meaning of Section 12(1), then a different interpretation of 12(1) is *possible,* and thus preferable. The Commission also dealt quickly with the legislative history of Section 13(a) of the ICA, calling its enactment "the more authoritative indication of the Congressional intent as to our regulatory jurisdiction over passenger trains and service." [14] Again, this is a curious notion.

2. *Supreme Court cases:* The Commission cited *United States v. Pennsylvania RR Co.,* 242 US 208 (1916), a case based on a situation entirely different from that of the "Adequacies" case. That case held that Section 12(1) cannot be used to enforce 1(4)—the real issue in the case at hand—but such a conclusion can be clearly overridden in 1969 by the reference to the enactment, in 1941, twenty-five years after the decision cited, of the National Transportation Policy. This preamble to the Interstate Commerce Act gives the ICC broad power to carry out its responsibilities to

> provide for fair and impartial regulation of all modes of transportation subject to the provisions of this Act, so administered as to recognize and preserve the inherent advantages of each . . . to the end of developing, coordinating, and preserving a national transportation system by water, highway, and rail, as well as many other means, adequate to meet the needs of the commerce of the United States of the Postal Service, and of the national defense.[15]

The Supreme Court has ruled that the National Transportation Policy is "the yardstick by which the correctness of the Commission's actions will be measured," [16] and the Interstate Commerce Commission itself used the National Transportation Policy in 1967 as successful justification for its issuing rules making "TOFC" (piggyback) service available to the nation's truckers.[17] There the Commission used the National Transportation Policy correctly to help a powerful transportation industry. Here, where the nation's states and its rail passengers petitioned for assistance, the Commission made no mention of a National Transportation Policy.

3. *Findings of Congressional Committees:* The Commission's citations of the reports of several Congressional Committees in the enactment of Section 13(a) are another exercise in illogic. The enactment of 13(a) was due to the inability of railroads to obtain permission from various state regulatory bodies to take their trains off the tracks. If 13(a) has anything at all to do with this case, it would seem that its enactment meant that Congress was recognizing that only the federal regulatory agency has the capacity to tackle this truly nationwide problem. Instead, the ICC took the enactment of 13(a) to mean exactly the opposite—that Congress intended to give the ICC "a very limited regulatory power over a field generally occupied by the States." [18] The Commission states that "Congress [in 1958] recognized that the States have long occupied the field in considerable depth and it chose not to disturb this situation except to the minimal degree necessary to deal with specific problems considered to have become Federal in scope." [19] This is an outrageous example of misinterpretation. Examination of debate reveals a full awareness of the inherent "interstate" nature of much of the nation's rail industry. The purpose of the provision was not to define the outer limits of federal authority, but the inner limits. The provision was an elucidation of minimum federal powers exercisable to the exclusion of state authority. There is absolutely no basis for interpreting the section as a maximum limit standard—it was intended as precisely the opposite. And, indeed, logic as to the deficiencies of state regulation of an inherently interstate mode, makes this interpretation sensible as well as representative of congressional intent.

4. *Past ICC Decisions and Practice:* In 1967, the United States Supreme Court, referring to the Interstate Commerce Commission, said:

> [F]lexibility and adaptability to changing needs and patterns of transportation [are] an essential part of the office of a regulatory agency. Regulatory agencies do not establish rules of conduct to last forever; they are supposed, within the limits of the law and of fair and prudent administration, to adapt their rules and practices to the Nation's needs in a volatile, changing economy. They are neither required nor supposed to regulate the present and the future within the inflexible limits of yesterday.[20]

The Interstate Commerce Commission, in citing its past cases as authority for denying that it has jurisdiction over the adequacy of rail passenger service, is flouting the obvious dictates of the Supreme Court that it ignore its own prior decisions when changing times have provided changing conditions in the regulatory field. The Commission places most of its reliance on a 1924 ICC decision, *Wisconsin R. Commission v. Chicago & N.W. Ry. Co.*, 87 ICC 195. Wisconsin has usually been used by the Commission to justify inaction in this field, but, as stated in the dissent by Commissioner Tierney in the "Adequacies" case, *Wisconsin* provides scant actual authority: it is a short, three-and-a-half-page report, with a scant two paragraphs discussing Section 1(10), and with no discussion whatever on Section 1(4). Even if the Commission could claim to be bound by prior decisions, which the Supreme Court has time and again said is not so, *Wisconsin,* decided in the manner it was, before the enactment of the National Transportation Policy, would provide little or no support for its position.

5. *Laws and Practices of the States:* The Commission stakes out its final justification on the grounds that states have always exercised power over intercity passenger service, and thus ought to be allowed to continue. This position is another futile attempt to avoid its regulatory duties, for it ignores the very facts of the case. This part of the Commission's report assumes that the states are jealously guarding their regulatory power over railroads, and do not want the federal government to intervene. The ICC states: "A State and its cities still look upon the long-line passenger train as a thing of local concern too—even though they may constitute but a small segment on the train's route." [21] One can only wonder how the Commission could reach the above conclusion when it was faced by five state regulatory agencies seeking help from the Commission, telling the Commission that their powers were too limited, and appealing to the federal regulatory agency to take the appropriate national view to a national, and not a local, problem.

Finally, the Commission, in its policy of expressing, in the words of Chairman Virginia Mae Brown, "only those legalistic concepts which serve its purpose," [22] failed even to take up the arguments used by the ICC hearing examiner, John Messer, in his recommended report to the full Commission. Incredibly, no mention was made by Examiner Messer in concluding that the Commission had the requisite jurisdiction to enforce Section 1(4) of the Interstate Commerce Act. The cases he cited provided the legal framework for Examiner Messer's decision, and one would think that the full Commission would at least refute the arguments used by their examiner, rather than simply ignore them.

Why the ICC decided the way it did is open to question. It appears that the decision is an exceedingly political one, in the sense that the decision appears to have been made not entirely on the merits of the case. This is certainly the view of one legal observer of the ICC in action, who wrote the Washington *Evening Star:* "The decision itself, with the circumstances surrounding it, establish beyond any doubt that the ICC is now nothing more than an extension of the railroad lobby within the United States government." [23]

The authors have not attempted to discuss the "Adequacies" case in depth, but, instead, to indicate only a few points of concern. What the decision reflects overall is the outdated philosophy of regulation to which the ICC still holds—that the regulator never lifts a remedial finger in the public interest unless specifically told when, where, and how by Congressional language. The Transportation Act of 1941 gave to the ICC broad powers and means equal to those available to any federal agency. Modern court decisions and regulatory construction urge agencies like the ICC to assert their jurisdiction to the fullest, and leave the task of limiting the scope of that jurisdiction to the courts. [24] But the ICC takes the narrowest possible view of its powers, and waits for the courts, Congress, or the industries to prod it forward.

The reasoning behind the ICC's decision aside, the most important fact in this case is that the Commission muffed a clear opportunity to investigate the basic question it has only occasionally approached, and that is the chicken-and-egg controversy described in Chapter 8. Although it has warned for several years that the government is facing the now-or-never stage in rail passenger service, the ICC failed to rise to the occasion when it had the chance.

APPENDIX 21 Letter from Nader to Finch about Dumping

19 December 1969

The Honorable Robert Finch
Secretary of Health, Education,
  and Welfare
Department of Health, Education,
  and Welfare
Washington, D.C.

Dear Secretary Finch:

I wish to bring to your immediate attention some documentation of what must be considered the most blatantly outrageous corporate pollution that your Department regulations permit to continue unabated. Reference is made to the dumping of raw human excrement directly on railroad right-of-ways, street crossings, stations, watersheds and other land areas.

The scope of the problem. The American Public Health Association lists twenty-seven communicable diseases which could be passed on by raw waste. It is one of the most elementary principles of public health and sanitation that raw feces and urine not be dumped onto the land. Buses and aircraft are required by Public Health Service regulations to retain all wastes and direct disposals are prohibited. Not so with the favored railroad industry. A double standard is at work here. Over tens of thousands of miles of railroads are permitted to dump human excrement wholly untreated just as soon as an employee or a passenger relieves himself in the toilet. The only possible restriction on this repulsive corporate practice is contained in 42 C.F.R. 72.154(b) which states that "Toilets shall be kept locked when conveyances, occupied or open to occupancy by travellers, are at a station or servicing area unless means are provided to prevent contamination of the area or station." This regulation has never been enforced; it is outrageously violated and there is no record of any penalty ever being assessed against a railroad. The Surgeon General has not designated any other prohibited areas in the regulations.

Although your Department has long been aware of this dumping of raw sewage, there has been no study conducted about the volume deposited; where deposited in rough percentages; and the consequences. This is not because public health officials are not worried; indeed they are very concerned. Rather, they have been intimidated by the Association of American Railroads which is intent on perpetuating the freedom of enterprise to defecate on open land and in crowded stations.

A very recent study of Monogram Industries, a producer of waste disposal equipment, provides statistics on the extent of the waste volume dumped directly without treatment onto the tracks from locomotives and cabooses. This study was conducted with the knowledge and assistance of the U.S. Public Health Service but has not been made public by any government agency. PHS's assistance was purely technical and indicated a long familiarity with this major public health hazard. On the most conservative estimate, the Monogram study reports that 30,000 locomotives, and 15,000 cabooses with a total of 45,000 toilets dump 51.5 million pounds of feces per year on the land and the total sewerage output per year is 30.5 million gallons of waste. These figures are based on the most conservative calculations. In addition, there are 17,600 passenger cars which carried 296 million revenue paying passengers in 1968. It can be prudently estimated that the total waste dumped wholly untreated by the railroad industry per year is around 200 million pounds of feces and 90 million gallons of waste.

The general hazards to human health need no elaboration, except to the primitive insensitivities of railroad executives. The last time the railroads tried to whitewash this disease-breeding sewage disposal was in the late 1940's when they attempted to dismiss the problem as (a) inconsequential, (b) subject to air and sunshine purification, (c) the rights of private property which did not need to recognize trespassers. If such responses were crude then, they are even cruder today. Demographic patterns have changed; once rural areas through which railroads passed are now built up residential areas. Easements come closer to the tracks than before. House pets of nearby residents roam the area. More freight trains are in operation. Further, as before, railroad laborers maintaining or replacing track are exposed to human waste material surrounded by flies in their work. The stories of their experience heap shame and disgrace on company management. Toilets are kept in the filthiest condition by this management which has chosen this way to cut costs. Railroad chiefs rarely make field trips here.

Even the railroads' advanced planning does not take into account the necessity of being toilet trained. Every year there are about 3,000 locomotives and cabooses built and put into operation. Over 90% of the toilets in these brand new vehicles are primitive toilets that empty directly onto the tracks. Like their predecessors they will be a threat to humans, watersheds, and provide animal carriers with their diseased burdens. Japan and the nations of Western Europe have far stricter laws and take greater precautions in practice. In Sweden, direct disposal is banned and retention toilets are required. Some states, such as Pennsylvania and New York, are beginning to show other than verbal concern. But the national remedy belongs inescapably to the federal government. Canada has now passed legislation prohibiting direct dumping of human waste and as this law is implemented, it will be felt by five U.S. Railroads who operate about 1200 miles of track inside Canada.

The technical and economic remedies are quite simple and even compatible with the dreams of avarice that are inspiring railroad conglomerates to range far and wide in their acquisitions and downgrade their passenger service. I have made inquiries as to the cost of replacing all existing toilets known as gravity feed flushing hoppers. The minimum costs to refit some 80,000 units for all existing locomotives, cabooses and passenger cars would be $3,750,000. This relatively trivial expenditure for an industry, that has shown a net yearly income after taxes from its railway operations of between $676 million to over $1 billion during the past six years, must be imposed immediately by the effect of new Public Health Service regulations. This expenditure would permit the purchase and installation of retention type buckets with appropriate chemicals in the tank. Disposal would then be accomplished when the trains are at a service station or arrive at their destination.

Even the most superior kind of equipment—a complete, self-contained retention asystem which recirculates the fluid, disinfects and deodorizes the waste with an electrically driven filter pump—would cost a total of $35 million for all locomotives, cabooses and passenger cars.

In the list of the foregoing facts, I urge you to immediately initiate the proceedings for revision of 42 C.F.R. 72.154 to prohibit direct disposal onto land of human waste by railroads and establish criteria for sanitary waste disposal procedures that are enforceable. If this requires that you investigate or seek investigation of the Association of American Railroad's collusive lobbying at the Public Health Service, then let such an inquiry be made openly and in public. Unlike other public health decisions, this is not a difficult one to make. The facts are clear; the hazards recognized and banned on other transportation vehicles. Only the railroads remain outside the rule of law. I would hope that you act with firmness and dispatch.

I am forwarding copies of this letter to Mr. T. M. Goodfellow, President of the Association of American Railroads and to Mr. Stuart T. Saunders, Chairman of the Board of Penn-Central. Both of these gentlemen are tidy enough not to expose themselves to the filthy conditions which their policies subject railroad employees and passengers to endure. They will now be asked to concede that corporations are not immune from the standards of decency common to men even if they be railroad corporations.

Sincerely yours,
Ralph Nader

RN: smf
CC: Mr. T. M. Goodfellow
    Mr. Stuart T. Saunders
    Senator Edmund Muskie
    Senator Vance Hartke

APPENDIX 22 The Other Side of the Railroad Poverty Game

While the railroad industry plays the poverty game before the ICC and Congress, many of the same railroad companies which cry the loudest rake in profits by the millions from non-railroad holdings. Railroads are among the largest owners of real estate in the United States; the railroads have "made great progress in exploiting their potentials." [1]

The leading railroad land owner is the Penn-Central Company. According to the Hayden Stone Company, "the Penn-Central may well be the *largest single owner of real estate in the United States.* Total receipts from all Penn-Central real estate operations and sales amounted to $273 million in 1968 as compared with only $137.3 million in 1966." [2] (Emphasis added.) The total value of the Penn-Central's landholdings may well be $1 billion. [3]

The construction of the Madison Square Garden Center atop the old Penn Station site in Manhattan has proved a boon to the Penn-Central as well as the New York Knicks and Rangers. Penn-Central owns 24 per cent of the stock of the Garden, and as a result of the new Center, the Penn-Central will probably make a profit on the operation of Penn Station. Additional income from this area will come with the construction of a modern shopping center with connections with a new bank at 7th Avenue and 33rd and 34th Streets. [4]

Penn-Central owns valuable air rights over its properties in the New York City area, "which should provide the railroad with substantial revenues, when ultimately leased, or sold." [5] These air rights include:

1. Passenger and freight yards five to ten minutes from Grand Central Station by subway, in Queens.
2. Bay Shore yards in South Brooklyn.
3. Yards facing the Hudson River adjacent to the West Side Highway.
4. Yards facing the Hudson River west of 11th Avenue at 32nd to 36th Streets.
5. Yards in Weehawken, New Jersey, one minute from the Lincoln Tunnel and ten to fifteen minutes from Times Square. [6]

Other valuable New York landholdings are at the Grand Central Terminal area. This real estate, "probably the most valuable . . . in the United States," produced nearly $45 million in rental income in 1968. [7] This $45 million from that real estate alone, representing just the rental income, represents 37 per cent of the deficit from eight major railroads' passenger service for 1968, before taxes. After taxes, it represents 58 per cent of that deficit. According to the experts, this sum may be "enhanced substantially

(1) when a multi-million dollar renovation of the Barclay, Biltmore, Commodore, and Roosevelt Hotels is completed,
(2) if and when the company is able to clear the roadblocks posed by the City of New York to the proposed 55-story office building over the Terminal itself, and
(3) when $2 million, formerly paid to the New Haven annually is obtained by the Penn-Central, following final absorption of that property." [8]

The Penn-Central's holdings in Philadelphia include five major office buildings; a major hotel, the Penn Sheraton; and a motel, the Penn Center Inn; along with several cooperative apartments, near the old Broad Street station site. The value of the company's holdings will increase substantially with the rehabilitation of the area between the 30th Street station and 18th Street. In preparation for the possible principal location of the United States' 200th Anniversary celebration in Philadelphia, Penn-Central is planning the development of eighty-four acres of air rights over the 30th Street Terminal.[9]

The Company is not inactive in other major cities, either. In Pittsburgh, the Penn-Central Company has a 127-acre industrial park adjacent to the Golden Triangle. The federal government is putting up a $50 million postal center there, and plans are under way for a convention center and an exhibition hall. In Washington, D.C., plans to transform the Union Station into a national visitors center will reduce the tax burden of Penn-Central and B & O by one million dollars each. In Chicago, Mayor Daley's plans to consolidate four passenger stations into one will "make much more pleasant reading" for Penn-Central, which now operates Union Station at a deficit. But completion of a third office building in Chicago will reduce that deficit anyway by increased revenues from air rights. In Cleveland and Detroit, plans have begun to redevelop Penn-Central holdings into major urban complexes.[10]

In addition, consolidation of dual facilities of the New York Central and the Pennsylvania Railroad will undoubtedly free many acres for use for industrial purposes.[11] These developments would add millions of dollars to the already gigantic Penn-Central real estate holdings.

The above-described landholdings are near the tracks which carry the Penn-Central's age-old passenger equipment. But the company also owns substantial property hundreds of miles from their right-of-ways. Three important properties have been acquired by Penn-Central.

The Macco Corporation owns one of the largest single blocks of real estate in burgeoning Orange County, south of Los Angeles. Earnings on this land have increased from $4.3 million in 1966, to $7.6 million in 1967, to $21.0 million in 1968, an increase in value of 388 per cent, in two years.[12]

Penn-Central owns 80 per cent of Great Southwest Corporation, which is developing industrial parks in the fast-growing areas of Dallas-Fort Worth and Atlanta, Georgia. Pre-tax earnings of these holdings grew even faster than the California holdings: *700 per cent from 1964 to 1968, and 125 per cent from 1967 to 1968,* when the property had $9.7 million in earnings. Development of a 3000-acre tract in Atlanta will further increase earnings.[13]

Fifty-nine per cent of Arvida Corporation is owned by Penn-Central. This corporation owns valuable properties in the most rapidly growing counties of one of the most rapidly growing states—Dade, Broward, Palm Beach, and Sarasota Counties, Florida. Real estate sales from these holdings reached $15.2 million in 1968, and will increase with expansion of new condominiums, apartment houses, hotels, motels, and golf courses. Earnings for Arvida have increased

921 per cent since 1964, rising from $235,000 to $2.4 million, after taxes.[14]

Penn-Central owns 100 per cent of Buckeye Pipe Line, which distributes oil products over a 7600-mile system, including airports like Kennedy, Miami, International, Greater Pittsburgh, and air force bases in three states. The company is considering adding La Guardia and Newark Airports. Buckeye's earnings have increased substantially over the past eleven years, and were $13.8 million in 1968.[15] Buckeye supplies 3,000,000 gallons of jet fuel to Kennedy International Airport daily, with a two-and-a-half-fold increase seen in five years. It would seem that here it is in the Penn-Central's interest not to disturb the supremacy of the passenger airline in many areas across the country. The ICC should investigate *this* aspect of the Penn-Central's holdings, at least.[16]

The whole story behind the Penn-Central's vast landholdings indicates that this is a very rich company which can well absorb losses from passenger operations, at least in the short run. As estimated by railroad financial experts Pierre Bretey and Karl Ziebarth, real estate net could double to almost $100 million by 1975.[17]

But Penn-Central is not the only major railroad with vast landholdings which is carrying around a huge crying towel over its passenger losses. The Illinois Central owns property in Chicago worth $200 million, and property in other areas worth another $100 million.[18] This compares to an after-tax avoidable expense of $5,418,857 for the Illinois Central from 1968 passenger operations.[19]

The Illinois Central sold air rights on which the Prudential office building was constructed, and has sold eighty-three acres of additional Loop properties for more than $83 million, through its 98 per cent-controlled Illinois Center Corporation. The ultimate value of the Loop property owned by Illinois Central Industries could exceed $1 billion, with the construction of a mixture of office and residential buildings in conjunction with other developers.[20]

Additional holdings by Illinois Central industries include several hundred acres of air rights south of 11th Street in Chicago; large holdings thirty miles south of Chicago, being developed as Park Forest South, with 20,000 homes and a college complex planned; an industrial park seven miles from downtown New Orleans; and a recently sold tract of land adjacent to the New Orleans train station, on which New Orleans will construct a municipal dome stadium.[21]

Another land-rich railroad is the Southern Pacific, beneficiary of the recent "Adequacies" decision. As of one year ago, Southern Pacific owned, in addition to land directly involved in rail operations, 3,854,831 acres of land; this includes 36,250 acres of land which are available for sale to users of the S.P.'s freight service. Gross income from real estate operations for the S.P. amounted to $13.4 million, from properties such as the Fontana Apartments in San Francisco.[22] In addition, Southern Pacific is active in other non-rail businesses besides landholding, making it one of the richest corporations on the West Coast.

The Nofolk & Western is active in developing residential, industrial, and even forest lands. N & W owns most of the land in Hammond, Indiana; Kansas City, Missouri; and Cincinnati real estate projects, with a total investment of $525 million. By 1980, Norfolk

& Western expects that income from these projects, plus a complex vacation-residential development in Coral Gables, Florida, will total $50 million a year.[23]

Several railroads are actively involved in mining operations which present a gigantic opportunity for increased income. Union Pacific has mineral rights on nearly 10 million acres; Northern Pacific, on 8 million. These companies are making substantial amounts of money, and will increase this flow with further development of oil and gas, trona, titanium, and beryllium, ores, iron ores, coal, lumber, and other mineral resources.[24]

Union Pacific's oil operations are making that company richer by the day. A wholly-owned subsidiary, Union Pacific Resources, Ltd., will carry out new explorations and development in Canada and the Arctic, in conjunction with Husky Oil. In the Rockies of the United States, Standard Oil of Indiana has announced plans to explore for oil and gas on over 7 million acres of land the mineral rights of which are held by Union Pacific. U.P. will retain 25 per cent of development rights, and will receive $9 million for the first three years of the project as a cash bonus from Standard Oil. The latter has also purchased options from Union Pacific for further use, upon payment of additional rentals and exploration payments. In August, 1969, Union Pacific purchased two oil companies owned by Celanese, for $240 million; these companies have facilities for production, refining, and marketing—some 1400 service stations. U.P. also holds a 15 per cent interest in a group which bought six Alaskan oil tracts in the recent bidding in the north slope.[25]

U.P. has also spent $56 million in the past four years to add to its real estate development holdings. One purchase was a 309-acre estate midway between Los Angeles and Long Beach. Real estate holdings near Salt Lake City may develop into a $25 million chemical complex. U.P. has recently expanded into residential real estate, including a $3.8 million investment in a residential development in Whittier, California, that is expected to become worth $25 million. An investment of $1.8 million in Costa Mesa, California has been made for a fifty-acre residential development. U.P. has also formed a new company, Upland Industries, to provide finished lots to builders of residential areas in the Los Angeles area.[26]

The St. Louis-San Francisco Railway (the "Frisco"), which has not been very active in landholdings, recently announced that a 50.1 per cent-owned subsidiary has found a uranium deposit on its lands, which could provide substantial earnings to the company.[27]

Each of the major railroads has an industrial development department with the responsibility of attracting new industry to the land owned alongside the tracks, thus producing greater freight income. It is estimated that aggressive marketing techniques have brought the Class I carriers $180 million in new revenues each year from 1962 to 1968.[28]

In addition to these landholdings described above, most railroads derive "other income" from other sources, such as bond holding, miscellaneous real estate sales, and dividends from stock held in other railroads. This income is not modest for many railroads. The following table from the *Railroad Industry Review 1969* illustrates the impact of such "other income" on rail operations.[29]

SELECTED CARRIERS' OTHER INCOME COMPARED
TO PRE-TAX NET RAILWAY OPERATING INCOME

1968	Pre-Tax Net Railway Operating Income (millions)	Net Other Income (millions)	% Other Income to Pre-Tax Net Railway Operating Income
Southern Pacific *	$102.2	$54.5	64.1
Northern	16.1	23.8	147.8
C & O	48.8	20.4	41.8
Seaboard Coast Line	21.7	14.2	65.4
Missouri Pacific	25.5	14.0	54.9
Illinois Central	17.6	11.6	65.9
B & O	18.7	11.1	59.4
Great Northern	21.8	11.0	50.5
Milwaukee Road	7.2	9.4	130.6

* Including subsidiaries.

Perhaps even more illustrative of the impact of "other income" is the fact that six major railroads were able to offset 50 per cent or more of their net railway operating losses through their "other income." The following table is also from the *Railroad Industry Review 1969*,[30] and includes those carriers with major passenger operations.

SELECTED CARRIERS' OTHER INCOME AS COMPARED
WITH PRE-TAX NET RAILWAY OPERATING LOSS

1968	Pre-Tax Net Railway Operating Loss (millions)	Net Other Income
Penn-Central	$45.4	$119.6
Chicago & NW	2.3	13.4
Rock Island	7.3	3.0
Chicago & Eastern Ill.	1.2	1.4

What this means is that for every dollar lost in running its railroad operations, the giant Penn-Central Company made $2.63 from holdings too diffuse to be called by any name other than "other income" —not reflecting the vast landholdings from which Penn-Central makes much more money. The Chicago & North Western System did even better, making $5.82 for every dollar lost in rail operations. The Rock Island did worse, making only $0.41 for every dollar lost in rail operations. And the C & EI made $1.17 for every dollar lost in rail operations.

The foregoing is not meant as a complete description of non-railroad holdings of companies operating passenger trains. Doubtless, there are other holdings in other areas. But this description is meant to make clear that when railroad executives come to Washington to plead poverty—and predict disaster if passenger trains are forced to continue to run—they are leaving out some of the most salient facts of their total financial picture.

APPENDIX 23 Thirteen-a Cases Since 1958

1. 13a(1)

Year	Petitions	Granted in Full	Granted in Part	Granted Without Investigation	Trains Off
1958	12	7	5	1	26
1959	33	25	2	3	93
1960	12	8	1	1	22
1961	13	9	0	6	36
1962	13	9	1	4	28
1963	20	10	5	0	77
1964	14	8	3	2	55
1965	34	24	1	1	92
1966	31	23	1	8	59
1967	50	28	6	7	72
1968	66	38	4	27	95
1969	41	9	0	5	22
		(27 pending as of 9/23/69)			
Total	339	198	29	65	673

2. 13a(2)

Year	Petitions	Granted in Full	Granted in Part	Granted Without Investigation	Trains Off
1958	7	2	2		10
1959	10	8	0		22
1960	4	3	0		11
1961	5	2	1		11
1962	2	0	1		1
1963	2	2	0		4
1964	7	4	1		271
1965	5	2	0		4
1966	3	1	0		2
1967	4	2	1		2
1968	4	1 + 1 pending	0		2
1969	2	2 pending			
Total	55	27	6		345

Source: ICC Compilation of 13a Cases.

Notes

All agency interviews, unless otherwise noted, took place in Washington, D.C. at the main office of the ICC during the summer of 1969.

CHAPTER 1

1. *Wall Street Journal*, September 26, 1969.
2. See especially 49 Code of Federal Regulations 1100.95–1100.102.
3. James C. Nelson, "The Effects of Entry Control in Surface Transport," *Transportation Economics*, Conference of the Universities–National Bureau Committee for Economic Research, New York, Bureau of Economic Research, 1965, p. 413.
4. Interview with Department of Transportation attorneys and economists.
5.*Agency interview, Tierney.
6. Agency interviews, Forbes, Stillwell.
7. Agency interview, Stillwell.
8. Agency interview, Cheseldine.
9. Agency interview, Stillwell.
10. Agency interview, Stillwell.
11. 49 CFR 1000. 735-14(a).
12. 49 CFR 1000. 735-14(b).
13. *Washington Post*, September 26, 1969.
14. *Chicago Tribune*, July 27, 1968, p. 7.
15. Interviews with lobbyists, ICC practitioners, and ICC employees, Charles Roberts, "The Other Ev Dirkson," *Newsweek*, June 16, 1969, pp. 26–28.
16. *Toward an Age of Greatness*, Published by State Committees on Voter Education, Washington, D.C., 1965, p. 35.
17. *Washington Post*, September 26, 1969.
18. *Report of Basic Policy Matters Under Consideration by the ICC*, ICC, June, 1969, p. 107.
19. *Id.*, p. 110.
20. The foregoing information about Mr. Schmid and the U.S. Freight Company was revealed to us by several individuals, including present or former ICC officials, and several sources within the transportation industry.
21. *ICC Manual of Administration*, 20-062.
22. *Id.*
23. *Id.*, 20-064.

CHAPTER 2

1. R. L. Banks & Associates, *Study of Cost Structures and Cost Finding Procedures in the Regulated Transportation Industries,* 1959, pp. 1–3.
2. John Meyer, Merton Peck, John Stenason, and Charles Zwick, *The Economics of Competition in the Transportation Industries,* Harvard University Press, Cambridge, Mass., 1964, p. 205.
3. Ann Friedlaender, *The Dilemma of Freight Transport Regulation,* Brookings Institute, Washington, D.C., 1969, p. 108.
4. See U. S. Bureau of Public Roads, Highway Statistics, 1966, pp. 123, 127.
5. Secretary of Commerce, *Supplementary Report of the Highway Cost Allocation Study,* H. Doc. 1924, 89 Cong. 1 Sess. (1965).
6. R. L. Banks and Associates, *Intermodal Competition,* Washington, D.C., January, 1966, v. 1, p. III-44 (prepared for Union Pacific and Rock Island Railroads).
7. For a full discussion of intermodal coordination, see Merril J. Robert and Associates, *Intermodal Freight Transportation Coordination: Problems and Potential,* Pittsburgh University, December, 1966, p. 498.
8. Meyer, Peck, Stenason, and Zwick, *op. cit.,* p. 99.
9. *Id.,* p. 100.
10. Data derived from *Eighty-First Annual Report on Transport Statistics in the United States,* prepared by the Bureau of Accounts of the ICC, Washington, D.C., (1967).
11. Association of American Railroads, *Yearbook of Railroad Facts,* April, 1969, p. 5.
12. Meyer, Peck, Stenason, and Zwick, *op. cit.,* p. 205.
13. Chart taken from Josephine Olson, *Discrimination in Motor Carrier Class Rates,* unpublished thesis, p. 23.
14. James C. Nelson, *op. cit.,* p. 401.
15. ICC 82nd Annual Report, 1968, Appendix G, Table 1, p. 137.
16. ICC 81st Annual Report, 1967, Table 33, pp. 152–3.

CHAPTER 3

1. The history of rail mergers under the ICC is described in *National Transportation Policy,* a Report Prepared for the Committee on Interstate and Foreign Commerce, United States Senate, by the Special Study Group on Transportation Policies in the United States, January 3, 1961 (hereinafter cited as the "Doyle Report"), pp. 236–242. The citation of the 1929 report including the "master plan" is *In the Matter of Consolidation of the Ry. Properties of the U.S. into a Limited Number of Systems,* 159 ICC 522 (1929), modified 163 ICC 188 ICC 663, 185 ICC 403.
2. 49 USC (2) (c).
3. Ann Friedlaender, *The Dilemma of Freight Transport Regulation,* Brookings Institute, Washington, D.C., 1969, p. 140.
4. See the comments by Judge Lovett of the Union Pacific at hearings on the Fess-Parker Bill in 1928, where he stated that the crucial matter in mergers was not improved service, but "cold business in every instance." Quoted in *Rail Merger Legislation,* Hearing before the Subcommittee on Antitrust and Monopoly of

the Senate Judiciary Committee, Pursuant to S.Res. 258, June–July 1962, p. 74.

5. "Chiefs of Northern Lines Sure Merger Will Work," *The New York Times*, Section 3, February 8, 1970, p. 1, col. 1.
6. Robert Gallamore, Ph.D. dissertation quoted in D.O.T. Staff Study, *Western Railroad Mergers*, 1969, p. 10.
7. Doyle Report, p. 270.
8. *Penn Central Merger Cases*, 389 US 486, 493 (1968).
9. Interview with ICC accountant, August, 1969.
10. Interview with ICC accountant, August, 1969.
11. *Baltimore and Ohio R. Co., v. U.S.*, 386 US 372, 391–2 (1967).
12. *Penn Central Merger Cases*, 389 US 486, 493 (1968).
13. *Id.*, 501.
14. Transcript of Hearings, "Northern Lines" merger, p. 268. The statement was made by the head of Wyer-Dick Associates, economic consultants who have worked on many occasions for railroad companies. They were chosen by the Department of Transportation and the ICC to assist in the *Investigation of Costs of Intercity Rail Passenger Service* (1969). Wyer-Dick has appeared on behalf of railroad companies in the following mergers: Rio Grande-Western Pacific; Milwaukee Road-C & NW; MoPac and Associated carriers; Seaboard Air Line-Atlantic Coast Line; Northern Pacific-C & EI; C & O—B & O; and Erie Lackawanna-Penn-Lehigh Valley; among others.
15. *Review of ICC Policies and Practices*, Hearings before the Subcommittee on Surface Transportation, Senate Commerce Committee, 91st Cong., 1st sess., Ser. No. 16, p. 99. (Hereinafter referred to as "Oversight Hearings.")
16. Gallamore, *op. cit.*
17. Oversight Hearings, p. 100.
18. "Mergers: Hidden Costs of Delay and Indecision,"166 *Railway Age*, 58, February 24, 1969.
19. Kent Healy, *Economics of Scale in the Railroad Industry*, Yale University Press, New Haven, 1961. See also *The Railroad Merger Problem*, Report of the Subcommittee on Antitrust and Monopoly, of the Senate Judiciary Committee, Pursuant to S. Res. 258, 87th Cong., February 26, 1963, 17–18.
20. *The New York Times, op. cit.*
21. Friedlaender, *op. cit.*, pp. 89–90.
22. *Id.*, pp. 94–97.
23. *B & O R. Co. v. U.S.*, 386 US 372, 436–437 (1967) (concurring opinion).
24. Letter from ICC Practitioner to Robert C. Fellmeth, January, 1970.
25. Exceptions of the United States to Examiner's Report and Order in Northern Lines Merger, FD 21478, 79, 80, pp. 6–8.
26. Exceptions of the State of Minnesota and the Minnesota Railroad and Warehouse Commission to Examiner's Report and Order in Northern Lines Merger.
27. *Id.*
28. This practice is outlined in the Justice Department's brief before the Supreme Court in the "Northern Lines" Merger, October, 1969.
29. Oversight Hearings, p. 99.

30. For the problems of shippers with the new merged carriers, see "Shippers Hit Deterioration of Railroad Freight Service—Blame Merger," *Journal of Commerce*, February 24, 1969, p. 1, col. 1; "Seaboard Lays Problems to P-C," *The New York Times*, April 28, 1969, p. 55, col. 5.

31. 386 US, at Appendix B.

32. *Id.*, at 450.

33. 386 US, at 424 (1967) (concurring opinion).

34. *Id.*, at 425.

35. *Id.*, at 430.

36. *Id.*, at 441–442 (1967) (dissenting opinion in part).

37. 386 US, at 438.

38. *Id.*, at 444.

39. *Id.*, at 447.

40. D.O.T., *Western Railroad Mergers*, 1969, p. 1.

41. *Report of the Interagency Committee on Transport Mergers in The President's Transportation Message of April 5, 1962* (March 6, 1963).

42. Oversight Hearings, p. 99.

43. D.O.T., *Western Railroad Mergers*, 1969, pp. 2–3.

44. 386 US 372, 399.

45. George E. Leighty, *Rail Merger Legislation*, Hearing before the Subcommittee on Antitrust and Monopoly of the Senate Judiciary Committee, Pursuant to Senate Resolution 258, June–July, 1962, p. 80.

46. Oversight Hearings, p. 283.

47. 73 H.R. 7373, H.R. 7374, and S. 1398, virtually identical with H.R. 7374, 91st Cong., 1st sess, 1969. H.R. 8261, 8322, and 8323 would similarly apply to takeovers of air carriers.

48. *Traffic World*, April 30, 1968.

49. Eighty-first Annual Report on Transport Statistics in the United States, ICC Bureau of Accounts, Washington, D.C., 1967, p. 53.

CHAPTER 4

1. Fox-Smythe Transportation Company, Extension, Oklahoma, 106 M.C.C. 1.

2. *Inventory of Motor Carrier Authority Study*, ICC (not released), p. 1.

3. *Id.*, p. 8.

4. *Id.*, p. 41.

5. James C. Nelson, *op. cit.*, p. 391.

6. *Id.*, pp. 391–3.

7. Robert A. Nelson, "Economic Structure of Highway Motor Carrier Industry in New England," in *Public Transportation For New England*, The New England Governor's Conference, November, 1957, pp. 31–32.

8. IMCA Study, p. 42.

9. *Id.*, p. 44.

10. *Id.*, p. 43.

11. James C. Nelson, *op. cit.*, p. 401.

12. *Id.*, p. 405.

13. *Id.*, p. 406.

14. *Id.*, p. 404.

15. ICC 81st Annual Report, 1967.
16. James C. Nelson, *op. cit.*, p. 421.
17. *Id.*; p. 417.
18. See Meyer, *et al.*, *op. cit.*, p. 216.
19. See Hough Transfer Inc., Gateway Eliminations, MC—66800 (Sub—no. 30).
20. Walter Miklius, "Agricultural Exemption," updated study for D.O.T., unpublished, p. 1.
21. Mildred De Wolsfe, *For Hire Carriers Hauling Exempt Agricultural Commodities: Nature and Extent of Operations*, Washington, D.C., USDA, Marketing Economics Division, ERS, Marketing Research Report 585, p. 5.
22. R. N. Farmer, "The Case for Unregulated Truck Transportation," *Journal of Farm Economics*, Vol. 46, May, 1964, p. 404.
23. *The Role of Truck Brokers in the Movement of Exempt Agricultural Commodities*, MRS No. 525, February, 1962, p. 23.
24. Miklius, *op. cit.*, p. 21.
25. *Interstate Trucking of Fresh and Frozen Poultry Under Agricultural Exemption*, MRS No. 224, March, 1958, pp. 1, 3–4, 67–68.
26. *Interstate Trucking of Frozen Fruits and Vegetables Under Agricultural Exemption*, MRS No. 316, March, 1959, pp. 1, 3–4, 50–65.
27. *The Role of Truck Brokers in the Movement of Exempt Agricultural Commodities*, MRS No. 525, February, 1962, p. 23.
28. *Supplement to Interstate Trucking of Frozen Fruits and Vegetables Under Agricultural Exemption*, Supplement to MRS No. 316, July, 1961, p. 3.
29. James C. Nelson, *op. cit.*, p. 415.
30. Robert A. Nelson, *op. cit.*, p. 24.

CHAPTER 5

1. See Section 5(a) of the Interstate Commerce Act, Appendix 1.
2. For a defense of the rate bureau, see Charles Taff, *Commercial Motor Transportation*, Irwin, Homewood, Illinois, 1955.
3. Walter Adams, "The Role of Competition in the Regulated Industries," *American Economic Review*, May, 1958, Vol. XLVIII, p. 533.
4. *Id.*
5. James C. Nelson, *op. cit.*, p. 406.
6. See also, "Midwest Emery Freight System, Inc. *v.* Lee Brothers, Inc. *et al.*, Docket 34110, 322 ICC 701 (1964) and "Oilfield Equipment, Materials, and Supplies to and between the Southwest," Docket MC–C-1891, 313 ICC 577 (1961).
7. Some ICC hesitation about granting great numbers of these orders is expressed in 313 ICC 577, 602 (1961).
8. *Tobacco—North Carolina to Central Territory, Interstate Commerce Commission*, Division 2, 1960, 309 ICC 347.
9. *Id.*
10. *Id.*
11. Friedlaender, *op. cit.*, p. 85.
12. *Id.*, p. 86.
13. *Id.*

14. Systems Analysis and Research Corporation, *Coast-Based Freight Rates—Desirability and Feasibility*, August, 1966, p. 45.
15. Statement No. 6-64, Washington, D.C., June, 1964.
16. See *Procedures for Developing Rail Revenue Contribution by Commodity and Territory*, Bureau of Accounts, Statement No. 1-68, Washington, D.C., February, 1968.
17. See *Distribution of the Rail Revenue Contribution by Commodity Groups*, Bureau of Accounts, ICC, 1961, p. 23.
18. Walter Y. Oi and Arthur P. Hurter, *Economics of Private Truck Transportation*, W. Brown Company, 1965.
19. Friedlaender, *op. cit.*, p. 61.
20. Meyer, *et. al., op. cit.*
21. *Id.*, p. 196.
22. 332 ICC 820.
23. See Chapter 2.
24. See Meyer, *et. al., op. cit.*, p. 195.
25. *Id.*
26. 1961 Commodity Statistics, see n. 17.
27. See *New Orleans, Cotton Exch. v. Cincinnati, No. & T.P. R.R.*, 2 ICC 289, 293 (1888).
28. See Senate Committee on Interstate and Foreign Commerce, *Merchant Marine Study and Investigation*, S. Rep. No. 2494, 81st Cong., 2d Sess., 1950.
29. See Locklin, *Economics of Transportation*, p. 201.
30. Donald Turner, *Economic Regulation Materials*, available from Harvard Law School Distribution Center, p. 90.
31. See especially Dockets No. 34971, 34875, and 34970.
32. 335 ICC 143.
33. *Ex Parte 256.*
34. *Review of ICC Policies and Practices*, Hearings before The Subcommittee on Surface Transportation, Senate Commerce Commission, 91st Cong., 1st Sess., ser. 16, 77–84.
35. *Id.*, Commissioner Walrath.
36. AAR, *Yearbook of Railroad Facts*, 1969, pp. 35, 80.
37. Bretey and Ziebarth, *Railroad Industry Review*, 1969, New York: Hayden Stone, p. 56.
38. *Id.*, p. 57.

CHAPTER 6

1. ICC Bureau of Accounts, *Cost of Transporting Freight by Class I and Class II Motor Common Carrier of General Commodities, Performing Transcontinental Service 1966*, Statement No. 5-68, Washington, D.C., June, 1968, p. 58.
2. U.S. Department of Transportation, Federal Highway Administration, Bureau of Motor Carrier Safety, 1967, *Accidents of Large Motor Carriers of Property*, Washington, D.C., December, 1968, p. 2. The large interstate motor carriers were involved in 25,981 *reported* accidents in 1967, accounting for 1291 deaths and 14,882 injuries. The property damage came to $55,989,610.

CHAPTER 7

1. A.M.C. 1967 Annual Staff Report to Special Committee on Industrial Practices, p. 6.

2. *Ex Parte MC-19.*
3. 95 M.C.C. 138, 166.
4. Docket # MC-48374 Sub. 7.
5. Joseph Liantino, Executive Director, Affiliated Van Owners Association Inc., *Movers' News*, July, 1969.

CHAPTER 8

1. *Special Agents Manual,* ICC (First Reissue, July, 1959), p. A-6.
2. See Appendix 6.
3. *Id.*
4. *Id.*
5. *Id.*
6. *Id.*
7. *TRINC's Bluebook of the Trucking Industry,* Dun and Bradstreet, 1968, pp. 5–8.
8. See Appendix 6.
9. Agency interview, Pfahler.
10. See Appendix 6.
11. Agency interview, Oaks.
12. Agency interviews in the field.
13. *Id.*
14. *Id.*
15. Hearings, 91st Congress, June 24, 25, p. 273.
16. Agency interview, O'Brien.

CHAPTER 9

1. Association of American Railroads, *Yearbook of Railroad Facts,* 1969.
2. Interview with Frank Lawrence, Railroad Special Agent, Interstate Commerce Commission.
3. Interview with Paul Reider, Chief of the Railroad Division, ICC.
4. Public Law 89-430.
5. Letter of Senators Hartke, Magnuson, and Pearson, April 7, 1969.
6. Statement of Virginia Mae Brown before Committee on Commerce, United States Senate, Summer, 1969.
7. *Ex Parte 252.*
8. Before the Interstate Commerce Commission: Petition for Reopening, Reconsideration and Modification of Price Reports and Orders, and for an Order Prescribing an Increase in Per Diem Charges on Plain Unequipped Boxcars. Docket Nos. 31358, 33145.
9. Interstate Commerce Commission Report to United States Senate Regarding Freight Car Shortage.
10. *Id.*
11. Before the Interstate Commerce Commission: Petition for Reopening, *op. cit.*
12. Association of American Railroads, *op. cit.*
13. *Id.*

CHAPTER 10

1. *Report of Basic Policy Matters Under Consideration by the*

Interstate Commerce Commission, ICC, June 23, 1969, Appendix E.

2. *Investigation of Costs of Intercity Rail Passenger Service*, ICC, July 16, 1969, p. iii.

3. *The New York Times*, January 16, 1970, p. 1.

4. *The Janesville Gazette*, Janesville, Wisconsin, October 21, 1969, p. 6.

5. *The New York Times*, January 16, 1970, p. 44.

6. *Trains*, Vol. XXVIII, No. 8, June, 1959, p. 3.

7. Pierre E. Bretey and Karl Ziebarth, *Railroad Industry Review 1969*, Hayden, Stone, New York, 1969, pp. 80–85.

8. *Investigation of Costs, op. cit.*, p. iv.

9. *Report on National Transportation Policy*, prepared for the Senate Committee on Interstate and Foreign Commerce by the Special Study Group on Transportation Policies in the United States ("Doyle Report"), January 3, 1961, p. 324.

10. 133 Congressional Record 11936 (daily edition, October 3, 1968).

11. *Id.*

12. *Id.*, 11940.

13. Claiborne Pell, *Megalopolis Unbound: The Supercity and the Transportation of Tomorrow*, Praeger, New York, 1966, p. 140.

14. Letter from Henry J. Kastell, St. Paul, Minnesota, to Interstate Commerce Commission, September 28, 1967.

15. Cited in "The Federal Interest in Railroad Passenger Service," W. B. Saunders & Co., for the Department of Commerce, November, 1959.

16. *Investigation of Costs, op. cit.*, Table 38.

17. *Id.*, Table 39.

18. Doyle Report, *op. cit.*, p. 334.

19. *The Pocket List of Railroad Officials*, Railway Equipment and Publication Company, New York, 1969.

20. Doyle Report, *op. cit.*, p. 329.

21. *Modern Railroading*, March, 1958.

22. *New Haven Discontinuance of All Interstate Passenger Trains*, 327 ICC 151, 221 (1966). (Emphasis in the original.)

23. *Santa Fe; C & O; B & O; Burlington; Milwaukee Road; Rio Grande; Erie-Lackawanna; Great Northern; Illinois Central; Kansas-City Southern; Louisville & Nashville; Missouri Pacific; New York Central; New Haven; Norfolk & Western; Northern Pacific; Pennsylvania; Richmond, Fredericksburg & Potomac; Seaboard Coast Line; Southern Pacific; Southern; Union Pacific* and *Western Pacific.*

24. Braniff, Continental, Delta, Eastern, National, Northeast, Northwest, TWA, United.

25. *Boston Globe*, October 29, 1969, p. 3, col. 1.

26. Interviews with Penn-Central and American Airlines officials, Boston, Massachusetts, and Philadelphia, Pennsylvania.

27. Doyle Report, *op. cit.*, pp. 335–6.

28. *Southern Pacific Co. Discontinuance of Trains*, 328 ICC 360 (1966); *Southern Pacific Co. Discontinuance*, D&O, May 24, 1966; *Chicago, Burlington & Quincy RR Co. Discontinuance*, 333 ICC 742 (1967); *Southern Pacific Co. Discontinuance*, 333 ICC 525 (1968); *Southern Pacific Co. Discontinuance*, 333 ICC 783 (1968).

29. *Docket No. 34733, Adequacies—Passenger Service—Southern Pacific Co. Between California and Louisiana,* Ultimate Findings of Hearing Examiner, April 22, 1968, p. 49.
30. *Id.,* pp. 39, 41.
31. Pierre Bretey and Dr. George Hilton of UCLA have made this claim.
32. Doyle Report; Testimony by Chairman Brown of ICC before Senate Subcommittee on Surface Transportation, September 23, 1969.
33. Testimony by Mrs. Brown, September 23, 1969.
34. See note 31, above.
35. *Southern Pacific Co. Discontinuance,* 333 ICC 525 (1968).
36. *Investigation of Costs, op. cit.,* p. 92.
37. *Id.,* Table 5.
38. *Id.,* Table 4.
39. *Id.,* p. 27.
40. Claiborne Pell, *Megalopolis Unbound, op. cit.,* p. 116.
41. W. B. Saunders and Co. *The Federal Interest in Railroad Passenger Service,* for the Department of Commerce, November, 1959, p. 71.
42. *Report of Basic Policy Matters, op. cit.,* 1969, pp. 36–54.
43. *Journal of Commerce,* September 26, 1969.

APPENDIX 8

1. "Equal Employment Opportunity," 2 ICC Manual 22-041, August 15, 1966.
2. U.S. Civil Service Commission, "Evaluation of Personnel Management," 1963, pp. 45–49.
3. Figure supplied by the ICC Personnel Office.
4. U.S. Civil Service Commission, *Study of Minority Group Employment in the Federal Government,* 1967, Table 1-32, p. 34.
5. *Id.,* Table 1-1, p. 3.
6. *Id.*
7. Figures for 1967 are from the C.S.C. *Study.* Figures for 1968 are adapted from figures on Minority Group Employment for December, 1968, supplied by the ICC Personnel Office, and figures from June, 1968, from the ICC's "Report of Annual Review for Classification Currency," July 31, 1969, p. 4.
8. *ICC Merit Promotion Plan* Handbook.
9. Agency Interview.
10. Agency Interview, Adams.
11. Agency Interview, Wheeler.
12. Agency Interview.
13. Letter to ICC Hearing Examiner Edward F. Conway, Jr., from former ICC employee.

APPENDIX 10

1. Ann Friedlaender, *The Dilemma of Freight Transport Regulation,* Brookings Institute, Washington, D.C., 1969, p. 206.
2. Friedlaender, *op. cit.,* p. 204.

APPENDIX 14

1. In the United States District Court for the Northern District of Ohio, Eastern Division, *United States of America v. Roadway Express, Inc.*
2. In the United States District Court for the Western District of Oklahoma, *Marcus Jones, Willie B. Hodge, and Clarence L. Irving v. Leeway Motor Freight, Inc.*
3. *Id.*

APPENDIX 18

1. R. L. Banks, *Intermodal Competition*, Washington, D.C., 1966, Vol. 2, Part III.
2. *Id.*

APPENDIX 20

1. *No. 34733, Adequacies—Passenger Service—Southern Pacific Company Between California and Louisiana*, 335 ICC 415 (1969).
2. *No. 34733, Adequacies,* Report of Hearing Examiner John S. Messer, April 22, 1968, 2.
3. Letter from William Symons, President, California Public Utilities Commission, to Richard E. Brodsky, October 30, 1969.
4. *82nd Annual Report of the Interstate Commerce Commission*, 1968, Appendix B, Table 2.
5. *The Evening Star,* Washington, D.C., July 28, 1969.
6. *U.S. v. Pennsylvania RR Co.*, 242 US 208 (1916).
7. See cases listed in note 3, Chapter 8.
8. *Southern Pacific Co. Discontinuance of Trains,* 333 ICC 783 (1968).
9. *The Evening Star,* Washington, D.C., April 8, 1969.
10. *The Evening Star,* Washington, D.C., August 8, 1969.
11. *Adequacies,* 335 ICC 415, 437 (1969) (dissenting opinion).
12. *Id.,* 421.
13. *Id.,* 422.
14. *Id.*
15. 49 USC preceding Sec. 1.
16. *Schaffer Transportation Co. v. U.S.*, 335 ICC 83, 87–8 (1957).
17. *American Trucking v. A.T. & S.F.R. Co.*, 387 US 397 (1967).
18. *Adequacies,* 427.
19. *Id.*
20. See note 17, above.
21. *Adequacies,* 428.
22. *Id.,* 437.
23. Letter from Pierre E. Dostert to *The Evening Star*, September 21, 1969.
24. See notes 17, 20, above.

APPENDIX 22

1. Pierre Bretey and Karl Ziebarth, *Railroad Industry Review 1969*, Hayden, Stone, New York, 1969, p. 80.
2. *Id.*

3. *Id.*, p. 81.
4. *Id.*, p. 80.
5. *Id.*
6. *Id.*
7. *Id.*, p. 81.
8. *Id.*
9. *Id.*
10. *Id.*
11. *Id.*, p. 82.
12. *Id.*
13. *Id.*
14. *Id.*
15. *Id.*
16. *Id.*
17. *Id.*
18. *Id.*, p. 83.
19. *Investigation of Costs of Intercity Rail Passenger Service*, Report of the ICC to Senator Warren G. Magnuson, July 16, 1969, Table 25, p. 63.
20. Bretey and Ziebarth, *op. cit.*, p. 83.
21. *Id.*
22. *Id.*
23. *Id.*
24. *Id.*
25. *Id.*
26. *Id.*, 85.
27. *Id.*
28. *Id.*
29. *Id.*, p. 97.
30. *Id.*